Ethnic Conflict in International Relations

edited by
Astri Suhrke
Lela Garner Noble

The Praeger Special Studies program, through a selective worldwide distribution network, makes available to the academic, government, and business communities significant and timely research in U.S. and international economic, social, and political issues.

Ethnic Conflict in International Relations

PRAEGER SPECIAL STUDIES IN INTERNATIONAL POLITICS AND GOVERNMENT

Praeger Publishers New York London

Library of Congress Cataloging in Publication Data

Main entry under title:

Ethnic conflict and international relations.

(Praeger special studies in international politics and government)
Includes bibliographical references and index.
1. International relations. 2. Race problems.
I. Suhrke, Astri. II. Noble, Lela Garner.
JX1395.E83 1977 327 77-83444
ISBN 0-03-040681-1

PRAEGER SPECIAL STUDIES
200 Park Avenue, New York, N.Y., 10017, U.S.A.

Published in the United States of America in 1977
by Praeger Publishers,
A Division of Holt, Rinehart and Winston, CBS, Inc.

789 038 987654321

Printed in the United States of America

PREFACE

This book began with a panel on "Ethnicity and International Relations Theory" at the meetings of the American Political Science Association in 1974. Participation in the panel convinced us that the relationship between internal and external conflicts involving ethnic issues was important, from both academic and policy perspectives, and deserved systematic analysis. We spent some time clarifying our ideas about that relationship; then identified instances of ethnic conflict which involved both internal and external factors; and then recruited people whose recognized expertise indicated that they could write case studies. In subsequent meetings the expanded group shared findings, sharpened issues and hypotheses, and eventually drew conclusions.

Thus the book is a result of a collaborative process. While we assume responsibility for the introductory and concluding chapters, and for the presentation of the book as a whole, all have benefited from the discussions involving all the participants. Particularly helpful was a series of sessions with all the contributors during the 1977 meeting of the International Studies Association.

Every effort was made to keep the case studies focused on common issues; nevertheless each case study remains the work of an individual writer and—like the ethnic conflicts with which they deal—each reflects a range of personal perspectives. Chapter 6 was, in fact, written by an Ethiopian scholar whose present position made it advisable to use a pseudonym.

Many colleagues contributed to the project by suggesting names of case study authors and ideas for chapters. Departmental chairpersons allocated travel funds and other support services. Secretarial staffs—particularly the one at San Jose State under the direction of Kathryn Marlatt—produced multiple drafts and copies of drafts. Our families and friends also made a contribution by tolerating—with varying degrees of grace—the tensions induced by a series of deadlines. We thank them all.

CONTENTS

Page

PREFACE v

LIST OF ABBREVIATIONS xi

Chapter

1 INTRODUCTION
Astri Suhrke and Lela Garner Noble 1

Policy Implications 2
Context and Characteristics of Ethnic Conflict 3
The Case Studies 7
The Interaction Process 9
The Nature of the Ethnic Conflict 11
Ethnic Characteristics of External Parties 13
Cross-Boundary Ethnic Links 14
Forms of Involvement 16
Notes 18

2 NORTHERN IRELAND
Terrance G. Carroll 21

Ethnic Conflict in Ulster 23
Parties to the Conflict 29
External Aspects of the Conflict 31
Conclusion 37
Notes 40

3 THE CYPRUS CONFLICT
Naomi Black 43

The Development of Ethnic Differentiation and Conflict 46
The Role of Greece and Turkey 53
Other External Parties 60
Conclusions 64
Notes 65

4 THE KURDISH CONFLICT IN IRAQ
George S. Harris 68

Origins of the Iraqi Kurdish Revolt 70
Course of the Conflict, 1961–63 73

Chapter

The Arif Brothers in Power, November 1963–July 1968 77
Return of the Baath: The March 1970 Accord 81
The End of Resistance: The March 1975 Agreement 85
The Conflict in Retrospect 89
Notes 90

5 THE WAR IN LEBANON
Leila Meo 93

Internal Dimensions: The Sociopolitical Dynamic 94
External Dimensions: The Major Powers, the Palestinians, and Lebanon 99
The Conflict and Syrian Intervention 104
The Conflict and Other Arab States 116
The United States and Israel 118
The End of the War 120
Conclusion 121
Appendix 122
Notes 125

6 THE ERITREAN-ETHIOPIAN CONFLICT
Ethiopiawi 127

Eritreans and Ethiopians 127
External Actors 138
Conclusion 143
Notes 144

7 THE KAZAKHS IN CHINA
June Teufel Dreyer 146

The Protagonists 146
The Course of Empire 148
The 1917 Revolution and Its Effect on Central Asia 150
Activities of the Soviet and Chinese Communist Parties in Sinkiang 153
Sinkiang Minorities and the Sino-Soviet Dispute, 1958–76 159
Conclusions 170
Notes 174

8 MUSLIMS IN THE PHILIPPINES AND THAILAND
Astri Suhrke and Lela Garner Noble 178

The Philippines 179
Internal Dimensions 179
External Factors 182
The MNLF 191

Chapter

The Philippine Government 192
Summary 194
Thailand 196
Internal Dimensions 196
External Dimensions 200
Conclusions 208
Notes 211

9 SPREAD OR CONTAINMENT: THE ETHNIC FACTOR
Astri Suhrke and Lela Garner Noble 213

Competitive Conflict Expansion 215
Simple Conflict Expansion 218
Simple Conflict Containment 220
Conflict Equilibration 220
The Ethnic Factor 223
Scope of External Involvement 223
Consequences of External Involvement on the International System 224
Ethnic Characteristics of the Outside Party 225
Policy Implications 226
International Stability and Conflict Regulation 226
Parties to the Domestic Conflict 228
Conclusions 230

INDEX 233

ABOUT THE EDITORS AND CONTRIBUTORS 247

LIST OF ABBREVIATIONS

ASEAN	Association of Southeast Asian Nations
CCP	Chinese Communist Party
CENTO	Central Treaty Organization
CIA	Central Intelligence Agency
CPM	Communist Party of Malaysia
CPSU	Communist Party of the Soviet Union
DPK	Democratic Party of Kurdistan
EEC	European Economic Community
ELF	Eritrean Liberation Front
EOKA	Ethniki Organosis Kypriakou Agonos (National Organization of Cypriot Struggle)
EPLF	Eritrean People's Liberation Front
ETR	East Turkestan Republic
IRA	Irish Republican Army
IRFED	Institut International de Recherche et de Formation en vue de Développement
KMT	Kuomintang
MIM	Muslim Independence Movement
MNLF	Moro National Liberation Front
MPR	Mongolian People's Republic
NATO	North Atlantic Treaty Organization
NCNA	New China News Agency
NICRA	Northern Ireland Civil Rights Association
NLP	National Liberal Party
NSA	National Security Agency
Noraid	Irish Northern Aid Committee
OAU	Organization of African Unity
PAS	Parti Islam
PDFLP	Popular Democratic Front for the Liberation of Palestine
PLA	Palestine Liberation Army
PFLP	Popular Front for the Liberation of Palestine
PLA	People's Liberation Army (China)
PLF	Popular Liberation Front
PLO	Palestine Liberation Organization
PMIP	Pan-Malaysan Islamic Party
PRC	People's Republic of China
PSP	Progressive Socialist Party
SDLP	Social Democratic and Labour Party
SUAR	Sinkiang Uighur Autonomous Region
UK	United Kingdom
UMND	United Malays National Organization
UUUC	United Ulster Unionist Council

Ethnic Conflict in International Relations

CHAPTER

1

INTRODUCTION

Astri Suhrke
Lela Garner Noble

Increasing concern to cross the disciplinary border between comparative politics and international relations probably reflects more than an academic disposition alternately to erect and demolish analytical boundaries. Terminological innovations such as "penetration," "dependency," "interdependence," and "transnationalism" seem to be efforts at describing a reality that does not allow for fixed distinctions between domestic and international phenomena. It is therefore proper that "ethnicity"—a much-studied phenomenon in comparative politics—should be placed in an international context and, conversely, that students of international relations should consider the findings of political scientists regarding the causes and consequences of ethnic identity.

This volume attempts to explore further the relationship between internal ethnic conflict and patterns of international conflict and cooperation. Clearly, there are important questions here that deserve examination. Are domestic ethnic conflicts particularly explosive in terms of attracting outside intervention and developing into international conflicts? Or, on the contrary, are such conflicts more likely to be isolated from international rivalries—do they perhaps even facilitate international cooperation by encouraging states to contain and regulate them? Do ethnic links that cut across state boundaries serve as channels for outside participation in the conflict, or are such ethnic ties subordinated to other considerations by interested outside parties? More generally, what is the significance of ethnic factors in determining foreign involvement or non-involvement in a domestic ethnic conflict, and do those factors suggest particular forms of external response?

These questions form the main themes of this book. They are developed in seven contemporary case studies: the civil war in Lebanon, the recurring conflicts in Cyprus and Northern Ireland, the Kurdish rebellion in Iraq, the

Muslim separatist movements in the Philippines and Thailand, the Eritrean secessionist struggle in Ethiopia, and the problem of the Kazakh minority in China. In all these cases we are interested in the relationship between the domestic conflict and patterns of international cooperation or conflict: how and why the domestic conflict can "feed on," and in turn shape, international conflict; how and why the domestic conflict is affected by, and affects, structures of international cooperation. To focus on this interaction process, the authors of the individual case studies were first asked to explain the nature of foreign involvement in the conflict, and then to assess the consequences.

Two reasons account for this choice of focus. First, as we shall explain more fully below, we assumed that the interaction between internal and external forces is particularly significant in ethnic conflicts. Second, the literature that has a bearing on this subject is fragmented. In the international relations literature, several themes that deal with contemporary manifestations of ethnic conflict can be distinguished: the effects of domestic ethnic lobby groups on foreign policy formulation; the causes and consequences of boundary disputes in cases where state and ethnic boundaries do not coincide; and the consequences of permanent or temporary migration of ethnic groups on the state-to-state relations of the governments concerned.[1] These themes are more specific than and/or different from those followed in this volume. The international relations literature that thematically is closest to our perspective—the relationship between external and internal conflict—has largely ignored the ethnic factor as a separate variable that deserves systematic attention.[2]

Within the field of comparative politics, there is a massive and still growing literature on the subject of ethnic identity. However (and this is by now a commonplace observation), there have been relatively few efforts to place ethnic issues in the context of the external environment.[3]

This is not to suggest that the questions addressed in this volume are novel. In one form or another, they were prominent in the political debate over national self-determination in nineteenth-century Europe, further emphasized at the Versailles Conference and in its aftermath, and revived by the decolonization process following World War II. Indeed, a main issue in the debate has been whether or not multinational entities were a more likely cause of international conflict than were ethnically homogeneous states. We are simply sharpening and reconsidering this question as it applies to the contemporary international system, where—after multinational empires have been dismantled—we are witnessing the fragility of states trying to maintain national integrity or to build a viable nationhood.

POLICY IMPLICATIONS

At one level, then, the policy implications of the questions raised here have "some bearing on mankind's collective survival," as Ted Robert Gurr phrased it.[4] At another level, there are important policy implications for the parties involved in the conflict. Whether the normative and/or political injunction is to expand or contain the conflict, the question of how to expand or contain is a problem of formulating an appropriate policy strategy.

For the ethnic groups involved in the domestic conflict, the policy problem is how to exploit external tension or cooperation for their own purposes. They may choose between two opposite strategies: to limit outside involvement or to attract outside support, or they may select from a variety of intermediary or mixed strategies, such as channeling external interest into conflict mediation or blocking the external links of the competing ethnic group. Choices are affected by the group's access to governmental power and, more generally, by the relative strength of the domestic protagonists, by the intensity of the domestic conflict, and by the kind of external support available. If, for example, a domestic ethnic group has privileged access to governmental power, the initial strategy is usually to limit external involvement in the conflict. For an ethnic group with less access to governmental power, the initial strategy is often the opposite, since it needs to develop its own external contacts to compete with the group that, because of its privileged access to governmental power, already maintains a range of international contacts that are either actually or potentially supportive.[5]

Whatever status a group has, the central policy question remains how to evoke and/or regulate outside involvement. Even when the conflict is not intense, in many multiethnic states considerations of how a given foreign policy will and should affect the domestic ethnic balance continuously and decisively influence foreign policy formulation. For instance, Canadian foreign aid policies carefully balance assistance to English- and French-speaking states in Africa. How, or if, major questions of national security policy can be isolated from the treatment of a minority group at home constitutes a troublesome issue in the Soviet Union with regard to Soviet-American relations and Soviet Jews.

For outside parties with a potential or actual interest in an ethnic conflict, the central policy questions can be subsumed under similar headings. How can an internal conflict be exploited to serve the interests of the outside party? How can costs be minimized and benefits maximized by different forms of intervention? Conversely, how can a domestic conflict elsewhere be isolated and contained?

CONTEXT AND CHARACTERISTICS OF ETHNIC CONFLICT

The assumption that stimulated the undertaking of this volume is that ethnic conflicts have peculiar characteristics that place them in the area where domestic and international politics interact. They seem to link internal and external forces of conflict and cooperation and, to some extent, to result from such interaction; consequently they must be understood in this context.[6]

One reason that state boundaries do not necessarily contain ethnic conflicts is suggested by the definition of "ethnic identity." Despite the variety of definitions used by social scientists, there is general agreement that ethnic identity eschews functional specificity (that is, an ethnic group is functionally diffuse) and generational specificity (it is transgenerational). Ethnic association refers to a total identity of the group—as Talcott Parsons notes, "for the member it characterizes what the individual *is* rather than what he *does.*"[7] This identity stems from a real or believed common ancestry of the group, symbolized or expressed in shared characteristics such as common race, language, religion, customs, or—even more intangibly—in a historically derived consciousness of being a separate group. The Eritreans, for instance, do not share language, religion, race, or culture; but the group identity is derived from being administered as a separate entity in the past. Indeed, some anthropologists, following Fredrik Barth, would argue that the Eritreans constitute an ethnic group simply because they perceive themselves, and are perceived by others, as being a separate group. For Barth, the critical features of an ethnic group are that it is ascriptive and exclusive: its continuity depends on the maintenance of a boundary.[8]

The point here is that the properties of ethnic groups suggested by these definitions are quite similar to properties commonly used to define "nationalities." Some scholars have emphasized the distinction between ethnic groups and nationalities. Crawford Young, for example, argues, "Ethnicity in the great majority of instances in the developing world differs from nationalism in its lack of ideological elaboration and in the absence of any serious aspiration to the total autonomy required by nationalism."[9] The early writings on "cultural pluralism" did not link ethnic or cultural identity with nationalism, nor did they discuss goals of "communities" in terms of self-determination. On the other hand, Clifford Geertz and Harold Isaacs exemplify a school of thought that sees ethnic groups as "candidates for nationhood" precisely because they possess the characteristics that nationalities have or claim to have.[10]

Paradoxically, both schools of thought support our argument. Ethnic groups in many cases do not claim the right of "national self-determination" with goals of autonomy or separate statehood. Others do; indeed, in most ethnic groups there is at least an extremist fringe that does aim at independence. But whether or not a group explicitly expresses political-ideological goals, the fact that ethnic groups resemble nationalities in some very important aspects will often cause them to be perceived as potential nationalities. Certainly ethnic discontent provides a potential for politicization and, implicitly or explicitly, in stating or justifying goals, calls into question the nature of the state. To cite an example from one of the case studies: in southern Thailand the Muslim population has long had a politicized elite that has demanded greater rights for the Muslims on the grounds that they constitute a distinct group and that they suffer discrimination as a group. Clearly, one logical extension of this argument is that group distinctiveness warrants a distinct territorial entity and administrative unit. This is indeed the conclusion drawn by some members of the minority, as well as by other parties at home and abroad.

The argument, then, is that while national self-determination is not necessarily the only form that demands of aspiring ethnic groups can take, this form is likely to be considered a possibility in a historical era that retains the coincidence between the state and the nation as a powerful ordering myth for political societies. As long as this possibility is implicit in the situation, it will evoke international concern. Disgruntled ethnic groups in other states may be stimulated to think of self-determination for themselves, even if the group involved in the original conflict has not advanced that goal. Governments of multiethnic states may fear such a demonstration effect and take measures accordingly, whether or not their fear is justified.

As long as the nation-state is recognized as the norm—and principal actor—of the international system, a "domestic" conflict that even implicitly questions that norm and the nature of that actor ceases to be purely "domestic" and automatically acquires international dimensions. If the ethnic conflict explicitly raises the question of national self-determination, it naturally evokes a broader international response (at the very least in the form of recognizing or not recognizing the new claimants of statehood), and may be linked structurally to the international environment in other obvious ways (such as through irredentist demands). Thus, like revolutions—which frequently are assumed to be motivated by ideologies claiming universal validity and, hence, to have international implications, whether or not there is evidence of external intentions, initiatives, or involvements—ethnic conflicts raise an ideological issue with international implications.

Second, historical experience suggests that ethnic conflicts have a peculiarly festering quality.[11] During some periods they are latent, then erupt, only to subside again, and so the cycle continues. This festering quality has two likely international implications. The duration and repetition of the conflict mean that the domestic protagonists have ample opportunity to identify outside friends and enemies and to establish contacts accordingly. When the conflict intensifies, the outside connections can be more easily and rapidly activated than if it were a "new" conflict. To illustrate from the case studies, over a period of years the Kurds in Iraq and the Eritreans in Ethiopia developed outside contacts that constituted an infrastructure available in times of intensified conflict. As George Modelski notes in his study of international aspects of civil strife, the absence or presence of such an infrastructure influences the form and degree of outside involvement in internal conflict.[12] It would follow that, all other things being equal, the festering quality of ethnic conflicts facilitates rapid external involvement because knowledge and contacts across state boundaries have been established, or at least explored, during earlier eruptions.

The festering quality has another dimension that suggests that ethnic conflicts are particularly prone to attract outside intervention. If dissatisfaction is continuous and latent, it provides a tempting opportunity for outsiders to use it for their own ends. The temptation lies in the fact that a situation exists that can be exacerbated easily; a minimal intervention produces a proportionately greater effect. This is demonstrated in the case study of Sino-Soviet relations with respect to the Kazakhs, as well as in the Kurdish conflict.

The festering quality typical of ethnic conflict should be seen as an intervening variable that interacts with other determinants to facilitate foreign involvement. If an outside party has some reason to become involved, the prospect of a relatively "cheap" intervention will suggest cost-benefit calculations in favor of such action. Similarly, if the domestic ethnic conflict intensifies, and if the domestic protagonists seek outside support, they are likely to have existing links to the outside that facilitate external involvement.

A third characteristic of ethnic conflict also seems to facilitate external involvement. Ethnic identification usually involves strong, affective group ties, and a consequent we-they dichotomy that feeds on the memories of past conflicts. This suggests that when ethnic conflict and animosity break into violence, it is likely to be particularly intense and vicious—indeed, it may be perceived by the parties as threatening genocide. This is not to say that ethnic divisions necessarily lead to violent conflict. There is ample evidence of dualism in ethnically plural societies: some forces working toward conflict, another set of forces working toward accommodation.[13] However, when the forces of conflict take precedence and result in violence, it seems to be particularly vicious. This is likely to lead the combatants to look for additional sources of support. If one group controls domestic resources, the other is likely to need outside resources to balance this advantage. Hence it may try desperately to gain international attention, as by terrorist acts or by charges of genocide.

For outside parties, intensification of conflict can stimulate concern and a desire to influence the situation. As James Rosenau suggests, conflicts that are particularly vicious do seem to arouse international interest and to result in demands that "something be done" to regulate the situation.[14] If genocide seems a possibility, there are additional moral and legal pressures for outside parties to intervene. On the other hand, when ethnic discontent takes a violent form, it rarely reaches the level of full-scale warfare. Rioting and protracted insurgency seem to be more typical expressions.[15] Since both of these forms of violence allow the state to function internationally much as it did before, they may have little material effect on the outside world.

The fourth, and perhaps most generally recognized, characteristic of ethnic conflict stems from the fact that ethnic identities rarely coincide fully with state boundaries. In many—perhaps most—cases ethnic kin inhabit different sovereign states. Hence ethnic conflict in one state has implications in other states where ethnic kin are located and affects official and unofficial transactions between or among these states. For example, an ethnic group may demand that its own government support embattled kin elsewhere; if unsuccessful in influencing government policy, it may render unofficial assistance. It may also fear repercussions for its own group (particularly if it is a minority) and remain passive, or the ethnic ties may not be sufficiently strong to affect it. The government's actions will likely be influenced by its own ethnic composition and by that of the state. If its dominant majority is the protesting (or persecuted) minority in the other state, it may offer to help facilitate a peaceful settlement; if the states share minorities, the "outside" state may supply arms to the other government.

Thus the presence of ethnic links cutting across state boundaries may serve to resolve, contain, or spread the conflict. These international ethnic links constitute the most obvious structures connecting domestic ethnic conflicts with the external environment. They may be severed, used, or ignored, just as the issues raised by ethnic conflicts with regard to the basis of the nation-state may be ignored, exploited, or combated. The contention here is simply that a response will occur outside the domestic arena in which the conflict takes place.

THE CASE STUDIES

So far we have only argued that ethnic conflicts have certain attributes that are likely to evoke strong international concern, both official and unofficial. Some of these attributes suggest competitive partisan involvement by outside forces, while others suggest the opposite response, that of containing or isolating the conflict. The nature of the external response, its determinants, and its consequences are the subjects of the case studies that follow.

The cases vary with respect to the characteristics of ethnic conflict noted above. In some cases separatism is the central issue. In others the dispute centers on formulas for sharing power within the existing state. In still others, demands range from changes in policies through changes in structures to independence. To generalize, the cases vary in the extent to which the integrity of the state, and hence its identity as an international actor, are called into question. The variation should permit conclusions about the relevance of this issue in explaining different forms of international response to the conflict, as well as different domestic pressures to solicit external support.

Second, while all of the cases have a festering quality, the form and intensity of domestic conflicts have varied over time within, as well as among, the countries studied. In Lebanon and Ethiopia, the term "civil war" is appropriate; conflicts involving Muslims in Thailand and the Kazakhs in China have involved scattered violence of limited scope, intensity, and organization. This variation invites analysis of the impact of the form of ethnic conflict on the nature of external involvement. Finally, in all cases there were ethnic links across state boundaries, but their nature varied greatly with regard to strength and the role of the ethnic kin in other states.*

Another issue should also be treated. To what extent is ethnicity the source of conflict in the cases studied? Most of these conflicts must be understood as multidimensional, involving economic, political, and ideological dimensions that interact with ethnic aspects. In some cases, particularly in Lebanon, economic aspects clearly are extremely important; and some observers may hesitate to describe them as "ethnic conflicts." We have included them because they conform to the main criteria for ethnic conflict used in this volume: that the principal alignments of political forces in the initial conflict reflect ethnic divisions, and that to a great extent the parties to the conflict define the issues in terms of the rights and obligations of ethnic groups as they relate to each other. In other words, we used a criterion of relative emphasis on ethnic identities and issues in the totality of issues and alignments apparent in the conflict situation.

The problem, however, is still more complicated. Are ethnic identifications and antagonisms merely creations of the economic system? Do they, then, only mask—and hence distract attention from—the class divisions and conflicts in a society?[16] Or are ethnic identifications social-psychological realities that certainly interact with economic, political, and ideological factors, but may themselves produce groups, animosities, and ambitions that shape political alignments and provide the dynamics of conflicts? This is not the place to enter a prolonged discussion of this issue. The question is, or should be, an empirical one. As Donald Horowitz noted in an attempt to analyze what too often is settled by political-philosophical fiat: "Economic grievances do play a role in ethnic hostility, but they are operative in some connections and at some levels far more than others. A precise concept of ethnic conflict. . .must begin by differentiating the various strands of antagonism."[17]

This differentiation is a task for the authors of the case studies. The issue should be dealt with, since it has implications for the analysis of outside involvement in an initially domestic conflict. On one level, it can help to explain a particular event. For instance, an alliance between domestic and

---

*We recognize that a great deal of variation in a small number of case studies also presents problems: it is difficult to find sufficient "constants" against which to contrast and explain variations.

external parties that grossly violates ethnic kinship ties may be explained by the artificiality or superficiality of ethnic issues in the initial conflict. Or, a very forceful, partisan intervention may be explained by a coincidence of cleavages —ethnic and class.

On a more general level, a differentiation of factors (economic, political, ethnic) may help clarify the significance of ethnic factors in shaping international alignments and creating international conflicts. Specifically, an identification of parallel but independent structures of conflict in the case of the Kazakh minority in China, where the degree of Soviet involvement is clearly related not only to the presence of Kazakhs on both sides of the Sino-Soviet boundary but, more fundamentally, to other aspects of the Sino-Soviet split, may substantiate a minimalist view. Ethnic grievances and cross-boundary ethnic links, it would be argued, merely exacerbate existing international tensions that are not the product of ethnic antagonisms. By contrast, the case of Cyprus may suggest that the minimalist view is inadequate: parallel, reinforcing ethnic antagonisms on both the domestic and the international level may have the capacity to create particularly intense interstate conflict that modifies a wide range of relationships between the states in question.

THE INTERACTION PROCESS

In trying to develop a framework for the analysis of the cases that appear in this book, we were struck by the absence of theoretical literature upon which to draw. Three sets of literature deal with the subject matter in one way or another, but they all have serious shortcomings for our purposes.

First, there is the literature on modern nationalism in Europe and, more specifically, on the attempts by the Versailles Conference to accommodate the self-determination principle when reconstructing the state system after World War I. The literature from and on this period probably constitutes the most concentrated bulk of writings on the relationship between nationality (or ethnic) conflicts and questions of international peace and war. In one strain of thought, John Stuart Mill's argument that ethnically homogeneous states are more likely to be democratic, stable, and viable entities than are multiethnic states is a central premise. Nationalists like Johann Herder and Giuseppe Mazzini carried Mill's argument further, contending that the homogeneous states are also more likely to be peacefully inclined in their relations with other states. In their version, the redrawing of state boundaries to coincide with nationality boundaries would both remove a major source of international conflict (conflicts over national self-determination) and lay the foundation for future cooperation—the "international fraternity" in Mazzini's vision, the "harmonious flower bed" in Herder's metaphor. In what Inis Claude calls the "League philosophy" (it also might be called the "Wilsonian postulate," in tribute to Woodrow Wilson's role in popularizing it), "the realization of the ideals of democracy and self-determination was regarded as the essential means for minimizing the element of conflict in international relations."[18]

These assertions about the link between unsatisfied nationalism and international conflict obviously are relevant to our inquiry about when and how domestic ethnic conflicts become internationalized. However, neither their proponents nor their critics offer more than a starting point for a systematic examination of the linkage.[19] Proponents of greater ethnic self-determination have argued that nationality conflicts are intense and enduring because the challengers are fighting for a just cause, but have not explained how intensity and duration are related to internationalization. Further, they have maintained that conflicts involving minorities may provoke international conflict by leading to foreign intervention either on humanitarian grounds or in response to cross-boundary ethnic ties, but have not dealt with the question of whether either consideration is a sufficient cause for intervention. The critics, in turn, have argued that implementation of national self-determination is extremely difficult and may be counterproductive in terms of international stability; when ethnic conflicts do become internationalized, national ambitions are subordinate to—or a catalyst for—other forces of "power politics." But there is still no systematic delineation of the specific circumstances in which nationality conflicts occur, either domestically or internationally.

This literature does, however, help us to identify some central variables and emphasizes the need to distinguish between two basic types of outside involvement in the internal conflict: affective involvement (based on ethnic ties) and instrumental involvement (unrelated to, or in the absence of, ethnic ties).

Second, there is the Marxist-Leninist school of thought, which—quite apart from its secondary emphasis on ethnic conflict—provides a model of conflict extension.[20] According to Lenin's classic formulation, the capitalist class seeks external sources of raw materials and markets to dispose of its surplus capital and to prevent the internal class struggle from coming to its inevitable climax. Competitive capitalist demands abroad then lead to war among the capitalist states, and between them and the oppressed peoples. The Leninist model thus assumes similarity of problems at home, similarity of elite responses directed externally, and competition for the same scarce resources abroad that eventually leads to interstate war.

Some international conflicts that relate to ethnic grievances may be explained by such a dynamic. But, more generally, even if one can conceive the multiethnic states as having, broadly speaking, similar problems at home, there is no reason that internal problems should necessarily produce similar, competitive external policies leading to interstate war. One may even discern an interesting reversal of the original model when it is applied to ethnic conflict. To the extent that the domestic problem is similar in two states (for instance, the problem with Muslim minorities in Thailand and the Philippines), and to the extent that this does lead to similar elite responses directed externally (Thai and Philippine governments attempting to neutralize external sympathy and support for the Muslim rebels), this suggests interstate cooperation rather than conflict (such as parallel Thai and Filipino efforts to use a regional organization, ASEAN, to isolate ethnic problems in their respective countries from international rivalries in the region). In an extreme case, one could envisage a sort of Holy Alliance of governments with similar minority problems. Lenin's conclusions might still be accurate, of course, in cases where ethnic manifestations actually mask deeper class conflicts, resulting in competitive attempts at economic expansion and, hence, international conflicts.

Finally, there have been many efforts to relate domestic and foreign conflict behavior in the contemporary international relations literature. Much of the theory underlying these efforts concerns conflict transformation rather than conflict extension, and follows the pioneering ideas of Lewis Coser.[21] Social conflict, according to Coser, has system-maintenance functions, as scapegoating clearly exemplifies. Internal conflict, of whatever kind, can be alleviated by focusing on an external enemy; but the two conflicts are not necessarily related in any other way. We are not concerned here with such possible transformations of the original conflict, but with the ways in which a specific conflict spreads or is prevented from spreading to involve outside parties. Furthermore, this analysis does not concern itself with the process of conflict interaction, and only rarely does it identify ethnic conflict as a separate variable.[22]

Lacking any firm theoretical guidance and being aware of numerous, generally nontheoretical case studies, we outlined an analytical framework for the case studies in this book by identifying a few variables and suggesting initial hypotheses about their role in conflict expansion or containment. Three variables relating to the ethnic dimensions of the initial conflict were selected: the nature of the ethnic conflict, the ethnic characteristics of potentially interested outside parties, and the nature of ethnic links cutting across state boundaries.

The Nature of the Ethnic Conflict

As suggested earlier, demands from ethnic groups can be placed along a continuum where, at one end, they concern resource allocation within the state and, at the other end, separatism and irredentism. Demands for autonomy or for other structural changes would be located somewhere around the center of this range. In any one case, obviously demands may change over time, or different demands may be expressed simultaneously by members of the group. It would seem, though, that the nature of the demands—whether unified, mixed, or inchoate, whether tending toward separatism or toward changes in resource allocation—has a bearing on the nature of external involvement in the conflict.

In regard to the relationship between the nature of the domestic dispute and the response of outside interested parties, we can stipulate different degrees of international concern: the more the conflict calls into question the legitimacy or territorial integrity of the state, the more likely it is to arouse international concern. It does not seem possible to deduce what form that concern will take—isolating the conflict, mediating, or giving direct, partisan support to one of the parties. However, we can be more specfic about the likely actions of the domestic protagonists.

Where the legitimacy and territorial integrity of the state are at issue, the challengers (the separatists) will have few qualms about seeking outside aid, precisely because they reject the legitimacy of the state and, hence, the scope of what is considered domestic. Moreover, separatist conflicts are usually perceived by the parties as being intense, since they involve disagreement on fundamental issues; and they frequently reflect a territorial grouping of ethnic communities into somewhat distinct zones.[23] Perceived intensity tends to reinforce the inclination to obtain outside (indeed, any) aid, and a territorial base facilitates tangible assistance from the outside (such as weapons and advisers). Since the government already has external links, the separatists are motivated to establish their own connections. The government, in turn, may be tempted to match the separatists' success in obtaining outside support; and a spiral of competitive efforts to involve external parties as partisans is likely to result.

When the central issue concerns allocation of economic, cultural, or political resources within the state, the local protagonists may be relatively more inhibited in seeking overt partisan aid from the outside. The problem is more clearly defined as domestic; hence it is difficult to legitimize overt foreign aid. Such aid may indeed be counterproductive. In the case of an ethnic minority, for instance, possible links with foreign states may be used by the local adversary to discredit the minority by questioning its loyalty to the state, and thus may lead to a deterioration in its position.[24]

Another, more general consideration also can serve to restrain the protagonists from seeking outside support. As long as most of the local parties see the issues as concerning resource allocation within the state, there is an element of shared interest in maintaining the sovereignty and territorial integrity of the state itself. Outside involvement in the dispute, however, may encourage a more extreme and total form of ethnic loyalty that is hard to reconcile with the continued integrity of the state. The dynamic may be similar to that discussed in the breakdown of multiethnic coalitions within a plural society. Political entrepreneurs realize they can easily outbid the advocates of multiethnic coalitions by taking extreme stands on ethnic issues. This very action raises the salience of ethnic identification and eventually undermines the moderate coalition.[25]

In our analysis, outside interested parties may play the role of "political entrepreneurs"—whether deliberately or unintentionally—if given a chance to intervene, and an invitation issued by the local parties naturally constitutes an excellent entry. One would consequently expect the local protagonists to be cautious when considering foreign assistance, for fear that they will not be able to control its consequences. This may be a particularly salient fear when there are extremist elements on the fringes of the more moderate protagonists, and when possible outside supporters are ethnic kin. Ties with the latter may be justified with reference to ethnic identity and thus raise the consciousness of ethnic cleavages in the dispute. As a result, the conflict may develop toward its logical extreme, where ethnic rights are seen to require autonomous administration or a separate state.

Focusing on the nature of the domestic conflict, then, involves consideration of a number of characteristics that cluster and interact in various ways and that, separately and together, seem to have international implications. Conflicts that concern resource allocation within the state have been, and may be, solved relatively peacefully; separatist conflicts have not been. Conflicts of the former kind need not involve territorial grouping of communities; the latter type almost always does. So conflicts with a strong or predominant separatist element are more likely to generate internal pressures for overt support from the outside. However, if conflicts concerning resource allocation have or acquire the territorial and intensity characteristics of separatist conflicts, there likely will be pressures to involve outside parties in a similar manner. Since partisan intervention may not only strengthen the extreme elements among the domestic protagonists, as discussed earlier, but also generally raise hopes that more extreme goals (like separatism) are realizable, it may lead to changes in the definition of the conflict. Several of the case studies should probe this dynamic further.

Ethnic Characteristics of External Parties

Students of African affairs commonly conclude that the multiethnic character of most states on that continent heightens their feelings of vulnerability and leads to a restrained policy toward boundary disputes.[26] By extension, one would expect governments of multiethnic states to pursue a restrained policy toward ethnic conflicts in other states. Aware of their own vulnerability and anxious about precedents that might be established, they would try to mediate, contain, or isolate conflicts elsewhere.

This may well be too facile an assumption. If the government is anxious to establish the normative validity of the multiethnic state, it may support the local protagonist who champions the legitimacy of the existing state. The crucial question, however, is how anxious the government has to be before embarking on such a policy. Is the ideological precedent posed by possible dismemberment of another multiethnic state sufficient to produce active, partisan intervention in support of the status quo? A reverse question can also be asked: under what circumstances would the government of a multiethnic state be prepared to give active support to the challengers of multiethnicity in another state?

That both forms of partisan intervention have been undertaken by governments of multiethnic states clearly demonstrates that multiethnicity does not in itself guarantee a restrained policy toward ethnic conflict elsewhere. Indeed, it should be recalled that in the European state system after World War I, the victorious powers considered a combination of multiethnicity, new boundaries, and cross-boundary ethnic ties to be highly volatile. States with these characteristics, they assumed, would be prone to intervene in ethnic disputes elsewhere, in ways likely to create major international conflicts.

Thus, in the contemporary context, when even more states have these characteristics, a government may be distressed by the ideological precedent posed by a conflict elsewhere (that is, it may regard the conflict as a challenge to the principle of multiethnicity as a basis for the state structure). This distress may be reinforced by ethnic kinship ties, if ethnic kin are dominant in the other state and/or would suffer from a weakening of central authority there. Under these circumstances the government has strong incentives to intervene in a partisan fashion to restore the status quo.

But if there is a conflict between ideology and kinship ties—if the ethnic kin are the challengers to the multiethnic status quo elsewhere—then a typical response may be official restraint but active, partisan "unofficial" assistance.[27] A third variation is also possible. Even if ideology and kinship produce conflicting interests, a government may have moderate incentives to support the challengers to the status quo in the other state if the kinship links involve its own dominant majority or a politically significant minority.

All these combinations, of course, may be decisively changed by nonethnic factors, such as a desire to weaken a rival state or to preserve government-to-government cooperation. But before considering these, as will be done in the case studies, it is necessary to appreciate the strength of the incentives to intervene on grounds of ideology and ethnic kinship ties.[28]

Cross-Boundary Ethnic Links

Ethnic kinship ties may or may not influence the policy of outside parties toward ethnic conflict; in some cases this variation can be explained by the priority given to nonethnic factors, but it is also likely to reflect differences in the strength of ethnic ties. If a group that is divided by state boundaries has a common language, religion, and culture, for instance, it can be said to be united by stronger ethnic ties than if it shares fewer symbols of ethnic identity. Strong ties are more likely to result in partisan alignments than are weak ones.

Yet geographical proximity seems to have a paradoxical effect on this relationship. While it is frequently accompanied by strong ethnic ties that encourage partisan intervention, and while it facilitates the logistics of providing assistance, proximity also may inhibit such action. Partisan intervention creates at least one enemy, and effective retaliation by that new (or more enraged) enemy is facilitated by geographic proximity. This calculus of vulnerability may not be irrelevant in explaining, for instance, why distant Libya has supported Muslim rebels in the Philippines more actively and openly than has neighboring Malaysia, where the majority population is linked to the rebels by more than religious ties.*

In situations where the links involve minorities in both (or all) states, ethnic ties—however strong—are likely to be subordinated to other considerations. Giving aid to kin engaged in rebellion in another state clearly identifies the supporting minority group as potential rebels in their own state, and hence encourages retaliation from the dominant majorities, individually or collectively.

It is also possible that the local protagonists may consider ethnic ties as having comparatively little significance in providing support to achieve their goals. As discussed earlier, the inclination to seek outside aid tends to vary with the nature of the original conflict; but even when a decision to seek external assistance is made, the ethnic group may well look beyond kinship ties. One could argue, to the contrary, that the parochial element in ethnic groups (the we-they dichotomy) suggests an alliance policy limited to ethnic kin. However, it is equally possible that the intensity of the motivations resulting from that we-they dichotomy will lead to a pragmatic alliance strategy: support will be sought where it is thought to be available and significant, regardless of ethnic ties. Very possibly, there is a simple correlation between the intensity with which goals are pursued and alliance strategy. When the situation seems desperate and/or the goals are critically important, ethnic

---

*A similar argument has been made in the African context: "The continued support of armed liberation movements seems certain to add an unstable element to the politics of numerous states bordering on troubled areas. It may be partly for this reason that most direct military aid for rebel movements in Central and Southern Africa has come from North Africa, which is geographically insulated from the disturbances." William J. Foltz, "Military Influences," in Vernon McKay, ed., *African Diplomacy* (Baltimore: John Hopkins University Press, 1966). However, this statement clearly is modified by recent developments in southern Africa; geographic proximity or distance is at most a partial explanation.

groups are likely to regard an ethnically pure alliance strategy as a luxury, and to opt for pragmatism. According to this logic, an ethnically pure strategy would be followed only when kin elsewhere control significant resources.*

FORMS OF INVOLVEMENT

The preceding discussion has dealt with both internally and externally generated pressures for outside involvement or noninvolvement in a conflict. Particular pressures influence decisions by the local protagonists to seek or discourage assistance; but their invitations to intervene, or pleas to abstain, are judged by the outsiders according to a different calculus. Indeed, for their own reasons outsiders may take the initiative and leave the local protagonists to respond as best they can. The form that involvment takes—partisan cooperation, mediation, policies of containment, or isolation—thus depends on the interaction of internal and external pressures.† Although it is difficult to disentangle these in any given case, it is analytically useful to distinguish them.

The ethnic nature of a conflict seems to shape outside involvement in two peculiar ways. First, where intervention is motivated primarily by ethnic ties (that is, where it would be classified as affective), the timing and magnitude of external partisan support appear directly related to the vulnerability of the local protagonist. For the external kin, the worst possible contingency is the extermination of the local kin; but their success is not necessarily viewed with equal fervor. A typical attitude is probably "It would be nice if they won or improved their position, but it would be disastrous if they lost totally." When "loss" is likely to mean stringent assimilationist policies, expulsion, or genocide, the external kin may make sharp, unprecedented increases in support

*The central argument made by Rabushka and Shepsle in *Politics in Plural Societies* (Columbus, Ohio: Charles E. Merrill, 1972)—that ethnic disputes are characterized by high intensity of goal preferences—would suggest a flexible alliance strategy. If an ethnic group is desperately committed to its goal, it is likely to align with anybody who endorses that goal. Cynthia Enloe argues, from a different direction, that ethnically pure alliances are likely to result. Approaching the question from the viewpoint of the "outsider" (a nonmember of the ethnic group), she suggests that ". . . ethnic groups have a difficult time winning the confidence and trust of potential allies. Their objectives seem too parochial and their leadership too alien to excite active participation within the majority" (*Ethnic Conflict and Political Development* [Boston: Little, Brown, 1973], p. 222). The term "the majority" suggests that she is speaking of alliance building within the state, yet the context clearly shows that she is referring to external allies as well. The parochialism of the ethnic group is seen as inhibiting alliances with nonkin—whether internally or externally.

†Indifference and inaction are other possible responses to the conflict, and sometimes require explanations. Both can constitute indirect intervention. Inaction can be a deliberate policy; indifference, by definition, is not.

even if they have previously limited their involvment to sympathy and marginal assistance. The contrary—and pragmatic—inclination to disengage when a group is obviously losing would grossly violate sentiments of ethnic solidarity. The cases of Northern Ireland and the Muslims in Thailand and the Philippines may yield insights: what level of loss would the Republic of Ireland be willing to tolerate in regard to the Catholics in Ulster, or Islamic states with regard to the two Muslim minorities?

This reasoning implies that ethnic ties cutting across state boundaries serve to hold the initial conflict within the bounds of total defeat and total victory. Clearly, this effect would be most marked where external kin command power of some consequence, as when they control a state that is able to intervene decisively.* In these cases, the outsider will have to juxtapose the cost of intervention against the "cost" of seeing the death or displacement of embattled kin, and is likely to conclude that preventive action is a political and moral imperative. It can be argued, of course, that precisely when the external kin are in a position to rescue their relatives from total defeat, they also will be tempted to bring them to victory. However, that goal involves different costs and benefits, and the external kin may well perceive themselves as bearing most of the costs while the relatives reap most of the fruits of victory. Unless victory brings rewards to the supporting kin group that exceed the mere sentimental satisfaction of seeing the local kin victorious, intervention in pursuit of total victory seems rather unlikely.

There is another factor affecting calculations of cost. If total victory means the dismemberment of another state, it is likely to require considerable investment and risk. The tenacity with which states have succeeded in maintaining themselves as sovereign territorial units—however fragile internally—is a striking feature of the post-World War II era; and the dismemberment of the multination empires of the past, it should be recalled, took place in the context of world wars.† The poor prospect of victory, or its probable cost under the circumstances of a generalized war, is likely to act as a disincentive to intervention for this purpose. By comparison, the prospect of preventing total defeat for an ethnic kin group seems somewhat better.

Finally, the ethnic nature of a conflict affects involvment simply because, as argued earlier, its characteristic festering constitutes a continuously convenient opening for outside parties that wish to intervene for their own "instrumental" reasons—to weaken a rival state, to build up bargaining chips for use

---

*The level of destruction is a different matter. If intervention is anticipated, it should restrain the stronger of the local parties and thus limit suppression and attendant destruction. If this deterrence fails and intervention occurs, destruction may or may not be limited.

†There are exceptions, notably the case of Bangladesh. Moreover, it is possible that irredentist disputes have been "solved" more frequently in modern history than have separatist conflicts.

in other matters, and so on. Ethnic ties are irrelevant or secondary in these cases, and the form and magnitude of intervention vary according to a different dynamic. But when partisan involvement in an ethnic conflict occurs on this basis, it seems typically to be limited: sufficient to have a nuisance value but insufficient to compel a settlement satisfactory to one or all of the local protagonists. The outside party has in fact considerable incentives to keep the conflict from being settled either way, as long as it serves a useful purpose. When that is no longer the case, it has no incentives to be involved at all.

Moreover, since ethnic conflict characterizes a majority of the states in the contemporary world, this type of conflict extension is likely to occur frequently—and to add further hostility to already acrimonious relationships. We are thus back to the starting point of this study: the need to examine more carefully the international dimensions of domestic ethnic conflicts, in view of the frequency of such conflicts and their peculiar location on the "borderline" between domestic and international politics.

NOTES

1. A few examples indicate the scope of this literature. On cultural pluralism and foreign policy formulation, see Abdul Asiz Said, ed., *Ethnicity and U. S. Foreign Policy* (New York: Praeger, 1977); George A. Codding, *The Federal Government of Switzerland* (Boston: Houghton Mifflin, 1961); and Cynthia W. Frey, "Ethnicity in the Yugoslav Theory of International Relations," paper read at the American Political Science Association annual meeting, Chicago, August 1974 (mimeographed). On boundary disputes, see Ravi L. Kapil, "On the Conflict Potential of Inherited Boundaries in Africa," *World Politics* 18 (July 1966): 656–73; and Saadia Touval, *The Boundary Politics of Independent Africa* (Cambridge, Mass.: Harvard University Press, 1972). On migrant workers and foreign policy, see Roger Leys, "South African Gold Mining in 1974: The Gold of Migrant Labour," *African Affairs* 74 (April 1975): 196–208; V. M. Briggs, *Mexican Migration and the U. S. Labor Market* (Austin: University of Texas Press, 1975); and Samuel L. Sharp, "Ethnicity and Migration in Yugoslavia," *Studies in Comparative International Development* 10, no. 3 (1975): 63–70. Among several works on foreign policy implications of the permanent migration of Chinese, an excellent volume is David Mozingo, *Chinese Policy Towards Indonesia, 1949–1967* (Ithaca, N. Y.: Cornell University Press, 1976).

2. A notable exception is Istvan Kende, *Local Wars in Asia, Africa and Latin America* (Budapest: Hungarian Academy of Sciences, Center for Afro-Asian Research, 1972) and his "Twenty-Five Years of Local Wars," *Journal of Peace Research* 8, no. 1 (1971): 5–22. He concludes that internal ethnic conflict is less likely to be externalized than "anti-regime conflict" is.

Major works by other scholars using aggregate data analysis fail to treat ethnic conflict as a separate variable. See Jonathan Wilkenfeld, ed., *Conflict Behavior and Linkage Politics* (New York: McKay, 1973); Ivo K. and Rosalind L. Feierabend, "Level of Development and Internation Behavior," in Richard Butwell, ed., *Foreign Policy and the Developing Nation* (Lexington: University of Kentucky Press, 1969), pp. 135–88; and, for a review article of this literature, Andrew Mack, "Numbers Are Not Enough," *Comparative Politics* 7 (July 1975): 597–618. The main work dealing with the same problem but using a different methodology—James N. Rosenau, ed., *International Aspects of Civil Strife* (Princeton: Princeton University Press, 1964)—similarly ignores ethnic conflict.

3. Recent studies that include an international dimension are Cynthia H. Enloe, "Multinational Corporations in the Making and Unmaking of Ethnic Groups," paper read at the Conference on Challenges to the Nation-State, Denver, June 1976 (mimeographed); Stephanie G. Neuman, ed., *Small States and Segmented Societies* (New York: Praeger, 1976); Judy S. Bertelsen, ed., *Non-State Nations in International Politics* (New York: Praeger, 1977); and Robert G. Wirsing, "The International Politics of Cultural Pluralism," paper read at the International Studies Association annual meeting, St. Louis, March 1977 (mimeographed).

4. Ted Robert Gurr, "Social Change and the Interplay of Internal and International Political Conflicts," position paper prepared for the International Political Science Association meeting, Montreal, August 1973, p. 9 (mimeographed).

5. George Modelski makes this a central point in arguing that civil strife inevitably acquires international dimensions. "International Relations of Internal War," in Rosenau, op. cit., pp. 14–15.

6. For efforts at systematic identification of the links between domestic and foreign policy, see James N. Rosenau, ed., *Linkage Politics* (New York: Free Press, 1969); and his "Pre-Theories and Theories of Foreign Policy," in his edited volume *The Scientific Study of Foreign Policy* (New York: Free Press, 1971). Again, ethnic conflict is not discussed as a separate variable in this literature.

7. Talcott Parsons, "Some Theoretical Considerations on the Nature and Trends of Change of Ethnicity," in Nathan Glazer and Daniel P. Moynihan, eds., *Ethnicity: Theory and Experience* (Cambridge, Mass.: Harvard University Press, 1975), p. 56. Italics in the original.

8. Fredrik Barth, ed., *Ethnic Groups and Boundaries* (Boston: Little, Brown, 1969), p. 14.

9. Crawford Young, *Politics of Cultural Pluralism* (Madison: University of Wisconsin Press, 1976), p. 72.

10. Clifford Geertz characterizes ethnic groups "as possible self-standing, maximal social units, as candidates for nationhood" in "The Integrative Revolution: Primordial Sentiments and Civil Politics in the New States," in Clifford Geertz, ed., *Old Societies and New States* (New York: Free Press, 1963), p. 111. A similar concept is used in Harold Isaacs, *Idols of the Tribe: Group Identity and Political Change* (New York: Harper & Row, 1975). By contrast, M. G. Smith, *The Plural Society in the British West Indies* (Berkeley: University of California Press, 1965), exemplifies the early writings on cultural pluralism.

Cynthia H. Enloe, *Ethnic Conflict and Political Development* (Boston: Little, Brown, 1973), is more difficult to categorize. She views ethnic groups as potential nationalities (see esp. pp. 12–13); indeed, this is one of the starting points for her analysis of ethnic groups as entities of political development. On the other hand, she sees ethnicity as "not primarily ideological or political; rather it is cultural and social" (p. 222). The term "nationality" is used in a very specific sense: "Nationality ethnicity is characterized by communal identity having its roots in association with a foreign country. Ethnic groups referred to as 'nationalities' usually are made up of relative newcomers" (p. 24).

11. The ascriptive element in ethnic identity partly explains why ethnic conflicts are difficult to solve and, hence, tend to acquire a festering quality. Nevertheless, ethnic identities can and do change, as discussed, for instance, in Donald Horowitz, "Ethnic Identity," in Glazer and Moynihan, op. cit., pp. 111–40.

12. Modelski, op. cit., p. 28.

13. At the analytical level, Schermerhorn sees this dualism reflected in "power-conflict theory" and "system analysis," which he describes as "dialectically related perspectives" on ethnic relations. R. A. Schermerhorn, *Comparative Ethnic Relations: A Framework for Theory and Research* (New York: Random House, 1970), esp. pp. 50–64. Other writers have used different terms in making similar observations.

14. James Rosenau, "Internal War as an International Event," in Rosenau, *International Aspects of Civil Strife*, pp. 53–57.

15. If Ted Gurr's categories of turmoil, conspiracy, and internal war are used, the point would be that ethnic violence typically occurs as turmoil and conspiracy. For a discussion of his categories, see Ted Gurr, *Why Men Rebel* (Princeton: Princeton University Press, 1971), pp. 9–11.

16. For examples of Marxist intepretations of ethnic conflict, see Oliver Cromwell Cox, *Caste, Class and Race* (New York: Monthly Review Press, 1959); Joel C. Edelstein, "Pluralist and Marxist Perspectives on Ethnicity and Nation-Building," in Wendel Bell and Walter E. Freeman, eds., *Ethnicity and Nation-Building* (Beverly Hills, Calif.: Sage, 1974), pp. 45–57; and for an application to one of the case studies in our volume, Anders Boserup, "Power in a Post-Colonial Setting: The Why and Whither of Religious Confrontation in Ulster," paper prepared for the Sixth European Congress of the Peace Research Society (International), 1969 (mimeographed).

17. Donald Horowitz, "Multiracial Politics in the New States," in Robert J. Jackson and Michael B. Stein, eds., *Issues in Comparative Politics* (New York: St. Martin's, 1971), p. 167.

18. Inis L. Claude, *Swords into Plowshares* (New York: Random House, 1964), p. 48.

19. See especially Alfred Cobban, *National Self-determination* (London: Oxford University Press, 1945), versus C. A. Macartney, *National States and National Minorities* (London: Oxford University Press, 1934).

20. V. I. Lenin, *Questions of National Policy and Proletarian Internationalism* (Moscow: Foreign Languages Publishing House, n.d.), contains Lenin's basic writings on "the national question." The model of conflict extension across national boundaries is, of course, developed in his classic treatise *Imperialism: The Highest State of Capitalism* (International Publishers, 1939).

21. Lewis Coser, *The Functions of Social Conflict* (New York: Free Press, 1956).

22. See note 2.

23. As Crawford Young notes, "Territorial contiguity is an obvious but fundamental prerequisite for separatism to be a practical policy." "Nationalism and Separatism in Africa," in Martin Kilson, ed., *New States in the Modern World* (Cambridge, Mass.: Harvard University Press, 1975), p. 62.

24. This if further discussed in John A. Armstrong, "Mobilized and Proletarian Diasporas," *American Political Science Review* 70 (June 1976): 393–408. A similar theme is found in the literature on the relationship between the overseas Chinese and China, illustrating more fully some of the restraints on the minority group once it has a stake in the polity where it resides.

25. Alvin Rabushka and Kenneth A. Shepsle discuss this dynamic more fully in *Politics in Plural Societies: A Theory of Democratic Instability* (Columbus, Ohio: Charles E. Merrill, 1972).

26. See Kapil, op. cit.; and Touval, op. cit.

27. The possibility that ethnic kin will take matters into their own hands will be particularly strong in states where, as Walker Connor observed with reference to sub-Sahara Africa—in "Nation Building or Destroying?," *World Politics* 24 (April 1972): 353—"ethnic nationalism is the most momentous political fact . . . [and] earlier estimates of the strength of the central governments proved exaggerated. . . ."

28. For a detailed analysis of conflict interaction in irredentist disputes, see Myron Weiner, "The Macedonian Syndrome," *World Politics* 23 (July 1971): 665–83.

CHAPTER

2

NORTHERN IRELAND

Terrance G. Carroll

Self-identification by ethnic group members is very strong in Ulster. During the 1970s both Protestants and Catholics are likely to have strengthened their group identification as the perceived (and real) threat to members of both communities increased. Even during the 1960s, which until 1969 was one of the most peaceful periods in the province's history, virtually every member of the population identified with one group or the other. In the 1961 census less than 0.03 percent of the population failed to indicate membership in a Roman Catholic or Protestant church, and the proportion was still well under 1 percent when Richard Rose carried out his major opinion survey seven years later.[1] The few Jews, atheists, and other non-Christians in the province are assigned to one or the other religious group as a matter of course. Thus one distinguishes between Protestant Jews and Catholic Jews.

While the identifying characteristic is religion, the groups have also developed separate nationalities. Three-quarters of Rose's Catholic respondents identified themselves as Irish, while more than 70 percent of Protestants described themselves as British or Ulstermen. And the religious-cum-national identity is not limited to political and religious aspects of life. Four-fifths of both groups indicated that it would make a significant difference to their friends and family if they were to change their religion.[2]

The strength of ethnic identification in the province becomes even more impressive when one considers that the religious factor is not supported by other characteristics, such as race or language. Both the Irish ancestors of Ulster's Catholics and the Scots ancestors of the Protestants were Gaels. In both cases the Gaelic language was replaced by English, and the racial heritage was diluted through intermarriage with the Anglo-Normans and their descendants. A myth of nationality based upon race exists in Ireland, but it is almost entirely the product of the aspirations of eighteenth- and nineteenth-century historians.[3] We have a sort of inverted pyramid with the huge segment of social life that is shaped by ethnicity resting on the narrow base of religion.

There *are* cultural differences between the two groups, but they seem to be kept alive and exaggerated precisely in order to make the distinction greater. Catholics and Protestants play different games, sing different songs, and revere different heroes. Both groups support organizations that exist solely to maintain these differences. At the same time Catholics and Protestants are very similar in their general attitude toward authority, similar in their willingness to experiment and try new things, similar in their degree of trust in their fellow man, and even similar in the fundamentalism of their religious beliefs.[4] M. W. Heslinga has argued that different patterns of historical development have created a single culture in Ulster that is different from that in southern Ireland,[5] and this is also the case when one compares the province with Britain.

As a result, less than half of Rose's Protestant sample thought that the British were "about the same" as themselves, and less than half of the Catholics thought that people in the Republic of Ireland were the same as their group. Two-thirds of Protestants and four-fifths of Catholics said that Ulstermen of the other religion were the same as themselves.[6] The fact that Ulstermen identify with different groups but perceive few differences between members of these distinct collectivities is almost certainly a function of their common culture and common environment.

Both the Catholic and Protestant communities in Northern Ireland are biologically self-perpetuating. Only 4 percent of Rose's respondents had married members of the other religious group, and more than 80 percent of both groups felt that it was important that children be brought up with the same religious views as their parents.[7] By the late 1960s, however, rules governing intergroup relations other than marriage seemed to be weakening. Two-thirds of Protestants and three-fourths of Catholics claimed to have at least a few friends from the other religious community, and similar proportions had neighbors who belonged to the other group. Fifty-eight percent of both groups felt free to discuss controversial subjects like politics with people of the other religion; and less than a third thought it important that their children share their political views, even on such fundamental matters as the unification of Ireland. Three of every four respondents indicated a desire for friendlier ties with members of the other group.[8]

These replies may in part have represented a desire for a new state of affairs, rather than being a reflection of existing relations between the communities. The salience of religious identification seems to have been a source of embarrassment to many Ulstermen, and thus may have been understated.[9] Certainly the importance of exclusiveness in social interaction has increased, as the level of violence has grown since 1968. Thousands of people living in religiously mixed areas have abandoned their homes for the greater security of communities dominated by their own group. In a 1972 survey of people active in politics in four Catholic districts, one-third of the sample mentioned losing contact with Protestant friends as one of the consequences of the violence.[10]

To summarize, then, ethnic groups in Northern Ireland have but one identifying characteristic. Ethnic identities in Ulster remained surprisingly strong despite this narrow base, but the importance of maintaining these identities declined in the absence of intergroup conflict. In a sense ethnic identification would seem to be a function of the existence of issues dividing the groups, but it is important to note that it was not perceived in this way by members of the groups. While the group identity may not have seemed of vital import in periods of peace, neither Protestants nor Catholics believed that the time would ever come when religion would make no difference to the way Ulstermen feel about each other.[11]

ETHNIC CONFLICT IN ULSTER

Two great gulfs divide the population of Ireland. The first is based upon the geographical and historical isolation of Ulster from the rest of the island.[12] Rugged mountains limited north-south communications, while the thirteen sea miles to Scotland formed not a barrier but a well-traveled highway. While improving technology eventually overcame the barrier to north-south intercourse, centuries of differentiated historical development had created a culture in the north distinct from that found in the south.

The second gulf developed after 1603, when the British completed their conquest by defeating the Gaelic forces of Ulster, and thus united Ireland under a single effective government for the first time in its history. Following this victory the Scottish Presbyterian community was established in the north of Ireland. It was also during the seventeenth century that the modern, English-speaking, Catholic-Irish nation came into being as the Gaelic Irish and the descendants of the twelfth-century Anglo-Norman invaders finally merged. With these developments the foundations were laid for the modern division between Protestants and Catholics in Northern Ireland.

Protestants see Ulster as their homeland, just as the descendants of seventeenth-century settlers in Virginia and Quebec identify with North America. Catholics feel a part of the Irish nation, but at the same time they see themselves as different from their southern compatriots in many ways. Ulster is also their home. Neither Protestants nor Catholics can leave, yet they are equally incapable of living together.

Until the beginning of the nineteenth century, however, social divisions in Ireland were based as much upon class as religion. Protestant dissenters were treated almost as harshly as Catholics by the Church of England Ascendancy class, and working-class Presbyterians found that they had more in common with their Roman Catholic neighbors than with their Episcopalian masters. The unsuccessful rebellion by the United Irishmen in 1798 was led by Protestants, and its leaders provided the philosophical basis for modern Irish republicanism. Increasingly, however, lower-class Protestants and Catholics found themselves in economic competition. Catholics, who were even worse off than Presbyterians, would accept farm tenancies under less favorable conditions and would work for lower wages simply so that they might earn a livelihood at all. The Ascendancy class encouraged Protestant dissenters to view Catholics as their rivals and enemies; and the Orange Order, which was created by middle-class Anglicans, soon attracted scores of Presbyterian members. From the 1830s on, Belfast regularly experienced sectarian riots, frequently after demonstrations and parades by the Orange Order.

The desire among Catholics for political independence also grew during the nineteenth century, culminating in the home rule debates between 1885 and 1914. It soon became obvious that Catholic Irishmen would no longer accept British rule, while Protestant Ulstermen would fight rather than become a minority in an independent Ireland. By the beginning of World War I, both sides had well-organized private armies of more than 100,000 men. With the Dublin uprising of Easter week 1913, and the savage guerrilla war of 1916–21, Ireland became ungovernable. Finally, in 1922, Britain recognized the independence of the Irish Free State, while six Ulster counties remained as a province within the United Kingdom.

In 1922–23 both the Irish Free State and Northern Ireland experienced bloody civil war. In the south the more fully committed republicans of the Irish Republican Army (IRA) fought the forces of the new government, which had compromised by accepting the continuation of formal ties with Britain (Commonwealth membership and the monarchy) as the price of independence. The IRA simultaneously fought the Protestants and British in the north, attempting to prevent the division of Ireland into two jurisdictions. Both efforts failed in the short run, but the IRA has never accepted either failure as permanent.[13]

At its inception the new regime in Ulster was faced with a Catholic minority that made up one-third of the population of the province. Many of these people were undoubtedly disloyal, refusing to accord legitimacy to the regime. The regime reacted by treating all Catholics as inherently disloyal, and the political institutions of Ulster were explicitly designed to ensure Protestant domination.[14] Periodic riots by Orangemen reinforced Catholic ethnic identification by creating a constant fear of a pogrom. Periodic raids by the IRA, and the major campaign it waged from 1939 to 1945, reinforced Protestant ethnic identification and kept alive the determination to suppress the rebellious Catholic minority.

After World War II, Ulster entered a period of relative prosperity and sectarian hostility declined. Between 1956 and 1962 the IRA waged yet another campaign to force the British out of Ulster, but was unable even to seriously inconvenience the authorities in the north. Unlike the situation that developed at the end of the 1960s, in 1956–62 the IRA could not justify its efforts on the ground of defending Catholics against attack, or by pointing to any reforms within Northern Ireland that could be attributed to its campaign. The only justification for the battle was the desire for a united Ireland, and this goal was not sufficient in itself to engender significant support for violence among northern Catholics. When the campaign was finally abandoned, the IRA admitted that it had failed because of the lack of support among Catholic Ulstermen.[15]

During the 1960s the Protestant Unionist government for the first time made an effort to win the allegiance of Catholics, and that effort seemed to be succeeding. Catholic politicians accepted the role of official opposition in the provincial parliament; and when a civil rights movement began to develop in the late 1960s its demands were for full participation within the existing system, rather than for its abolition. The concerns of the new Northern Ireland Civil Rights Association (NICRA) centered upon such issues as the adoption of a universal franchise for local government elections, the need for an independent revision of gerrymandered electoral districts, and the elimination of discrimination in public employment and in the allocation of public housing.

Many Protestants, including a majority of Protestant politicians, remained convinced that this movement was simply republicanism in a new guise. They opposed making concessions that would strengthen the hand of a group they thought disloyal, and they regularly staged counterdemonstrations when the NICRA sponsored protest marches.[16] Widespread rioting broke out after several of these confrontations, pitting Protestant civilians and the police (whose membership was largely Protestant) against Catholic demonstrators. A judicial inquiry established by the government found that police violence was "... indiscriminate ... and wholly without justification ... " in Londonderry in October 1968; that a "police riot" took place in that city in January 1969; and that the police were guilty of " ... assault occasioning personal injury and of malicious damage to property ... " in Derry in April of that year.[17] A series of bomb attacks against public utilities in the spring of 1969 was almost universally attributed to the IRA, and strengthened the hostility of many Protestants. These attacks were later found to be the work of Protestant extremists who hoped to force the moderate prime minister, Terence O'Neill, from office. They were successful, for he resigned in April.[18]

The worst violence in Ulster since the 1920s broke out in Londonderry and Belfast in August 1969. The police used all the weapons at their disposal, including machine guns, in an attempt to suppress rioters in Catholic districts; but they were fought to a standstill. Catholics believed that the pogrom had begun; that the combined forces of the police and Protestant civilians were staging an armed invasion with the goal of destroying their communities. The authorities, on the other hand, believed that they were faced with a

". . . conspiracy of forces seeking to overthrow a Government democratically elected by a large majority."[19] The British government was finally forced to intervene, sending troops into Belfast and Derry. They were welcomed as saviors by the Catholic population of both cities.

The British had pressured the Northern Ireland government to make some reforms after the violence of 1968, and a new package of concessions was announced in the fall of 1969. By the end of that year all but one of the demands of the civil rights movement had been met. The sole exception was the refusal of the government to abandon its emergency powers legislation. Protestant reaction to these reforms was extremely bitter. Many Protestants had suggested all along that the civil rights movement was a front for subversion, and the violence convinced them that they were right. The government, in their view, was giving in to the demands of violent rebels. Catholics, on the other hand, remained unmollified. The concessions were made so hesitantly and with such obvious reluctance that they could do little to win the allegiance of the minority. During the following months it became clear that by focusing upon specific issues, the civil rights movement missed the heart of the problem. Catholics formed a permanent minority, and in the British parliamentary system they would remain totally excluded from power no matter how "fair" the rules.[20] Their well-being was dependent upon the whim and will of the Protestant majority, which had given Catholics no grounds for trust.

Almost inevitably, relations between the British army and the Catholic minority began to worsen. The IRA had virtually withered away after the disasterous 1956–62 campaign, and its remaining members had turned from a total reliance upon violence to the promotion of left-wing causes. Its complete inability to protect the Catholic ghettos in 1969 resulted in a bitter rejection of the "official" IRA by many former members and supporters. After the riots a new "provisional" IRA was born in the Catholic slums of Belfast and Derry. It returned to the traditional commitment to the unification of Ireland, and the traditional means to that end—the gun.

As occasional small-scale clashes between the provisional IRA and the British army developed, the troops began massive arms searches in Catholic areas. While this alienated many Catholics, it was always seen as too little, too late by Protestants who remembered the ease with which they had handled the 1956–62 IRA campaign. By early 1971 polarization was almost complete. Officially recorded "security incidents" averaged 318 per month during the first half of the year, and the rate was doubled in July.

The reaction of the authorities was to institute internment without trial for suspected subversives, and by mid-November more than 1,100 Catholic men had been arrested. In the six months preceding internment 24 people had been killed. In the next six months 171 people died in civil violence. The battle has continued undiminished. In 1972, 468 people were killed, and the Northern Ireland government was replaced by direct rule from Westminster. In 1973 a new form of government that gave Catholics proportional representation in both the assembly and the executive was created by the British. It foundered within a year in the face of massive Protestant opposition. In addition to giving power to a minority that was seen as disloyal, this system also was seen by Protestants as the first step on the road to a united Ireland, since it gave the government of the Republic of Ireland a role on an advisory "Council of Ireland." In 1973, 250 people died in civil violence, and another 216 perished in 1974. In 1975 a constitutional convention was established to try to find a system acceptable to both sides. The Protestant majority united behind the notion of restoring the old Ulster regime, however; the idea was unacceptable to both the British and the Catholics of Ulster. During this period 246 people were killed.

The roots of this conflict are complex, but they have become somewhat clearer over the last several years. It is not a fight about civil rights, not a battle over reform proposals. If the system incorporates any version of the majority rule principle, a self-identified minority will be dependent upon a majority it does not trust. For the committed republicans who form the core of the IRA, the solution is the unification of Ireland. Majority and minority would find their positions reversed, although the IRA claims that Protestants would suffer no disability in the new republic. In the 1968 survey a majority of Catholics indicated a preference for a united Ireland, but only 13 percent thought that this goal justified the use of violence.[21] Even after the violent clashes of 1968–72, only one-third of the Catholic political activists in this author's survey supported the use of violence to bring about the unification of Ireland.[22] Similarly, a survey carried out in May 1973 found that while a majority of Ulster Catholics favored some form of united Ireland, less than 10 percent were prepared to try to sabotage the power-sharing proposal.[23]

For a few Catholics, then, the battle has the unification of Ireland as its goal. In the eyes of a far greater number of Catholics, the conflict has a more limited aim. It is seen as being primarily a defensive battle, and any outcome providing them with increased security would be acceptable. Thus, 70 percent of the respondents in my 1972 study indicated that they felt the IRA's campaign of violence had some worthwhile results, and 60 percent specifically mentioned "defense" as a beneficial consequence. Less than 40 percent of these Catholic activists were so committed to the unification of Ireland that they rejected all possible types of Northern Ireland regimes as unacceptable. While there was no concensus on the format of an acceptable system, the types of changes commonly suggested included "power sharing," as proposed by the British in 1973, and local control over the police.

Among Protestants the division of opinion is less stable and less clear, but it does seem that there has been a steady movement toward an uncompromising position in recent years. Surveys in early 1973 found that while only one Protestant in ten thought that "power-sharing" was the best solution, about half were willing to give such a system a try.[24] When the 1973 elections for a power-sharing Assembly were held under a proportional representation system, 59 candidates who opposed the unification of Ireland were elected. Of these, 27 opposed power-sharing and 32 supported it (albeit with some reservations). The 19 members of the Catholic Social Democratic and Labour party (SDLP) who won seats also supported power-sharing.

By February 1974 when the British general election was held, Protestant opinion had shifted considerably. Eleven of the 12 Ulster seats were won by Protestant hardliners who opposed power-sharing, and candidates taking this position received about 60 percent of the total vote. Three months later a Protestant general strike made the province ungovernable, and the Assembly had to be abolished. In May 1975 delegates to a constitutional convention were elected, again on the basis of proportional representation. This time the United Ulster Unionist Council (UUUC)—a coalition of Protestant opponents of power-sharing—won 46 seats, a clear majority. Although a few members of the UUUC expressed interest in a limited version of power-sharing, and leaders of Protestant militia groups gave some support to this position, the hardliners held firm and pushed through a recommendation for a return to the pre-1972 regime.

Security for Protestants has two aspects. There is the immediate physical threat from armed members of the IRA, of course, but in the longer run there is also the danger of losing security by being forced into a united Ireland. There is little doubt that most Protestants believe the short-term threat could best be handled by reconstructing a Protestant government in Ulster and giving it a free hand. There is disagreement on how the long-term threat can best be minimized.

Some Protestants favor complete integration into the United Kingdom (UK). In their view the present distinction between Ulster and the rest of the UK gives Irish republicans hope, and increases the possibility that Britain may someday decide to abandon the province. Some Protestants favor the power-sharing model, either with the hope of winning the allegiance of Catholics, or because they calculate that this is the greatest degree of provincial autonomy that Westminster is prepared to grant. A majority of Protestants, however, see the restoration of majority rule—meaning Protestant rule—as the only means of meeting either the short-term or the long-term threat.

We have three general views of the conflict, then. Committed republicans see it as an effort to separate Ulster from the UK, and to make it a part of a united Ireland. This group would include not more than one-third of Catholics and one-tenth of the population, and probably is considerably smaller than this estimate. A more conservative estimate could be made on the basis of the 1973 survey that found that only 10 percent of Catholics wanted to see the power-sharing Assembly fail.[25] This would put the proportion of unqualified republicans at less than 4 percent of the population. In the middle are those Catholics and Protestants who believe that security may be attainable in a reformed system that gives Catholics a bigger role. Despite the considerable differences among the people in this group, it would seem to include only 40 percent of the population. The largest group, constituting about half of the total population, are Protestants who believe that security can be attained only in a system in which the Protestant majority is free to suppress those who oppose the regime.

PARTIES TO THE CONFLICT

These segments of the population of Ulster, and the groups that represent them, are the direct internal parties to the dispute. Protestant "loyalists" have carried on their part in the conflict with little significant external aid in recent years. The ethnic ties with Scotland, and with the Scotch-Irish in America, are relatively weak. There have been a few incidents in which outside supporters have provided money and weapons to the Protestant cause, but these have had little effect on the ability of Protestants to continue the battle. Protestants are strong enough not to require extensive aid, and their internal resources overshadow such assistance as they do receive. Within Ulster they have a two-to-one superiority in numbers; and they are probably the most powerful group in Ireland as a whole, with the possible exception of the British army. It seems clear that they are stronger than the Irish Army and the IRA taken separately or (an unlikely situation) in combination.

Protestant political groups have changed and multiplied since 1974, when the Ulster Unionist partly split in two.[26] The various "loyalist" organizations together form the strongest political group in the province, as is demonstrated by their current coalition, the UUUC, which received 55 percent of the vote in the 1975 constitutional convention elections. Its position in the convention debates was clear: Ulster must be governed by a Protestant-controlled government with significant powers. No other solution would be accepted. The Unionist party of Northern Ireland is made up of the minority of moderates who accepted power-sharing and followed the former prime minister, Brian Faulkner. When the old Unionist party split, its support declined from more than 25 percent of the electorate in the 1973 Assembly elections to only 8 percent in the 1975 convention vote. The Alliance and Northern Ireland Labour parties have been the main hope of liberals with their combination of accepting the British tie and an explicitly nonsectarian appeal, but together they receive the support of only one Ulsterman in ten.

The greatest strength of Protestant Ulstermen comes not from their voting power but, rather, from the realization that the state cannot continue to function in the face of their noncooperation, even if noncooperation is confined to more or less peaceful measures. The general strike of 1974 proved a devastating weapon that even the resources of the British army could not counter. Without the cooperation of the Protestant workers, electricity could not be provided, sewage could not be disposed of, gasoline could not be supplied.[27] Being incapable of ensuring the provision of the essential services of modern life, the regime could not survive.

More explicitly violent weapons are required when the enemy is a guerrilla group or a disaffected segment of the population, however, than when the target is a government and regime constrained by its own sense of its duties and obligations. Protestants also are well prepared to move from industrial action to violent confrontation. The two institutions that provide weapons training to large numbers of Ulstermen are the Royal Ulster Constabulary, with an authorized strength of 6,500, and the Ulster Defence Regiment, a 7,700-man militia force under British army command. In both cases more than 90 percent of the members are Protestant. Paramilitary groups with a claimed membership of some 100,000 drill openly in the street, and Protestant terrorist organizations have assassinated more than 200 Catholics since 1972.

Representatives of the Catholic community are less easy to classify within an internal/external dichotomy, since they frequently deny the legitimacy of the division of Ireland and organize on a cross-border basis. The most important Catholic political force is the SDLP. While it favors the unification of Ireland, its activities are confined to Ulster. It consistently appeals to about one-quarter of the voting public, and it was the only Catholic party to win seats in either the Assembly or the convention. Its success has convinced the British authorities that no long-term solution can be achieved without the consent of the SDLP, acting as representatives of the minority. Many Ulster Protestants, however, still believe that they could govern adequately in the face of SDLP opposition if given a free hand.

Peaceful demonstrations proved a more effective weapon than voting power for Catholics in 1968–71, as they did for Protestants in 1974. While the Catholic-dominated NICRA could not bring normal life to a halt through noncooperation, it was able to generate considerable support at home and abroad, and to force the authorities to take steps aimed at halting the protest marches. These steps ranged from legal bans and police attacks to concessions and a major package of reforms. Again, however, Protestants were less convinced than the British that the way to meet the demands of the civil rights movement was by making concessions. A firmer stand, they felt, would soon bring the rebels back into line.

Protestants pointed to the increasing activity of the IRA to support their argument that concessions served only to encourage rebels. The IRA sees itself as a primary party to the dispute. While its participation is more effective when it is seen as playing a part in the general struggle of the Catholic community, its main goal of creating a united Ireland by force of arms is endorsed by only a minority of Ulster's Catholics. The IRA would wish to continue the battle even if some less dramatic solution acceptable to a majority of Catholics could be achieved.

Like the Irish government, the IRA has never recognized the legality or the morality of the division of Ireland. As a result, it is organized on an all-Ireland basis. Headquarters is in Dublin; many IRA guerrillas are based in the Republic of Ireland, where they have been somewhat more secure than they would have been in Northern Ireland; and most of the weapons and explosives used in Ulster arrive from the south. There is also a "Northern Command" in Ulster, however, and large IRA units exist in most of the Catholic communities in the province.

By early 1971 there were an estimated 2,000 active IRA men in Northern Ireland.[28] Since then their number probably has fluctuated greatly, depending on both the success of the British forces and the strength of Catholic support at any given moment. Following "Bloody Sunday" in 1972, when British soldiers killed 13 Catholic demonstrators in Londonderry, for example, the IRA had more volunteers than it could handle. Six months later a bomb attack by the IRA killed nine people and, as a result, a peace movement grew rapidly among Catholics. IRA strength almost certainly fell at that time. Despite such ups and downs, and despite the efforts of the British army, the IRA has proved able to carry on a large-scale guerrilla war since 1971. There is every reason to believe that it will remain able to carry on the battle as long as it receives even a modicum of support from the Catholic population.

The horror of the strife since 1969 has led some Catholics and Protestants to unite, forming an active, public opposition to men of violence no matter what their political goals. Peace movements developed significant strength in 1972, and again in 1976. They demanded that the IRA, Protestant extremists, and the British army all withdraw from the battle. The courageous efforts of members of the peace movement have resulted in brief, temporary cease-fire periods, but they have been unable to establish a permanent peace because they have no answer to the real disputes that underlie the conflict.[29] Simple desire for a peaceful solution may be an essential prerequisite to the achievement of agreement, but such an aspiration is not enough in itself to bring an end to the violence.

EXTERNAL ASPECTS OF THE CONFLICT

The internal politics of Northern Ireland became of interest to the student of international relations because of the involvement of the British and Irish governments and publics, the involvement of Irish-Americans (and, to a lesser extent, Irish-Canadians), and the reaction of other international actors. Perhaps the most noteworthy aspects of this external involvement have been the general reluctance of outside governments to become involved in Ulster's affairs, particularly in a partisan fashion, and the importance they have attached to avoiding the internationalization of the dispute.

British Conservatives explicitly allied themselves to the Protestant cause between 1880 and 1914, going so far as to condone open rebellion against the Crown.[30] With the "Irish Question" apparently settled by the division of 1922, however, British interest in Irish affairs waned. Not until the late 1960s did happenings across the Irish Sea again become of central concern at Westminster. The role of the British government in Ulster has undergone considerable change since the first intrusion in 1968. At that time the goal was to prod the Northern Ireland government into making reforms that might settle the grievances of the minority, and thus win their allegiance. Between 1969 and 1972 the IRA came to be seen as the enemy, and the British authorities tried to suppress republican guerrillas while restraining Protestant hardliners (and the British troops on the ground) so as not to alienate the Catholic population completely. Both of these attempts failed.

Since 1972 there has been an increasingly desperate struggle by both Conservative and Labour governments to find a solution—any solution—that both Protestants and Catholics would accept. Continuing to pour human and financial resources into Ulster while pleasing neither party in the province is a singularly unappealing prospect for the British, but allying with either side would be just as unpalatable. Ruthless suppression of the Catholic minority is a prospect that no British government can stomach, while the expulsion of a population in which the overwhelming majority wish to remain in the UK is equally impossible.

The British are left with two policies to pursue. One is to meet force with force, attempting at least to reduce the level of violence. At best this is a holding action. There is no evidence that any level of coercion the British would be willing and able to employ could successfully repress the combatants in Ulster. The longer-term policy, then, is to encourage Ulster's Catholics and Protestants to discover a means of living together peacefully. So far this policy also has failed.

The main British initiative was the Assembly proposal.[31] It was intended to win acceptance from Catholics by ensuring that their representatives would be included in the executive, and by recognizing through the Council of Ireland that the Republic of Ireland had a legitimate interest in Ulster's affairs. Protestants were to be induced to accept these changes by having the Irish and British governments assert clearly that Ulster's position in the UK could be altered only by a majority decision, and by a crackdown on the IRA in the Republic. Many Protestants opposed power-sharing in principle, and they found the declarations on the status of Northern Ireland unconvincing. They remembered that in 1971, when Prime Minister Harold Wilson was in the opposition, he had suggested that the unification of Ireland could and should come about within fifteen years. They noted that Irish Prime Minister Liam Cosgrave was forced to equivocate on the question of respecting Northern Ireland's position because of a clause in the Republic's constitution that claimed jurisdiction over the north.[32] And, although Dublin undertook stringent measures to combat terrorism, the IRA proved able to continue its battle despite the efforts of authorities throughout the British Isles.

With the failure of the Assembly plan, the British decided that Ulster's Protestants and Catholics must themselves find the solution. To this end they established the constitutional convention in 1975.[33] Some back-benchers at Westminister had, by this time, come to favor a unilateral withdrawal of British forces from Ulster, and the Labour government tried to encourage convention members by noting that continued British military and financial support depended upon the efforts made by Ulstermen to solve their own problems.

When pushed, however, the government firmly rejected the notion of bringing the troops home in the absence of a settlement. The recommendation by the convention that the pre-1972 regime be reconstructed has been turned down by Westminster. Both the Labour and Conservative parties remain convinced that some form of power-sharing is essential. What the British will do if these efforts prove no more successful in the future than they have been in the past is unclear. The public record suggests that British leaders would prefer not to think about that possibility.

The British public has displayed similar changes in opinion, but its current position seems to be more extreme than that of the government. Initially public opinion favored the Catholics who were seen as victims of bigotry and discrimination. Gradually, as the IRA campaign escalated and the mortality rate among civilians and British soldiers increased, opinion shifted away from the Catholic minority. When the IRA extended its bomb attacks to British cities, sympathy for the side they represented disappeared almost completely. At the same time, however, the intransigence of Protestant leaders and the growing Protestant involvement in violence prevented British public support from simply switching sides. The common reaction now seems to be "a plague on both your houses." By November 1975, 64 percent of the British public favored a unilateral withdrawal of the troops in Ulster, leaving Ulstermen to sort out their own affairs however they choose.[34]

The position of the Irish government is more confusing. The constitutional claim to authority in Ulster was symbolic of the general Irish attitude from 1922 to 1969. Dublin accepted the de facto division of the island, and opposed the IRA's efforts to end that situation through force of arms. At the same time, however, the Irish government attributed Ulster's problems to the

British tie, and held that the ultimate solution could be found only in a united Ireland. Thus, when British troops were sent to Belfast and Londonderry in 1969, the Irish foreign minister condemned this action at the United Nations:

> Our history has meant that British troops are a hindrance not a help to a lasting settlement of our differences. We have maintained that differences between Irishmen can only be settled by Irishmen. . . .[35]

The riots of 1969 were generally perceived in the Republic of Ireland as an all-out attack on Ulster's Catholics. Irish army hospital units were sent to the border, and Catholic civilians from Northern Ireland were enlisted in the army reserve for one-week periods so that they could be given weapons training. Some reports indicate that an actual invasion of the north was considered, despite the relative impotence of the Irish army. The Dublin government gave £ 100,000 to a fund for relief work in the north, but the Public Accounts Committee of the Dail (Commons) later found that less than one-quarter of this money was used for the purpose authorized. The remainder almost certainly went to the IRA.[36] Two ministers were forced to resign in connection with allegations of illegally importing arms for the guerrilla force.

Once the initial fear of a pogrom passed, the actions of the Irish government became considerably more restrained. The greatest domestic challenge to the authority of the government comes from the IRA, and this makes Irish authorities understandably reluctant to support violent republicans even when their efforts are concentrated in Ulster. Beyond this, it gradually became apparent in Dublin that the notion of an imperial Britain holding on to an unwilling Ulster was untenable. Thus it was that Cosgrave's government supported the power-sharing proposal, agreed to participate in the Council of Ireland, and joined British and Northern Irish representatives at the Sunningdale conference in 1973 to work out details of this plan.

Faced with a legal challenge to the constitutionality of his declaration at Sunningdale that a change in Ulster's status would require majority approval in Northern Ireland, Cosgrave and his government were forced to equivocate. At the conclusion of the court case, however, he made his position clear by telling the Dail, "The factual position of Northern Ireland is that it is within the United Kingdom, and my government accepts this as a fact."[37] He repeated his statement that only a decision by a majority of Ulstermen could change this situation, and the government received the support of the Fianna Fail opposition on this stand.

The increasing Protestant violence, and the strength and determination they demonstrated during the general strike of 1974, gave further pause to Irish politicians. The prospect of trying to govern a country that included a million embittered Protestants must be daunting indeed. In the spring of 1976 the Irish Parliament passed tough antiterrorist legislation that permitted it to try guerrillas for crimes committed in Northern Ireland.[38] Membership in the IRA was already a crime, and a system of special criminal courts that did away with jury trials had been instituted.

Charges of membership in the IRA can be brought in these courts whenever a senior police officer is willing to state that he believes someone is active in the banned organization. The burden of proof rests with the accused. In July 1975 the chief of staff of the provisional IRA was convicted and imprisoned by means of these procedures.[39] By the end of the year the efforts of the Irish government were such that British Prime Minister Harold Wilson told the House of Commons that " . . . the Government of the Republic is as determined as Her Majesty's Government to stamp out cross-border banditry and murder. There is now close and valuable cooperation between the R.U.C. [Royal Ulster Constabulary] and the Irish police."[40] In August 1976 the Irish government proposed that constitutional safeguards be suspended, and that it be given emergency powers to deal with the IRA.

Irish public opinion remains mixed. A significant minority regularly supports the IRA, and the republican tradition is important for even the majority that does not give general approval to the activities of the guerrilla force. On a number of occasions since 1969 events in the north have aroused a great emotional response among Irishmen. After "Bloody Sunday," for example, the British embassy in Dublin was burned to the ground by a mob of some 30,000 people.[41] It is clear that most people in the Republic of Ireland sympathize with the position of Catholics in Ulster, and identify with them. When the northern minority appears to be threatened, support for the IRA and pressure on the Dublin government to intervene become overwhelming. When there is no immediate threat, however, Irishmen as a whole seem able to accept the reality of Ulster's position in the UK.

Anglo-Irish relations have never been particularly warm, and the Northern Irish situation has increased the strain. From 1969 to 1972 the Dublin government consistently and publicly held Britain responsible for the violence. Westminster responded by repeatedly condemning Ireland's failure to clamp down on the IRA terrorists operating from the south. Even during this period, however, neither government yielded to the temptation to alienate the other completely. When enraged Dubliners burned the British embassy, for example, the Irish government immediately offered to pay for the damage, and the British authorities accepted that such a gesture would discharge Dublin's responsibilities.

The improvement in relations between the two countries that began in 1972 seems to have been based upon a perceived similarity in interests with regard to Ulster, rather than on a fear that the conflict might have a deleterious effect on other binational concerns. In 1972 Britain admitted that Ireland had a legitimate role to play in Ulster's affairs, and in the south new antiterrorist legislation was introduced. Britain has since consulted regularly with Dublin on Northern Ireland, and with the Council of Ireland proposal the UK tried to create an institutionalized role for the south. Ireland reciprocated by accepting the reality of Ulster's position within the UK and making its antiterrorist measures more stringent year by year.

The cooperative approach by Britain clearly was motivated by the need to reduce the level of violence in the north, and by the desire to reduce the level of disaffection among Catholics. Ireland's overriding motivation seems to have been to prevent the spread of violence into the south. This concern was reinforced by the growing belief that terrorism in Ulster did not further the interests of northern Catholics. A desire for good relations with Britain per se does not seem to have been an important factor. Indeed, the Dublin authorities have had to make some effort to ensure that they were not perceived by the Irish public as too close to the UK.

This has been done by pursuing charges against Britain in the institutions of the European Community. Ireland alleged that the UK had tortured suspected terrorists in 1971 and later, and that it had discriminated on religious grounds in arresting and detaining suspects. In September 1976 the European Commission on Human Rights upheld the first charge and rejected the second. Britain then accepted the torture finding, stated that the condemned procedures had been discontinued and compensation had been paid to victims, and pledged not to use such techniques in the future. Given this admission and pledge, Westminster took the view that Ireland should drop its case. In what seems to have been an effort to balance the antiterrorist emergency legislation introduced in the fall of 1976, however, Ireland decided to pursue the case against Britain in the European Court of Human Rights. What is likely to be a long, drawn-out process began with hearings in February 1977.[42]

These human rights hearings have constituted the only formal involvement in the Ulster problem by Britain and Ireland's fellow European Economic Community (EEC) members. In the United States the Nixon and Ford administrations carefully refrained from taking a partisan position in the conflict, and they managed to avoid becoming involved in any way at all. Despite the emotional impact of "Bloody Sunday," Secretary of State William Rogers made the American government's position clear in February 1972. He replied to appeals from the Irish foreign minister and from a number of Congressmen for a condemnation of Britain by saying, "It would be inappropriate and counterproductive for the United States to attempt to intervene in any way."[43] Later that month the House Foreign Affairs Committee's subcommittee on Europe provided a forum for representatives of Ulster's minority, but the hearings did not lead to any action by either Congress or the administration.[44]

Among active, vocal Irish Catholics in North America, support for the IRA and opposition to the British seem to be common. The traditional source of American arms and money for the IRA was Clan na Gael. While it provided very limited amounts of money, this financial support was essential to armed Irish republicanism from the 1880s through the IRA campaign of 1956–62. During the 1960s, however, the Clan splintered and disintegrated. After the violence of 1969 a new American organization was formed—the Irish Northern Aid Committee (Noraid)—and it has since become the most important source of foreign assistance for the IRA. Noraid claims to have 80 branches and 80,000 members in the United States, and to have raised more than $1 million since 1971. British authorities estimate that 85 percent of the IRA's arms have come from the United States.[45]

While a considerable portion of the money donated by Americans probably is intended for general relief rather than weapons, hostility to the British and support for the IRA seem to be strong among Irish Americans. Such prominent American politicians as Senator Edward Kennedy and Paul O'Dwyer, president of New York City Council, have urged the British to withdraw. It should be noted that this view has been publicly criticized by members of the Irish government, as well as by British leaders. By the spring of 1977 revulsion at the violence had become strong enough even among Irish Americans to lead Senators Kennedy and Daniel P. Moynihan, House Speaker "Tip" O'Neill, and New York Governor Hugh Carey to issue a joint statement calling on their followers to refrain from contributing to the IRA.[46]

The passive neutrality of the U.S. administration is typical of governmental reaction outside of the British Isles. Colonel Muammar al-Qaddafi of Libya is the only foreign leader who has taken a strong, active position in the dispute. In 1972 he publicly announced that his government was supplying arms to the IRA,[47] and leaders of both Catholic and Protestant extremist groups have since met with him. While the Irish and British governments criticized Libya's intervention, authorities in both countries seem to feel that it is of little importance.

CONCLUSION

Few external parties have become involved in the Ulster situation at all; and those that are involved have, to a remarkable degree, avoided partisan forms of participation. Why has this been the case? The limited number of foreign participants can be credited to the lack of any discernible advantage to be gained from participation. There would seem to be at least three kinds of considerations that might lead an external party to intervene in a domestic dispute. The dispute might be used as a convenient rationalization for an attack on an enemy state already caught up in the conflict. The possibility of establishing a beneficial relationship with the eventual victor might motivate an external actor to intervene if apparent strategic, ideological, or material rewards exist. Finally, a desire to receive credit for settling a dispute, or to avoid undesirable consequences of its continuation, could lead outside parties to become involved as mediators, restrainers, or peacekeepers. To these general (or instrumental) causes of intervention we must, in the case of ethnic conflict, add a fourth. Affective ties with one of the internal parties to the dispute might lead an external actor to intervene to assist ethnic kin, or to engender support from members of the ethnic group within the external government's own population.

Catholics and Protestants in Ulster have not themselves been international actors, and consequently neither side has general enemies (apart from ethnic opponents). Ireland has no foreign enemies, and even Britain has few opponents who are so malevolent that they would wish to attack the UK in the absence of some possible benefit beyond simply weakening Britain. Fortunately for Westminster, the few regimes that are this hostile to the UK are, like Libya, distant and relatively impotent.

Additional incentives could come from the hope of establishing a friendly regime in Ulster. Northern Ireland lacks the natural resources that might attract the involvement of some outside parties, however, and only the Soviet Union could hope for any strategic advantage from a change in the Northern Irish regime. Given the general conservatism of both Catholics and Protestants in Ulster, there is little reason to suppose that either group would move Ulster to a radical new course in international politics if it controlled the province's affairs. Indeed, the possibility that a change in Ulster would affect global politics is so slight that even the British would not try to maintain control of the province for strategic reasons alone.

The desire to avoid the consequences of a continued battle in Northern Ireland is the primary motivating factor for British involvement. Since its legal jurisdiction cannot easily be abandoned against the wishes of the Protestant majority in Ulster, Westminster must find a peaceful solution or countenance civil war within its domain. No other party has become involved in a peacekeeping role because the consequences of the Northern Irish problem for foreign governments are minimal, and the chances of gaining credit by solving the dispute are slim.

Finally, the ethnic factor is the reason for the involvement of the Irish Republic. With 95 percent of its public sharing the ethnic identity of Ulster's Catholics, and with the Republic and Ulster sharing a relatively small island, the Irish government could not hope to remain uninvolved in Northern Ireland. Only the U.S. government has faced similar ethnic pressures, but they have not been nearly as strong. The Irish form a minority group in America, and they are counterbalanced to some extent by people of British and Scotch-Irish descent. Any slight political advantage that might have been gained by adopting the position of Irish-Americans was far outweighed by the dangers involved in alienating America's most powerful ally.

In a sense the fact that this is an ethnic conflict has restricted the number of foreign participants. If either side in Ulster represented an ideological position, other regimes might find they had an identity of interests. Given that the only goal of the immediate parties to the dispute is to maintain or improve the position of its ethnic group, however, only external members of the groups can easily identify with either side. And only the Irish Republic is dominated by members of one of the groups concerned.

The British have attempted to restrain the conflict rather than act in a partisan way because they do not identify with either side in the dispute, and because they do not believe that either side can so repress the other as to ensure peace and stability. The Irish are involved precisely because they identify with one side in the conflict, so one might expect that they would act to aid their fellow Catholics. Their resistance to the pressure to act in a partisan way, however, and to exacerbate the conflict, does not necessarily indicate that the ethnic ties are weak.

Ethnic identification leads directly to a sense of "oneness," and to empathy for the other group members. It need not lead to an overpowering commitment to the creation of a homeland in the form of a nation-state. Clearly, few Irish-Americans wish to return to Ireland to live, or wish to have all Irishmen join them in Boston (although this might solve Ulster's problems). The feeling of empathy is as strong among the Irish as any other group, and this becomes obvious when Catholics in Northern Ireland seem threatened with extinction as a community. The impulse of all Irishmen at such times is to join the battle.

When the northern minority seems more secure, however, Irishmen can and do differ about the proper policy to pursue. The IRA can opt for unification through force of arms, while the government and a majority of the public prefer to look for a solution that seems less likely to result in a bloodbath. External support for an ethnic group in conflict may increase if the group seems strong enough to hope realistically to win. In Ulster we have seen that significant support is also likely to be provided if complete defeat seems imminent. Between these extremes, however, factors other than simple identification with an embattled group seem to determine the response of external parties; and the aims of the external parties themselves are likely to be of greater importance than the specific situation of the ethnic participants in the conflict.

The two fundamental questions identified in the introductory chapter were, What is the significance of ethnic factors in determining the pattern of foreign involvement or noninvolvement in a domestic conflict? and, Do they suggest particular forms of external response? No one case study can hope to answer these questions, but the conflict in Northern Ireland does provide some relevant evidence. The Ulster case would seem to indicate that ethnic conflict (as opposed to other types of disputes) encourages internationalization only insofar as there are other states in which one of the combatant ethnic groups is important. If outside parties are not affected by the relevant ethnic ties, the prospects for internationalization are, at most, no greater than would be the case with any type of domestic strife. Indeed, the concerns that are so typical of ethnic groups as to come close to being definitional characteristics are of interest only to other group members. Thus, by increasing the difficulty of finding common interests between the internal and external actors, ethnicity may actually discourage foreign involvement in some domestic conflicts.

Turning to the second question, the nature of external involvement seems to depend in large part upon the balance between the opposing sides. Partisan involvement is most likely when one side seems to be in danger of complete defeat. In less extreme cases ethnic identification will still provide an impetus toward partisan participation, but this may be counterbalanced by other considerations. Indeed, ethnic identification and empathy may act as moderating forces in some instances, because the cost of losing the contest is greater for the external party than it would be in another sort of clash.

Cuba can intervene in Angola, for example, and thus exacerbate the dispute—even if the chance of losing is high—because the costs of losing are not especially great. Defeat may cost some manpower, some money, and some loss of face, but it will not result in any great emotional feeling of defeat among Cubans. Complete defeat for Catholics in Ulster, on the other hand, would represent a terrible emotional blow to all Irishmen. If an ultimate test of strength is unavoidable, the ethnic partner is likely to throw all of its resources into the battle; but if a peaceful solution seems even remotely possible, the external party may prefer to try to moderate the dispute rather than force the issue and thus increase the potential costs. Ethnic identification and empathy may breed partisan commitment, but they may also breed caution.

NOTES

1. Richard Rose, *Governing Without Consensus: An Irish Perspective* (London: Faber, 1971), p. 248.

2. Ibid., p. 208.

3. See M. W. Heslinga, *The Irish Border as a Cultural Divide* (2nd ed.; Assen, Netherlands: Von Gorcum, 1971), p. 18.

4. See Rose, op. cit., pp. 474–510, for the results of his survey. On cultural matters note questions 6a–6e, 31a, 44a–44d, 46a, and 59a–59c.

5. Heslinga, loc. cit.

6. Rose, op. cit., p. 214.

7. Ibid., pp. 341, 362.

8. Ibid., pp. 270, 307, 362.

9. See Cynthia Enloe, *Ethnic Conflict and Political Development* (Boston: Little, Brown, 1973), p. 16. Enloe cites Michael Moerman's warning that if people are aware that a researcher is interested in ethnicity, they may exaggerate ethnic distinctions. In this case the reverse may have been true.

10. This study, which had a sample of 259, is described in T. G. Carroll, "Political Activists in Disaffected Communities: Dissidence, Disobedience and Rebellion in Northern Ireland" (Ph.D.

diss., Carleton University, Ottawa, 1974). On the migration that resulted from the violence, I estimate that 7 percent of the Catholic population of Belfast had been forced to move by mid-1972. See pp. 241–42.

11. Rose, op. cit., p. 477, question 4.

12. Here and throughout this section I am indebted to J. C. Beckett, *A Short History of Ireland* (4th ed.; London: Hutchinson, 1971); Edmund Curtis, *History of Ireland* (6th ed.; London: Methuen, 1950); and T. W. Moody and F. X. Martin, eds., *The Course of Irish History* (Cork: Mercier Press, 1967).

13. Ireland did leave the Commonwealth and became a republic in 1949, but this was not a direct result of IRA pressure. For an informative history and analysis of the IRA, see J. Bowyer Bell, *The Secret Army* (London: Sphere, 1972).

14. For a description of the institutions see Nicholas Mansergh, *The Government of Northern Ireland* (London: Allen & Unwin, 1936). Examples of Protestant manipulation of the system are given in Government of Northern Ireland, *Disturbances in Northern Ireland,* cmd. 532 (Belfast: Her Majesty's Stationery Office, 1969) (*The Cameron Report*), paras. 126–43; and in Campaign for Social Justice in Northern Ireland (CSJNI), *The Plain Truth* (2nd ed.; Dungannon, N.I: CSJNI, 1972).

15. Bell, op. cit., pp. 394–95.

16. On the development of the NICRA, and Protestant reaction to it, see *The Cameron Report,* paras. 185–93 and passim.

17. Ibid., paras. 49–51, 177, 180.

18. See the Government of Northern Ireland's second judicial inquiry on the troubles, *Violence and Civil Disturbances in Northern Ireland in 1969,* cmd. 566 (Belfast: Her Majesty's Stationery Office, 1972), para. 5.10.

19. Ibid., para. 2.1.

20. See the statement made by the Catholic Social Democratic and Labour party when its members withdrew from Parliament in 1971. It is quoted by Henry Kelly, *How Stormont Fell* (Dublin: Gill and Macmillan, 1972), pp. 51–55.

21. Rose, op. cit., pp. 193, 213.

22. Carroll, op. cit., pp. 350–51.

23. "Fortnight Poll," *Fortnight* no. 62 (May 21, 1973): pp. 6–7.

24. Ibid.; "How to Win Polls," ibid. no. 58 (March 16, 1973): pp. 6–8.

25. Ibid.

26. For a review of events in Northern Ireland to the beginning of 1976, see Richard Rose, *Northern Ireland: Time of Choice* (Washington: American Enterprise Institute, 1976).

27. See Robert Fisk, *The Point of No Return: The Strike Which Broke the British in Ulster* (London: Andre Deutsch, 1975).

28. J. Bowyer Bell, "The Escalation of Insurgency: The Provisional Irish Republican Army's Experience, 1969–1971," *Review of Politics* 35, no. 3 (July 1973): 406.

29. Lucinda Franks," 'We Just Want Peace,' " *New York Times Magazine,* Dec. 19, 1976, pp. 29 ff.

30. See Liam de Paor, *Divided Ulster* (2nd ed.; Harmondsworth, Eng.: Penguin, 1971), pp. 58–67.

31. See Government of the United Kingdom, *The Future of Northern Ireland* (London: Her Majesty's Stationery Office, 1972); and *Northern Ireland: Constitutional Proposals,* cmd. 5259 (London: Her Majesty's Stationery Office, 1973).

32. Keith Kyle, "Sunningdale and After: Britain, Ireland and Ulster," *The World Today* (Nov. 1975), pp. 443–45.

33. See Government of the United Kingdom, *The Northern Ireland Constitution,* cmd. 5675 and Northern Ireland Discussion Paper 2—*Constitutional Convention Procedure* (London: Her Majesty's Stationery Office, 1974).

34. *Belfast News Letter,* Feb. 3, 1972.

35. Quoted by Kyle, op. cit., p. 439.

36. See Sunday Times Insight Team, *Ulster* (Harmondsworth, Eng.: Penguin, 1972), pp. 176–91; and *The Times* (London), Aug. 24, 1972, p. 2.

37. *The Times* (London), Mar. 14, 1974, p. 1.

38. *Toronto Globe and Mail,* March 4, 1976, p. 12.

39. *The Times* (London), July 25, 1975, p. 2.

40. Ibid., Jan. 13, 1976, p. 8.

41. Ibid., Feb. 3, 1972, p. 1.

42. "Irish 'Torture' Row Grows," *The Guardian Weekly,* Sept. 12, 1976, p. 4; and "Ireland and Britain," *The Economist,* Feb. 12, 1977, pp. 55–56.

43. *New York Times,* Feb. 4, 1972, p. 2.

44. Ibid., Feb. 29, 1972, p. 3.

45. "Helping the Old Country Kill," *The Economist,* Jan. 10, 1976, p. 52.

46. *The Times* (London), Mar. 17, 1977, p. 2.

47. Ibid., June 12, 1972, p. 1.

CHAPTER

3

THE CYPRUS CONFLICT

Naomi Black

The most important fact about Cyprus is that it is an island. This means that it looks, and is treated like, a self-contained political entity, when it is really a combination of fragments of Greece and Turkey. This overlap of borders cannot easily be adjusted, though the island's shores are as arbitrary a political delineation as any imperially imposed administrative district line in Africa. Within that small territory, moreover, there are two separate, autonomous political communities. Their shared isolation means they cannot avoid confrontation. But their conflict is only in part generated or controlled by the mainland sectors of the larger nations. For the second most important fact about Cyprus is its location, more than 400 miles from one mainland and only 40 from the other. Consequently, one mainland—Greece—finds nationalistic identification (and influence) diluted by distance while the other—Turkey—finds identification strengthened by the security implications of an offshore island, and by the ease of sending in troops or arms. In the meantime, international intervention has persisted in treating this ethnic dispute as colonial, with independence the appropriate solution.[1]

Certainly, the history of the Republic of Cyprus can be made to sound typical of the history of many troubled former colonies. Predominantly Greek, Cyprus had been part of the Turkish Empire for three centuries when it came under British control in 1878. It was part of the British Empire until attaining independence in 1960, after several years of guerrilla warfare and appeals to the United Nations. Its president, Archbishop Makarios, was exiled by the British to the Seychelles for leading the fight against them; he now seems set for lifetime tenure in office. At independence Britain retained bases on the island, and Cyprus became part of the Commonwealth and of the group of nonaligned nations. Three years later a civil war broke out. International concern then generated a United Nations (UN) peacekeeping force that is still in place.

Yet such an account omits the most important occurrences in recent Cypriot history: the coup of 1974, provoked and regretted by mainland Greece, and the subsequent and continuing Turkish occupation of 40 percent of the island. More generally, such an account ignores the element of "enosis." It thus fails even to refer to the communal conflict that is the basis of Cypriot politics.

"Enosis" is the basis of Cyprus' involvement with irredentist Greek nationalism, with Greece, and with Turkey. The Greek word itself means "union"; Lawrence Durrell notes that before the Cyprus struggle "enosis" also referred to "the S-shaped pipe used in plumbing."[2] Since the emergence of Cyprus into world news, even for hellenists "enosis" refers to the "Megali Idea" of reuniting under a single political leadership all the territories once part of the Byzantine Empire and still inhabited by Greek-speaking, Greek Orthodox peoples. The inspiration of the builders of modern Greece, this ideal has continued to be central to Greek politics, and for some years Cyprus has been the only Greek area still unredeemed. Four-fifths of the island's population is Greek Cypriot, for whom enosis is their ideal and Greece their spiritual homeland. Unfortunately for Cyprus, however, another 18 percent of the population is Turkish Cypriot—Turkish-speaking, non-Christian descendants of Ottoman garrisons. They are devoted to Turkey and responsive to Turkish national interests, which correspond to their own. In the 1950s it was the Greek Cypriots who, in the guerrilla organization Ethniki Organosis Kypriakou Agonos, "National Organization of Cypriot Struggle," (EOKA), fought against the British. Their battle was not for the independence finally awarded, but for enosis. After Cyprus' independence, the Greek Cypriot goal changed to a demand for majority rule and unitary, sovereign independence —but union with Greece was still hoped for. The possibility of enosis was what produced Turkish Cypriot and Turkish concern, and the ethnic conflict that continues in Cyprus. Enosis also has been the main contemporary activator of the Greco-Turkish antagonisms that threaten the unity of the North Atlantic Treaty Organization (NATO) and the strategic control of the eastern Mediterranean. It is thus the key to both the internal conflict and the external linkages of the Cypriot communities.

In 1954 Greece took the cause of enosis to the United Nations, over the protests of Turkey and Britain. The conflict has thus been international for more than 20 years. It has drawn in nearly every element and institution of international relations, from the Conferences of Islamic and Non-Aligned Nations to NATO, from the General Assembly to the Security Council and the secretary-general of the United Nations, and from the national legislatures of the United States, Britain, Greece, and Turkey, to the leading organs of the European Communities and of the Communist party of the Soviet Union. It could be studied as a microcosm of the international political system, including as it does both crisis and noncrisis diplomacy, multilateral and bilateral negotiation, peaceful and violent management of conflict, and the whole gamut of issue areas and goals.

Our interest here, however, is not in the way the Cyprus struggle epitomizes the growing interdependence of international politics. We are concerned, rather, with the role played by the ethnic dimension of the conflict's international linkages. It seems clear that for most of the international actors involved, the nature of the two Cypriot communities was of little interest. Strategic and other power concerns were central. Since Cyprus was not yet free to align itself, the preferences or even the actions of its populations attracted international attention only as they might influence possible sponsors. That the majority community was or claimed to be Greek was of interest only because it guaranteed Greece's involvement in the island's fate. This enlarged the strategic role of Cyprus, which became the key not just to the eastern Mediterranean but also to the southern flank of NATO and thus to the basic unity of the alliance. That the minority community was or claimed to be Turkish mattered rather less, for Turkish involvement was already guaranteed by the location of the island and the concern of Greece. In general, in relation to Cyprus the NATO powers have been concerned mainly to reduce intra-alliance conflict, and the Soviet Union mainly to increase it. The latter has shown a particularly wide range of policies, backing Greek or Turkish Cypriots with a callousness that has devastated the large Greek Cypriot—and therefore enosist—Communist party of Cyprus. It is significant that the Soviet Union has not felt it advantageous to make the nod to ethnic linkages that would have called on the brotherhood of the Soviet and Cypriot Moslems.

Similarly, the important role of the United Nations has been to override the ethnic nature of the disputes in Cyprus, handling the situation first as a case of anticolonialism, and later as civil war and denial of minority rights. It was Cyprus' first encounter with the United Nations, in the years 1954–58, that produced the imposition of independence on an island whose majority community wanted union with its motherland and whose minority community would have preferred self-government under continued colonial protection. The second and continuing relationship has deepened the deadlocked de facto partition of the island, preventing a resolution by force of arms. The specific appeals of the communal leaders have been disregarded, forced into the frames of reference accepted by the larger international community.

There is perhaps a parable in the way Greek and Turkish Cypriots must communicate with international organizations or actors. They cannot use their own languages, but must shift to French and English, the languages of diplomacy—and of anticolonialism and anticommunism. Ethnic linkages seem likely to be significant only where appeals can be made in the mother tongue and, in general, in the language of blood ties and irrational sympathies. For Cyprus, the main ethnic links therefore must be with Greece and with Turkey, and those connections will be my main concern here. However, we must add a brief consideration of those few other involved parties who might perhaps respond to ethnic linkages: the Moslem powers appealed to by Turkey, plus Britain and the United States. The first of these is obvious, and Turkey did go to both the (Muslim) Regional Cooperation for Development pact and the Islamic Conference. Britain must be discussed because of its long tradition of philhellenism even among leading politicians, and its large Greek-Cypriot population. The United States is relevant because of its large and influential Greek-American minority, and their apparent success in imposing an arms embargo on Turkey after the 1974 invasion of Cyprus.

The important question for all of these involved countries is the following: to what extent are these ethnic involvements? That is, to what extent are there interventions on behalf of, in response to the wishes of, and in conformity with the goals of the ethnic communities involved outside the intervening actors? I shall argue here that none of the ethnic linkages, including those intimate ones with Greece and Turkey, had much impact on the policies adopted by the outside parties involved. Ethnic connections contributed to the attention paid—indeed, rendered involvement inevitable—but they had surprisingly little influence on what the interveners actually did. Certainly, there was far less influence than is generally believed.

The discussion here will outline the development of ethnic differentiation and ethnic conflict in Cyprus, showing how they are connected with each other and with the notion of enosis. I shall also show the involvement of Greece and Turkey in these processes, and in the internationalized conflicts that followed. Finally I shall discuss briefly the roles played by ethnic linkages in the Muslim, British, and American connections with the Cyprus conflicts. I shall not attempt to give any complete account of a long and confusing history, of which almost all the "facts" are subject to partisan dispute. I shall hope, however, to touch on those aspects that demonstrate the autonomy of both the Cyprus communities and their quarrel—and the sad lack of response either have really had from all those who were drawn in.

THE DEVELOPMENT OF ETHNIC DIFFERENTIATION AND CONFLICT

The present communal division of Cyprus dates back to the Turkish take-over toward the end of the sixteenth century. Before then the population was essentially Greek in language, religion, and culture, having resisted the influence of a succession of Latin Catholic overlords. The Turkish regime was a minimalist one, interested in revenue and security. But the Ottomans did two important things that guaranteed future enosism, and future resistance to it. First, they created a Moslem community by planting soldiers and their dependents as colonists, much in the Roman pattern. The descendants of these soldiers multiplied enough to produce a substantial continuing minority, reaching as high as one-third of the population and then gradually declining in the twentieth century to probably somewhat less than the widely used approximation of 20 percent of the population. This community dispersed widely over a very small island; but it kept its identity, extending down to separate Turkish sections in tiny mixed villages.

From the beginning, Turkish rule showed the same motives that characterized its continuing interest in the island. Already, by that time, there were only preemptive reasons for holding once-prosperous Cyprus: to prevent its domination by any hostile power interested in the Bosporus. An established Turkish population was the easiest form of preemption, against the Russians in particular. It also established a permanent basis for Turkish claims to a right to intervene against any sort of take-over. Even after the British assumed the administration of the island, the existence of a Turkish community there made it an extension of the motherland. Hence the importance Turkey has always attributed to sustaining the minority as a community—and the importance Greece gives to the assertion that the Turks of Cyprus are no different from the Turks of Thrace or Macedonia.

Thus Cyprus, when it came under British rule, possessed the population pattern common to the successor states of the Ottoman Empire. It was unusual in the origin of the minority population, since conversion and invasion have been far more common than plantation. The island was also unusual in having only two substantial communal groups, instead of a number of competing Christian communities, and more than one group of Moslems. The power of Cypriot ethnic identification may owe something to the relative simplicity, and consequent directness, of the confrontation of communities.

Turkish rule also established the basis of differentiation of the two communities. In Cyprus the Ottomans revived the office of "ethnarch," making the religious leader of the Greek Cypriots also their secular administrator, backed by the power of the empire. The central government concerned itself mainly with revenue (handled through the communal leadership) and with a minimal level of public order. The communal leadership took care of health and social welfare, education, charity, and village self-government. For the people the visible authority in their lives was thus linked to their membership in a specific religious group. One result of this was, obviously, a significant strengthening of the Greek Orthodox church in Cyprus. Another was to establish the church's interest in maintaining the identity of the Greek community and its differentiation from any broader secular organization. Shared religion was reinforced by shared language, and by a shared history going back to the glories of Byzantium.

The identity of the Greek Orthodox community was thus linked to the incipient nationalism of the other Greek segments of the Ottoman Empire. The Greek Cypriots were bound to be enosist as soon as there was a Greek nation to join. The Turks were well aware of this—in fact, they contributed when they took draconian measures against a revolt not yet ready to occur in nineteenth-century Cyprus. George Grivas, the Cypriot-born former Greek officer who headed the enosist guerrillas in Cyprus in the 1950s, reflected the origin of Greek nationalism by his nom de guerre: Dighenis, from Dighenis Akritas, a legendary hero of Byzantine frontier battles against the Arabs. That Cyprus has never been part of an independent Greek nation is irrelevant; neither have the other territories self-defined as Greek because of language and religion. Cyprus, after all, has an Autocephalous Orthodox church older than that of the mainland. Nor does the remoteness of this small island from the Peloponnesus matter; contemporary Greece includes most of the other islands of the same archipelago, and claims them all.

Greek Cyprus' commitment to enosis has continued to the present. In 1965 a poll showed well over 50 percent of Greek Cypriots still yearning for it, and in 1974 the biographer of Archibishop Makarios explained that His Beatitude is obliged to make "emotional appeals to enosis" to retain popular support in Cyprus. "For the first time since antiquity," says P. N. Vanezis, "there exists a separate Hellenic state outside of an independent Greece." His final remark exemplifies Greek Cypriot ideas: this independent Greek nation exists only because Turkey "has interposed, for the present, its veto on enosis."[3] In that "for the present" is the whole history of ethnic conflict in Cyprus.

During the first, most important period of British rule, Cyprus was only leased from Turkey. The patterns established then continued until Cyprus became independent. Obligations of noninterference coincided nicely with ease and cheapness of administration, and the British continued the Turkish system of indirect rule. The Ottoman administrators returned home, and the Muslim community began slowly to develop native leaders. As in other possessions, the British respected the separate legal systems of the communities. When public education and other social services were instituted, they were organized through, and largely by, the communities. School books and other cultural materials came from the two mainlands, and by the 1920s were militantly and competitively communal. A constitution provided a Legislative Assembly (abolished in 1931), but this also was organized in terms of communal representatives. Therefore, as Cyprus slowly modernized, the institutions that might have provided national or class solidarity developed instead on a communal basis. Both ethnic groups were relatively slow to secularize, perhaps in part because of the economic backwardness of Cyprus in the interwar period. The religiously defined communities in Cyprus reached the period after World War II with a continuous tradition of internal self-government, a high level of identification with kinsmen, marked mutual hostility, and powerful entrenched leaderships whose advantages were linked to nonassimilation of their communal groups.

However, as commentators are quick to point out, this ethnic differentiation in Cyprus did not become ethnic conflict until well into the 1950s. Ethnic differentiation is, logically, a precondition for ethnic conflict. But even when communities are separate and competitive, it does not seem logically necessary that their relationship should be characterized by violence. To move to this state requires certain types of goals and communal solidarity. We can articulate this by adapting a definition of international conflict, formulated by Jean-Baptiste Duroselle, and applied by François Crouzet to the struggle of the Greek Cypriots against the British:

> A process of relations between political units which amounts for a considerable period of time, to a contradiction between their respective objectives, along with enough collective will for obtaining them, [make] an eventual recourse to force seem possible.

Crouzet, using this definition, focuses on the Greek Cypriot demand for enosis; he calls it a "brutal" contradiction of British goals.[4] Surely it was equally contradictory for the Turkish Cypriots, whose communal identity would end if Cyprus joined Greece. The terms of Cyprus's independence excluded enosis; but notions of "majority rule" and "unfettered sovereignty" became stand-ins, outlining the process that would establish Greek control of an island that could then vote to join Greece.

It was the identification of the Greek Cypriot community with enosis that produced the communal or ethnic conflict in Cyprus. This conflict became violent to the extent that the enosis struggle itself became violent. The involvement of both Greece and Turkey follows from the turn toward communal conflict.

The growth of enosist activity was steady during the British occupation. It was paralleled by Turkish Cypriot rejections, first defensive and then, like the enosis agitation, violent. The first British official to land in Cyprus was greeted by a "memorial" appealing for union with Greece; the Turkish *molla* (religious leader) was also there to demonstrate the continuing role of Turkey. The memorials continued steadily through the twentieth century, answered at least since 1898 by countermemorials pleading for continued British or renewed Turkish rule. The British seem never to have taken the nationalist element in these demands seriously. Even when a small revolt broke out in 1931 and the Government House was burned down, most administrators remained convinced that Greek Cypriots were not basically interested in union with Greece. They were, of course, encouraged in this belief by the government of Greece, which disclaimed support for the outbreak and reprimanded and recalled a hotheaded young enosist consul from Cyprus. After the revolt, political activity was virtually abolished in Cyprus. The leaders of the Greek Cypriot community were exiled. Not until 1943 were municipal and archiepiscopal elections permitted.

In the 1940s popular, even mass, politics began in Cyprus. It was a boom time, and the British believed that this activity would encourage allegiance to the Commonwealth. Instead, it probably encouraged social mobilization, group identification, and dissatisfaction based on rising expectations. As many as 34 Greek Cypriot political groupings seem to have appeared, most importantly a very powerful trade union-allied Communist party. Only the leftists were willing, very briefly, to discuss constitutional change with the British, along with the Turkish Cypriots and the members of the other smaller minorities. But after 1949 the Communist party adopted a policy summed up as follows by their secretary-general: "What we want is national liberation, and on Cyprus this means—enosis."[5] The whole range of Greek Cypriot politics was thenceforth enosist, and so was that of trade union and communal organization. In 1950 a church-organized plebiscite (in which Greek Cypriots of all shades of belief voted) showed 95 percent in favor of union with Greece. In the following quarter-century, many splits and hostilities appeared among the Greek Cypriot community, but the rhetoric of the personal and political quarrels took the form of accusations of lack of enthusiasm for enosis. No party or significant Greek Cypriot political figure ever opposed it.

The enosis struggle thus became a mass one after World War II, mediated and encouraged through such mass organizations as unions, political parties, cooperatives, and women's and youth groups, organized competitively by the Orthodox church (under a new American-trained young archbishop, Makarios III) and the Communist party of Cyprus. On April 1, 1955, the movement became violent, with a series of bomb explosions on the island. The British still did not recognize the agitation for what it was, considering it then and later as an independence movement. It is true that the guerrilla organization EOKA had missed its intended kickoff date of March 25—Greek Independence Day. But the symbolic importance of this date probably would have escaped British leaders such as Anthony Eden. In his memoirs, Eden stated that the Greek community in Cyprus was majoritarian only because of emigrants from Asia Minor in the 1930s. On the topic of enosis, he wrote, "Cyprus has never belonged to Greece."[6]

Eden did at least recognize that there was bound to be Turkish interest in the last strategic redoubt off the Bosporus. On the other hand, he also seems to have been unaware of the autonomy, and therefore the crucial role, of the Turkish Cypriot community. This supposed nonexistence of the minority community is, of course, a central element of the Greek arguments in favor of enosis.

In general, the Turkish Cypriots have inspired less sympathy than their Greek counterparts, and their opponents have had a good deal of success in arguing away the reality of the minority's communal existence. They are less modernized, less politically mobilized, and far less skillfully led than the Greek Cypriots, and they have the ungrateful role of opposition. Mainland Turkey's self-interest has been more blatant than has Greece's: Turkey tends to urge her kinsmen on to action, while Greece has most often restrained hers.

Yet we should not overlook the importance of the tradition of Turkish Cypriot responses to Greek Cypriot agitation for enosis, beginning with the continuing countermemorials. An early governor noted that the Turks consistently sided with him in the Legislature, against the Greeks. A Turkish National Congress in Cyprus met as early as 1931, and voiced resentment at sharing the repressive consequences of the enosist Greek Cypriot revolt of that year. In 1941, when the British allowed resumption of political activity on Cyprus, a Turkish Cypriot party existed alongside the ethnarchy-organized Greek Cypriot efforts; and later representatives of the minority community met with the governor to discuss self-government for the island. By 1945 there were two Turkish Cypriot political parties, which survived to merge in 1949; the resulting Party of Cypriot National Union became the Cyprus Is Turkish party in 1955. In 1943 a Turkish trade union movement appeared.

In the same period, the Turkish Cypriot leaders rejected the British nomination of a Turkish-born religious leader, and insisted on replacing him with an elected native representative. Modernization seems to have made great progress during this period, including secularization of family law, although *sharia* judges apparently continue to apply religious law in Moslem courts and there is an important foundation administering substantial religiously based philanthropic funds. There is also a Turkish, as well as a Greek, central bank in the cooperative movement, 274 Turkish cooperative societies (as opposed to 700 Greek), and (in 1964) four Turkish-language daily newspapers besides the six Greek and one English.[7] There is also, of course, a tradition of village self-rule that continues without interruption from the days of the Ottoman Empire, for Turkish just as for Greek villages—and these village councils also run the school system.

It was the EOKA campaign that transformed communal differentiation into communal conflict. Until then, the goal of enosis was only threatening to the leaders of the Turkish Cypriot community, whose status and power depended on survival of their own communities and on protection by the British. In a Greater Greece they would have no importance at all. EOKA transformed Cypriot politics from the British colonial model to a primitive version of the Balkan model. Weapons were distributed widely, and adolescents were encouraged to use them. As Peter Loizos notes, this population had little knowledge of politics, and its structures of social trust barely extended beyond village boundaries.[8] The ideology of the conflict was heavily loaded with memories of past mutual brutalities. And, like minority groups in many other countries, the Turkish Cypriots were overrepresented in the Cyprus police force, and naturally enough made up the larger part of the new auxiliary police forces recruited to serve against EOKA.

The pattern of casualties during the EOKA campaign tells the story of what happened: In 1955–59, 22 Turkish Cypriot policemen were killed (15 Greek Cypriot policemen), and 62 Turkish Cypriot civilians (236 Greek Cypriot civilians)—but among the civilians 55 of the Turkish Cypriots were victims of communal battles and only 60 of the Greek Cypriots. EOKA was responsible for the deaths of the Turkish Cypriot policemen, and of most of the Greek Cypriot civilians.[9]

Apart from scattered episodes, communal conflict in Cyprus appeared only when the restraining influence of Archbishop Makarios on EOKA was removed by his exile early in 1957. That year a Turkish counterterrorist organization appeared, and George Grivas warned Greek Cypriots against using Turkish Cypriot facilities and planned countermeasures against anticipated Turkish attacks. Communal riots took place, and an incoming British governor feared that "at any time some EOKA outrage would set off Turkish resistance." The next summer the conflict had developed into what he described as "a civil war between the Greek Cypriots and the Turkish Cypriots."[10] It was during these latter battles that the Turkish Cypriots withdrew into their own quarters, which from then on they administered themselves. This was the origin of the demand for legally separate municipalities that was written into the Cyprus Constitution, and of the Turkish Cypriot organization of its population into armed enclaves.

After 1958, there can be no doubt of the existence of an ethnic conflict. The British were still the primary enemies of the enosists—the Greek Cypriots —but the Turkish Cypriots had responded to the goal of union with Greece, and as a community were the major obstacle to it. Unfortunately, by 1959–60 both communities were armed, and the pattern of division between them had been sharpened by violence. During 1960–63 there was an increasingly bitter, communally defined political struggle during which the Turkish Cypriot leaders lost any reason they might have had to trust the majority. The Christmas season of 1963–64 saw a conflict whose brutality destroyed any remaining likelihood that the Turkish Cypriots would see themselves as individual members of a Hellenic society; under the leadership of such former EOKA thugs as Nicos Sampson, there is no doubt that kidnapping and murder of hostages took place—and that the Turkish Cypriots in turn reciprocated. The Greek Cypriots thus reinforced the hostile solidarity of their fellow citizens, and they continued to do so by economic blockades extending to food and water, and by attacks on Turkish Cypriot redoubts.

The conflict thus continued to be related to the composition of the two communities, and to the consequent actions of the Greek Cypriots that brought them into conflict with the Turkish Cypriots. None of the outside powers could settle or dispose of the majority commitment to enosis that was at the root of communal conflict on the island—and its outside linkages.

To see how this worked, we must look more closely at how Greece and Turkey were involved in the periods of the EOKA struggle, of Cyprus' early independence, and after the disturbances of 1963–64 that brought in the UN peacekeepers.

THE ROLE OF GREECE AND TURKEY

We should begin with Greece, whose role was always crucial. Only after World War II did it give any practical assistance to Cyprus enosists. In 1915 a neutralist Greek government refused the British offer of the island, preferring nonbelligerence to the "Megali Idea." In 1931 the Great Liberator himself, Eleutherios Venizelos, tarnished his record in Greek history by refusing to back Cypriots against the British. After the war, as after earlier ones, Greece confidently expected that the Labor Government of Britain would carry out earlier policy intentions. Disappointed, it nevertheless continued private and discreet efforts to exert pressure, efforts doomed to failure because of extreme dependence on Britain and the United States. When George Grivas wanted to start fighting the British, he could get only grudging and limited promises of Greek support. It took a personal affront by Anthony Eden to spur Greek Prime Minister Alexandros Papagos to take the hardly drastic step of an appeal to the United Nations. And only when that appeal was rejected (in 1954) did he reluctantly unleash—and supply—Grivas for guerrilla activity on the island. To Grivas' fury, he was forbidden all-out terrorism, restrained in assassination attempts, and constrained to truces.

From a Greek point of view, EOKA was a propaganda weapon, and the United Nations was the main forum of activity. Enosis, it was hoped, could be smuggled in under the rubric of self-determination. These tactics proved unsuccessful, however. Accordingly, in 1958 the Greeks declared that they accepted the Third World definition of self-determination as independence. Archbishop Makarios agreed with this capitulation. He believed independence would mean straight majority rule, and that a majority vote would be for enosis; the Greek Cypriots, 95 percent for enosis, constituted, after all, 80 percent of the island's population. He did not, however, agree with the next thing Greece did, which was to meet secretly with Turkey and dictate the constitution of the new state of Cyprus.

These Greco-Turkish arrangements in no way represented a shift in Greek policy. The initial move to the United Nations has to be understood in the context of Greek dependence on first Britain and then the United States. Greece had always been a client state, and always resented it. In the postwar period the dependence was very much an issue of domestic politics, with the son of Eleutherios Venizelos on the right, and the Papandreous on the left, pressing a series of centralist governments that held precarious power. The cession of Cyprus to Greece would have been the only visible compensation and reward for allegiance to NATO. Britain's haughty refusal even to discuss reasonable arrangements added insult to injury, fortifying the broader desire to demonstrate something like independence. Greece hoped that the neutralist majority in the United Nations could be mobilized. But by 1958 it became clear that the Afro-Asian majority would not support enosis even if it was disguised as self-determination. By that year it was also clear that the other NATO powers would not back Greece against Britain (and Turkey). The United States in particular was flatly opposed to enosis. A Greek historian of this period attempts to turn it into a victory: "By yielding first . . . ," he writes, "Greece had sided with the [anti-colonial] victor."[11] The main loser was, in any case, the Greek Cypriot community.

The terms of the 1958 settlement were initially and understandably rejected by all Greek Cypriot leaders. It enshrined the separate identity of the Turkish Cypriot community, giving it separate representation (including powers of taxation and separate municipalities), along with weighted representation in all key institutions and veto power in all crucial areas. The Greek leaders brutally enforced Greek Cypriot compliance, threatening abandonment of support in the inevitable civil war and Turkish invasion that would follow a continuation of the battle for enosis. Settlement and constitution included a tripartite right of intervention and enforcement, with Greek and Turkish troops stationed on the island in perpetuity along with British troops in sovereign base areas. Greek policy thus focused on Greek interests, Greek initiative at crucial points, Greek control—totally disregarding the Greek Cypriot preferences in respect to goals, tactics, and timing.

Looking back, in a period that has seen the rise and triumph of many liberation movements, we may be surprised at the Greek Cypriots' dependence on the Greeks. But it follows logically from the nature of their goal: it is not possible to merge with a country that will not accept the merger. Psychologically, acceptance of enosis as a goal produced in the Greek Cypriots a certain deference to the mainland leaders and, for a while, a willingness to allow them to decide the tactics for Hellas. Only later did Grivas and Makarios acquire independent international stature, both personal and national, automatic access to the forum of the United Nations, and a national budget that could be expended on arms purchases. In the 1950s they did not even have access to a radio station, unless they could use Greece's.

After independence, the balance of power between the two Greek communities shifted. On the island Makarios controlled the machinery of national government and communication. The Turkish Cypriots were able to block establishment of an army under Greek control, but the Greek Cypriots constituted the major portion of the police and security forces. Above all, they had weapons, both those purchased by the new nation and those retained by the former members of EOKA.

We know now that the Greek Cypriots never tried seriously to make the constitution work. Makarios himself, elected president of the new republic, may have been prepared to be relatively conciliatory toward the Turkish Cypriots. However, internal political conditions made enosis the only cause around which he could rally support. In the first independent elections he had a clear warning: extreme right-wing forces allied with the Communists to garner one-third of the Greek Cypriot votes. Their joint platform charged the archbishop with having abandoned the cause of enosis. Grivas had returned to Greece, but obviously was ready to reappear as the head of an ultra-enosist party on the island. Makarios bought off the Communists by allocating them a fraction of seats in parliament. The others he outflanked by policy and rhetoric, co-opting the more prominent EOKA leaders by including them in his cabinet. Makarios' biographer explains how he managed to reconcile independence and enosis:

> Since independence and sovereignty implies a right to self-determination, the Greek leadership could interpret the disappearance of enosis as a temporary pragmatic expedient which could very well be set right in the future. This has been the line adopted by Archbishop Makarios after his signature of the Agreement [that ended the fighting in 1959].[12]

Contemporary observers failed to note that, even before independence, the Greek Cypriots were already stalling about legalization of separate municipalities and the prescribed communal ratios in the civil service, issues later cited as crucial to the breakdown of the government. Within two months of Cyprus' independence, the archbishop was hinting at the forbidden goal of enosis when he spoke of the island's "Hellenic ideals" at a ceremony commemorating an EOKA hero. By 1962, President Makarios was describing himself publicly as "the Greek leader of a Greek island," while the leader of the Turkish Cypriots was somberly telling a Turkish Cypriot audience at Lefka that they must stay united as "during the days of the [EOKA] struggle," but that the "mother nation stands always by our side."[13]

It should not have been surprising that Archbishop Makarios and his cabinet proceeded to disregard all the provisions of the constitution that protected the communal identity of the Turkish Cypriots—and that the Turkish Cypriots responded by using all the many methods of interference legally provided by the constitution. By 1963 the government of Cyprus was reduced to a complete deadlock, unable to collect taxes, administer justice, run a civil service, or set up unified armed forces. Both sides had retained arms and had acquired new ones in anticipation of another violent confrontation, which again would be basically about the prospect of enosis.

In the fall of 1963, just three years after the proclamation of independence, President Makarios made his move, suggesting amendments to the constitution that in effect would have removed all recognition of the communal existence of the Turkish Cypriots. Minority rights were to remain, but on an individual basis. No one has yet established what the archbishop expected to happen—most likely a fait accompli achievement of majority rule followed by a vote of cession to Greece. He seems to have been surprised by both the violence of the Turkish response—flat refusal and preparations for intervention—and the lack of enthusiasm shown by the Greeks. A civil war broke out with brutal fighting and heavy casualties, especially in the cities; the Greek troops on the island refrained from assisting the Greek Cypriots, and Greece itself joined the other two guarantor powers to call for a cease-fire and British-commanded peacekeeping. By March 1964, a UN peacekeeping force was installed, though not before a second Turkish threat of invasion (this time met by Greek countermeasures). Overt intercommunal violence stopped, apart from intermittent Greek Cypriot attempts to pressure the "rebels" into submission. The two communities remained heavily armed, and over the next few years were reinforced clandestinely by men and arms from the two mainlands, including former General Grivas (1964–67, and 1971–74). About half of the Turkish Cypriots were crowded into armed enclaves comprising 2 percent of the territory of Cyprus. An uneasy peace prevailed, with the assistance of a UN force that found itself unable to do more than could prevent the Greek Cypriots' repeated attempts to resolve things by force of arms.

Thus, by 1964, the relationship between Greeks and Greek Cypriots had visibly moved into a new phase. In 1958 Greece had disavowed active support for the radical solution of enosis. It had also pledged itself to a form of independence that would recognize the existence of the Turkish Cypriot community. The islanders were now the ones to take initiatives toward enosis, or unfettered majority rule. The mainland's main concern was to minimize the impact on itself. The only source of leverage—a weak one—was the ability to veto enosis by refusing to accept union. Prime Minister George Papandreou refused such an offer in 1964, and so did the Crown Council in May 1965. In 1967 there was a confused episode in which the Greek Cypriots on the island tried once again to reduce a Turkish Cypriot redoubt by force of arms—Grivas may have been responsible, most likely acting against the wishes of both Greece and Archbishop Makarios. This attempt to establish at least the dominance of the majority, and perhaps union with Greece, provoked a violent Turkish reaction: strafing and invasion preparations. It also produced what the Greek Cypriots most feared: "secret bilateral negotiations with Turkey over the heads of the Cypriots."[14] The result was withdrawal of the clandestinely introduced (Greek) troops and of "Mr. Enosis," Grivas himself.

A former Greek diplomat summed it up in 1971: Greece, he wrote, was "a power just as indifferent to the people of Cyprus as Turkey, the United Kingdom, the U.S., or the U.S.S.R. (i.e. pursuing her own interests and calculations regardless of whether they are acceptable to the Cypriots)."[15] In the words of Makarios' biographer, "Athens and Ankara . . . had a common interest in reaching a deal at the expense of Cypriot interests."[16] This dominance of mainland interests was unrelated to the ideology of the Greek governments: George Papandreou interfered with Makarios' attempts to obtain heavy weapons from the Warsaw Pact nations, General George Papadopoulos attempted to have the archbishop defrocked and assassinated, General Demetrios Ioannides fomented a coup that intended to depose Makarios and acquire a nonneutralist Cyprus. All regimes but the last feared a war with Turkey most of all, and the last thought of its own survival rather than of the welfare of Cypriots. What is interesting is the way Greek Cypriot initiatives which were unable to produce enosis against Greek wishes, nevertheless were able repeatedly to reactivate Turkish Cypriot and Turkish responses—and, thereby, Greek ones. The unsettled, UN-administered potential civil war of 1964–74 was alarming because of that possibility. And it was particularly alarming to Greece precisely because of its lack of control of the situation—a lack of control that consisted of the Greek Cypriots' ability to prevent any externally arranged settlement, and their ability also to provoke the continuing nationalist hostilities between Greece and Turkey.

Turkey's relation to its island kin is somewhat different. Here the predominant mainland interests—nationalistic and strategic—coincide with the communal ones. Turkey's need of the island means the need for survival of a Turkish entity there. The basic line of Turkish policy therefore is culturally and politically—and, if need be, militarily—to sustain the group's identity. This follows lines of natural sympathy, including formal and informal links. Moslem religious leaders in Cyprus came from the mainland, to which the Turkish Cypriot middle class had emigrated in some numbers after the British occupation. Turkey encouraged emigration from Cyprus in the interwar period; although it was never very substantial, it presumably reinforced the connections based on the islanders' going to the mainland for post-secondary education. There is thus an overlapping of cadres that parallels the better-known one connecting the Greek Cypriots to Greece.

Turkey's interventions on behalf of the Turkish Cypriots have always occurred, however, in response to overtly enosist acts by either Greeks or Greek Cypriots. It was Greece's appeals to the United Nations, and the beginning of EOKA's campaign on the island, that produced the Turkish objections sustained throughout the first UN episode of the 1950s. Admittedly, its moves tended to be drastic and heavy-handed. It was in the 1950s Turkey began the pattern of manipulating mob action at home (attacks on Greeks in Smyrna in 1955, for instance, were used to stress the seriousness of the Turkish stance at the Tripartite Conference then being held under British auspices), and of encouraging and subsidizing the armed territorial consolidation of the Turkish Cypriot community. Pressure against the remaining Greek populations in Turkey began at this time, though they were most intense in the 1960s, when the Greek Orthodox patriarchate in Constantinople was harrassed and threatened with expulsion.

It was only after independence that Turkey moved to the threat of invasion, overflights, and bombing (1964 and 1967), troop mobilization, and preparation of an invasion fleet. These overt interventions were justified in reference to the constituent Treaty of Guarantee's provisions that a guarantor power might act alone if the others refused to cooperate (and they were always requested to cooperate). Such actions, moreover, were taken only when intercommunal warfare was occurring and the Turkish Cypriots seemed physically endangered. The invasion of 1974 seems to have been a more direct response to the likelihood of an attempt at enosis. It also should be noted that the puppet president, Nicos Sampson, who had first made his reputation in EOKA, had been the leader of one of the more ferocious anti-Turkish groups of fighters in the bitter intercommunal warfare of 1963–64.

On the covert side, of course, Turkey was involved in arming its community from the beginning of the EOKA struggle. It seems to have continued support through the brief period of undivided independence, and certainly sent in substantial quantities of arms and materiel in 1964–67, when the Greeks were engaged in their main clandestine support. The Turkish Cypriot refugees and armed forces of 1964–74 were supported from Turkey. Since the 1974 invasion, the northern, occupied sector has been administered by Turkish military and civilian officials, and heavily subsidized from the mainland. But there has also been a careful continuing attempt to build up and support at least a symbolic Turkish Cypriot governmental structure, a "federated state" that would eventually be part of a communally divided new government of Cyprus.

On the whole, the Turks and Turkish Cypriots have been relatively willing to discuss settlements, the Greeks and Greek Cypriots the ones to break off discussion. The one irreducible Turkish requirement is the prevention of enosis, which has come to mean also the prevention of a simple majoritarian system. It should be noted that in 1977, the Turkish Cypriot leadership has once more taken an initiative to open discussions under the UN aegis. These are stalled once again, but seem slightly more promising than in the past. A solution involving a communally organized state is easier since the invasion, whose aftermath included a population exchange grouping the Turkish Cypriots mainly in the northern, occupied part of the island and the Greek Cypriots in the southern part. The juridical role of the central government is the main issue, since the physical and legal existence of the Turkish Cypriot community is no longer open to question. The radical solution, unacceptable to Turks and Turkish Cypriots, is now permanently ruled out. It remains to be seen what version of moderation will emerge.[17]

We thus have a pattern where the majority community on the island took initiatives with the reluctant acquiescence of its sponsors—provoking minority community response and a double response by the minority's sponsors, both to defend that community and to oppose Greece. Underlying and envenoming the situation is the Greco-Turkish hostility that dates back to, and is inseparable from, their two nationalisms. Both nations are offsprings of the Ottoman Empire, Greece being among the earliest nationalities to break away and modern Turkey being the survivor of the wreck. Built into Greek nationalism is resentment of the former masters, who still control the Byzantine capital and the site of the Orthodox patriarchate; built into Turkish nationalism is the great victory over Greece that consolidated commitment to Kemalism in 1922. Neither has the glory, the recognition, or the control over its own destiny that it feels entitled to. Sentimental, romantic Greek nationalism of the "Megali Idea" is always in conflict ideologically with a Turkish nationalism that sees national security as central and holds persistently onto what it can get of the Greek archipelago. On Cyprus these conflicts coincide, embodied in communities whose ratios are reversed, so that Greeks might perhaps dominate Turks, and thus perhaps dominate the entry to Turkey.

This is the period bracketed by the Truman Doctrine and the current disputes over Aegean oil; the two may stand for the two nations' mutual dependence and mutual, continuing hostility. In any direct confrontation between Greece and Turkey, the outcome would not be at issue. Greece is decisively smaller in both population and military might. Any battle specifically dealing with Cyprus, furthermore, could not be fought on that distant island, but would have to occur, probably disastrously for Greece, in Thrace. Greece's only strategic advantage is other nations' interest in having it cooperate with Turkey in order to form a solid military or economic barrier across the eastern Mediterranean. Hence this period is characterized by the two mainlands' competitive appeals to NATO, to the European Communities, and particularly to the United States, all of whom have proved reluctant to espouse either side of a quarrel between two nations seen as equally backward and difficult. The hostility between two nations that ought to cooperate is the main policy concern of the others appealed to. The ethnic dimensions of the quarrel are of little interest to the other concerned allies; there has never been any chance of partisan response. The shared importance of the two powers led other sympathetic nations to act, as far as they could, to dampen the conflicts. Greece, therefore, never obtained the allies and support in connection with Cyprus that it would have needed to counter its disadvantages. Consequently it seems, in general, to have acted with a caution disproportionate to its long-standing enmity to Turkey.

We may thus conclude that even close ethnic ties, with reinforcement in long-term enmities and in the nationalist rhetoric of domestic politics, may nevertheless produce only limited and cautious partisan support of a militant ethnic group. This is the more likely if that ethnic group is countered by another whose sponsor has both practical and emotional or ethnic reasons for supporting it, and has a will to use advantages of situation or power. Given this, we would expect that ethnic links with less psychological and political force, would have even less effect in drawing partisan support for an ethnic group. And this is the theme of the three other ethnically linked interventions in relation to Cyprus that will be discussed briefly: Islamic, British, and American.

OTHER EXTERNAL PARTIES

The Islamic case can be disposed of quickly. The Turkish Cypriots do not seem to have attempted to activate Muslim links. Turkey, however, used such links to get a hearing and endorsement of the reality of the island community. But Turkey's own relationship with Islam is a little peculiar. The Turkish National Pact defines Turkish identity in terms of language and of commitment to the secular Kemalist ideals. As a result, it did not associate itself with the Islamic Conference until its seventh meeting, in 1976, which it solicited and sponsored at Istanbul. Here the 42 Islamic countries agreed to support the demand for "equality of treatment" voiced by the "fraternal people of the Turkish Muslim Community of Cyprus," as well as their right to be heard in all international forums including the Islamic Conferences.[18] Turkey announced, slightly evasively, that it planned full membership in the group. And it was clear that the Islamic nations had found symbolic value in meeting in the ancient capital of the Ottoman emperors. In return for a fairly cynical statement of identification with a religious affiliation it usually shunned, Turkey received an equally inexpensive statement of symbolic support. It should be noted that symbolic approval was what the establishers of the "Attila Line" were vainly seeking in 1976; the Turkish Cypriots did not need the more concrete aid sought by other Muslim groups, such as the Philippine insurgents.

The other Muslim support shows even more clearly the nonemotional and highly instrumental nature of such linkages. This is the Iranian and Pakistani backing that Turkey (and hence the Turkish Cypriots) has as a part of the Regional Cooperation for Development pact founded in 1964. Considerations of regional power are clearly dominant, with the key element being shared hostility to Nasser's Egypt, which has aided enemies of all three regimes. An Iranian commentator is explicit: "The other parties to the disputes . . . Greece and Turkey, played no . . . role in Iranian diplomacy, nor were they traditionally viewed as Middle Eastern States, and both tended to be oriented in terms of their primary goals outside of the diplomacy of the Middle East."[19] The same commentator notes that the three nations also had in common their being non-Arab and pro-Western. Again, Muslim ties provided a rhetorical vehicle, but the nature and value of Turkey was the link. The same reasoning, of course, appears powerfully in relation to the NATO powers that are linked with neither Muslims nor Greeks; their avoidance of partisanship reflects concern with the likely behavior of both the sponsor states, Greece and Turkey.

The cases of Britain and the United States are somewhat different. The tradition of British philhellenism, dating to before the death of Lord Byron, must be noted because it was so important to Greek and Greek Cypriot politicians. The last British governor of Cyprus was responsive to it; writing in his *Memoirs,* he said: "There is a natural affinity between Greeks and English—stronger, I often think, than between any other two peoples." His affectionate comments go on to include the real substance of what was happening along with this friendliness: "We were in blank disagreement with the Greek leaders right up to the end. . . ."[20] William Gladstone and Winston Churchill share with many less distinguished British politicians the experience of having urged enosis in a private capacity and having prevented it, even refusing to discuss it officially. The Greek historian of the first UN episode makes it clear that well into the period of EOKA the Greeks still hoped that, if not the whole British people, still the Labour party would somehow make effective their feelings of affinity. When we add to this a population of about 90,000 Greek Cypriots in London, in Labour constituencies, we can understand why the Greeks (and Greek Cypriots) put high hopes on Labour party support of the Cypriot struggles (as in 1957), and why Archbishop Makarios chose a Labour member of Parliament (and minister), Barbara Castle, as messenger to announce his conversion to independence as a goal for Cyprus (in 1958). Here we need only note that the Labour party supported enosis well before World War II—before it was in office. In office, it retreated to a niggardly version of self-government. Even in irresponsible, and therefore carefree opposition, the Labor party—through the even more irresponsible medium of the party conferences—never moved further than to a very reduced commitment to eventual independence. Thus sympathies and concrete electoral pressure together were not able to get even a verbal commitment to the goals of the Greek Cypriots in Britain and Cyprus. Therefore it seems reasonable to argue that the ethnic linkage was as ineffective as possible. It should further be noted that the only poll data we have on British public opinion during the emergency (1954–59) show the British public unaware of enosis, and classifying Cyprus as merely one of a number of colonies that wanted, and were being denied, independence.[21]

Britain's active impact on Cyprus really ended, however, in the winter of 1963–64. It did the initial peacekeeping after the outbreak of civil war (1963–64); but after an abortive series of meetings of the protagonists in England, it raced to dump the problem in the United Nations' lap, beating the Greek Cypriots by hours. The British bases have served certain residual functions in Cypriot ethnic politics: Archbishop Makarios made his escape that way in 1974, and Turkish refugees from the same coup sought British protection there. Later, the British allowed these refugees to be shipped to Turkey and then back into the northern, Turkish-controlled part of the country. This made possible the effective regrouping of the populations, and presumably earned Britain the enmity of those few Greek Cypriots not yet anti-English.

The United States' importance is, however, acknowledged to have continued. Secretary of State Henry Kissinger is often blamed for the 1974 coup and invasion, much as he and the Central Intelligence Agency (CIA) are blamed for the accession of the colonels, and for their departure. More important, for our concerns here, is the fairly common assumption that the U.S. embargo of

Turkish weapons and its general attempt to put pressure on Turkey in respect to the occupation of Cyprus are linked to the efforts of the substantial Greek-American community. This is, of course, inconsistent with the general argument that the United States wished to partition Cyprus and establish a NATO base there, rather than having it independent and neutralist, or a source of friction between Greece and Turkey.

In fact, U.S. policy in regard to Cyprus was consistent throughout the period preceding the coup and occupation of 1974. Concern for the stability of NATO was always predominant, so that peace between Greece and Turkey was more important than what happened to the island. A secondary concern, was to preclude neutralist or Communist control of that strategic location. The British had nuclear-armed V-Bombers based on Cyprus. More important, Cyprus was a valuable listening post and something of a spying center. These interests meant support of Turkey's opposition to enosis, but also great efforts to avoid any sort of military confrontation between the two segments of the painfully constructed southern wing of NATO. One has to assume American concern during the 1950s, but there is little evidence of their having taken an unmistakable stand against enosis before the 1958 sessions of the United Nations—and when the Greeks finally realized this, they moved toward compromise with Turkey. It should be noted that the compromise included secret agreements to convert the Greek and Turkish contingents on Cyprus into a NATO base.[22] Indeed, the Zurich and London settlements, and the new constitution, would seem to answer all the American desiderata, disregarding any residual enosism of the Greek-American population.

The 1960s and 1970s show a constant pattern, with the United States playing a slightly more active role in suggesting possible solutions. Thus, the Acheson Plan of the summer of 1964, allowed for enosis but with repatriation of Turkish Cypriots to Turkey, a Turkish base and territory on the island, and the transfer to Turkey of other small, strategic islands. No one seems to have liked this suggestion very much, though there are some indications that Grivas favored it. It was not a solution likely to appeal to Greek-Americans, though they would have been glad of the American role in inhibiting a threatened Turkish invasion that fall (the famous "Johnson letter"). The Greek-Americans seem, in fact, to have aided the American government in urging restraint on Greece as well.[23] Once the junta came to power, the question of policy toward Cyprus was overshadowed by the far more contentious question of relationships with it. The colonels' caution about Cyprus was surely reassuring for the United States; they also could share concern about the headstrong behavior of the Cypriots, and the likely results of a war with Turkey.

As for the American role and reaction to the coup-invasion on Cyprus in 1974, it seems implausible that the United States would have provoked these occurrences, given the serious risk of Soviet intervention. This was the summer of Watergate and of preoccupation in the Washington Establishment. In general, the standard policy of reducing tension and trying to inhibit confrontation seems to have continued, though with less impact on Turkey than under conditions of less provocation in the previous ten years. Later in the year, however, there appeared to be a shift in U.S. policy—and an important one, in that it seemed to respond to ethnically motivated pressures from the Greek-American lobby. This was the congressionally imposed arms embargo that was still partially in force in 1977.

There is no doubt that the Greek-Americans have made their voices heard; they number several million and have such spokesmen as former Senator Kenneth Keating, Senator Thomas Eagleton, and Representative John Brademas, as well as, periodically, the mayors of New York City. The identity of these representatives shows how the lobby works—as part of pressure groups (Keating, Eagleton) and through ethnic spokesmen (Brademas). The group's seeming success, however, can be attributed to a combination of events having little to do with any general U.S. responsiveness to Greek-American goals. We should look briefly at these factors, for they are unlikely to be combined again.

In 1974 the Greeks in the United States were unusually united in their views about what U.S. policy toward the eastern Mediterranean should be. For once there was no disagreement about the ideological complexion and orientation of the Greek regime, newly restored to political openness and preparing for an election. Furthermore, all Greeks could agree in opposing Turkey's invasion and occupation, without the usual need to dispute justifications. In London, during the invasion, Communist and anti-Communist Greek Cypriots, recruiting separately, had agreed on resistance to the Turks; much the same happened in the United States. Furthermore, the U.S. government was more prepared than usual to be anti-Turkish: a long-standing dispute about heroin production had revived when the Turkish government had reintroduced the growing and marketing of poppies under "controlled conditions." In addition, the brutality of the Turkish invasion made it difficult for the Americans to maintain any sort of evenhandedness. And they felt obligated to support Constantine Karamanlis' new, respectable, middle-of-the-road Greek regime that would soon be facing elections and a serious threat from the left.

On the other hand, Turkey remained the more valuable NATO party, Greece was newly dependent, and a chance of settling the Cyprus dispute was thoroughly welcome. Immediately after the July coup, Kissinger apparently had even hoped to replace the deposed Makarios with John Clerides, one of the few Greek Cypriots acceptable to Turkish Cypriot communal negotiators. Clerides, willing to act temporarily as Makarios' replacement before the latter's return to Cyprus in December 1974, realistically bowed to the charisma of the unkillable ethnarch. In the meantime, however, communal talks had begun again in the fall of 1974; and the Greek Cypriots were for the first time talking of a bizonal federal state. The American administration, wanting Turkey out of Cyprus, was nevertheless inclined to walk softly.

The U.S. Congress stepped in to force through measures suspending arms aid to Turkey if used for "offensive purposes" (that is, in Cyprus) unless the president could certify that "substantial progress" was being made in the Cyprus talks. The president stalled, but eventually imposed the cut-off (in December 1974). Turkey responded furiously, putting in question the lease of U.S. bases in Turkey and suspending intelligence-gathering operations there.

By the summer of 1977, the situation had moved no further. Greece's effective withdrawal from participation in NATO continued (its troops were in effect lined up against Turkey instead of within the NATO strategic alignment, and it had withdrawn from information-gathering activities), while Turkey had reduced NATO access to facilities, in part realigned its own armies, and was suffering from and complaining about shortages of equipment needed for its NATO missions. It had, obviously not withdrawn from Cyprus. As for negotiations, the old pattern continued, with the Greek Cypriots still intransigent. Turkey occupied some 40 percent of the territory of the island, and the Turkish Cypriots' negotiating figure was about 32 percent, estimated as equivalent to the land titles held by Turkish Cypriots. Rumors abounded, however, that they would settle for 27–28 percent. It seemed clear that Turkey was indeed refusing to withdraw from the island—but that it was the Greek Cypriots who were balking at negotiating a federal or cantonal state. And neither invasion nor U.S. or mainland pressure had made much impact.

Thus the Greek-Americans can hardly be said to have achieved their goal. Nor, I think, can they be said to have produced the policy change to overt pressure on Turkey. That is, rather, a result of an unusual congressional initiative into foreign policy. Its motives were not so much concern for the fate of Greece or Cyprus as a desire to reassert congressional powers in foreign policy. In particular, after the war in Vietnam and Cambodia, Congress wished to restrain the executive use of military aid to sustain undemocratic regimes that used the aid for their own purposes. The Turkish invasion gave the Congress an opportunity to please the general antiwar, antiexecutive public opinion and to slap down an autocratic executive, in particular an autocratic secretary of state. The Greek-Americans were, in brief, pushing against an open door. But the practical ineffectiveness, even counterproductiveness, of their policy seems likely to have encouraged a return to the traditional, more balanced policy. The instrumental goals, not of the foreign policy establishment but of the legislative sector of the government, produced the unusual intervention. This could only be exceptional.

CONCLUSIONS

Today it is hard to say just what is happening in Cyprus. Early in President Carter's tenure of office, Archbishop Makarios was mentioned as one of the foreign leaders subsidized by the CIA. If so, it failed in this case to get its money's worth, for the archbishop looms larger and larger as the explanation of the failure to achieve a federal solution on the island: thus he is the main cause of Cyprus' role in sustaining Greco-Turkish tensions. In the early months of 1977, however, there seemed to be a movement toward solution. Rauf Denktash, Turkish Cypriot vice-president of Cyprus, who had not met with President Makarios for 13 years, requested discussions between the communities. The two leaders agreed that negotiators should work for an independent, nonaligned, bicommunal federal republic. The basic principles stipulated by the Turkish Cypriots and Turks seem to have been accepted by the other side. There are rumors of U.S. pressure applied by a new administration, but the only, and very slight, indication of reasons for a break comes from the announcement that Archbishop Makarios suffered a mild heart attack early in April. The symbol of Greek Cyprus has perhaps accepted his own mortality, and wishes to leave some legacy of peace.

It probably is unrealistically optimistic to think that the tangled affairs of Cyprus are near to being sorted out. The renewed communal negotiations stalled in April. All one can say is that the radical solution of enosis has now been rendered impossible by the Turkish invasion, although even most Greeks accepted the unlikelihood of enosis long ago. It is possible that the Greek Cypriots have finally come to this realization. They seem also to have given up the substitute vision of a unitary Greek island theoretically able to rejoin the motherland.

The quarrels of the motherlands continue, where the nationalistic and emotional heritages of the past continue to play a large role, even if the ostensible subject of dispute is something as concrete as the resources of the Aegean seabed. Now that enosis is impossible, the dispute no longer takes place in Cyprus. But if the Cyprus dispute no longer seems a possible cause for a Greco-Turkish confrontation or even war, its settlement and the withdrawal of the Turkish forces are still prerequisites for any cooperation between Greece and Turkey. The struggle on the island was often a sufficient condition for igniting old Byzantine enmities; its ending is now a necessary, if not a sufficient, one for their settlement.

NOTES

1. The bibliography on the Cyprus struggles is voluminous, but most of its items are more or less well-disguised propaganda. It is particularly difficult to find information on the Turkish Cypriots. I shall list here the studies that proved consistently useful. For the period before the emergency, I found Sir George Hill, *History of Cyprus* (Cambridge: Cambridge University Press, 1952), most helpful; Doros Alastos, *Cyprus in History* (London: Zeno, 1955) and *Venizelos* (London: Percy Lund Humphries, 1942), give an objective Greek Cypriot viewpoint. François Crouzet, *Le conflit de Chypre 1946–57* (Brussels: Emile Bruylant, 1973), covers the earlier period

very extensively, and gives the only full account of the Turkish Cypriots. Stephen Xydis, *Cyprus: Conflict and Conciliation, 1954–58* (Columbus: Ohio State University Press, 1967) and *Cyprus: Reluctant Republic* (The Hague: Mouton, 1973), draw extensively on official and unofficial records of the Greek government. Stanley Kyriakides, *Cyprus: Constitutionalism and Crisis Government* (Philadelphia: University of Pennsylvania Press, 1968), gives a good account of the early days of the republic from a moderate Greek Cypriot viewpoint. Thomas Ehrlich, *Cyprus 1958–67* (Oxford: Oxford University Press, 1974), is slightly more objective. J. A. Stegenga, *The United Nations Force in Cyprus* (Columbus: Ohio State University Press, 1968), is the authoritative account of that force, but it was also necessary to use Michael Harbottle, *The Impartial Soldier* (Oxford: Oxford University Press, 1970).

For internal conditions on the island since the late 1960s, I found two books helpful: Peter Loizos, *The Greek Gift: Politics in a Cypriot Village* (Oxford: Basil Blackwell, 1975); and P. N. Vanezis, *Makarios: Pragmatism and Idealism* (London: Abelard-Schumann, 1974). The best account of the strategic significance of Cyprus is Robert Stephens, *Cyprus: A Place of Arms* (London: Pall Mall Press, 1966). Thomas W. Adams, *U.S. Army Area Handbook for Cyprus,* Dept. of the Army pamphlet no. 550–22 (Washington, D.C.: U.S. Government Printing Office, 1964), gives social and demographic data hard to find elsewhere; and his *AKEL: The Communist Party of Cyprus* (Stanford: Stanford University Press, 1971) illuminates an important area of Cypriot political life. Halil Ibrahim Salih, *Cyprus: An Analysis of Cypriot Political Discord* (Brooklyn, N.Y.: Thomas Gaus's Sons, 1968), is the only book-length Turkish or Turkish Cypriot version I know; it is probably unreliable on details but nevertheless useful. For U.S. policy in the 1960s, see Edward Weintal and Charles Bartlett, *Facing the Brink: An Intimate Study of Crisis Diplomacy* (New York: Scribner's, 1967), ch. 2; and Andreas Papandreou, *Democracy at Gunpoint* (New York: Doubleday, 1970), esp. chs. 7 and 12. Weintal and Bartlett give a detailed account of shuttle diplomacy and the text of the "Johnson Letter"; Papandreou, the Marxist version of U.N. manipulation but a good account of the actual events as perceived in Greece. My version of the development and nature of Greek nationalism depends on the writings of C. M. Woodhouse (e.g. *Apple of Discord,* New York: Hutchinsen, 1948) and on John Campbell and Philip Sherrard, *Modern Greece* (London: Ernest Benn, 1968).

2. Lawrence Durrell, *Bitter Lemons* (London: Faber, 1957), p. 114.
3. Vanezis, op. cit., pp. 186–87.
4. Crouzet, op. cit., pp. 23–24.
5. Adams, *AKEL,* p. 126.
6. Anthony Eden, *Full Circle* (London: Cassell, 1960), p. 395.
7. Adams, *Handbook,* pp. 197, 311–18.
8. Loizos, op. cit., esp. p. 6.
9. Xydis, *Conflict and Conciliation,* p. 654, ftn. 93.
10. George Grivas-Dighenis, *Guerrilla Warfare and EOKA's Struggle,* trans. A. A. Pallis (London: Longmans-Green, 1964), pp. 44, 96. Also see Charles Foley, ed., *Memoirs of General Grivas* (London: Longmans-Green, 1964).
11. Xydis, *Conflict and Conciliation,* p. 528.
12. Vanezis, op. cit., p. 168.
13. Cited in Kyriakides, op. cit., p. 110.
14. Vanezis, op. cit., p. 136.
15. A. G. Xydis, "The Military Regime's Foreign Policy," in Richard Clogg and George Yannopoulos, eds., *Greece Under Military Rule* (London: Secker and Warburg, 1972), p. 206.
16. Vanezis, loc. cit.
17. Malvern Lumsden, "Field Research of Conflict: First Results from an Empirical Study of Cyprus," in *Proceedings of the International Peace Research Association Inaugural Conference* (Assen, 1966).
18. Embassy of Turkey press release, "Resolution on Cyprus," May 17, 1976.

19. Sharam Chubin, *Iran and International Organization: The Use of the U.N. in Selected Issues 1960–1971* (Teheran: Institute for International Political and Economic Studies, 1976), p. 36.

20. Sir Hugh Foot, *A Start in Freedom* (London: Hodder and Stoughton, 1964), p. 151.

21. Social Surveys, Ltd., International Survey XX-6, November 1955.

22. Xydis, *Reluctant Republic,* pp. 413, 457–58 ("Agreed Minutes"), 458–59.

23. Weintal and Bartlett, op. cit.

CHAPTER

4

THE KURDISH CONFLICT IN IRAQ

George S. Harris

The Kurds have long been celebrated as stubborn strugglers for an independent way of life. Resistance to outside domination and control has been their hallmark. This fierce determination to remain free caught the fancy of colorful chroniclers, from Justice William O. Douglas to a band of intrepid journalists. Hence, much of the narrative of their recent years of conflict was reported by Western observers. Yet these accounts of derring-do and heroism in personal combat did little to explain the abrupt collapse of the 15-year-old Kurdish rebellion in northern Iraq in March 1975. Unfortunately for the Kurds, fundamental, if little-appreciated, changes rendered individual bravery and fortitude under fire insufficient currency for successful ethnic conflict in the mountains of Iraq. In the end, their struggle had become such an integral part of the international environment that it depended not on the will and resources of the combatants but, rather, on the balance of external forces over which they had no control.

How and why the Kurdish movement lost its independence and came to be manipulated by political actors from abroad are questions that offer useful insight into the larger problem of the role of ethnicity in international relations. The Kurds of Iraq represent the case of a separatist conflict in which the ethnic group is divided among several neighboring states. Forming a majority in none of these countries, the Kurds nevertheless present a potential danger to the governments in their states of residence while lacking a voice in determining the policy of any. The experience of the Kurds sheds light on the effects of the interaction of such factors as geography, political legitimacy, and leadership on the fate of ethnic movements.

Geography plays an important part in this story. The stereotype of the Kurds as doughty mountain warriors is the natural consequence of their resistance to intrusions into their geographic refuge area north of Mesopotamia. Here, the Kurds have lived, set apart from the larger ethnic groups around them, in the first instance, by language. This chief distinguishing mark also has frequently been complemented by differences in religious rite (most Kurds are Shafii Suniis as opposed to the predominantly Hanafi Sunii Turks, Shiite Iranians and Arabs, and Hanafi Sunii Arabs that are their neighbors). Moreover, many Kurds are members of the Nakshbandi or Kadiri dervish orders; some belong to offbeat Islamic sects, such as the Nurcular and the Ali Ilahis. Especially in the more remote areas, the characteristics that differentiate Kurds from the outside world effectively discourage intermarriage or cultural assimilation.

At the same time, geographic isolation in these regions of difficult terrain has posed an obstacle to the creation of a broadly based ethnic independence movement. Living in valleys often cut off from each other, as well as somewhat inaccessible to their non-Kurdish neighbors, has contributed to the perpetuation of internal rivalries and traditional disunity. In fact, the Kurds are divided in dialect (Zaza, Kirmanji, and Kurdi), separated by bitter tribal feuds, and intermingled with other peoples in such a way as to frustrate a clear sense of overarching ethnic or national purpose. Moreover, with the sole exception of the short-lived Mahabad Republic formed during the turbulence of the Soviet withdrawal from northern Iran, Kurds have no historical state of their own to which they can look back. Rather, tribal memories provide the framework in which most operate. Their segmented society is further fragmented by the emergence of growing numbers of detribalized urban Kurds with goals and perceptions different from those of their mountain brothers.

To add to the complexity of the Kurdish situation, the drawing of international frontiers after World War I left the Kurds divided between Iraq (2 million), Turkey (4 million), and Iran (2.5 million), with smaller concentrations in Syria (600,000) and the Soviet Union (100,000).* While these borders imparted distinctiveness to the fortunes of the Kurds in each country, national boundaries did not sunder tribal and commercial ties. Except in unusual circumstances, when frontiers were sealed, customary tribal movement continued with little impediment. And in times of crisis, the border areas could provide embattled tribes sanctuaries from their enemies.

The emergence of a strong Kurdish separatist movement in Iraq had its effect on neighboring countries. The Turks still vividly remember the stubborn tribal revolts that they crushed by military force in the 1920s and 1930s in

---

*Accurate census data on the Kurds is lacking, so these figures are merely rough estimates. They represent a plausible maximum number of those of Kurdish origin. Some included may have lost their Kurdish identity and may no longer consider themselves Kurds for most practical purposes. For claims by the Kurds themselves, see Jamil Rojbeyani, "Facts on the Kurds: Reply to 'The Story of the Kurds,' Part 2" *Kurdish Journal* 5, no. 3 (September 1968): 15.

order to bring the Kurdish population of Anatolia into line. As a result, Ankara has always considered that the formation of an autonomous—let alone an independent—Kurdish entity just over the border would be a profoundly disturbing example for its own Kurdish population. Moreover, for a number of reasons—not least Mulla Mastafa Barzani's years of refuge in the Soviet Union—the Turks long worried lest a resurgent Kurdish movement in Iraq export Communist influence among the Kurds in Turkey. Thus Ankara has been prone to favor good relations with regimes of all political hues in Baghdad that seek to prevent Kurdish separatism in Iraq. Other factors may for a time have supervened to trouble Turkish relations with the Iraqi government, but over the long run the tendency to cooperate has proved irresistible.

The presence of Kurds in Iran has not been similarly decisive in determining the shah's policies toward the Kurdish problem. While suspicious of the possibility of revival of separatist aspirations in his country, he became increasingly confident of the effectiveness of the stringent security measures imposed on the Kurdish areas after 1946. By about 1960, the power of the central government relative to that of the tribes had risen to the point where the shah's armed forces were clearly more than a match for any conceivable domestic Kurdish dissidents. In these circumstances, the threat of Kurdish separatism became less immediate for the shah than did the challenge of outstanding issues in dispute with Iraq. The Shatt al-Arab boundary, which had been set by treaty in 1937 along the low water line on Iran's shore, was a growing irritant, particularly after the revolutionary regime in Iraq sought to collect pilot fees from ships proceeding to the Abadan refinery upstream. The shah's main concern, however, seems to have been that, following the brutal overthrow of King Faisal and Nuri al-Said in July 1958, Iraq might be seeking to export its own brand of political radicalism. Gestures such as allowing the tiny Khusistan Liberation Movement and dissident Iranian security chief Timour Bakhtiar to operate from Iraqi soil were taken as proof in Teheran of the danger emanating from Baghdad. In this situation, the shah did not let reservations about the possible spillover of Kurdish separatism into Iran impede friendly contact with the leaders of the Iraqi Kurdish movement. The supply of arms and money through Iran played an increasingly central role in keeping the Kurdish nationalist movement alive until 1975.

ORIGINS OF THE IRAQI KURDISH REVOLT

The Kurdish tribes in the north of Iraq had traditionally been restive under rule from Baghdad. On a number of occasions in the 1930s and the early 1940s, for example, the leaders of the Barzani tribe—one of the major Kurdish formations—had led insurrections against the Iraqi central government in the name of Kurdish independence. Exploiting their prestige as local religious chiefs as well as hereditary tribal overlords, the Barzanis were a formidable foe. Yet their military force was not sufficient to prevail over that of the Baghdad regime (reinforced by the British), particularly since important Kurdish tribes traditionally hostile to the Barzanis assisted the government troops. In 1943, Mulla Mustafa Barzani, the most active and charismatic of the leaders of this tribe, fled with a band of loyal supporters to Iran and thence, after the collapse of the Mahabad Kurdish Republic in 1946, to the Soviet Union.[1]

With the absence of Mulla Mustafa, with more astute government in Baghdad, and with the reimposition of firm control over adjacent areas in Iran, the Kurdish region of northern Iraq remained relatively quiet during the final decade of the Iraqi monarchy. Separatist sentiment had by no means disappeared, but there was little overt agitation for Kurdish rights and no tribal movement to provide a focus. Even though the United Democratic Party of Kurdistan was formed by detribalized Kurds in the larger urban centers of northern Iraq during the burst of political freedom in connection with the 1954 elections, its demands were modest and did not involve autonomy or independence.

The Iraqi revolution of 1958 ushered in a period of fundamental change for the Kurds as well as for Iraq as a whole. The new regime's lack of traditional legitimacy both encouraged and allowed Kurds in Iraq, though less numerous than their fellows in Turkey or Iran, to launch a bid for autonomy. Moreover, the 1958 revolution laid the ground for the return of Mulla Mustafa Barzani, whose commanding personality was central to the subsequent drive for Kurdish self-rule.

Both the Baghdad revolutionary government of General Abdul Karim al-Kassem and the Soviet regime in Moscow actively assisted in Mulla Mustafa's return. Yet Kassem certainly had no intent to foster a Kurdish separatist movement. When he moved on September 3, 1958, to pardon the Barzanis for their past insurrectionary activity and to welcome them back from the Soviet Union, he was no doubt attempting to secure Kurdish support for the new Baghdad regime. Likewise, Moscow—at least initially—probably did not intend to promote divisiveness in Iraq. The Kremlin regarded Kassem's government as a potentially important foothold for the Soviet Union in the Middle East and had no wish to undercut its position or to alienate the Baghdad revolutionaries. The Soviets probably believed that Mulla Mustafa had become a well-disposed ally during his dozen years in their country. Certainly they must have hoped that their sympathizers among his large entourage would prove useful in future. Joined with the Communist-oriented Kurds already on the scene in Iraq, these émigrés must have appeared likely to increase Soviet leverage in a rapidly improving climate.

The falsity of such assumptions was not immediately visible. Mulla Mustafa's involvement in Kurdish separatism developed slowly after his return on

October 6, 1958. While he assumed command of the United Democratic Party of Kurdistan and joined in demands for a degree of autonomy for the Kurds, he sought for a time to collaborate with Kassem. Barzani called on the Kurds to back Kassem against the Nasserite insurgents in the Mosul mutiny of March 1959. At first, too, both Kassem and the Kurds seemed to be moving leftward with increasing speed. Mulla Mustafa's party concluded a Covenant of Cooperation with the Iraqi Communist party on November 10, 1958; and in the Kirkuk rioting between Kurds and Turcomans in July 1959 the Communists aided the Kurds. It was not long, however, before Barzani's traditionalist orientation showed through. He repudiated such intimate association with the Communists and suspended those Kurds who had signed the cooperation agreement.[2]

Mulla Mustafa's relations with Kassem soon deteriorated as well. Although the Baghdad government had granted Barzani's party a license for legal operation under the name of the Democratic Party of Kurdistan (DPK) in January 1960, Kassem from the first was wary of its separatist orientation. His concern was compounded by the appeals of European Kurdish exiles for Barzani to take the initiative and by the agitation of these exiles at DPK congresses inside Iraq.[3] To counter Mulla Mustafa's aspirations, Kassem encouraged the Baradost and Zibari tribes, traditional rivals of the Barzanis, to burn crops, seize animals and grazing land, and raid the villages of the latter. The last straw was Kassem's move to withdraw privileges from Mulla Mustafa's family, who had been treated with great deference in the early days after the overthrow of the monarchy.[4] In June 1961, therefore, Mulla Mustafa took to the hills of his tribal area, which centered on the village of Barzan in northern Iraq, and prepared to resist the central government in traditional fashion.

At this stage, Barzani's aims were limited; he was principally reacting to Kassem's moves against his tribe. His main goal was to secure an end to political restrictions through clarification of the basic rights accorded the Kurds in Kassem's constitution. In this context, he sought no more than some form of self-administration for the Kurdish region, within the Iraqi state. Though he was not yet precise in his demands, he apparently did not seek the overthrow of Kassem. But under pressure from more radical elements in the DPK and the European Kurdish exiles, who stood for social change as well as for more far-reaching autonomy, he also favored demands for economic and cultural concessions from Baghdad.[5]

Domestic grievances, therefore, rather than foreign stimulus lay at the base of the Barzani rebellion. Nonetheless, Kassem wasted no time in branding Mulla Mustafa an agent of the "oil imperialists," asserting American and British complicity in the Kurdish movement. Baghdad promptly arrested several British civilians on charges of instigating the Kurdish revolt.[6]

Kassem's allegations of foreign intervention to the contrary, external response to the Kurdish rebellion at this time was minimal. The fact of the matter was that the Kurds had no strong foreign champion to trumpet their cause in world forums, nor were they ever able to overcome this deficiency. The West remained largely oblivious to the events in northern Iraq. While the Kremlin turned critical of Kassem for his active suppression of the Iraqi Communist Party, it was unprepared to support Mulla Mustafa in any effective way. The Soviets clearly regarded moves against Kassem as an embarrassment; Moscow no doubt appreciated the pronounced anti-Western tone of the revolutionary regime in Baghdad, and certainly was disturbed by Barzani's repudiation of the Communists. Hence, in spite of the temptation to recognize the Kurdish cause as a "national liberation movement," the Soviets did not take an unequivocal stand in favor of Mulla Mustafa.

Likewise, Middle Eastern states took little notice of Barzani's movement. The appeal to the United Nations on November 16, 1961, to demand an end to what the DPK Central Committee termed Baghdad's "genocide," was met with apathy. Egypt, which had become bitterly antagonistic to Kassem since the defeat of the "Nasserists" in Iraq, made some noises in favor of the Kurds; but these were halfhearted. Arab solidarity ran too deep for any Arab state to lend strong encouragement to a separatist movement in a brother country.

The only significant external assistance to the Kurds came from Iran. Thanks to Teheran's sympathetic stance, light weapons and ammunition flowed across the Iranian border, although from the first the Kurds probably were well enough equipped for guerrilla-style warfare in which they made no attempt to confront Iraqi regular army units. At least soon after the fighting began—and probably even earlier—Teheran had arranged behind-the-scenes contact with Barzani, a move that infuriated Kassem when he promptly became aware of it.[7] Also, the Iranian radio gave sympathetic coverage to the Kurdish movement through the remaining years of Kassem's rule. Yet judging from the scanty evidence at hand, Iranian support does not appear to have been unstinting or crucial to this phase of the Kurdish insurrection. And Teheran was unwilling to run interference for the Kurds in bodies like the United Nations or to speak out publicly in support of Barzani's cause. Quite clearly, therefore, encouragement from Teheran was not the main impetus for Mulla Mustafa's revolt.

COURSE OF THE CONFLICT, 1961–63

The Baghdad central government did not fight effectively against the Kurds during Kassem's remaining period in power. The conflict began as a fight between the Barzanis and rival Kurdish tribes. Next the police became involved, and gradually the regular armed forces of Iraq were committed to the fray. Even then, after mid-1961 the Iraqi army was distracted by the contemporaneous requirement to press Kuwait in the south. Morever, military morale was badly hurt by extensive purges as Kassem sought desperately to assure army loyalty to himself. In fact, the regime was far too busy pursuing other domestic enemies and attempting to reassure its position by playing off forces within Iraq against each other to concentrate fully on the Kurds. Barzani thus never faced Baghdad's full military power in the Kassem era.

In this situation, the central government was able to control only the urban centers and roads in northern Iraq. Indeed, during the rigorous winters the regular Iraqi forces had to fall back from their summer gains in this mountainous region. In the hinterland, where the bulk of the Kurdish forces were positioned, often in inaccessible caves, the Baghdad military could only bomb. Far from weakening the Kurds, however, the bombing of villages and largely civilian targets merely generated antipathy toward the government on the part of those Kurdish factions and tribes who had viewed the Barzani movement with reserve or open hostility at the start.[8]

Nonetheless, the Kurdish forces remained divided. Barzani commanded the tribal units in the northern, more mountainous area, but he refused to welcome the urban-oriented DPK in his sector. As a result, this ideologically directed, radical socialist organization, which was late to leave Baghdad for the hills, was compelled to establish its base of action in the rugged area to the southeast of Barzani's territory. The DPK Central Committee organized its units from detribalized Kurds, including deserters from the regular army and urban professionals. These units, therefore, were a formally organized standing force, as opposed to the tribal formations of Mulla Mustafa, which served as needed. Though its area was more exposed than the Barzani homeland, the DPK, once it began its military operations in the spring of 1962, defended its sector well. Indeed, DPK Central Committee member Jelal Talabani supposedly displayed a "flair for military command."[9] But although Mulla Mustafa, still nominally the leader of the DPK, eventually found it necessary to turn some of his tribal units into standing forces like those of Talabani, the division in the Kurdish camp continued strong and deep.

This split was reflected in tactical considerations as well. Mulla Mustafa, having failed to secure Soviet support on his terms, was all the more interested in obtaining Western approval and attention. Accordingly, he launched a campaign to attract Western correspondents to publicize the Kurdish movement. Through the good offices of the Kurdish émigrés in Europe, he facilitated the travel of such prominent journalists as Dana Adams Schmidt of the *New York Times* and Eric Rouleau of *Le Monde* to the Kurdish-held areas.[10]

A faction of the DPK, however, favored far more radical means of publicizing their cause. This group viewed disrupting Western oil operations in the Mosul region as an effective way to bring home to Baghdad the dangers of war in the north and to mobilize international opinion to press Baghdad to offer concessions. They may also have hoped to gain support from the Soviets and other anti-Western forces that were critical of the international oil companies. To these ends, Kurds blew up a part of the Iraq Petroleum Company pipeline on August 30, 1962; two months later they kidnapped British and American technicians; and on November 25, 1962, they hit oil installations in Kirkuk itself. The use of terror and destruction against Western interests, however, did not commend itself to Mulla Mustafa, since he did not want to close doors to the West and was seeking a share of the oil profits derived from production of the Mosul fields. Without his support, violence against oil facilities never became a major Kurdish tactic, although occasionally some damage was inflicted on oil installations.

For all their efforts, however, the Kurds made little progress in gaining international support. Despite deep differences with the Kassem regime, the United States announced in September 1962 that Washington would offer neither moral nor material support to Barzani.[11] Nor were the Kurds more successful in exploiting the temporary breach in Baghdad's relations with Ankara in the summer of 1962. At this point, Kassem accused Turkey of complicity with Mulla Mustafa, a charge that the Turks vigorously denied. It was undoubtedly true, however, that Ankara's stringent efforts to seal off the frontier notwithstanding, some assistance to Mulla Mustafa did leak over the border from tribes sympathetic to the Barzanis. But such leakage was minimal. After Iraqi planes, probably by mistake, hit a Turkish border post and killed two Turkish soldiers, Ankara retaliated by downing an Iraqi plane and in August 1962 temporarily recalled its ambassador for consultations. Yet this estrangement quickly passed; before the end of August the Turkish Foreign Ministry announced that Turkey would cease patrolling its borders with Iraq "in the interest of good neighborly relations."

Kassem's failure to handle the Kurdish issue successfully played a major part in his overthrow in February 1963. The military stalemate irritated powerful factions within the army and elsewhere in the power structure. Some military groups even made contact with the Kurdish rebels. Colonel Tahir Yahya approached DPK officials to solicit support for the Baath party, then being vigorously persecuted by Kassem. These talks resulted in an oral agreement in January 1963 in which the Baath apparently promised the Kurds autonomy and cabinet representation in exchange for an end to the Kurdish insurrection.[12] But this plan was never formally ratified and became a bone of contention between the parties almost from the first.

The early days of the Baath regime, therefore, were a time of probing and testing. In response to the Baath's appeal for the end of the "glorious insurrection of Kurds," Mulla Mustafa declared a cease-fire and quickly dispatched representatives to negotiate with the new regime on the basis of the promised local autonomy for the Kurdish areas.[13] Indeed, with the Baath party preoccupied with the larger Arab world, Mulla Mustafa found it possible to reach agreement with Baghdad on March 9, 1963, on the modest principle of recognizing Kurdish "nationalist rights" "on the basis of decentralization"—a vague formulation that Barzani interpreted as satisfying his minimum demands. A Baath party spokesman, however, stressed that in his view the agreement meant neither "secession nor . . . [even] delegation of powers on . . . internal political matters."[14]

Despite the interest of both the Baath and Barzani in preventing a new outbreak of war at this time, the accord was not carried out. The Baath leadership could not foresake its doctrinal commitment to Arab domination of Iraq. On the other hand, the Kurds in Europe and the dominant wing of the DPK had long pressed for greater concessions from Baghdad. They desired more complete autonomy and a guaranteed share of Iraq's oil revenue as the irreducible minimum. In fact, their terms stiffened notably once the possibility of an Iraqi federation with Syria was raised by the Baath party coup in Damascus in March 1963. To protect their interests in this situation, the Kurdish radicals insisted that the new constitution provide for a Kurdish vice-president, a Kurdish deputy chief of staff in the Iraqi armed forces, and one-third of the cabinet seats. Nor could Mulla Mustafa ignore their argument that the Kurds would be submerged if a greater Arab state should come into being.[15]

In this situation, the Kurdish demands escalated. In April 1963 Barzani's delegate, Jelal Talabani, demanded that the Baath include Kurdish representatives at future unity talks with Cairo and Damascus. Talabani further stipulated that if Iraq joined a federation of Arab states, the Iraqi Kurds must have complete autonomy within the federation; and that if Iraq united with another Arab state, the Kurds must have their own independent state linked to this Arab union. Provided that Iraq remained a fully independent state, however, Barzani indicated he would be willing to accept merely "national rights" on the basis of "decentralization," as previously agreed. But when Baghdad ignored this note, the Kurdish delegation presented a further plan on April 25, 1963, calling for a fully autonomous Kurdish area in an Iraqi state with very limited central government.[16] The Kurds rejected without second thought the Baath counterproposal of June 1963, which offered a small single province where Kurdish rights would be respected, but without any guarantees against the central government. Nor did Mulla Mustafa consider accepting the ultimatum to surrender within 24 hours that accompanied the publication of this Baath plan on June 10, 1963, and the simultaneous resumption of hostilities.

Moscow's stance encouraged Barzani to hold firm in his demands. The Soviets were shocked by the virulence of the anti-Communist strain in the Baath regime, which saw the Communist party as its chief rival. The Kremlin may also have counted on the sympathy of many of the members of the DPK Central Committee, who were strongly leftist. In any event, at Moscow's instigation Outer Mongolia put the Kurdish question on the UN agenda in May 1963 (this motion was withdrawn in the somewhat changed situation four months later). On May 6, 1963, *Pravda* gave notice that Moscow supported the "Kurdish struggle for autonomy" and condemned the Baath government for employing a "policy of terror and repression" toward the Kurds. *Pravda*'s tone grew more angry on June 12, in denouncing Baghdad's renewed military operations against Barzani. A few days later, *Krasnaia Zvezda* complained that the Baath had undertaken a "genocide operation" against the Kurds, and Moscow warned that it might end aid to Iraq if these operations continued. In a note of July 9, 1963, Moscow accused the Central Treaty Organization (CENTO) of interfering in northern Iraq, while leveling the charge of "genocide" against the Baath regime, an accusation that Iraq quickly and categorically rejected.[17]

The Baath leadership had for some time been preparing to reopen military action. As early as May 1963, Baghdad had moved its army north to bring it into position for operations against Barzani. Not committed to pressing Kuwait, the Baath regime was able to devote about three-fourths of its total force to combat with the Kurds. On June 10, 1963, when Baghdad launched its offensive against Barzani, all hopes for an accommodation with the Kurds were ended.

Unlike Kassem, the Baath could also field allied forces. The Baath regime in Syria pledged its solidarity with Baghdad. These words were followed a few months later by the dispatch of a brigade of troops from Syria to join in the operations against Barzani. Cairo, too, lent verbal support to the pan-Arab regime in Iraq, talking of a possible federation—although this talk rapidly petered out as Baath rivalry with Nasserism came to the fore.

In this situation, Mulla Mustafa did not do well on the ground. The Baath attack pushed him back into his mountain refuge areas. The Kurds apparently did not use their heavier weapons well (the bazooka was the heaviest arm ordinarily available), were perennially short of ammunition, and lacked artillery to stop Iraqi tanks and airplanes.

But the Barzanis were soon saved from military defeat by the inner strains that beset the Baath regime and led to its fall after only nine months in power. Thus, with the end of the fighting season in the fall of 1963, the Kurds began to stabilize their position. Although it was not Kurdish strength but the weakness of Baghdad that limited the damage to the Kurdish movement, both the Iraquis and outside observers shared the impression that within their rugged fastnesses the Kurds could hold out indefinitely, but could not successfully venture forth to impose their terms on the Baghdad government.

THE ARIF BROTHERS IN POWER, NOVEMBER 1963–JULY 1968

Like his predecessors, Abdul Selam Arif, who engineered the ouster of the Baath government in November 1963, called for peace with the Kurds immediately on assuming power. Arif stood for close relations with Nasser's Egypt and retained the commitment to join in the general Arab opposition to Israel. These pan-Arab aspirations eventually prepared the ground for a renewed conflict with the Kurds. But at the outset, the problems of establishing itself firmly gave the new regime little alternative to seeking an accommodation with Mulla Mustafa. This process took some months, since Arif evidently had not been in touch with the Barzanis before the coup and did not want to pay a high price for the end of the Kurdish insurrection. Thus it was not until February 10, 1964, that a cease-fire was reached on the basis that "Kurdish national rights would be recognized in a provisional constitution" through the principle of "decentralization."[18]

The cease-fire caused a major breach in the Kurdish ranks: the defection of most of the DPK leadership. The DPK had been only imperfectly associated with the negotiations with Arif after the ouster of the Baath regime. The Kurdish radicals saw the disruption of the Iraqi armed forces as the opportunity to gain lasting advantage over Baghdad by continuing the war. But, perhaps far more important, they clearly hoped that their activist stance would gain the DPK the allegiance of the Kurdish movement as a whole and would discredit the leadership of Mulla Mustafa. They therefore accused Barzani of selling out the revolution by agreeing to the cease-fire without securing a specific commitment to autonomy for the Kurds.[19]

Mulla Mustafa had little trouble in turning back this challenge. His base of power was built solidly on the prevailing tribal structure in the Kurdish area. Moreover, the Barzani family, through its traditional claim to religious leadership, inspired additional loyalties. Mulla Mustafa not only worked through the tribal chain of command but also controlled the main Kurdish armed forces. With his personal charisma and reputation, he was invincible. Although the DPK stalwarts used the winter of 1963–64 to attempt to build a political infrastructure, their efforts were attuned more to the urban intellectual environment from which they had emerged than to the realities of northern Iraq. Even detribalized Kurds did not universally support the DPK activists: the Communist party, which had made inroads among urbanized Kurds, backed Mulla Mustafa. And the efforts of the disaffected Kurds to negotiate Iranian backing for their faction did not succeed in procuring effective support from this quarter against Barzani.[20]

To break the resistance of the DPK and to reverse its attempts at social reform in the southern sector that it controlled, Mulla Mustafa sent his forces south in May 1964. In June, Ibrahim Ahmed, leader of the rival faction, organized a DPK congress that condemned Barzani and the cease-fire. But by July 1964 Barzani's pressure had grown too great for the dissidents; the DPK activists were forced to take refuge in Iran. There, after an abortive effort to return, the rebel faction was disarmed by the shah, who did not relish having armed Kurds inside his territory. Meanwhile, Mulla Mustafa, as nominal head of the DPK, convened a party congress in July to pack the governing boards with his supporters. In September 1964 Barzani's full mandate to lead the Kurds was reaffirmed by the new leadership. A few of the DPK dissidents, including Jelal Talabani, made their peace with Mulla Mustafa and were readmitted to the fold. The others eventually went over to the Baghdad side in frustration, and actively assisted the government in operations against the Barzanis.[21]

Mulla Mustafa's purge of DPK activists did not head off conflict with the Arif regime. Instead, by weakening the Kurdish military apparatus it may have encouraged Baghdad to attack. The Iraqi government saw the Kurds as disrupting the wider schemes for Arab unity propounded in the constitution proclaimed on May 3, 1964. The Baghdad regime had come to regard the Barzanis as effectively frustrating national unity, and in particular as a focus of subversion toward the government. In fact, Mulla Mustafa was seeking allies in the Communist party and even in the Baath party, which now, out of power, was willing to endorse autonomy for the Kurds. Moreover, once the DPK dissidents were brought to book, Barzani advanced more radical proposals than were envisaged in the February cease-fire or the constitution, although the final Kurdish plan presented in March 1965 was in the main merely a reiteration of long-held demands for Kurdish self-rule and the "right to private political organizations."[22]

When the spring fighting season opened in April 1965, therefore, Baghdad launched an offensive to regain control of the north. Arif's forces scored some successes, mostly in the initial two months of their campaign. Government troops continued to advance along the roads during the summer, but with increasing cost, as the Kurds were acquiring heavier weapons from Iran and capturing some from ambushed Iraqi units. By autumn 1965, Baghdad had begun to pull back from its summer gains to consolidate its position for the winter, when fighting usually ceased. This winter was an exception, however, and in December 1965 military operations resumed in what Kurdish sources called an Iraqi "winter offensive." While the results of this action were inconclusive, the government's forward positions remained exposed, prompting Baghdad to mount a spring offensive in hopes of gaining decisive advantage. This campaign was not seriously interrupted by the accidental death of Abdul Selam Arif in April 1966 and his replacement by his brother Abdul Rahman Arif. But the government's effort to smash through to the Iranian border from Ruwandiz ended in disastrous defeat, with the Kurds capturing much military booty, including artillery. As a result, Baghdad proclaimed a cease-fire in June 1966, a move that ended major military action for two years.[23]

In these engagements foreign support for the Kurds appeared to be of growing importance in determining the outcome. The involvement of Iran in particular became considerably more prominent. The supply of heavier weapons played a significant role in Kurdish successes. The increasing Iranian involvement took place in the context of deteriorating relations between Iraq and Iran. In fact, both sides reached the point of trading accusations of frontier violations; Iranian antiaircraft guns fired on Iraqi jets. In January 1966, President Arif accused the Iranian prime minister of personally meeting with Mulla Mustafa to formulate plans for "interference in Iraq's internal affairs," charges that Teheran not surprisingly rejected in toto.[24] While larger interests soon led these two states to reach a border accommodation to reduce the likelihood of general hostilities, it was clear that the Kurdish issue had become a major bone of contention between them. It was also noteworthy that for the first time Baghdad began to complain of Israeli assistance to the Kurds, evidently believing reports that Iran was acting "as a conduit of arms shipped to the Kurds from Israel."[25]

The Soviet factor, on the other hand, now appeared ambiguous in its impact on the conflict. To be sure, the advent of Abdul Selam Arif was greeted with relief in the Kremlin, where his regime was seen as more sympathetic, if not more malleable, than that of his Baath predecessors.[26] In August 1964, therefore, under pressure from Baghdad to resume large-scale deliveries of arms to the Soviet-equipped Iraqi military forces, Moscow agreed to return to a relatively open-handed policy of supplying modern weaponry and to expand commercial dealings between the two countries. It is not clear whether the Soviets sought any limitations on the use of these weapons against the Kurds. But in the era of hopefulness following the February 1964 cease-fire, such a restriction might not have seemed urgent. What terms the Soviets proposed for the use of military equipment during Abdul Rahman Arif's visit to Moscow in April 1966 also are not known. Coming in the midst of Baghdad's spring offensive against the Kurds, however, these negotiations must have posed considerable difficulties for the Soviets. In any event, the talks were interrupted by Arif's need to return to take power on his brother's death; with the June 1966 cease-fire, the Kremlin was given a temporary reprieve.

Despite the supply of weaponry to Baghdad, however, Moscow was far from ready to end its largely verbal support for the Kurds, particularly the DPK wing, which appeared more sympathetic to the Communist party of Iraq. It is difficult to ascertain whether the Kremlin was actually sending military equipment to Barzani at this period—though it is evident that Soviet-manufactured small arms were widely used by the Kurdish forces. What is certain is that such authoritative publications as the *World Marxist Review* carried articles defending the Kurdish movement and condemning Arif's regime as a "dictatorship."[27]

Although Abdul Rahman Arif continued much of the policy of his brother, he lacked the personal commitment to combatting Mulla Mustafa that had animated the regime. Moreover, there was a peace party of growing importance, led by Prime Minister Abdul Rahman Bazzaz, who appreciated the difficulties flowing from the war. The failure of the spring offensive in 1966 bolstered the position of civilians who believed that modest concessions and sympathetic treatment could satisfy Barzani. The latter, in fact, on a number of occasions reiterated his willingness to remain within the Iraqi state, though his more extreme colleagues usually stressed the need for complete autonomy for the Kurdish areas. Accordingly, Bazzaz promulgated a 12-point program on June 29, 1966, that offered elections, amnesty, reparations, and decentralized administration.[28] Mulla Mustafa lost no time in accepting this concession.

The 12-point program offered what seemed a reasonably workable compromise between the extreme demands by both sides, but it was given little chance to succeed. The day after Bazzaz announced his peace plan for the Kurds, Arif Abdul Rezzak, a former air force general and prime minister, attempted a coup in Baghdad. While his effort failed, it ushered in a period of increasing military restiveness that ended in the resignation of Bazzaz on August 6, 1966. Although the successor government under Naji Talib announced its adherence to the 12-point program and actually took some limited steps—releasing Kurdish prisoners and restoring property to Mulla Mustafa—pressure from die-hard military elements frustrated any substantial compliance with the plan. Unhappy though they were over the failure to carry out this program, the Kurds remained quiet. Thus an uneasy truce continued while both sides regrouped and prepared for the expected resumption of hostilities.

Mulla Mustafa's willingness again to accept a compromise from Baghdad gave his opponents new ammunition for attacks on him. The old DPK leadership, headed by Jelal Talabani, sought anew to establish its independence of the Barzanis by agitating for a resumption of hostilities. Their actions triggered clashes with Mulla Mustafa's forces. It was, however, an unequal contest: the Barzanis quickly reestablished their predominance, with even less difficulty than they had experienced a few years earlier.

RETURN OF THE BAATH: THE MARCH 1970 ACCORD

Uncertain in its philosophy, lacking a firm political and military organization, and increasingly beset with factional feuding, the Arif regime collapsed in July 1968. The Kurdish issue apparently played little role in Arif's fall; perhaps more important was disappointment with the performance of Iraqi troops in the Six-Day (Arab-Israeli) War. The only surprise about the overthrow of Arif was that it was so long in coming.

As in the past, the unsteady new government sought to propitiate the Kurds at the outset. At its ninth National Command Congress in Beirut in 1968, even before returning to power, the Baath had cautiously advocated ethnic rights for the Kurds, but within the "Arab homeland," and called for cooperation between the two peoples. Once in office, the new rulers opened negotiations to explore limited compromise with the Kurds. These gestures, however, did not allay Mulla Mustafa's suspicions, especially when the Baath made separate overtures to Jelal Talabani and soon sought to support him militarily against the Barzanis. In this situation, on November 18, 1968, Mulla Mustafa sent another protest to the United Nations against what he termed Baghdad's efforts at "genocide," and requested a UN mediator.[29] As always, however, such an appeal fell on deaf ears, since it lacked strong backing from a UN member state.

From the start, the Baath leaders had little interest in a prolonged truce with the Kurds. Once solidly entrenched in power, they opened a major offensive against Barzani. Kurdish separatism—especially with its Iranian entanglements—represented such a challenge to the dedicated pan-Arab leadership of the Baath party that a renewed effort to bring the Kurds to heel was all but inevitable. Within the armed forces, moreover, the desire to avenge the humiliation of past military failures apparently ran deep. In addition, the improvement in armament effected by supplies from the Soviet Union, with which the Baath sought to solidify relations, must have suggested that an offensive stood a good chance of success.[30]

Victory did not prove easy for the Baghdad regime. Midwinter seems to have been chosen for a swift attack in hopes of catching the Kurds off balance—a reasonable assumption, as it turned out. But weather precluded sustained operations. And before the Iraqi armed forces could drive to the Iranian frontier, the Kurds had time to regroup and were able to give good account of themselves. The government's drive stalled, and the campaign during 1969 proved indecisive.

The Baath regime's slowness in consolidating its internal position undoubtedly played a part in this stalemate. The Baath remained an elitist organization that relied heavily on its military wing for power to maintain itself in office. The party was divided not only into civilian and military cadres, but also into factions based on personality as well as on differences over the nature of the proper relationship with the Syrian wing of the Baath pan-Arab movement.

Even after squeezing out Colonel Abdul Razzaz Nayif and his military allies, who had cooperated in overthrowing Arif, the Iraqi Baath rulers had prolonged trouble settling in. For several years, the regime seemed only half a jump ahead of its opponents. In the fall of 1968, the government announced that a group including army officers had been arrested for attempting a coup. Secret trials and arrests followed; in January 1969, in the wake of another coup attempt, nearly a dozen Iraqis were hanged as spies for the United States, Israel, imperialism, and Zionism. Unrest continued through 1969, making it impossible for Baghdad to commit its forces to a maximum effort against the Kurds. Moreover, infighting within the 15-man Revolutionary Command Council kept the regime further off-balance as the civilian wing increasingly challenged the dominant military leaders of the Baath party.

Equally important in helping the Kurds stand off the Iraqi army was the sudden deterioration in Baghdad's relations with Teheran. In April 1969 the long-simmering controversy between Iraq and Iran over use of the Shatt al-Arab estuary took a sharp turn for the worse. In mid-April, 1969, Baghdad demanded that Iranian ships strike their colors in the Shatt and not carry Iranian naval personnel. The shah thereupon denounced the 1937 treaty that had set the boundary in Iraq's favor, and he sent naval escorts for freighters plying this waterway. The escalating confrontation led the Baath to withdraw forces from operations against Mulla Mustafa, especially after the shah put his forces on alert. By January 1970, following Baghdad's grant of political asylum to the shah's bitter opponent, General Timour Bakhtiar, relations between these countries sank to a new low: Baghdad and Teheran broke diplomatic relations.[31]

But it was more than the mere threat of war between Iraq and Iran that worked to the advantage of the Kurds. The flow of supplies across the border from Iran apparently increased markedly as Iranian relations with Iraq worsened. Again border clashes were reported, this time between the Iraqi army and Iranian troops said to be on their way to provide military assistance to Barzani. Although Iranian forces were not accused of having made deep incursions into Iraq, it was clear that Iran was being sucked further than ever into the military conflict. Indeed, there now appeared to be a direct link between the growing Iranian fear of the Baath regime's intentions and the degree of Iranian backing for the Kurdish movement.

Other external factors played a far smaller role in the success of the Kurds. To be sure, Baghdad chose this time to charge CENTO and the CIA with encouraging the Kurds. These accusations were part of the general media campaign to expose conspirators that the Baath launched in 1969, in an effort to mobilize support against its still numerous domestic challengers. This campaign was no doubt also stimulated by the continuing shipments of weapons from Iran. It was equally fueled by the frustration of the Baath at its inability to defeat the Kurds and cut off their flow of sympathetic reporting by Western journalists who persisted in making their way to the Kurdish area. But Baghdad did not actively press these charges for long. Significantly, by 1970 those incarcerated as enemies of the state came increasingly to be called Iranian agents rather than servants of the United States or Israel.[32]

With the advent of the Baath, the discomfort of the Soviets at the Kurdish dispute became more obvious. Neither the new rulers in Baghdad nor the Soviet leaders in Moscow wished to revive the feud that had marked the Baath's term in power in 1963. The Baghdad government held out something of an olive branch to the Communist party, therefore, and repeatedly dangled the possibility of forming a united front regime that would share rule with the Communists. The Baath's intention may have been not only to diminish the potential danger from this quarter, but equally to induce Moscow to withdraw its support from the Kurds. Saddam Husayn, who was the rising star of the Baath party, forcefully argued in 1969 that Communist leaders could not be accepted as partners in the government as long as their members were joining in the Kurdish struggle against the central authorities.[33]

Moscow, for its part, did not want to disturb the cooperative relationship that the Soviet Union had enjoyed with the Arifs despite the occasional critical rhetoric. Recognizing that military assistance lay at the bottom of their entree into Iraq, the Soviets took pains not to discourage the Baath by interrupting the flow of weapons, as they had done in 1963. But while continuing to deliver arms and to receive Iraqi military delegations, the Kremlin apparently used all means at its disposal to induce the Baath to come to terms with the Kurds. For example, in May 1969, during the stalemated fighting, when an Iraqi delegation came to ask for aircraft and other military equipment, Moscow apparently insisted that the Baath pledge not to use the new arms against the Kurds.[34] As a result, the Iraqis evidently returned from this foray somewhat disappointed, though Soviet interest in the Persian Gulf port of Umm Qasr gave the Iraqi leaders an attractive card to play. Moscow's pressure was exerted not just from behind the scenes. *Pravda,* on October 3, 1968, lauded the "just fight" of the Kurds and urged the Baath to work out a peaceful settlement with Barzani, arguing that this would strengthen the front against Israel.

Continuing Soviet pressure, together with the inconclusive results of the military action, the persistent power struggle within the Baath party, and the dangers of direct Iranian intervention, inclined the Baghdad regime to seek a more fundamental accord with Barzani. On March 11, 1970, after lengthy negotiations with the Kurds, President Ahmad Hasan al-Bakr announced agreement on a 15-point peace plan.

This agreement again called for Kurdish autonomy in a unified area in northern Iraq; a Kurdish vice-president; proportional representation of the Kurds in the Revolutionary Command Council and the government; Kurdish educational and linguistic rights, including eventually their own television station; the acceleration of the development of the Kurdish area; and indemnity for Kurdish losses. The Kurds were to surrender their heavy weapons and radio station only in the final stages of implementation of the provisions of the accord—a term of four years.[35]

Mulla Mustafa, having surrendered nothing to the central government, had won a major victory. He had gained somewhat more than the 1966 Bazzaz plan had accorded the Kurds. He had secured four years in which to consolidate his grip on the north without interference from Baghdad. The prestige of his victory also reinforced his towering stature in the north. Though even after a decade of the insurrection not all the Kurdish tribes had overcome their traditional rivalry toward the Barzanis, it would become even more difficult for those who had thrown in their lot with Baghdad to resist Mulla Mustafa's dominance. Despite his age—he was then over 70—his leadership had become unassailable. Even the perennial dissenters, such as Jelal Talabani, would find it necessary to make their peace with the charismatic Barzani.

THE END OF RESISTANCE: THE MARCH 1975 AGREEMENT

The climate of optimism that accompanied the 1970 accord masked troublesome trends for the Kurds. Long the odd man out of the Arab world, the Bakr government used the respite from the inconclusive Kurdish war to strengthen its position at home and to develop a prosperous economy based on increasing oil revenues devoted to industrial development in the Arab areas of the country. Overcoming its domestic opposition and steadily gaining internal cohesion, the Baath slowly tightened its grip on the Iraqi power structure. At the same time, while the Baath regime continued to nourish its pan-Arab aspirations, it began to moderate its differences with the rest of the Arab world —perhaps an easier task once Gamal Abdel Nasser had been succeeded by Anwar Sadat in Egypt. The intensity of conflict with Syria did not abate, and indeed at times reached new peaks of invective; but the general course of Iraq was toward composing its fundamental differences with the other Arab states. Moreover, the Baath's growing recognition of the interdependence of the oil producers, including Iran, was laying the base for a significant decrease in Iraqi isolation. In short, the developing strength and unity of the Iraqi regime and its Arab orientation boded ill for a lasting accommodation with the Kurds.

The Soviet relationship as well was evolving in ways that would not benefit the Kurds. Mulla Mustafa was becoming known increasingly as the ally of the shah. His opposition to the Communist sympathizers among the Kurds further reduced his appeal in Moscow's eyes. At the same time, the Baghdad regime's relations with the Iraqi Communists were reaching the point where, in May 1972, party members were included in the cabinet.

On the larger front, the cooling of Soviet relations with Sadat's Egypt stimulated the Kremlin to pay more attention to reinforcing its state-to-state links elsewhere in the Arab world, especially with regimes, like the Baath, that appeared receptive. In February 1972, Saddam Husayn, Command Council vice-president, returned from Moscow and gave notice that relations would be raised "to Treaty form."[36] And in April 1972, at the end of Aleksei Kosygin's visit to Baghdad, a 15-year treaty of friendship was concluded between the two powers. This treaty was perhaps more symbolic than substantial, but it gave clear indication of the trend in Iraqi-Soviet affairs. There could be no doubt that general policy considerations were committing the Soviet Union ever more firmly to support of the Baath regime, whether or not Iraqi policy toward the Kurds harmonized with that of Moscow.

Mulla Mustafa, on the other hand, could do little more to strengthen his forces. The general cease-fire made it difficult to keep his men on full martial footing. Moreover, the absence of fighting weakened the justification of the urgency of his need to stockpile heavy arms and ammunition. While Teheran remained deeply estranged from Baghdad, the shah was apparently interested in keeping the Kurds supplied only to the point where they could defend themselves against a Baath offensive, but not to the point where they would stand a good chance of delivering a decisive defeat to the central government forces or setting up an independent entity. Furthermore, the shah was exploring the possibilities of a limited improvement in relations with Iraq; indeed, in October 1973 diplomatic ties between the two states were restored. As a result, the Iranians were not prepared to make an all-out effort to provide the Kurds with heavy weapons, although aid did continue during these years.

Taken together, these trends doomed the detailed negotiations over the application of the March accord with the Kurds. While the talks dragged on, the government refused to carry out the census that was to determine the limits of the Kurdish area; the Kurds claimed that the Baath had meanwhile settled Arabs in the vicinity of Kirkuk. The Baghdad regime refused to seat the Kurdish candidate for vice-president. Further, in September 1971, Barzani narrowly escaped assassination in a plot that the Kurds suspected was linked to the central government. By April 1972, Mulla Mustafa was openly complaining of the government's bad faith and warning that the war might resume if there were no change in Baghdad's attitude. In July 1972 another attempted assassination was attributed to the Baath regime.

In this situation, Barzani's relations with Baghdad steadily deteriorated. The Baath party memorandum of September 1972 requesting KDP cooperation in working out differences proposed no compromise on the main points at issue. Nor was Mulla Mustafa willing to risk accepting the Baath offer to form a united front including the KDP as well as the Communist Party—a proposal that Talabani's faction was tempted to accept. Thus by 1974 it was clear that Barzani and Baghdad were on a collision course.

The Iraqi government's proclamation of local self-rule for the Kurdish minority on March 11, 1974, was, therefore, meaningless. The negotiations had already reached an impasse: Baghdad's plan was issued as an ultimatum with a two-week deadline. The limited autonomy granted by the Baath in this program was by no means as extensive as that agreed upon four years earlier. Baghdad reserved its veto over local legislative and executive councils, and refused to assure a division of oil revenues with the Kurdish region.[37] Thus it was hardly surprising that fighting broke out almost at once, while the Baghdad regime was still in the throes of preparing decrees to enforce its limitations on Kurdish autonomy.

The chances that the Barzanis would accept Baghdad's terms were further reduced by the major clashes between Iraqi and Iranian border forces that erupted to end the modest warming trend that had appeared in relations between the two states. In February 1974 artillery duels flared across the border, leading to numerous casualties on both sides. Iraq charged Iran with arming Barzani; Teheran in return accused Baghdad of inciting the Kurdish population in Iran. As usual, the increase in tension along the frontier coincided with heightened Iranian interest in the Kurdish cause. But while the Iraqis and Iranians managed to arrange a cease-fire before the end of March 1974, the border remained tense and support for the Kurds increasingly flowed across it.

Leaks from congressional sources investigating the American intelligence community allege that arms supplied to the Kurds from Iran and, at the behest of Iran, from the United States, were central to inducing Barzani to resume hostilities at this time. The version of the report of the House Select Committee on Intelligence as published in the *Village Voice,* however, makes no such claim in respect to the United States.[38] Indeed, its pertinent passage reads: "As our ally's aid dwarfed the U.S. aid package, our assistance can be seen as largely symbolic." Further, this document assesses the total American assistance as only $16 million. Whatever the precise facts of the matter, given the rising interest within the Baath in reimposing authority in the north, the supply of weapons to the Kurds from outside sources could have been only one of the many factors that triggered the war. In any event, to encourage Barzani to resist Baghdad would have been to preach to the converted.

The Kurdish conflict, which began in March, became more intense toward the end of April 1974, when the central government forces started bombing towns to cover their advance. The Baath troops aimed to cut the major supply lines from Iran, thereby isolating the Barzani tribal heartland to the west. Since Syria joined Turkey in closing the Iraqi border in order to prevent the fighting from spilling over into their territories, the Kurdish sector faced disruption of food supply as well as the loss of arms and ammunition.

Baghdad's advance was slow through the summer of 1974; the government tanks and heavy artillery were largely road-bound and unable to move into the hilly Kurdish terrain. But the tide of battle went steadily against the Kurds. By fall only one supply route remained open to the Iranian border, and Baath forces had seized almost all the cities and towns in the Kurdish area. This led to a major exodus of Kurds—reportedly a total of some 120,000—who fled into Iran. And Barzani's counterattack in mid-September failed to ease the pressure on his troops.[39] Thus, by midwinter it was clear that the Kurds were hanging on by a thread—their tenuous supply route to Iran, which was constantly threatened by Iraqi air activity.

The success of Baghdad's offensive reflected the all-out effort of the Baath regime to bring the Kurds to heel. Saddam Husayn committed his personal prestige to the campaign. He was well aware that failure against the Kurds had brought down previous regimes, and he recognized that his personal association with the Iraqi offensive left him vulnerable to criticism from the military faction of the Baath if his gamble did not succeed. Thus the government's resolve was firm; Baghdad was willing to commit a large proportion of its armed forces, giving it considerable numerical superiority over Mulla Mustafa's combined standing forces and tribal irregulars. Moreover, supplies from the Soviet Union had been arriving in a steady stream, particularly after the 1972 treaty; hence, the Iraqi armed forces were far larger (twice the size they had been in 1963), better equipped, and better trained than in the past. The all-or-nothing approach increased the level of the conflict and the advantage of the regular Iraqi forces over their Kurdish guerrilla opponents.

The constellation of foreign factors was not favorable for the Kurds. The Soviets, who had previously pressed Baghdad to reach an accommodation with the Kurds, urged Barzani to accept the Baath offer of limited autonomy in March 1974.[40] There is no evidence that Moscow sought to persuade the Iraqi regime to eschew military action against the Kurds.

The declining fortunes of the Barzani movement were reflected in a rising tide of appeals for American military equipment and "political understanding."[41] Correspondents visiting the Kurdish area in the spring of 1974 reported Mulla Mustafa's fervent pleas for American aid. According to several reporters, he offered the lure of "concessions for unexploited oil and minerals" in "unabashedly" bidding for support.[42] To one journalist from the United States, Barzani's representative complained: "We asked for American help as long as ten years ago, and to this day we have had no answer."[43] These appeals no doubt reflected Mulla Mustafa's desire that Washington reveal itself as openly behind his cause. In this vein, he noted bitterly that American officials around the world refused to welcome Kurdish representatives for discussions at embassies.

Despite Barzani's faith that the United States could, if it would, redress the unfavorable balance, it was clearly Iran that held the key to the destiny of the Kurds. Significantly, as the level of fighting increased, Teheran became increasingly embroiled in military operations. With the Kurds losing ground to the advancing Iraqis, Iranian border forces bore an ever-expanding share of the combat. During the summer of 1974 there were repeated border violations by the forces of both countries; at the end of August, Baghdad accused the shah of massing troops on the frontier in contravention of the terms of the cease-fire agreed upon the previous March. In December several Iraqi planes were shot down by Iranian missiles near the border. So tense did the situation become, with a clear threat of major war between these protagonists, that Turkey and the United Nations attempted mediation. But by early 1975 it was evident that the shah faced the necessity of deciding whether or not to make a major military commitment to the Barzanis when the season for renewed operations opened in the spring.

In these circumstances, the shah's decision to accept mediation by Houari Boumedienne of Algeria and to agree to a comprehensive settlement with Iraq in March 1975 had logical antecedents, though it came with unexpected suddenness. The Iraqis offered to relocate the disputed border in the Shatt al-Arab to the middle of the navigable channel, thus conceding a persistent demand by the shah and removing a continuing irritant in relations. And the lure of a rapprochement with Baghdad held out the possibility, according to the shah, of easing the Soviets out of the Persian Gulf as a whole.[44] Against these advantages, the risk of continuing to support the Kurds appeared unacceptable and the mounting refugee and other costs too high. To seal this arrangement, the shah agreed to close his border to Iraq and to cease all assistance to Barzani.

The March 1975 agreement sounded the death knell for the Kurdish separatist movement in Iraq. Mulla Mustafa's forces could not withstand the closing of their supply base and sanctuary. In desperate straits, Barzani and his colleagues took refuge in Iran, where the government carefully kept them far from the frontier. Indeed, Teheran strongly encouraged the mass of refugees to accept Baghdad's offer of amnesty and to return to Iraq. Most soon availed themselves of this last chance and threw themselves on the mercies of the Baghdad regime, the Kurdish movement inside Iraq having collapsed once its leadership had departed. The advancing Baath forces quickly established effective control over northern Iraq. By April 1975 the Kurdish insurrection was over.

THE CONFLICT IN RETROSPECT

In conclusion let us draw some perhaps paradoxical conclusions with respect to the question of why domestic conflict spread or was contained.

An important distinguishing characteristic of the Barzani revolt was its tribal nature. Yet in a multitribal environment, ethnic unity clearly is hard to achieve. Thus the Barzani movement—though it gradually gained general acceptance among the Kurds—was constantly beset by Kurdish opponents of Mulla Mustafa both inside and outside the Kurdish insurrectionary ranks. But internal unity was not the essential ingredient for the Kurdish revolt to achieve success. A less capably led and more divided movement might have come apart more readily and might not have survived so long. On the other hand, even full unity would not have been enough to spare the Kurds defeat once the Iranians joined Iraq's other neighbors in cutting the Kurdish lifeline to the outside world.

That the Kurdish conflict lasted so long was due in significant measure to the fact that it was confined to Iraq and did not spill over to involve Kurds struggling for autonomy in adjacent countries. The first hint that Kurds in Turkey, Syria, or Iran were about to embark on conflict with their respective mother countries would have arrayed all these states in a cooperative venture to eradicate all traces of Kurdish separatism, wherever situated. While some

Kurds in Europe and the United States might on occasion talk idly about a larger Kurdish state, it clearly was not in the Barzani interest to raise such a specter.[45] It was only because the shah saw no real threat from his own Kurdish population that he could discount this factor in working with Barzani.

Particularly in ethnic conflict based on tribal units, the assistance of detribalized émigré agitators in countries far removed from the scene of fighting may be of mixed value to the leaders on the ground, if the Kurdish case is a model. The overseas Kurds proved more radical than did Mulla Mustafa. They complicated his delicate negotiations with the central government. He, closer to the scene and less extreme in his desires, stood a better chance to work out a compromise that might have avoided the ultimate debacle even if it had fallen short of true autonomy. Perhaps moderation and compromise were the only course that gave any realistic promise of lasting success.

NOTES

1. For the Mahabad Republic, see William Eagleton, Jr., *The Kurdish Republic of 1946* London: Oxford University Press, 1963), passim.

2. On the Communist issue, see Edgar O'Ballance, *The Kurdish Revolt: 1961–1970* (Hamden, Conn: Archon, 1973), pp. 63–69.

3. On Qasim's relations with the Kurdish activists in Europe, see Ismet Cheriff Vanly, *Le Kurdistan irakien entité nationale* (Neuchâtel: 1970), pp. 90–92.

4. Lettie M. Wenner, "Arab-Kurdish Rivalries in Iraq," *Middle East Journal* (hereafter *MEJ*) 17 (Winter-Spring 1963): 72.

5. For the views of the more radical Kurds, see Vanly, op. cit., pp. 89–94.

6. Wenner, op. cit., p. 78; "Chronology: Iraq," *MEJ* 16 (Winter 1962): 66.

7. O'Ballance, op. cit., p. 83.

8. Wenner, op. cit., p. 75.

9. O'Ballance, op. cit., p. 87.

10. See Dana Adams Schmidt, "Kurdish Rebels Confident of Victory in Iraq," *New York Times* (henceforth, *NYT*), Sept. 10–13, 1962; Eric Rouleau, "Le Kurdistan irakien a dos de mulet," *Le Monde,* Apr. 10–16, 1963.

11. "Chronology: Iraq," *MEJ* 16 (Autumn 1962): 488.

12. O'Ballance, op. cit., p. 96. Also see John F. Devlin, *The Ba'th Party* (Stanford: Stanford University Press, 1976), pp. 265–69, who points out that the Kurds were not in touch with the dominant Baath leadership. Dana Adams Schmidt, *Journey Among Brave Men* (Boston: Little, Brown, 1964), calls the Baath agreement "the great double cross."

13. O'Ballance, op. cit., p. 99.

14. Vanly, op. cit., pp. 181–86; Devlin, op. cit., p. 266.

15. For the various Kurdish demands, see Vanly, loc. cit. Significantly, it was Kurdish radicals who served as the negotiators. They were, therefore, well placed to sabotage the talks. In fact, Barzani himself complained about the independence of his negotiator, Jelal Talabani. Also see Devlin, op. cit., pp. 265–69.

16. For the complete text of this plan and the Baath counterplan, see Vanly, op. cit., pp. 369–75.

17. "Chronology: Iraq," *MEJ* 17 (Autumn 1963): 425. Also see *Iraqi News: The Movement of Defending Iraqi People* no. 5 (1963): 3–5. This pamphlet, issued by the "High Committee" in Vienna in late spring or early summer, reflected the viewpoint of the Iraqi Communist party and the Kremlin. According to this source, the "High Committee . . . proclaims its full support for the aims of the Kurdish people for autonomy and other demands put forward by the Kurdish negotiators."

18. O'Ballance, op. cit., pp. 116–17; "Chronology: Iraq," *MEJ* 18 (Spring 1964): 219.

19. Vanly, op. cit., pp. 220–21. The political bureau of the DPK issued a document on April 19, 1964, "The Arif-Barzani Accord, a Peace or Capitulation?," which amplified these charges against Mulla Mustafa.

20. O'Ballance, op. cit., pp. 119–20, claims that the shah backed the DPK wing because he wanted to weaken Iraq. While the shah was no doubt hostile to Baghdad, the claim that he was supporting the DPK against Barzani appears to be based largely on inference from the fact that Iran accorded the dissidents refuge without initially disarming them.

21. Vanly, op. cit., pp. 222–24; O'Ballance, op. cit., pp. 120–21.

22. "Chronology: Iraq," *MEJ* 19 (Summer 1965): 341; O'Ballance, op. cit., pp. 124–25.

23. O'Ballance, op. cit., pp. 133–37; Vanly, op. cit., pp. 259–66.

24. "Chronology: Iraq," *MEJ* 20 (Spring 1966): 210. O'Ballance, op. cit., p. 126, believes "there was some measure of cooperation" between Teheran and Baghdad in trying to seal the border. But if cooperation existed, it was far overshadowed by the profound hostility that led to the exchange of charges.

25. Shahram Chubin and Sepehr Zabih, *The Foreign Relations of Iran* (Berkeley: University of California Press, 1974), p. 180; "Chronology: Iraq," *MEJ* 20 (Winter 1966): 74.

26. Y. Bochkaryov, "New Orientation in Iraq," *New Times,* Sept. 16, 1964, pp. 12–14; *Pravda,* Aug. 13, 1964.

27. Aziz al-Hajj, "Their Heroism Illumines the Path to Victory," *World Marxist Review* 8 (Oct. 1965): 55–57.

28. For the text of the 12-point program, see Vanly, op. cit., pp. 379–80; Majid Khadduri, *Republican Iraq* (New York: Oxford University Press, 1969), pp. 268–78.

29. "Chronology: Iraq," *MEJ* 23 (Spring 1969): 197.

30. George Lenczowski, *Soviet Advances in the Middle East* (Washington, D.C.: American Enterprise Institute for Public Policy Research, 1972), p. 139, estimates that the Soviet Union supplied "200 jets, more than 500 tanks" over 10 years.

31. "Chronology: Iraq," *MEJ* 23 (Summer 1969): 370; Harvey H. Smith et al., *Area Handbook for Iraq* (Washington, D.C.: U.S. Government Printing Office, 1971), p. xv.

32. Smith, op. cit., p. x; Dan Morgan, "Kurdish Leader Visits U.S.," *Washington Post,* Nov. 28, 1975. According to the *Village Voice,* Feb. 16, 1976, pp. 85, 87(fn 459), the House Select Committee on Intelligence asserted that CIA support for the Kurds began later, in 1972, and took place at the behest of the shah.

33. Lenczowski, op. cit., p. 141, quoting the Beirut paper *Al-Sayyad,* Oct. 9, 1969.

34. The mission of Foreign Minister Abd al-Karim Abd al-Sattar Shaykhli. For an earlier Soviet view of Baath-Kurdish relations, see G. Mirsky, "Developments in Iraq," *New Times,* Aug. 21, 1968, pp. 11–13.

35. For a summary of the agreement, see Smith, op. cit., p. xiii.

36. "Chronology: Iraq," *MEJ* 26 (Summer 1972): 296.

37. "Iraq Gives Kurds Limited Autonomy," *Washington Post,* Mar. 12, 1974.

38. "The CIA Report the President Doesn't Want You to Read," *Village Voice,* Feb. 16, 1976, p. 85; Nicholas M. Horrock, "U.S. Role Hinted in Cypriot Coup," *NYT,* Jan. 20, 1976.

39. James F. Clarity, "Iraqi Forces Seize Most Kurdish Towns," *NYT,* Sept. 27, 1974; "Chronology: Iraq," *MEJ* 29 (Spring 1975): 188.

40. *Pravda,* March 14, 1974; Joseph Fitchett, "Kurds Seize Area Along Iraqi Border," *Washington Post,* Mar. 19, 1974.

41. "The Plight of the Kurds," *Washington Post,* Mar. 22, 1974.

42. Fitchett, op. cit.; Gwynne Roberts, "Kurdish Leader, Facing Possible Civil War, Looks to West for Support," *NYT,* Apr. 1, 1974.

43. Smith Hempstone, "The Middle East War Nobody Knows," *Washington Star,* Sept. 1, 1974.

44. Geoffrey Godsell, "Shah Tells Why He Made Peace with Iraq," *Christian Science Monitor,* May 7, 1975.

45. Israel T. Naamani, "The Kurdish Drive for Self-Determination," *MEJ* 20 (Summer 1966): 294, ftn. 29.

CHAPTER

5

THE WAR IN LEBANON

Leila Meo

In mid-October 1976, a minisummit of Arab states hosted by Saudi Arabia in Riyadh produced an agreement that haltingly brought to an end the 18-month-old civil war in Lebanon. Though there continued to be some skirmishes in various places and occasional fighting in the south, the war was officially over; and Lebanon's new president, Elias Sarkis, and his government of technocrats took up the enormous task of physical and social reconstruction. Under the auspices of the Arab League, 30,000 Arab peacekeeping troops, 25,000 of them from neighboring Syria, began to enforce the cease-fire and to collect heavy weapons from the rival militias. Without the presence of the peacekeeping force there could be no peace and no possibility of reconstruction.

The Lebanese civil war stunned the world by its length and destructiveness, for the image of Lebanon before the war was one of a stable, pluralistic democracy with a free and prosperous economy. Since its independence in 1943, it seemed that Lebanon had succeeded in institutionalizing ethnic diversity and balancing the interests of varied religious sects in ways that promoted mutual accommodation and avoided conflict. Its geographic location at the eastern end of the Mediterranean had assured it steady economic growth and prosperity through the role it assumed as entrepôt for commerce and banking between the other Arab states and their trading partners.

Yet despite all these advantages, in 1975–76 Lebanon suffered a bitter civil war that provoked external intervention in this country of only 4,062 square miles and a population of 2.5–3 million people. The conflict took an estimated 40,000–60,000 lives, and injured and maimed thousands more. It destroyed the country's economy, turned hundreds of homes and public buildings into piles of rubble, caused an estimated 1 million Lebanese to flee, and brought about major population shifts from one area of the country to another. The Lebanese army was factionalized, as was the government of former President Suleiman Franjieh. Effective authority was exercised by rightist factions in one-fifth of the country, by leftist factions in another fifth, and by a Syrian army of occupation in the remainder.

What caused the war? What were the reasons for this traumatic event that differed sharply from the image of a stable, balanced, and enlightened democracy? The purpose of this study is to explain the war's origins, its expansion, and its sudden end. To do this we will look into three areas that we expect to yield relevant information: the interaction between ethnic-socioeconomic forces and the political structures and processes within Lebanon; the role of the Palestinian community living in exile in Lebanon, and more broadly the impact of the Palestine question on Lebanon's internal politics and external relationships; and the specific motivations behind Syria's diplomacy in Lebanon and open military intervention in the war, as well as the motives and roles played by other Arab states and by Israel and the United States.

INTERNAL DIMENSIONS: THE SOCIOPOLITICAL DYNAMIC

The structure and function of the Lebanese political system are very much a reflection of the country's historical heritage, religious diversity, and class structure. Historically, Lebanon consisted primarily of the chain of high mountains, known as Mount Lebanon, running through the present state from north to south. It maintained its internal autonomy through the successive Byzantine, Arab, and Ottoman empires that ruled the eastern Mediterranean region. The inaccessibility of Mount Lebanon made it the refuge of disaffected Christian and Muslim sects and enabled Lebanon to maintain its autonomy under a system of feudal leadership *(iqta')* that paid tribute to the imperial suzerain. The two major sects inhabiting the Mount Lebanon were the Maronites, an Eastern Rite Catholic church, and the Druze,* a small Muslim community with minority views and beliefs.

In the mid-nineteenth century, Mount Lebanon experienced a Maronite peasant rebellion against Maronite feudal families in the north; but the rebellion assumed religious overtones when the peasants encroached on the lands of the feudal Druze clans of the south. Civil strife continued intermittently for 20 years and prompted Britain, France, and Russia, the major European competitors for influence in the Ottoman Empire, to introduce various forms of sectarian representation, ostensibly to bring conflict to an end. In 1860 a

*In Arabic, the word "Druze" is plural for the singular "Durzi." However, for the purpose of simplification we shall use the plural form throughout this chapter.

Maronite peasant uprising against their Druze overlords led to a major intercommunal conflict and the massacre of predominantly Maronite peasantry. In 1861 the three European powers imposed the governorate of Mount Lebanon, a more stable sectarian regime that maintained peace until the Ottomans assumed direct control with the outbreak of World War I. However, during the fifty-odd years of the governorate, the traditional feudal families reasserted their leadership by dominating the sectarian balance in government.

Feudalism and sectarianism were reintroduced into Lebanese politics by France when it was given mandate over Syria and Lebanon by the League of Nations after World War I. First, in 1920 France created Greater Lebanon by detaching from Syria and attaching to Lebanon the fertile Biqaa Valley in the east,* Jabal Amil in the south, and the coastal plains with their ancient cities of Beirut, Sidon, Tyre, and Tripoli. It next provided the country with a centralized parliamentary system that nevertheless was circumscribed by the requirement for a sectarian balance in elective and appointive office reflecting the numerical strength of each sect. The sectarian demographic balance, however, had changed with the creation of Greater Lebanon, increasing the ratio of Sunni and Shiite Muslims and Greek Orthodox and Greek Catholic Christians, to the hitherto majority community, the Maronites, and the next largest community, the Druze.

But whereas the Maronites remained the largest single religious community, the Druze community became fifth in size, preceded by the Maronites, the Sunni Muslims, the Shiite Muslims, and the Greek Orthodox. The existence of other, smaller Christian minorities, to whom political representation was accorded, gave the totality of Christian sects a slight numerical edge over the totality of Muslim sects. Significantly, none of the Christian and none of the Muslim sects by itself represented a majority. France catered to the religious sects individually, bestowing special privileges on some; but overall it catered most to the Maronites, to whom it had traditionally been a protector and through whom it felt it could maintain its presence in Lebanon indefinitely. Muslim irredentism during the mandate years, seeking reattachment to Syria, encouraged Christian dependence on French protection. However, by the late 1930s it had become evident to both Christians and Muslims that French protection was entrenching French economic and political hegemony by manipulating their political institutions. The nation rallied to the cause of independence and achieved it in 1943 when France was weak from its wartime losses.

Because of earlier mutual suspicions between Christians and Muslims,

---

*Parts of the Biqaa had in the past been under the control of individual Lebanese feudal lords for various periods of time.

independence was launched on the basis of the 1943 National Pact *(al-mithaq al-watani),* negotiated verbally by two respected leaders, the Maronite Bishara al-Khouri and the Sunni Riyad as-Solh. It provided for a balance of power in both domestic politics and foreign policy.

In domestic politics, the pact established, on the basis of the last census (1932), that political representation in the Chamber of Deputies would be in the ratio of six Christian representatives to five Muslim representatives. Thus, whatever its size, the Chamber's total membership would always be a multiple of 11, and would give the Christians a narrow majority.* Seats in the Chamber were allocated to each sect in proportion to the numerical percentage it represented in the total population. Thus, of the three major Christian sects in the country, the Maronites constituted 30 percent of the population, the Greek Orthodox 10 percent, and the Greek Catholics 6 percent. Within the Muslim community, the Sunnis constituted 20 percent of the total population (the second largest group after the Maronites), the Shiites 18 percent, and the Druze 6 percent.

The pact further assigned the three most important offices in government to the three largest sects: the presidency of the republic to the Maronites, the premiership to the Sunnis and the presidency of the Chamber of Deputies to the Shiites. The Greek Orthodox were to fill the office of deputy premier in the cabinet and deputy president in the Chamber. Flexibility was allowed in filling other cabinet posts, including at times the deputy premiership, as long as a Christian-Muslim balance was maintained and the major sects were represented.

In foreign policy, the National Pact committed Muslims and Christians to the territorial integrity and political independence of Lebanon within its existing boundaries. The Christians also renounced their dependence on foreign protection and accepted Lebanon as an Arab country; in return, the Muslims promised to drop all demands for unification of Lebanon with Syria or any other Arab country.

The "sectarian balance" formula was in effect a continuation of the elaborate system of checks and balances among the sects introduced into the political structure of Lebanon during the mandate period. But after independence the "balance" became heavily weighted in the executive, legislature, bureaucracy, and armed forces in favor of the Christians, particularly the Maronite community. The "balance" further enabled traditional regional feudal leaders and city notables to maintain upper-class control of politics, regardless of sect.

---

*In 1960 the size of the Chamber was increased from 66 to 99 deputies. For the Christians the increase was from 36 to 54 deputies, and for the Muslims from 30 to 45 deputies.

The Chamber of Deputies became the center of extensive nepotism, patronage, and special privilege. The privileges of the cabinet, drawn generally from the Chamber, were even greater; and those of the president were practically limitless, except for a constitutional ban on a second consecutive term in office. Thus, through "sectarian balance" the feudal elite preempted higher public office, with little accountability to the public at large.

The sectarian formula in politics encouraged sectarian thinking, thereby distorting class interests. But class interests did not disappear. Coupled with a successful entrepôt economy, the sectarian "balance" tended to paper over the widening economic gap between Lebanon's poorer regions and more developed regions, and between its poorer classes and the bourgeoisie; it also favored trading interests over industrialization. In some 30 years of independence, Lebanon developed a strong service economy geared to banking, commerce, transit trade, tourism, and the needs of foreign firms that found Beirut a congenial regional base for doing business with the Arab world. Free trade was the key to Lebanese prosperity, but prosperity came primarily to the bourgeoisie and upper levels of public officials; some of it filtered unevenly down to employees of such services such as tourism and the transit trade, but it had little effect on workers in agriculture and industry. Thus,

> . . . agriculture and industry, which employ 40 to 45 percent of the labor force, provide less than 30 per cent of the gross national product; other estimates indicate that half of the national income is controlled by 5 per cent (or less) of the population. By contrast, workers in agriculture, industry and construction combined receive only 12 to 15 per cent of the national income.[1]

The laissez-faire economy was accompanied by corruption in high places and by widespread evasion of even limited taxes by the rich.[2] The growing economic polarization between the politicians allied with the commercial interests and the majority of the citizens with limited or falling incomes was highlighted by opposition to the regime of President Camille Chamoun in the 1958 civil war. A study undertaken by the Paris-based Institut International de Recherche et de Formation en vue du Développement (IRFED) at the request of the succeeding president, Fuad Shehab, pinpointed the source of the trouble and recommended a solution:

> Our study of Lebanon has revealed to us an enormous disparity in the standards of living which appears to be on the increase. . . .
>
> If the current situation does not change, the disparity in the standards of living is likely to pave the way for revolution in the Lebanese regions and on the part of the underprivileged classes—revolution which would plunge the country in chaos and place it at the mercy of its neighbors' ambitions. . . .

> To achieve national solidarity . . . the groups which are enjoying various privileges must as of now work toward narrowing the gap between their standard of living and the standard of living of less fortunate groups. . . .[3]

The IRFED study revealed the existence of a wide and widening discrepancy in income and social amenities between the bourgeoisie and the poorer classes and in development and social services between different regions of the country. The existence of abject poverty in the shadow of great wealth was best illustrated by conditions in the capital of Beirut before its disfigurement by the civil war and before the expulsion and flight of populations from whole neighborhoods. High-rise apartments and villas stood a few minutes' drive away from the city's poverty belt, an ever-expanding ring of ramshackle neighborhoods that housed the urban poor, rural immigrants fleeing underdevelopment in the south, east, and north, and refugees escaping from Israeli military raids on the south. Many of the migrating poor and refugees settled close to Palestinian refugee camps on the outskirts of the city. (The Palestinian presence in Lebanon is discussed in the next section.) The residents of this poverty belt of Palestinian refugee camps and Lebanese neighborhoods were mostly Muslims —Sunnis and Shiites—but included smaller numbers of various Christian sects.

The regions suffering most from underdevelopment were Akkar in the north, with a mixture of Sunni, Greek Orthodox, and Maronite villages; Hermel in the northeast, with a predominantly Shiite population; part of the Biqaa, especially areas where Shiites lived; and South Lebanon, with its mixture of Christian and Muslim sects, but with a predominantly Shiite rural population.

During the summer and fall of 1975, when conflict was interspersed with shaky cease-fires, a broad public debate was conducted on the causes of the crisis. The armed presence of the Palestinian resistance movement, as embodied in the Palestine Liberation Organization (PLO), was mentioned as a factor. But whereas right-wing Maronite political groups blamed the Palestinians for starting the crisis by acting as "a state within a state," left-wing and Muslim mass-based political groups, as well as individual religious and political leaders of all religious affiliations, saw the long-festering social injustices as the root of the crisis, and the presence of the Palestinians on Lebanese soil as a complicating factor.[4] Spokesmen for the left (which included both Christians and Muslims) and for Muslim groups demanded modification of the 1943 National Pact so that it would reflect the larger proportional growth of the Muslim community since independence. But some voices called for abolishing the National Pact altogether and secularizing elective and appointive offices throughout the government and armed forces. Spokesmen for the Maronite right (and not all the Maronite leadership was rightist) defended the "sanctity" of the National Pact and argued against any modifications that would deprive

Maronite interests of their special privilege and power in government. They also demanded the disarmament of the Palestinians and their confinement to their camps.

The debate did not divide the Lebanese into two neat opposing camps. Public-spirited religious and political leaders tried to find common ground between left and right in order to avoid conflict, but to no avail. In the domestic debate, the sectarian dimensions of the National Pact became the stumbling block to compromise, and prevented response to the more crucial issue of social justice for the poor. The Christian poor, including the Maronite poor, desperately needed social justice; the cause was taken up by the leftist groups and the Muslim popular forces. Christian-Muslim linkages existed in the leadership and among the followers of the leftist groups. These linkages were further encouraged and sustained by the close association with the left of the secularist Palestinian movement. Yet broad-based class solidarity between Christian and Muslim poor could not emerge because the rhetoric of feudal-sectarian alliances dominated the debate, and manifestations of sectarian behavior during the fighting created an atmosphere of terror intimidating Christians and Muslims alike. But there were other factors that prevented the untangling of sectarian interests from class interests and blocked serious consideration of social reform. These ranged from the presence of the Palestinian revolution on Lebanese soil, to the importance of Lebanon's strategic location in the making of either peace or war in the conflicts between Israel and the Palestinians and Israel and the Arab states, to regional and international disagreements over the Palestinians' demands for restoration of their individual and national rights in Palestine.

EXTERNAL DIMENSIONS: THE MAJOR POWERS, THE PALESTINIANS, AND LEBANON

For 500 years the Arabs of the Fertile Crescent lived as subjects of the Ottoman Empire. As Ottoman power declined in the nineteenth century, the Arabs underwent a cultural and political reawakening; and by the beginning of the twentieth century they had determined to fight for political independence. Their bid for independence was denied them, however, when at the end of World War I, Britain and France agreed to share hegemony over the eastern provinces of the defeated Ottoman regime. Along with czarist Russia, those two imperial powers had competed vigorously for influence in the Ottoman Empire in its declining years. The Arab provinces were prized because they provided land and sea routes to imperial interests farther east and because they provided markets and resources for European trade. After the war, the victorious European powers set up the mandate system under the League of Nations, ostensibly to promote the independence of liberated peoples but in reality as a screen for imperial control. Since the Bolshevik Revolution of 1917 temporarily removed Russia from the competition, Britain and France divided the Fertile Crescent—Iraq and the Syrian provinces—into mandates. Britain became mandatory power for Iraq, Transjordan and Palestine, and France mandatory power for Syria and Lebanon. Britain encouraged Jewish immigration into predominantly Arab Palestine, which served to break up Arab unity in the Fertile Crescent. It also created a Jewish dependency that could serve as an eastern buffer against possible French pressure on the Suez Canal, which Britain controlled. There was no threat on the western flank of the canal because Britain had occupied Egypt since 1882.

After World War II, Britain and France were replaced by the United States and the Soviet Union as the major competitors for influence in the Middle East. Both superpowers began by supporting the creation of Israel through the 1947 UN resolution to partition predominantly Arab Palestine. American support for Israel continued, but the Soviet Union sought friendly relations with the Arab states. The opportunity came in 1955, when, following the denial of Western arms to Egypt, the Soviet Union assisted President Gamal Abdel Nasser in securing Czech arms instead. This began a long Soviet-Egyptian friendship that extended to other Arab states as they sought to reject the remnants of European imperialism. The United States cultivated conservative Arab regimes and attempted to isolate those that opposed Western influence over their economies and defense capabilities.

Because the National Pact forbade military alliances with any external power, Lebanon kept its doors open to all powers except Israel. There was one aberration. When the United States announced the Eisenhower Doctrine in 1957, in order to increase American influence at the expense of the Soviet Union, President Camille Chamoun declared his adherence to the doctrine by claiming a (nonexistent) Communist threat to Lebanon. His intent was to obtain a second term in office; but his foreign policy digression, coupled with his denial of governmental powers to the traditional *za'ims* (feudal leaders) and continued executive neglect of Muslim poor areas, provoked the war of 1958. A new cabinet under a new President, Fuad Shehab, repudiated the Eisenhower Doctrine and returned the country to nonalignment.

With its sectarian formula in government keeping a rough balance between its pro-Arab and pro-Western tendencies, Lebanon became a marketplace for a variety of foreign and home-grown ideologies, and a listening post for foreign powers seeking information on and influence in the neighboring Arab countries. Lebanon's fairly extensive freedoms also provided a base and a haven for Palestinian nationalism. By the early 1970s, the Palestinian community in Lebanon was part of a Palestinian diaspora totaling 1.5 million people. In 28 years of exile, the Palestinian community in Lebanon grew from around 180,000 to some 400,000. By 1975, an estimated 100,000 Palestinians were living in refugee camps located in various parts of Lebanon, particularly in the south.

In the late 1950s, the Palestinian diaspora began to organize for a war of liberation. Following the defeat of Arab armies by Israel in the 1967 war, Palestinian commando groups surfaced, and in the next two years seized control of the PLO. That organization had been created in 1964 by the Arab League to channel Palestinian nationalism and prevent it from provoking a premature Arab military confrontation with Israel. But under the leadership of Palestinian resistance organizations, the PLO's dual mission became to secure the return of the exiles to their home and the reunification of partitioned Palestine into a democratic, secular state. The strategy of the resistance movement was to conduct guerrilla warfare against Israel from bases in the Arab world, but to postpone a final military showdown until regular Arab armies were strong enough to defeat Israel.

Inevitably, Palestinian political and military strategies created tensions and conflict with the host Arab governments. Support for the Palestinian resistance movement among the Arab masses following the 1967 war had at first forced the governments of Jordan and Lebanon—the main resistance bases—to accommodate the movement. But in both countries clashes soon began to take place between commando groups and the army. In Lebanon, army-commando clashes led to Egyptian mediation that produced the Cairo Agreement of November 3, 1969. In this agreement, the Lebanese government recognized the autonomous presence in Lebanon of the Palestinian resistance movement under the leadership of the PLO and its right to undertake operations from the country, subject to "coordination" with the government. The government also granted the resistance movement the right to control Palestinian refugee camps, to set up military bases in southern Lebanon, and to recruit Palestinians in Lebanon for armed struggle against Israel.

The Cairo Agreement could not solve the inherent contradiction between the Palestinian liberation struggle and a Lebanon committed by its political leaders to avoidance of a confrontation with Israel so it could continue to prosper through its service economy. Moreover, the Lebanese people were divided on whether to allow the existence of a Palestinian resistance movement on their soil. Those who supported the movement wanted to strengthen the defense posture of Lebanon to repel the massive Israeli retaliation raids not only on Palestinian refugee camps but also on Lebanese villages and farms in the south. Those who opposed the resistance movement argued that Lebanese territorial integrity could be better protected through proper diplomacy with Paris, London, and especially Washington than through a stiffened defense posture.

The argument over the Palestinians was never an academic one in Lebanon. And the argument over defense could not remain academic. Lebanon could not continue to be a haven of peace and prosperity catering to special economic interests while all around it tensions were escalating; the Palestinian revolution challenged both Israel and other Arab governments. To begin with, Israel had announced, with the emergence of the resistance movement, that it held Arab governments responsible for commando acts against it, and claimed the right to retaliate against nations that gave haven to the PLO. Retaliation was a policy that Israel exercised in Jordan, Syria, and Lebanon, the three countries where the Palestinian resistance movement was based. The operations included air raids, land invasions, and, in the case of Lebanon, sea invasions. Generally, very little could be done to repel the Israeli attacks, since Arab air defenses were practically nonexistent and Arab armies not sufficiently equipped to risk military engagements that could lead to a wider confrontation with Israel.

In addition, popular support for the Palestinians notwithstanding, Jordan and Egypt were willing to try the road to peaceful negotiation to recoup the territories they had lost to Israel in 1967. An American initiative for peace won support from both Egypt and Jordan in 1970, and led to the expulsion of the Palestinian resistance movement from its main base in Jordan in 1970 and 1971. The bulk of the commando groups expelled from Jordan settled in Lebanon, and southern Lebanon then became the main base of commando operations against Israel. Syria remained primarily a source of logistical and moral support for the Palestinians. However, when Syrian President Hafez al-Assad came to power in November 1970, he progressively imposed greater restrictions on the Palestinian resistance movement in Syria.

As the most active front against Israel, southern Lebanon was subjected to massive Israeli raids that provoked the flight of villagers to the slum areas of Beirut.[5] Making the Lebanese people the target of Israeli retaliation had two objectives: to create dissension between Lebanese and Palestinians, and to force the Lebanese army to suppress the resistance movement on its soil. However, strong support for the Palestinian cause among the Muslim poor and middle class, within the student movement, and among leftist parties and intellectuals made it inadvisable for the government to use the army to destroy the Palestinian resistance movement. Besides, there were serious doubts whether the army, dominated by a Christian majority in the officer corps but composed of Christians and Muslims in the ranks, could survive attempted destruction of the Palestinian movement.

Expanded to some 16,000 men, the army remained weak. Lebanon's air force, too, was weak. The army offered only occasional and limited resistance to Israeli land raids into Lebanon. Israeli air raids went unchallenged. But the combination of an expanded Palestinian resistance presence in southern Lebanon and more frequent Israeli raids after 1970 forced Lebanese leaders to look more seriously into the question of defense and into the possibility of reorganizing Lebanon's military forces. In 1975, Maronite Deputy Fuad Lahoud said that as chairman of the Parliamentary Defense Committee, he had drawn up a plan for strengthening the army, for army reorganization, and for more administrative control of the almost unlimited powers of the commander in chief. He also saw the need for agreement on a wise defense policy.[6] But, he said, the president rejected his recommendations and preferred to maintain the status quo. "More than that," Lahoud added, "a decision was taken to cancel the deal for the purchase of Crotale rockets from France. They canceled it because the Crotale is an effective weapon which could have angered Israel. . . ."[7] Maronite Deputy Pierre Gemayel, head of the rightist Phalange party, opposed strengthening Lebanon's defenses but seemed to agree with Lahoud on the existence of an Israeli threat. "Those in Lebanon and outside it who are demanding a defense plan for Lebanon," Gemayel said, "are in effect inviting Israel to launch a war against us and occupy our lands."[8]

Israel's continued massive raids on southern Lebanon produced no defense policy in Beirut, but they did have other repercussions. Villagers abandoned their homes by the thousands and joined other Lebanese and Palestinian refugees living in the outer ring of poverty around Beirut. In addition, mass protests were held in the south against the government for failing to provide protection against the Israeli raids and for its long-time neglect of the economic and social needs of the south.

Neglected villagers in the south, poor urbanites and transplanted villagers in Beirut, and the poor in cities like Tripoli, Sidon, and Tyre were coming increasingly under the influence of Palestinian liberation ideology and of such leftist ideologies as Baathism and Nasserism. In addition, Lebanon's Communist party, after half a century of semiclandestine existence, emerged in 1970 as a legal party and opted for armed action in the south on the side of the Palestinian resistance movement. It also supported the popular movement and parties championing the demands of the effectively disenfranchised masses.[9]

The polarization between Lebanon's political establishment and the poor, predominantly Muslim masses paralleled an increased polarization between Maronite rightist interests enjoying a dominant position in the establishment and the Palestinian resistance movement, which the rightists saw as threatening Lebanon's security and profitable role as middleman of the Middle East. This dual polarization became critical in the wake of the 1973 October War because of two developments.

First, the war had upset the status quo that had favored Israel and had threatened vital U.S. interests in the Middle East. The United States now sought to attain a final peace in the Middle East that would safeguard its interests in terms of the new political and military realities. The peacemaking formula was to be U.N. Security Council Resolution 242 of November 22, 1967, which visualized the return by Israel of occupied Arab territories in exchange for Arab recognition of Israel's right to exist. Egypt, Syria, and Jordan were ready to make peace on the basis of Resolution 242. The Palestinians, who were represented by the PLO, rejected peacemaking according to Resolution 242 because it ignored them both as a national entity and as a primary negotiating party.

Second, the inflationary spiral that affected capitalist markets in the early

1970s, particularly after the rise in the price of oil after the 1973 war, caused a comparable inflation in Lebanon, which imports most of its consumer staples. The rich could afford the higher prices, but the middle class and the poor lost much of their purchasing power despite governmental subsidy of certain food staples. Strikes and general discontent increased popular antagonism to the establishment. In this atmosphere of uncertainty, politicians in and out of government and ideological groups began to build private militias through arms purchases and training. For those on the ideological right, mainly Maronite groups, the army could not be depended on to protect Lebanon's security because it included Muslims. For groups and politicians on the ideological left, and for Muslim mass-based groups, the army could not be depended on to protect their rights because it was effectively under Maronite officer control. With Lebanon as the last viable base for the Palestinians, the PLO and its various commando organizations were determined to maintain their freedom in Lebanon against all possible efforts to curtail it.

These were the main social and political forces at work in Lebanon when the armed conflict erupted in 1975.

THE CONFLICT AND SYRIAN INTERVENTION

In January 1975 there were massive Israeli armored and infantry attacks on the Arqoub area in southern Lebanon which laid waste the countryside and a number of villages.[10] Protesting the apparent lack of concern by their government, the destitute Lebanese villagers found comfort and support among the Palestinians, who had been the primary target of the Israeli raids. "In these villages," the correspondent of *Le Nouvel Observateur* reported, "young people, attracted to the fedayeen [commandos], are beginning to join the Resistance out of idealism and interest. The Palestinians adopted by the population are not politically inactive. The interests of the fedayeen coincide with those of the population."[11]

The Israeli raids on the Arqoub provoked verbal attacks on the Palestinian resistance movement by the largest Maronite rightist party, the Phalange. On January 20, Phalange leader Pierre Gemayel called for "reestablishment of state authority" and on February 20 he called for a "referendum" on the Palestinian presence in Lebanon.[12] On April 13, a bus carrying 27 Palestinians and Lebanese through Ain al-Rummaneh, a Christian suburb of Beirut and a Phalangist stronghold, was shot at and its occupants killed. The massacre, which the Palestinians blamed on the Phalange, ignited generalized fighting in Beirut and incidents between Maronite groups and Palestinians in Tripoli, Tyre, and Sidon.

Before the April clashes, however, other incidents had already taken place in the port city of Sidon. On February 26, demonstrating fishermen had clashed with the Lebanese army, and there were deaths and injuries on both sides. The fishermen were protesting plans by a government-licensed, private stockholding company to industrialize fishing off the southern coast of Lebanon, which the fishermen feared would deprive them of their livelihood. Significantly, Palestinian workers marched with the Lebanese fishermen in support of their cause.[13] More protest demonstrations took place on March 6 and 7 in Sidon, Beirut, and other towns after a former deputy from Sidon, Marouf Saad, died of wounds he had received on February 26 when soldiers fired on the demonstrators.

The events of early 1975 marked the haphazard beginning of the Lebanese civil war. They could have subsided like events of previous years, but by then the country had lost its ability to reach a consensus. As the as-Solh government fell because of its inability to deal with the crisis, sporadic fighting ensued in May between Phalangist militias and Palestinian commandos, and general strikes by merchants and shopkeepers partially paralyzed Beirut.

On May 23, in an attempt to bring the situation under control, President Suleiman Franjieh appointed a military government. Instead, the military government caused widespread resentment in Muslim and leftist ranks and triggered a new round of violence. It was forced to resign three days later but remained in office as caretaker while a traditional Sunni leader, Rashid Karame, tried to form a new civilian government. Finally succeeding on June 30, Karame announced his six-man cabinet on July 1 and said a new cease-fire had been agreed to. The new cabinet provided sectarian balance by including one cabinet member from each of the six major sects and by apportioning the various ministries among the six members. The problems of Lebanon, however, could not be solved by the cabinet. There were the cabinet's own internal divisions, particularly between Premier Karame (Sunni), who as minister of defense came into conflict with his own political rival, Minister of Interior Camille Chamoun (Maronite) on how to maintain internal security.* Chamoun adopted a hard line on maintaining internal security and dispatched internal security forces to areas of conflict. Karame tried to elicit Muslim, leftist, and Palestinian cooperation by assuming a conciliatory tone toward them and promising army reforms.

Compounding the cabinet's difficulties was the fact that two ideological opponents, Pierre Gemayel of the Phalange, and Kamal Jumblatt, head of the Progressive Socialist Party (PSP), had to be excluded from cabinet posts because of Jumblatt's objections to Phalangist participation and his own refusal to participate. Holding the Phalange responsible for the Ain al-Rummaneh

---

*The rivalry between Karame and Chamoun dated back to the crisis of 1958, when Chamoun was president and Karame among those opposing a second term in office for him.

massacre, Jumblatt based his objections on Phalange refusal to cooperate with the authorities in apprending those responsible for it.[14]

However, while both Gemayel and Jumblatt were excluded from the cabinet, Gemayel's interests were represented by Chamoun, whose National Liberal party (NLP) stood ideologically on the extreme right with Gemayel's Phalange and later joined Phalange militia in fighting against the Palestinians and the leftist-Muslim alliance. The interests of Kamal Jumblatt remained unrepresented in the cabinet. A traditional za'im himself, the Druze deputy from the Shouf area nevertheless espoused a socialist secular philosophy as head of the PSP and outspokenly supported the Palestinian cause and the Palestinian resistance movement in Lebanon.[15]

As issues began to crystallize between conflict and dialogue in the spring and summer of 1975, Jumblatt adopted a gradualist approach to reforms in the political, economic, and social structure of the state to benefit the hitherto effectively disenfranchised poorer classes.[16] Most of these classes belonged to Muslim sects who felt that their total numbers now outweighed the total numbers of Christian sects, and therefore entitled them to a better deal from the state. But there were also many Christian poor who could equally benefit from the same reforms. Though there were several groups of militias representing the interests of Muslim sects on a regional or countrywide basis, other armed groups demanding social change were organized on an ideological basis, and included separate Muslim and Christian groups, as well as groups with mixed Muslim and Christian leadership and following. The Palestinian commando group that sympathized with the emergent Muslim-leftist alliance's demands for social change, but tried at first to avoid being drawn into the Lebanese civil war, included both Muslim and Christian Palestinians. (See last section of article for the composition of the military and political opposition forces involved in the Lebanese civil war.)

Specifically, spokesmen for leftist and Muslim mass organizations demanded (1) renegotiation of the 1943 National Pact in order to give the Muslim population, now generally estimated to be a slight majority, a greater share in decision making; (2) reduction of the powers of the presidency and availability of the office to Christian sects besides the Maronites; (3) secularization of the Maronite-dominated administration; (4) reforms in the army that would improve its defense capabilities and open its officer ranks to more Muslims. Spokesmen for the Muslim-leftist alliance also defended the PLO and the Palestinian community against charges made by spokesmen of groups on the right. The rightist groups, supported by their own militias, were Christian Maronites (though not all Maronites were rightists) and stood for no change in the status quo and no change in the 1943 National Pact. Their leading spokesmen were Pierre Gemayel of the Phalange, Camille Chamoun of the NLP, and, in time, President Franjieh, who maintained his own militia, the Zgharta Liberation Army.

Other, smaller rightist groups included a clerical faction, the Maronite Order of Monks, under Father Charbel Kassis. There was also undetermined rightist sentiment within the Greek Catholic community; it came to a head at the end of August, when the residents of the Greek Catholic town of Zahle in the Biqaa clashed with Shiite Muslim neighbors. A leading spokesman for the right, Phalangist leader Gemayel made it clear that the right was determined to curb the freedom of the Palestinian resistance movement in Lebanon. The antagonism between the Phalange and the PLO was an old one, and became particularly bitter after the murder by an Israeli raiding party of three PLO leaders in their Beirut homes on April 10, 1973. Having received no protection from Lebanon's security forces at that critical time, Palestinian commando groups took to guarding their own offices in urban centers and patrolling the approaches to Palestinian refugee camps; but by doing so they aroused the displeasure of the Phalange. In April and May there were sporadic clashes between Phalangists and Palestinians, and the PLO vowed full resistance to Phalangist aims "ultimately to remove the Palestinian presence from the Lebanese theater," as a PLO statement claimed.[17]

Although the left and right political camps seemed far apart, there were people in the middle who worked for a reconciliation. These included the heads of the religious communities who exchanged visits and issued conciliatory statements, some traditional political leaders like Maronite Deputy Raymond Edde and Premier Rashid Karame, and Christian and Muslim members of the newly vocal intellectual community. Their efforts to prevent the ideological and physical splintering of Lebanon were in vain: positions seemed irreconcilable and, furthermore, traditional Muslim political leaders appeared to have lost credibility among the Muslim masses.

Concerned about the developing crisis in Lebanon, Syria began to play the role of mediator late in May. On May 25, one day before the resignation of the military government, Syrian Foreign Minister Abdel Halim Khaddam arrived in Beirut for talks with Lebanese political leaders. He was accompanied by high-level military commanders. Along with Yasser Arafat, head of the PLO and of Fateh, the largest Palestinian commando group, Khaddam again participated in talks in late June with Premier-designate Rashid Karame. Syria became alarmed when heavy fighting broke out again in late August and continued until January 1976. Two things in particular troubled President Hafez al-Assad of Syria. First, he was concerned that Lebanon's domestic conflict might draw Israel into southern Lebanon and the Biqaa, and thus pose a wider threat to Damascus than that through the Golan Heights. He also wanted, at first, to keep the Palestinian movement in Lebanon intact while bringing it gradually and effectively under Syrian control. As such he could use the resistance movement to bargain with Israel for return of the Golan and at the same time prevent the resistance from disrupting his own plans for peace.

Assad, who had seized power in Syria in November 1970, had brought his country out of its estrangement from the conservative Arab oil states and had coordinated policy with Egypt in the October war of 1973 to force Israel to negotiate on the return of the Arab territories occupied in the 1967 war. His strategy was to maintain unity within Arab ranks in the negotiating process so that the United States would have to pressure Israel to return the occupied Arab territories. In March 1975, Assad had proposed a joint military leadership with the PLO. The Palestinian leadership accepted, because of its dependence on Damascus for logistical support, but its acceptance remained tentative both because it feared complete subordination of the PLO to the Syrian regime and because Damascus was also seeking closer ties with the Hashimite regime in Amman, an old enemy of the resistance movement. The record of the two regimes was not encouraging to the Palestinians. In Syria, PLO activities were already regulated and restricted by Assad. In Jordan, the PLO had effectively lost its base in the 1970–71 suppression of the Palestinians by the Jordanian army. Separated from Israel by the Sinai desert and the Suez Canal, Egypt could not provide an effective base for the PLO, and was at any rate unwilling to do so. Lebanon remained the only place where various PLO groups could operate and enjoy freedom to disseminate their views. The PLO groups were not willing to lose that freedom to an extension of Syrian hegemony over themselves or over Lebanon.

There was already a marked difference between the Syrian position and the PLO position on negotiating peace with Israel. Syria under Assad accepted U.N. Security Council Resolution 242 of November 22, 1967, as the negotiating formula. The resolution provided for the return of conquered Arab terrorities by Israel in exchange for Arab recognition of Israel's right to exist. The resolution treated the Palestinians simply as refugees, ignoring their identity as a national entity and the fact that they were a primary party to the conflict with Israel. Succeeding U.N. resolutions adopted by the General Assembly had rectified Resolution 242's shortcomings by recognizing Palestinian nationhood and the PLO as sole spokesman for the Palestinian people. Thus, for the Palestinians negotiation of a peace on the basis of Resolution 242 would mean denial of their national rights. Furthermore, while the outcome of the 1973 war had given Egypt and Syria hope for return of the Sinai and the Golan, respectively, it put the Palestinians in a quandary.

First, the war made possible the restoration of part of the West Bank and the Gaza Strip, but the PLO had to compete for the establishment of a Palestinian state in those areas with Jordan. A conservative Arab state and, like Israel, a client of the United States, Jordan aspired to a return of the West Bank, which it had officially annexed in 1950, and for control of the Gaza Strip. The possibility of a West Bank-Gaza Strip Palestinian state was an option favored by three members of the PLO: Fateh, the largest independent Palestinian resistance group, headed by Yasser Arafat, who was also PLO chief; the Marxist-oriented Popular Democratic Front for the Liberation of Palestine (PDFLP), headed by Nayef Hawatmeh, and the Syrian controlled Sa'iqa, headed by Zuheir Muhsin. These three groups postponed indefinitely the PLO objective of fighting for the establishment of a secular state in the whole of prepartition Palestine. They hoped that such a state might peacefully evolve in time, possibly a long time after establishment of a Palestinian state alongside Israel.

Three other groups rejected the proposal for a West Bank-Gaza Strip Palestinian state as only a partial solution to the Palestine problem, and mainly a negative solution, in that the state would become a Palestinian Bantustan controlled militarily and politically by either Jordan or Israel. These groups were the Popular Front for the Liberation of Palestine (PFLP), led by George Habash; the Iraqi-sponsored Arab Liberation Front (ALF); and the PFLP-General Command, led by Amhed Jibril. The last group eventually split into two factions, a Jibril faction that came to support Syria and therefore to accept the proposal for a West Bank-Gaza Strip state, and a rejectionist faction that abided by its original position, opting with Habash's group and the ALF for continued struggle for a democratic secular state in all of Palestine.

The Arab states were also divided on how best to solve the Palestine problem. Syria, Egypt, and the conservative Arab states (except Jordan) favored the establishment of a Palestinian state in the West Bank; the Gaza Strip, Iraq, Libya, and South Yemen rejected this plan as a partial solution and supported the PLO groups opting for the long-range solution of a democratic secular state in the whole of Palestine. These states and commando groups came to be known as the Rejection Front. Using their oil wealth, Libya and Iraq tried to influence Arab politics to reject peace with Israel on the basis of Resolution 242.

The inter-Arab struggle over rejection or acceptance of peace with Israel spilled over into Lebanon after the 1973 October war. Because Lebanon was militarily weak, shared common borders with Israel and Syria, and provided the Palestinian resistance movement with its last independent base, Lebanon became the arena of competitive Arab politics as the internal sectarian-influenced class struggle unfolded in 1975 and 1976. The internal struggle for a redistribution of power and benefits became inextricably mixed with the Arab states' conflicting policies on the question of peace or war with Israel, and on the role of the PLO in any possible arrangement for peace.

During 1975, Syria supplied arms to both the PLO and the leftist-Muslim alliance, which in March 1976 under the leadership of Kamal Jumblatt came to be known as the Progressive Front. Syria also used its arms and diplomacy to achieve several objectives: to enable the alliance to bargain with the rightist Maronite groups for a better deal in Lebanon without essentially changing the favorable balance of power the Maronite community enjoyed; to bring an early end to the conflict and to preclude Israeli intervention; gradually to extend

Syrian controls over the PLO in Lebanon in line with a policy of bringing it under Syrian hegemony.

A separate Egyptian-Syrian crisis developed and produced repercussions in Lebanon when, on September 1, Egypt and Israel concluded the second Sinai Disengagement Agreement under American auspices. Because, in article 2 of the agreement, Egypt and Israel undertook "not to resort to the threat or use of force" against each other, Syria effectively lost its defense alliance with Egypt, and Israel emerged much stronger militarily vis-a-vis Syria. Syria vehemently criticized Egypt, and so did the PLO and the Libyan government, both of which felt Egyptian policy undermined Palestinian interests. An Arab League meeting held at the foreign ministers' level in Cairo on October 15–16 to discuss the Lebanese conflict, which had again flared up, was boycotted by Syria, Libya, and the PLO. They demanded that if there were to be any discussions of the Lebanese crisis by the Arab League, they should be related to the second Sinai Disengagement Agreement. Egypt refused. Its countermove was to support the status quo in Lebanon, President Franjieh, and the Maronite rightists.

For Syria, Egypt's desertion of the two-front strategy, which they had forged together before the 1973 war, made imperative the construction of an alternative "eastern front" strategy that would confront Israel with the best possible argument for return of the Golan. This strategy called for stabilizing the internal situation in Lebanon, extending Syrian hegemony over Lebanese politics and over the Palestinian armed presence there, and coordinating a common defense policy with Jordan.

The PLO welcomed whatever support it could get, but tried to avoid manipulation or control by any state. In Lebanon, the general PLO stand was to conserve Palestinian energies for the Palestine struggle, but to defend Palestinian camps and establishments if attacked, to secure a clearer understanding with the Lebanese government on the 1969 Cairo Agreement, to offer the mediation of PLO leader Yasser Arafat, and to help with the policing of cease-fires in Muslim and Palestinian residential areas.

Cease-fires, however, did not last; and Syrian mediation could not produce a compromise, for essentially rightist and leftist positions remained incompatible. Speaking for the right, Pierre Gemayel insisted that change should come within the existing political framework (the National Pact). Speaking for the Progressive Front, Kamal Jumblatt demanded change that would lead to the demise of the sectarian system. In addition, the fighting strategies of the Maronite militias revealed a progression toward de facto partition and the carving out of a Maronite-controlled Christian state. The military response of the Progressive Front was to prevent partition, which was also denounced by the Arab states and the PLO.

On November 28, Saudi Arabia warned against any attempt to set up a Christian state in Lebanon, but the rightist militias continued to move in that direction. In January 1976, they attacked and destroyed a predominantly Palestinian Christian refugee camp, Dbaye, and poor Muslim neighborhoods, Maslakh and Karantina, all located in the suburbs of predominantly Christian east Beirut, and drove the inhabitants into west Beirut. At the same time Chamoun's NLP militiamen blockaded a major Palestinian refugee camp, Tell al-Zaatar, on the eastern outskirts of Beirut. With Palestinian camps becoming the targets of rightist militia attacks, Palestinian commandos joined actively in the fighting on the side of the Progressive Front. They attacked the Maronite coastal town of Damour, south of Beirut, and Chamoun's nearby residence of Saadiyat to ease the pressure on their enclaves in east Beirut. At the same time, and for the first time, some 1,000 Druze followers of PSP leader Jumblatt laid siege to Maronite mountain villages, in response to the Maronite militias' blockade of Palestinian refugee camps.

On January 16, Lebanese air force jets attacked Progressive Front and Palestinian forces besieging Damour. In spite of the air attack, those forces took Damour and Saadiyat on January 20 as Lebanese Christian townspeople fled to the Maronite port city of Junieh and to other parts of the Maronite-held coastal enclave. Inadvertently, the Progressive Front and the Palestinians thus contributed to the de facto partition they were trying to prevent.

The use of the Lebanese air force against the Progressive Front and the Palestinian forces was a blunder of the same proportions. The air attack was the first serious intervention by the Lebanese armed forces in the conflict between left and right factions, and it signaled the beginning of the breakup of the Lebanese armed forces. A few days after the raid, a Muslim Army officer, Lieutenant Ahmad al-Khatib, deserted and took with him a substantial number of Muslim soldiers and their equipment. He announced the formation of the "Lebanese Arab Army," which began to fight on the side of the Palestinian, Muslim, and left forces. The Maronite-dominated air force now openly sided with the rightist militias, as did Maronite troops deserting (with their equipment) under the leadership of Colonel Antoine Barakat. However, there remained troops who did not join either side. Still, with the breakup of the army, both sides now had tanks in addition to rockets and automatic weapons.

Alarmed, Syria moved to prevent further territorial fragmentation and put an end to the crisis. On January 19–20, the Syrian-based and Syrian-controlled Yarmouk Brigade of the Palestine Liberation Army (PLA) crossed the border and engaged Christian rightist forces in the Biqaa.* On January 22

*The PLA brigades were the regular armed forces of the PLO. They had been recruited among Palestinian refugees after the PLO was established by Arab governments in 1964 to channel and control Palestinian nationalism. PLA brigades were stationed in Arab states and were under the control of the host states. The brigades remained under the states' control even after the emergent Palestinian resistance movement captured control of the PLO in 1968.

Syria secured a new cease-fire and continued its mediation efforts. Syrian mediation induced Prime Minister Karame, who had announced his resignation on January 18, to stay in office. But Syrian mediation with the Maronite president and with right-wing Maronite factions met with resistance to any government reforms that might lead to a more equitable distribution of power. On February 14, President Franjieh announced on national radio and television a 17-point reform program that revealed an intention for continued Maronite domination. His reforms included proposals for a slight rectification of the existing political imbalance against the Muslims: a numerical parity would be established between Muslim and Christian members of the Chamber of Deputies, and the office of prime minister, still reserved for the Sunni sect, would be filled by an election by the Chamber instead of appointment by the Maronite president. However, in announcing the 17-point program, President Franjieh called for incorporating this new sectarian formula into law, whereas the old formula, the National Pact, had remained a verbal understanding. By insisting that the nation's political system be frozen into the sectarian mold, which would indefinitely favor the Maronite community, the president made the reform program unacceptable to the Progressive Front, which until then had hoped for gradual secularization and democratization of politics.

By the beginning of March the new cease-fire was already in disarray, and the split in the armed forces began to appear irreparable unless something was done to stop it. Thus, in an attempt to reestablish the unity of the army, on March 11 a nonpolitical Muslim commander of the Beirut area, Brigadier Abdul Aziz al-Ahdab, declared a state of emergency, demanded the resignation of President Franjieh and of the government, and assumed the title of "provisional military governor of Lebanon." For this "purely Lebanese solution" Ahdab had considerable backing from senior military officers, including the commander of the air force, the chief of Military Intelligence, and tacitly from the Maronite army commander, Major General Hanna Said.

But Franjieh refused to resign, and was supported by loyalist troops who guarded him in the presidential palace at Baabda, six miles southeast of Beirut. As Muslim rebel units from the now-divided army launched an attack on the palace to force his resignation, Syria intervened. On March 16 new units of the Syrian-based PLA and Syrian-controlled Sa'iqa commandos halted a two-pronged advance on the presidential palace, and took up positions between the rebel forces and the loyalists guarding the palace. This Syrian intervention brought warnings from Israel, but no Israeli counterinvasion of Lebanon.

The Israeli position can be explained only in terms of an earlier understanding between Damascus and Washington. According to Eric Rouleau, Middle East diplomatic correspondent of *Le Monde,* on October 16, 1975, U.S. Ambassador to Damascus Richard Murphy asked President Assad to work for an "equilibrium" solution in Lebanon. In exchange, Washington would subsequently seek Israeli acceptance of Syrian intervention within "reasonable" limits. Settlement of the Lebanese crisis would then open the door to broader Arab-Israeli understanding.[18]

Syria's intervention to keep President Franjieh in office was denounced by Deputy Kamal Jumblatt, who in late March assumed general direction of Lebanese leftist and Muslim forces (now constituted as the Progressive Front), demanded the immediate resignation of Franjieh, and vowed to continue the fight until Lebanon attained a democratic secular government. The Progressive Front now launched a coordinated and sustained attack on Maronite rightist positions and scored initial successes. On March 26 it forced President Franjieh to flee the presidential palace for the Maronite stronghold of Junieh. Seeking to restore "equilibrium" between Lebanon's leftist and rightist factions, Syria rushed Sa'iqa commando units heavily infiltrated with Syrian "volunteers" into Lebanon. But neither Sa'iqa nor the Syrian-officered PLA units already in Lebanon could restore the military balance between left and right. These troops proved unreliable for Syrian purposes, since many of Sa'iqa's Palestinian commandos and PLA brigades in the Beirut area and in the south defected to the PLO. Because of these defections Syria also failed to take control of the PLO command in Beirut through Sa'iqa.

Fearing further PLA defections to the PLO, Syria withdrew the rest of the PLA forces from Lebanon, and before mid-April sent in regular Syrian troops and armored tanks to establish the hitherto elusive "equilibrium." The Syrian forces occupied strategic points and villages along the Damascus-Beirut highway, displacing troops of the Lebanese Arab army.

Washington's hestitant acceptance of this new Syrian venture had been obtained at the end of March by King Hussein during a visit to the United States. Washington, however, remained unsure of the Syrian venture and alternated between praise and warning for the Syrians in its public statements. Thus on April 14, Secretary of State Henry Kissinger said the intervention was close to the borderline of Israeli tolerance; but on April 19, Presidential Press Secretary Ron Nessen said the Syrians "overall have played a constructive role," and on April 20 President Gerald Ford again used the word "constructive" in commenting on the Syrian intervention. Israel, which was being kept informed by Washington of the Syrian moves, warned Syria not to go beyond the "red line" (which remained undefined). On April 21, however, it was reported that for Israel the "red line" was the Litani River in southern Lebanon.[19]

In contrast, Iraq and Libya strongly condemned the Syrian military intervention in Lebanon. On April 10, Iraq cut off the flow of oil piped across Syria to the Mediterranean, depriving Damascus of both oil transit revenues and crude oil for the Homs refinery. Nevertheless, finding encouragement in Washington's attitude, President Assad persisted in his Lebanese venture and added a land and sea blockade to prevent arms and other supplies from reaching west Beirut, Tripoli, and the south, areas controlled by the PLO and the Progressive Front. The Syrian intervention was now beginning to tip the scales in favor of the rightist militias. It encouraged their political leadership to further consolidation of de facto partition, and it encouraged President Franjieh to hold on to political office after he had been asked by the Chamber of Deputies to resign in favor of a new president, Elias Sarkis, elected by the Chamber on March 8. Sarkis had been the candidate of the rightist Maronite parties and had also received the support of Syria over Raymond Edde, a moderate Maronite deputy who had looked with disfavor on the Syrian intervention and therefore had received the backing of the Progressive Front.

Despite the military and political advantage the rightist factions had received from the Syrian intervention, they remained uneasy over the Syrian military presence. This feeling was shared by the PLO and the Progressive Front, and at the end of May there were indications that the right and left factions in the Lebanese conflict and the PLO were ready for mutual accomodation without the need of Syrian mediation or the presence of Syrian troops. The rapprochement between the two sides was worked out by President-elect Sarkis, who, after his election, had made a conciliatory broadcast promising cooperation with all Lebanese, with the Arab states, and the Palestinians. The two sides were now ready to make a joint demand that Syria withdraw its forces from Lebanon. This certainly would not have helped extend Syrian hegemony over Lebanon and over the Palestinians there.

What happened next was interpreted by rightist and leftist leaders alike as a deliberate Syrian move to destroy the rapprochement. On May 25, there were attempts on the life of Raymond Edde, an avowed opponent of Syrian intervention and of the civil war; and on May 27, Kamal Jumblatt's sister, Linda, was murdered. Eric Rouleau of *Le Monde* said the crimes remained unexplained and were strongly denounced by several rightist leaders.[20] Pierre Gemayel of the Phalange absolved both Christians and Muslims, rightists and leftists of the crimes. On May 29, however, a Lebanese Muslim officer ordered the shelling of two Christian villages in Akkar. Palestinian and Progressive Front leaders called for an immediate halt to the shelling and accused the officer of working for Damascus. It was too late, however. The battle was joined on all fronts, and several Syrian columns rumbled into Lebanon in the next few days "to put an end to the bloodshed" and achieve a Syrian-mediated peace. As a footnote to this episode, the officer who had ordered the shelling proved to be Major Ahmad al-Maamari, the northern commander of the Lebanese Arab army, who had been won over by the Syrians in April.[21]

The large-scale June invasion, which expanded the Syrian military presence in Lebanon to some 20,000 troops, was welcomed by the top leadership of the right-wing Maronite camp, including President Franjieh, Interior Minister and NLP leader Camille Chamoun, Phalangist chief Pierre Gemayel, and Charbel Kassis, head of the Order of Maronite Monks. Some younger right-wing leaders at first expressed misgivings; but seeing that the Syrian military intervention was helping their side, they accepted it. As it advanced into various parts of Lebanon, the Syrian army pinned down the Palestinian and Progressive Front forces, shelled their main port of Sidon, occasionally engaged them in battle, and blocked their communcations lines. Gradually, it helped the rightist militias regain their military advantage and made it possible for them to resume their attacks on residential pockets of Palestinian and Muslim poor in Christian east Beirut and south of Tripoli. In east Beirut, the camps of Jisr al-Pasha and Tell al-Zaatar and the Nabaa enclave fell during the summer, and their populations were expelled.

For the same reasons that the Syrian military intervention was welcomed by the Maronite rightists, it was denounced by the Progressive Front and by the Palestinians. It turned the tide of battle against them. Was this what President Assad wanted?

As the strongman of Syria, President Assad had as his constant objective the assurance of a policy in Lebanon that would not turn it into a confrontation state with Israel and thus undercut Syrian security by exposing Lebanon to partition or to an Israeli invasion. To prevent Lebanese fragmentation, Assad was prepared to promote mild political reforms—sufficient, he hoped, to satisfy the Progressive Front, but not to the point of threatening the domination of the political system by the Maronite minority. To this end he was prepared during 1975 to support the Progressive Front (still known then as the leftist-Muslim alliance) and enable it to pressure the resistant Maronite rightists to concede limited reforms. As for the Palestinian movement in Lebanon, he prepared to deprive it of independent decision-making by proposing a joint Syrian-PLO military command in the spring of 1975. By the beginning of 1976, it had become more urgent for Assad to control the PLO and to seek a moderate political solution in Lebanon since his erstwhile ally, President Sadat of Egypt, had abandoned him in September by signing the second Sinai Disengagement Agreement with Israel. However, threatened with partition of Lebanon, by the right-wing Maronite parties and groups, he gave in to their demands to freeze—in writing—the sectarian political formula in their favor against any further reforms.

This was political expediency, for in Syria, Assad, himself a member of the Alawite Muslim minority, had taken tentative steps in the 1973 Syrian constitution toward political secularization. By doing this he braved a storm of protests and resisted strong pressures from conservative Syrian Sunnis to legislate the preeminence of Islam. Only the president was to be a Muslim, and he did not have to belong to any particular sect. In Lebanon, however, Assad was prepared to let the Maronite rightists legislate the preeminence of their sect. But the Progressive Front would not accept such a regressive step, so that Assad found it necessary, in February and March, to try to control the Front and its Palestinian supporters with Syrian-infiltrated Sa'iqa and PLA troops. When he failed, he intervened with the Syrian army. The intervention tipped the military balance in favor of the Maronite rightists and, unexpectedly for

Assad, it accelerated the de facto partition of Lebanon. The threat of final (de jure) partition then became the trump card for negotiating Maronite preeminence in a reunified Lebanon.

THE CONFLICT AND OTHER ARAB STATES

Syria's large-scale invasion of Lebanon came at a time when Saudi Arabia, Kuwait, and other Gulf oil states were trying to mend relations between Cairo and Damascus, estranged by Cairo's adherence to the second Sinai Disengagement Agreement. But the Syrian move in Lebanon only contributed to further mutual recriminations between Cairo and Damascus. President Sadat denounced the Syrian invasion, then recalled his ambassador from Damascus after students ransacked the Egyptian embassy, an act he blamed on the Assad regime. As other Arab states watched the growing Syrian military intervention with increasing apprehension, a decision was made to convene an Arab League meeting on the Lebanese crisis. Held at the League's Cairo headquarters early in June, the discussions could not produce resolute decisions because members were divided on many issues. The conservative states, including Egypt, would have liked to see Syria "clip the wings" of the Palestinian movement as a prelude to concluding peace with Israel. But at the same time the conservatives, like the Rejection Front states, were opposed to a Pax Syriana in Lebanon. So the Cairo meeting finally decided to send a 1,000-man "symbolic" peacekeeping force to Lebanon under the League's flag, as a prelude to a Syrian withdrawal.

The first unit of peacekeeping force, 100 Sudanese troops, arrived in Beirut on June 10. The peacekeeping force was completed and expanded in the next few months, but President Assad did not withdraw his forces from Lebanon and insisted on keeping them there until a settlement of the crisis was reached. Clearly, neither Egypt and its supporters on the second Sinai Disengagement Agreement (Saudi Arabia, Kuwait, and the smaller Arabian Gulf states), nor Libya, outspoken opponent of the agreement, wanted to leave mediation in Lebanon entirely up to Syria. Thus, as cease-fires were made and broken in the summer of 1976, mediation efforts were undertaken for Egypt and its supporters by Dr. Hassan Sabry el-Khouly, Egyptian diplomat and Arab League representative, and for Libya by Libyan Prime Minister Abdel Salam Jalloud. Though Libya supported the Rejection Front and opposed Egypt on disengagement with Israel, Egypt now, like Libya, was supporting the PLO and the Progressive Front against an arms and food embargo that Syria was using to pressure the PLO and the Front into submission.

President Sadat's move in Lebanon was a tactical one. After supporting the status quo in Lebanon in 1975, a position favored by the Maronite rightist camp, he now moved to rehabilitate himself in the eyes of the progressive forces in the Arab world and at the same time to counterbalance Syrian influence in Lebanon. He allowed the PLO to reopen its Cairo broadcasting facilities* to replace those denied the PLO by Damascus; he moved 1,500 men of the PLA's Ain Jallout Brigade from its Egyptian base to the PLO command in Lebanon;[22] and he began shipping foodstuffs and weapons to the Progressive Front and the PLO to counter the Syrian blockade and embargo. On September 6, Sadat sponsored full voting membership for the PLO in the Arab League.

From the beginning of the Lebanese crisis in 1975, Saudi Arabia's interest had been to prevent the partitioning of Lebanon, as well as any other change that might favor the left and thereby further radicalize the Middle East and increase the threat to the Saudi monarchy. On November 28, 1975, the Saudi prime minister, Prince Fahd, publicly warned Maronite rightists that any attempt to establish a Christian state would have "the most serious consequence" for Lebanese-Saudi relations.[23] Yet at the same time Saudi Arabia was financing Maronite rightists as a means of preventing a leftist victory in Lebanon. On July 21, 1976, *Washington Post* correspondent Joseph Fitchett reported that American bankers in Beirut had admitted the transfer of $200 million to the rightists by Saudi intermediaries. But the Saudi aid apparently ceased early in 1976, Fitchett added, shortly after newspaper photographs circulated in the Arab world showing cross-wearing Christian fighters (that is, rightist Maronite militiamen) mistreating and humiliating Muslims in Beirut's Muslim slum area of Karantina.

After Syria intervened militarily in Lebanon and began an accommodation with the rightist Maronite camp, Saudi Arabia, Kuwait, and the United Arab Emirates also suspended the economic and financial aid they had been giving to Damascus. Seeing the strain on Damascus, Libya's mediation now promised to ease President Assad's economic and financial difficulties if he would join the Rejection Front states and come to a friendly understanding with the PLO and the Progressive Front in Lebanon. Assad did not accept the Libyan offer, and was forced to divert funds earmarked for development to finance the Lebanese occupation. There were several other consequences of the occupation policy for President Assad: inflation at home, an increase in the number of Lebanese refugees in Syria to some 500,000 people, and economic and political discontent among the Syrian people.[24] But the Syrian president made a shrewd move. On August 1, he appointed a new prime minister, retired Major General Abdel Rahman Khleifawi, a Sunni and a good friend of Assad's.[25] Khleifawi succeeded in keeping the domestic situation under control and the armed forces under discipline, despite tensions within the officer corps.

---

*Both Syria and Egypt allowed the PLO broadcast time from Damascus and Cairo. However, they periodically cut off the PLO's broadcast privileges whenever they disagreed with PLO program policies.

THE UNITED STATES AND ISRAEL

Of the external actors on the Lebanese scene, two others deserve special mention: the United States and Israel. As noted earlier, the United States alternated between public expressions of hope and anxiety over the large-scale Syrian invasion. Washington tacitly welcomed the Syrian move, but remained worried because Palestinian and Progressive Front fighters had shown stalwart resistance to Syrian tank attacks on their strongholds, and because it did not quite know how the other Arab states might respond or whether it could restrain Israel from intervening.

Yet it appeared that there was more than tacit support for Syria in Washington's position. On April 20, John K. Cooley of the *Christian Science Monitor* reported that a former National Security Agency (NSA) staffer, Winslow Peck, charged the CIA and the NSA with using Athens as a main Middle East headquarters from which they were aiding the rightist Phalange party in Lebanon's civil war.[26] A spate of press reports in July said right-wing Lebanese leaders admitted, and some boasted, that their side was receiving weapons from Israel. In a dispatch from Beirut published in the *Washington Post* on Israeli transfer of arms to right-wing militias, Joseph Fitchett commented:

> The ready willingness of American and European diplomats here and elsewhere in the Middle East to confirm the Israeli connection has aroused some suspicion that the prominent Israeli role might actually be a cover for assistance from American and European countries.
>
> CIA sources here have confirmed that the agency assisted a Christian militia with a program of stockpiling light arms in the 1950s as part of the agency's use of minorities to stop any Communist advance.[27]

If the CIA had done its homework, it would have learned that in the 1950s Lebanon was not remotely threatened by a Communist advance.[28]

Israel's foremost interest in the Lebanese civil war was its effects on the PLO and the broader Palestinian movement. Demise of the PLO—which had achieved international recognition as sole spokesman for the Palestinian people—would eliminate the pressures that Israel was now feeling from outside to allow an independent Palestinian state to rise in the West Bank and the Gaza Strip. With the PLO out of the picture, the final peace that Israel's supporter, the United States, was insisting on could be concluded with Jordan. And peace with Jordan, Israel felt, would allow it to retain extensive military, economic, and political advantage in the West Bank and the Gaza Strip.

Though Israeli officials remained silent when claims were made by Maronite rightist leaders that they were receiving arms from Israel, Lebanese Christian politicians, Mediterranean ship captains, Palestinian intelligence, and

American and other Western diplomats confirmed "substantial Israeli supply of arms to the right—including large consignments of Soviet-made arms captured by Israel in the Arab-Israeli wars of 1967 and 1973."[29] Indirect Israeli confirmation of this aid was reported by John K. Cooley in the *Christian Science Monitor* on June 2, 1976:

> A trustworthy source in Israel told this reporter in Tel Aviv recently that a member of the Defense and Foreign Affairs Committee of the Israeli Knesset (Parliament) had confirmed that Israel was sending arms and other help to the Phalange through Cyprus.[30]

Israel involved itself in the Lebanese conflict in other ways. Israeli patrol boats facilitated the Syrian blockade of Palestinian and Progressive Front forces by seizing weapons from ships bound for the Muslim ports of Tyre and Sidon in south Lebanon. And, with the Palestinians distracted by the demands of the conflict elsewhere, Israel stepped up its armed patrols of Lebanese territory south of the Litani River and began arming Christian villagers and rightist militias in that area, supporting them to prevent the return of the Palestinian commandos to their traditional bases there.[31] The border between Israel and these villages was kept open for free communication. Israel and Lebanese rightist interests were agreed that the border area was to become a *cordon sanitaire* against the Palestinian resistance movement.

The Syrian invasion of Lebanon and the Israeli intervention were directed against the Palestinians and their allies in the Progressive Front. Both Syria and Israel wished to prevent the emergence of a democratic secular state in Lebanon. For Syria, such a state would be a threat to its diplomacy and defense posture; for Israel, it would be a threat to its future as "the sovereign state of the Jewish people."* Although Syrian and Israeli objectives differed with regard to the PLO, there was enough complementarity to facilitate Syrian military action against the main strongholds of the PLO-Progressive Front alliance, and to produce simultaneous Syrian and Israeli blockading of Lebanese ports controlled by the alliance.

As for the Soviet Union, it could do little to influence the direction of the Lebanese civil war, although its interests in the Middle East were damaged by war. Because Syria had become a cornerstone of Soviet Middle East policy, Moscow was unable to pressure Damascus to abandon its de facto alignment with the Lebanese rightists and to return to a more conciliatory relationship with the PLO and the popularly based Progressive Front.[32] To salvage its

---

*As the "sovereign state of the Jewish people" Israel does not grant political equality with Jews to its Arab citizens and denies the right of return to Arabs.

position, Moscow, through a *Pravda* statement of September 8, indirectly called upon the PLO and the Progressive Front to compromise in Lebanon.[33]

THE END OF THE WAR

Syrian military intervention in Lebanon had enabled rightist militias, in the summer of 1976, to win victories over the forces of the PLO and the Progressive Front and to clear rightist-held territory in east Beirut of Palestinian camp dwellers and of Muslim Lebanese slum dwellers. In August, the last symbol of Palestinian resistance in east Beirut, Tell al-Zaatar camp, fell to rightist militias. But Palestinian and Progressive Front forces continued to occupy mountain strongholds, west Beirut, the south, and the cities of Sidon, Tripoli, and Tyre. After the inauguration of Lebanon's new president, Elias Sarkis, on September 23, under Syrian auspices, Syria moved to impose a military solution on Lebanon. On October 12, heavily armed Syrian troops struck at the Progressive Front and Palestinian mountain strongholds. Their capture threatened the heavily populated urban areas under Progressive Front and Palestinian control.

At this point Saudi Arabia intervened diplomatically and forestalled the Syrian assault. Under Saudi auspices, an Arab summit was held at Riyadh on October 16–18 with King Khalid, Amir Sabah al-Salim al-Sabah of Kuwait, President Sadat, President Assad, President Sarkis, and PLO leader Yasser Arafat attending. A cease-fire was declared in Lebanon and resolutions were adopted for the reunification of Lebanon under President Sarkis and for the implementation of the 1969 Cairo Agreement between Lebanon and the PLO. As Egypt and Syria became reconciled, provisions were also made at Riyadh and at an Arab Summit Conference in Cairo on October 25–26 to confirm Syrian hegemony over Lebanon. Of a 30,000-man Arab League force authorized for peacekeeping duties in Lebanon, 25,000 men were to be provided by Syria. Syria, which already had 20,000 troops in Lebanon, was thus authorized to bring in an additional 5,000. Furthermore, because the Syrian troops were put under the official command of President Sarkis for Arab League peacekeeping duties, they would henceforth by financed by the League. To smooth PLO-Lebanese relations in the implementation of the Cairo Agreement, the Riyadh summit also authorized formation of the liaison committee with representatives from Saudi Arabia, Syria, Egypt, and Kuwait.[34]

If the Riyadh summit underlined the preeminance of Syrian power in Lebanon, it nevertheless confirmed Saudi Arabia as the balancer of power among the Arabs. Syrian power in Lebanon though presently high, remained mercurial and tied to the unpredictables of the conflict with Israel. Saudi power was more solidly based in oil wealth. As for Lebanon, the war was not offically over. President Sarkis was embarked on the painstaking road of national reunification, national reconciliation, and national reconstruction.

CONCLUSION

The war in Lebanon can be understood only in an analytical framework that recognizes a complex conflict situation in three respects: the internal conflict stems from several types of social divisions that are expressed in a multiplicity of issues; the internal conflict intersects structurally with other conflicts involving external parties; and the various conflict sets do not produce parallel or reinforcing alignments. To elaborate with specific reference to ethnic factors and the Lebanese case, this means the following:

First, ethnic identity in the Lebanese context rested on religious affiliation and cultural orientation that helped to shape political alignments, but such identification was by no means the exclusive—perhaps not even the primary—force in the conflict. The socioeconomic divisions in Lebanon produced a conflict potential that could neither be contained nor be moderated by a political system based on a sectarian (or ethnic) formula. When that conflict erupted, the ethnic identities further sharpened antagonisms. Consequently, ethnic and class issues were intermingled without any one of them being the predominant issue.

Second, the other principal conflicts, the Palestine question and the Arab-Israeli conflict, were structurally linked to internal developments in Lebanon. With respect to the first, by the mid-1970s Lebanon had become the only viable base from which the Palestinian movement could operate. As regards the second, Lebanon was physically adjacent to two of the main actors in the Arab-Israeli conflict, Israel and Syria, both of which attached increasing importance to Lebanon because some of the tensions on the southern flank (between Israel and Egypt) had been defused as a consequence of the September 1975 Sinai Disengagement Agreement.

Third, while these two intersecting conflicts (Palestinian/Israeli and Arab/Israeli) had ethnic elements, they were not the same ethnic antagonisms that were displayed in the internal Lebanese conflict. And while the Palestine conflict had an element of class (in addition to national) ideology that fused with the socioeconomic aspirations of leftist groups in Lebanon (exemplified in the PLO-Progressive Front alliance), the Arab-Israeli conflict did not. The different sources and issues in the three conflict sets produced an intricate network of different and shifting alignments.

Two consequences of this complexity should be noted. First, ethnic links cutting across state boundaries were not very significant channels of external, partisan support for the Lebanese; indeed, such links were grossly violated by the major intervening party, the Syrian government, which gave priority to the demands of the Arab-Israeli conflict and the Palestine questions as these affected its quest for influence in Lebanon. Second, the existence of three interrelated conflicts with diverse issues created a rudimentary balance of power in the Lebanese conflict theater. Partly this was seen in the internal correctives in Syrian policy, where contradictory stimuli tempered unqualified support for one or the other of the Lebanese parties.

There was also an external corrective, as exemplified by Egyptian support to the PLO-Progressive Front in order to counter Syrian influence in Lebanon and restore Egypt's image as champion of the Palestinian cause. This balance-of-power mechanism helped to prevent a total defeat or a total victory for the main Lebanese parties to the conflict. Thus, the outcome hypothesized for some ethnic conflicts in the initial framework for this study was brought about, but for rather different reasons (see Chapter 1).

As suggested in Chapter 1, the nature of the internal conflict did influence the form of external intervention. The intensity of the conflict (which to some extent reflected its ethnic aspects) clearly facilitated Syrian intervention by encouraging the Lebanese to accept Syrian assistance even though they were worried about Syrian control. More important, the Syrians decided to intervene regardless of local hesitations, because they feared that the intensity of the conflict would lead to partition of Lebanon. This, in turn, would harm Syria's position in the Arab-Israeli conflict. As it turned out, however, Syrian intervention at one stage brought the country closer to partition.

This sequence is relatively close to that suggested at the outset of this study: ethnic identification encourages intense conflicts once the "system maintenance" mechanisms fail, and intense conflicts promote territorial relocation of the protagonists into ethnically distinct zones that lend credibility to an eventual partition. Foreign partisan aid in turn encourages support within the client group to consider the extremist "solution" of partition, even though —as in this case—there is no common ethnic tie between the local client (Maronite rightists) and the foreign supporter (the Syrian government) that might raise the salience of exclusivist ethnic sentiments for the former, and despite the intention of the outside supporter to prevent partition.

APPENDIX

Political and Military Groups Involved in the Lebanese War (balance of forces as of September 1976)

Progressive Front

- The Progressive Socialist party, led by Kamal Jumblatt, supported by his 3,000-man Druze militia.
- The Lebanese Communist party, led by George Hawi and the independent Marxist Organization of Communist Action in Lebanon, led by Muhsen Ibrahim and

Palestine Liberation Organization (fully involved in support of the Progressive Front by January 20, 1976)

PLO groups involved:

- Fateh, largest Palestinian commando group led by Yasser Arafat (head of PLO). Controlled Yarmouk Brigade (Palestinian soldiers who had deserted the

Fawwaz Trabulsi. Both groups supported by well-trained, armed Muslim and Christian militias.

- The Murabitun, independent Nasserite movement under Ibrahim Koleilat, with a Beirut-based Muslim militia.
- The Syrian National Social party, faction headed by Inaam Raad. Membership predominantly Greek Orthodox. Militia operated in Beirut, Mount Lebanon, Kura, and Metn.
- The pro-Iraqi branch of the Baath party. Militia was strong in Tripoli, home of its leader, Abdel Megid el-Rafei.
- The 24th of October Movement. Militia based in and around Tripoli, under leftist leader Farouk al-Mokaddem.
- The Lebanese Arab army. Muslim soldiers led by L. Ahmad al-Khatib after deserting Lebanese army in spring of 1976. (Some officers with units defected to Syria in May and June.)
- Some small groups of undetermined strength: Union of Working People; Arab Socialist Union, pro-Libyan Nasserite group; Kurdish Democratic party, pro-Iraqi.

Jordanian army and founded regular units within Fateh in 1971).

- The Popular Democratic Front for the Liberation of Palestine, led by Nayef Hawatmeh. Fielded second largest commando group in Lebanon (after Fateh).
- The Popular Front for the Liberation of Palestine-General Command. Split politically and militarily after Syrian invasion of Lebanon in June. The Ahmed Jibril faction supported Syria; the Abul Abbas faction opposed the Syrian incursion.
- The Arab Liberation Front, a pro-Iraq Baathist commando group with some Iraqi membership. Played limited role in the conflict.
- The Hittine, Kazafiya, and Astal Brigades of the Palestine Liberation Army, which arrived from Syria in May, rallied to the PLO after the Syrian military incursion in June. The Ain Jallout also arrived from Egypt to join the PLO forces.

Progressive Front and PLO forces under arms estimated at 25,000 men (80 per cent of them Palestinians).

Right-wing Groups and Parties

Members of these groups and parties were predominantly Maronite, and enjoyed widespread, though not universal, Maronite support. They collaborated at times as the Lebanese Front or the Kfour Front. Rightist forces under arms were estimated at 25,000 men in the summer of 1976.

- The Phalangist party or Kataeb. Led by Pierre Gemayel, it controlled the largest militia in the

Syrian Forces and Groups Supporting Syria

- A 20,000-man Syrian force equipped with 450 tanks. The Syrian army invaded Lebanon in June, but its full strength of 20,000 was reached later in the summer. It pinned down a total of 9,000 Palestinian and leftist Lebanese troops, transforming the military balance in favor of the rightist opposition.

APPENDIX (continued)

rightist camp: 10,000 well-trained, well-equipped men who fought on several fronts.

- The National Liberal party (NLP), led by former President Camille Chamoun. It fielded 2,000 well-trained men. An extreme right-wing party opposed to any accommodation with the Palestinians and the Lebanese leftist movement.
- The Zgharta Liberation Army led by President Suleiman Franjieh's son, Tony. A regional militia of about 7,000 doing battle in areas close to the president's home town of Zgharta.
- Prominent among the smaller right-wing groups with their own militias were the Maronite League, led by Shaker Suleiman; the Maronite Order of Monks, headed by Father Charbel Kassis; the Guardians of the Cedars, headed by Said Aql; the Maronite Organization, led by Dr. Fuad Chemali; the Zahle Union, a Greek Catholic militia operating in the Biqaa.
- The Loyalist branch of the Lebanese Army included some 5,000 Christian troops who joined the rightist militias under the leadership of Col. Antoine Barakat after the disintegration of the army in the spring of 1976.
- Units of Sa'iqa, the Syrian-controlled Palestinian commando group and several brigades of the Palestine Liberation Army (PLA) stationed in Syria. These were sent to Lebanon in the spring of 1976 to oppose PLO and Progressive Front troops, but there were mass defections to the PLO from both the PLA and Sa'iqa.
- The Syrian National Social party, faction headed by Assad al-Ashkar. The faction remained primarily an ideological supporter of Syria.
- The Lebanese Arab Army. Though the bulk of these troops supported the Progressive Front, a few defected to Syria in May and June.
- The Ahmad Jibril faction of the Popular Front for the Liberation of Palestine—General Command. Ideologically, it supported Syria after the June invasion of Lebanon, and it clashed mainly with the anti-Syrian faction headed by Abul Abbas.

Special Category

- The Movement of the Deprived (Harakat al-Mahrumin), was a large amorphous movement of poor, primarily Shiite Lebanese led by Imam Musa al-Sadr, the spiritual leader of the Shi'a population. The movement was anti-establishment and represented those suffering most from discrimination. Some of its members no doubt supported the Progressive Front, but its leader began to show allegiance to Syria in the summer of 1976. He may not, however, have carried the entire movement with him.

NOTES

1. Eric Rouleau, "Civil War in Lebanon," *SWASIA* (Washington, D.C.), Oct. 16, 1975, p. 3.

2. Ibid.

3. "The Fulfillment of the IRFED Prophecy," *Monday Morning* (Beirut), Nov. 17–23, 1975, pp. 16–19.

4. The weekly issues of *Monday Morning* for 1975 give extensive coverage to the debate on the causes of the Lebanese crisis.

5. Tabitha Petran, "The Trials of South Lebanon," *Middle East International* (London), Sept. 1975, pp. 11–13; Arab Red Cross and Red Crescent Societies, *Violations of the Geneva Conventions of 1949: 1971–1974* (Beirut: the Societies, 1975) and *Facts* (bimonthly bulletins and supplements of the Lebanese Association for Information on Palestine, Beirut), support with extensive documentation the material presented by Petran.

6. "Why I Imported Arms to Lebanon," *Monday Morning,* Nov. 10–16, 1975, p. 27.

7. Ibid.

8. Maha Samara, "Should Lebanon Fight Back?" ibid., Jan. 6–12, 1975, p. 10.

9. For details on Communist party strategy in Lebanon, see Patrick Seale, "Lebanon at the End of Its Tether," *Middle East International,* Nov. 1975, pp. 9–10.

10. For detailed accounts see "The Battles of the Arqoub, January 2–18, 1975," *Facts: Supplement of April 1975;* also see Rouleau, op. cit., p. 6.

11. Hervé Chevalier, *Le Nouvel Observateur,* Feb. 3, 1975, as cited in "The Battles of the Arqoub . . .," *Facts,* op. cit.

12. Rouleau, loc. cit.

13. Randa Yammine, "Neptune on the Rampage," *Monday Morning,* March 3–9, 1975, pp. 6–9.

14. Maha Samara, "Jumblatt: Yes to a Christian President (but not Necessarily a Maronite)," interview with Kamal Jumblatt, *Monday Morning,* June 19–25, 1975, p. 28.

15. Ibid., pp. 27, 30.

16. Ibid.

17. Cited in *Keesing's Contemporary Archives,* Aug. 18–24, 1975, p. 27288.

18. Eric Rouleau, "Syria in the Quagmire," *SWASIA,* June 18, 1976, p. 2.

19. *Keesing's Contemporary Archives,* June 11, 1976, p. 27773.

20. Eric Rouleau, "Assad's Calculated Risk," *Manchester Guardian Weekly,* June 27, 1976, p. 13. The details that follow are based on Rouleau's report.

21. James M. Markham, "Christian Right in Lebanon Backs Syrian Incursion," *New York Times,* June 6, 1976.

22. Henry Tanner, "Syrian Troops Halt Drive in Lebanon East of Capital," ibid., June 3, 1976.

23. *Keesing's Contemporary Archives,* June 11, 1976, pp. 27768, 27769.

24. Very good coverage on Syria's involvement in Lebanon is provided by Eric Rouleau, "A Cop in the Supermarket?" *Manchester Guardian Weekly,* June 20, 1976, and in his "Assad's Calculated Risk."

25. Henry Tanner, "Syrian Premier Replaced by a Favorite of the Army," *New York Times,* Aug. 2, 1976.

26. John K. Cooley, "CIA, NSA, Accused of Involvement in Lebanon," *Christian Science Monitor,* Apr. 20, 1976.

27. Joseph Fitchett, "Israel Apparently Aiding Beirut Right," *Washington Post,* July 21, 1976.

28. Leila M. T. Meo, *Lebanon: Improbable Nation: A Study in Political Development* (Bloomington, Ind.: Indiana University Press, 1965), pp. 123, 168.

29. William Blakemore, "Israeli Aid to Lebanon: Touchy Issue," *Christian Science Monitor,* July 20, 1976.

30. John K. Cooley, "Foreigners Entering Lebanon Fight," ibid., June 2, 1976.

31. Jason Morris, "Self-defense Units Organized," ibid., Sept. 13, 1976.

32. "Brezhnev Hits Syrian War Role," *Washington Post,* July 21, 1976.

33. David K. Willis, "Soviets Urge 'Reasonable' Compromise in Lebanon," *Christian Science Monitor,* Sept. 9, 1976; "Denunciation by Moscow of 'Ultraleftists' Arouses Bewilderment in Lebanon," *New York Times,* Sept. 7, 1976.

34. For texts of the Riyadh and Cairo summit resolutions, see *Journal of Palestine Studies* 6, no. 2 (Winter 1977): 192–94.

CHAPTER

6

THE ERITREAN-ETHIOPIAN CONFLICT

Ethiopiawi

The Eritrean separatist movement has been active, first outside and later inside Ethiopia, since the mid-1950s. The first external impetus was the hostility of the Arab states to the U.N. decision (1950) to return Eritrea to Ethiopia. This opposition took the form of radio propaganda, arms, and funds to promote a movement in Eritrea for independence from Ethiopia. In the second stage, starting at the end of the 1950s, the movement shifted its bases of operation from Cairo to Damascus and Mogadisho, and by the mid-1960s to Eritrea as well. This third stage opened in 1974 with the revolutionary changes in Ethiopia and its rapid evolution into a Marxist state. During this stage, the secessionist forces in Eritrea profited from the explosion of violence in the rest of Ethiopia. At the same time, external support shifted from the radical Arab states—Syria, Iraq, and the People's Democratic Republic of Yemen, to include conservative Arab states—the Sudan, Kuwait, and Saudi Arabia in particular—that were bitterly opposed to consolidation of a Soviet center of power in Ethiopia and its presence on the Eritrean coast of the Red Sea.

The intent of this chapter is to identify the factors responsible for the development and escalation of the conflict between Eritrean separatists and the Ethiopian government and to explain how and why the conflict became "internationalized." Particular attention will be paid to the significance of ethnic identifications and linkages.

ERITREANS AND ETHIOPIANS

Ethiopia is prototypically a multiregional, multiethnic state, although at one level there is a great deal of ethnic similarity.[1] All ethnic groups except for a few isolated enclaves in the southwest and the southeast are either Semitic or Hamitic in origin, as are their languages. Ethiopia's regionalism is characterized by diversities in language, religion, and subsistence and land-tenure patterns. Language families are frequently formed around mutually unintelligible dialects. Christian, Muslim, and animist communities exist throughout, for the most part relatively peacefully. Settled agricultural and nomadic communities and land tenure patterns are necessarily differentiated by climatic and geographic influences. Suffused throughout these structures and patterns are tribal and kinship associations and influences.

Eritrea—one province of the state—is in many respects simply a microcosm of Ethiopia. Historically, it is the oldest part of the country, reflecting the Semitic origins of the Tigrinya-, Tigre-, and Amharic-speaking groups that originally migrated across the Red Sea from the Asir coast of Arabia. Adulis, the ancient center of Ethiopia, was located in Eritrea. The linguistic affinities among the Tigre, Tigrinya, and Amharic languages perpetuate shared semitic origins. The Baria and the Kunama, who inhabit the southwest corner of Eritrea, have more in common with the so-called Nilotic people who live along the western frontier of Ethiopia than with other ethnic groups in Eritrea. The peoples of the northern highlands around Keren—such as the Bet Asghede, Mensa, Bet Juk, and Bilen—are descendants of migrants from the ancient Ethiopian regions of Tigrai, Dembia, and Agew who settled in this area at different periods, though their contact with their original homes has declined with time and their conversion to Islam. The Afars in the eastern plain of Ethiopia are identical with their kinsmen who live across the provincial border in Dankalia and in the French territory (until 1977) of Afars and Issas. The Saho of Samhar and Akele Guzai are identical with those in the region of Agame in Tigrai province. Linked by blood, language, culture, and religion—with common traditions, administration, folklore, and mythology—the inhabitants of the central southern highland plateau are even more intimately interrelated with the people of Tigrai in northern Ethiopia.

Other Eritreans—those belonging to the Rashaida—are recent migrants from Arabia and retain their distinctive language, customs, and lifestyle—and doubtless their identity with kinsmen in their country of origin. The Beni Amer tribesmen have more affinity with fellow tribe members in Sudan than with any ethnic group in Ethiopia, though ties with their kinsmen the Hadendowa have been weakened because of conflicting claims to grazing rights and grudges over raids committed in the past.

Moreover, as with other Ethiopians, ethnic identifications in Eritrea are layered, then crosscut or reinforced by class, occupational, and ideological identifications, all of which—at least potentially—have political implications. The Muslim-Christian distinction, for instance, has tended to coincide with socioeconomic divisions, particularly between landowners (generally Christians) and landless peasants or nomads (generally Muslims), and with political affiliation. The Tigrinya-speaking population in Eritrea, for example, shares with Tigreans elsewhere a specific tribal, cultural, but not necessarily always a linguistic, identity. They are proud of their ancient heritage as a cradle of Ethiopia, and opposed Shoan—formerly Gondarine and Lasta—hegemony when the center of government moved to these areas.

Yet if a case can be made that Eritreans are characteristically Ethiopian in their patterns of fragmentation, and for historical and political reasons are part of "Greater Ethiopia," it is equally important to note that other factors move Eritreans to one end of the Ethiopian spectrum, and under certain circumstances encourage them to perceive themselves as being outside that spectrum. In the late nineteenth century, as part of a dispute over control of the Ethiopian throne, Emperor Menelik, motivated by personal ambition, acceded to Italian requests for territory in northern Ethiopia by allowing that nation to occupy Asmara and move up to the highland. The Italians consolidated their control there, and used it to launch their attack on Ethiopia itself in 1896 and in the 1930s. Success in the war made possible the creation of the "Italian Empire of East Africa," incorporating Eritrea, Italian Somaliland, and Ethiopia. The empire collapsed with the Italian defeat in 1941; the British subsequently took over Eritrea, administering it until 1952, when the United Nations reached an agreement on its future.

The periods of Italian and British administration had superficial but significant effects. While the Italians did little to improve living conditions for Eritreans generally (educational and health programs, for example, were very limited and designed primarily for the benefit of resident Italians), they did—for their own reasons—construct railroads and roads and provide employment, in war-related endeavors, for many. The result, particularly in the 1930s, was an economic boom that left Eritreans with memories of relative prosperity.

The British legacy was primarily political. By allowing trade unions, political parties, and a free press at a time when the future of Eritrea was being heatedly debated outside the territory itself, the British presided over the intense politicization of many sectors of Eritrean society. At least three positions—each represented by a distinct political group or groups—emerged: (1) support for unconditional union with Ethiopia, a position maintained by the Unionist party, which was predominantly Christian in membership but contained many Muslims of both upper and lower classes; (2) independence either immediately or after ten years of trusteeship, but with the inclusion of the province of Tigrai (which the Italians had linked with Eritrea), a position identified with the Liberal Progressive party, largely dependent on Ras Tesemma Asberom, his son Dedjazmatch Abraha, and Ato Wolde Ab Wolde Mariam, who had followers among a minority of the Christian population and some Muslims; and (3) complete independence from Ethiopia as a necessary condition for protection of Muslim rights, a position advocated by the Muslim League under Ibrahim Sultan, Abu Baker el-Marghani, and Osman Saleh

Sabbe, who had the support of many Muslims inside Eritrea and contacts with Arab states.

When the question was debated in the United Nations, there were shifts among these parties—the pro-independence parties cooperated for a while, then split, and the Christian independence party then sided with the Unionists —but there seemed little support in Eritrea for other options supported by outside states, specifically for a partition that would link a predominantly Muslim area of Eritrea with the Sudan, or for an Italian trusteeship. The final U.N. agreement for a federation between Eritrea and Ethiopia hence represented a compromise that had some reluctant support inside Eritrea but fully satisfied no one. It clearly did not satisfy the Ethiopian government, which regarded provision for Eritrean autonomy in matters other than defense, foreign affairs, currency and finance, external and interstate communications, and maritime matters, and for a separate Eritrean Assembly, as a serious infringement on its own authority.

Thus a combination of historical experiences, beginning about 1890, and particular political arrangements institutionalized under U.N. supervision in the late 1940s and early 1950s, created a sense of Eritrean identity distinct from an Ethiopian identity. Two other factors were also important in developing Eritrean consciousness and ultimately in facilitating separatism. One was the high level of participation of Eritreans in the government, armed forces, business, and commerce in Ethiopia—which heightened the sense of ethnic identity and clannishness. Second, because of its geographic location, Eritrea was readily accessible to other states and Eritreans had long been subject to foreign influences and had developed foreign contacts. That these contacts were primarily with Muslim states was both cause and result of the composition of Eritrea's population, divided rather evenly between Christians and Muslims. The combination of a sizable Muslim population and at least potential outside Muslim links made Eritrea receptive to Islamic and Arab influence.

However, it was primarily policies pursued by the Ethiopian government within Eritrea that led to the transformation of Eritrean consciousness into Eritrean separatism and of discontent into escalating violence, beginning about 1961. Generally the period of the federation was characterized by two trends. First, there were increasing attempts by the central regime to bring Eritrea closer to Ethiopia by downgrading the local linguistic and cultural factors, by appointing Shoans rather than Eritreans to federal positions in Eritrea, by fiscal subventions and controls, and by abusive commercial concessions in the federal area of foreign and interprovincial commerce and industry. Second, there was growing Eritrean opposition to the original federal institutions and/or their modification.

Ethiopian-Eritrean differences focused on political, economic, and ethnic issues. Politically, the Ethiopian regime consistently contended that Eritrea had no rightful claim to independent nationhood and perceived the administrative decentralization provided by federal institutions as a dangerous precedent, given the ethnic and political diversity of Ethiopia's provinces. International factors exacerbated the regime's fears. Somalia was fomenting irredentist sentiments among the Somalis in the Ogaden region of Ethiopia. Egypt intervened in Yemen, and there was increasing evidence of external Muslim support for the independence of Eritrea. Meanwhile, in Eritrea itself banditry—which was difficult to distinguish from at least incipient insurgency —was growing. Hence the regime determined to tighten its control:

> There was a steady pressure on the Eritrean newspapers, arrests of politicians and above all use of the unlimited patronage available to the imperial Government. Several politicians fled abroad. . . . More amenable members of the Unionist Party were appointed to top positions. In the elections of 1956 no political parties were allowed. In 1958 the assembly voted to discard the Eritrean flag, in 1959 the Ethiopian law code was extended over Eritrea, and in 1960 the Eritrean Government became the Eritrean administration. . . .[2]

Finally, in November 1962 the Eritrean Parliament voted to abolish the federation and unite with Ethiopia. This was ratified by the emperor the following day, and Eritrea was declared the fourteenth province of Ethiopia. While some Eritreans clearly benefited from and favored these moves, they fomented opposition among other sectors of the population. The drastic narrowing of the political base alienated many politicians, both Muslim and Christian. More generally, Eritreans saw the administration as corrupt, incompetent, and ineffectual. The perception was based in reality, since higher officials were generally chosen for their loyalty and were comparatively invulnerable to criticism; and lower officials, though Eritrean, lacked both training and authority.

Economic policies were equally controversial. The regime was obsessively aware that Eritrea constituted Ethiopia's outlet to the sea, but regarded its subsidies to Eritrea and the benefits Eritreans derived from the transit trade as generous compensation. Eritreans, in contrast, measured their benefits not in comparison with other Ethiopian provinces (Eritrea was second to Shoa in receipt of government revenues) but in comparison with memories of wartime prosperity and present needs. Major investment projects—such as a $2 million dam and an oil refinery—affected only a few Eritreans, and restrictions on unionization appeared likely to limit further the benefits gained from any "progress." Moreover, by the late 1960s and early 1970s economic circumstances were rapidly deteriorating under the cumulative impact of a worldwide recession, drought, and increases in oil prices.

Ethnic grievances involved some of the political and economic issues already discussed. Additionally, the regime's insistence on replacing Arabic (introduced by the British) and Tigrinya with Amharic as the language of instruction in schools at best blunted the potential praise it might have accrued for educational expansion; at worst it aggravated feelings of discrimination among both Muslims and Tigrean Christians. It is important to note, however, that ethnic grievances divided Eritreans among themselves as well as from other Ethiopians.

During the late 1950s Eritrean exiles began to organize in opposition to Ethiopian rule. By 1961 a separatist movement had emerged that had most of the characteristics it was to maintain during the next 13 years, until fighting escalated in late 1974: it was factionalized along both religious and ideological lines but was predominantly Muslim in its ideology, membership, and sources of support; its most organized and effective sector was the Eritrean Liberation Front (ELF); and its tactics were limited by the narrowness of its resource base both inside and outside Eritrea.

The Eritrean Democratic Front, out of which the Eritrean Liberation Front emerged, contained both Christian and Muslim politicians in exile, such as Ato Wolde Ab Wolde Mariam, Osman Saleh Sabbe, and Idris Mohammed. When the decision was made to resort to direct action within Eritrea in September 1961, however, the field operation was led by Idris Awate, and the militancy was justified by a proclamation of *jihad* (holy war), both within and outside Eritrea against the *kafir* (traitor, unbeliever) Haile Selassie. Furthermore, "Christian Eritreans were ostracized as *kafirs* and attacked as an enemy."[3] Since then the ELF has drawn most, though certainly not all, of its internal support from the Muslim half of the population, and particularly from the nomadic Beni Amer along the Sudanese border. ELF support has also come from Muslim and animist peoples living along the coast and, to a much lesser extent, in the Dankali desert.

To the extent that Christians have been involved, there has been friction. Near the end of 1965 the ELF split its forces into four divisions, according to regions. Then, in an effort to appease Christians who objected to being led by a Muslim, a fifth division was established under Christian leadership. Muslim-Christian conflict within the movement continued, and eventually led many Christians to surrender to Ethiopian authorities. In 1968 a second attempt was made at reorganization, with the divisions replaced by three units organized without reference to religious affiliation; in 1969 a general command was created. Again Muslim-Christian violence led to Christian surrenders. By 1970 this conflict, plus a growing one over ideology and tactics, had caused a splintering of the ELF and the formation of the Popular Liberation Front (PLF), which is identified as being more Marxist-oriented and—paradoxically, given its initial Christian support—more linked with the Palestinian freedom movements than the ELF. In 1972 the two groups engaged in internecine warfare.

Throughout this period the level and scope of the fighting fluctuated. One plausible estimate is that by 1967 the number of separatists involved in armed actions was 2,000–3,000, and that groups of near-battalion strength were engaged in open battles with Ethiopian forces. Much of the activity was north and west of the port of Massawa and in the western and northern parts of the province.[4] After 1967, however, the fighting capacity of the separatists decreased markedly because of the effect of the Arab-Israeli war on their sources of supply. The Ethiopian government took advantage of this temporary weakness, and of the concurrent ethnic tensions within the movement, to launch an offensive that was accompanied by a resettlement of people in fortified villages and by such reprisals as public hangings. The result was relatively calm, but at the cost of a marked increase in the number of refugees (according to Sudanese figures, 28,600 Ethiopian refugees arrived in the Kassala area in the Sudan in 1967), increased popular alienation from the government, and a deliberate attempt by at least one faction of the separatists to draw international attention to the struggle.[5]

The tactics chosen included both kidnapping foreigners and hijacking and destroying planes. The hijackings ended as the Arab states, recovering from defeat, began resuming arms aid and other assistance. Subsequently fighting again intensified within Eritrea. Assassinations of government officials (six in Asmara in April, and the general in command of the main Ethiopian army unit in Eritrea in November 1970, for example) brought severe military retaliation —destruction of villages, further resettlement of populations into selected fortified villages, and, according to the ELF, a number of massacres: 112 shot in a mosque at Bascacara in late November, 600 killed in a village near Keren on December 1, and 60 killed in a mosque at Elaberet.[6] Martial law was declared throughout most of the province, and the emperor's representative, Ras Asrate Kassa, who opposed martial law, was replaced by a general who could be trusted to introduce stringent security measures. Again the separatists' activity subsided, at least partially for other reasons: there was infighting within the movement, and the Addis Ababa Agreement of 1972—which was promoted by the emperor and ended the 17-year-old civil war in the Sudan—led to an Ethiopian-Sudanese agreement that limited ELF access to arms. By 1973, however, the ELF had reestablished its supply lines by shifting to South Yemen, and was again taking initiatives.

This, then, was the Eritrean context for the "creeping coup" that gradually replaced the government of Emperor Haile Selassie with a military council, the Dergue. The transition period—particularly in mid-1974—provided an opportunity to reach a negotiated settlement. In March, the minister of the interior entered into discussions with Eritrean members of Parliament in an effort to pave the way for a political solution of Eritrean grievances. From these discussions it became clear that the first condition was the abolition of martial law in Eritrea. This necessity was recognized in principle by the Cabinet of Ministers, but it was not implemented.

Meanwhile both the ELF and the Ethiopian government were engaged in international lobbying. In May 1974 the ELF attempted to draw other African states into the conflict by insisting that the Eritrean issue be placed on the agenda of the Organization of African Unity's (OAU) eleventh Summit Conference. It asked for an African fact-finding mission to assess the situation in Eritrea, immediate intervention by the United Nations, and relief assistance for the drought-stricken Eritrean people. It also demanded that the OAU recognize the ELF as "the legitimate and sole representative of the Eritrean people."

At the same time the ELF was soliciting foreign political support elsewhere. Its members visited neighboring Arab states to persuade them to use their good offices to mediate between Eritrea and Ethiopia. A spokesman for the Front, during an interview in Saudi Arabia with a reporter from *Al-hawath,* stated that the United States had contacted the ELF through Italy. Presumably this statement was an attempt to gain the favor of the conservative government of Saudi Arabia, which was known to be favorably disposed toward the United States. The spokesman added, "The fact that the US sought to establish contact with the Eritrean Liberation movement is an indication of the United States' belief that the movement is not dominated by leftist ideology."[7]

The Ethiopian government continued to insist that the Eritrean conflict was a purely internal matter and must be handled as such: it should be excluded from discussion in any international forum, such as the OAU or the United Nations. In July, however, Ethiopia's foreign minister did state in Khartoum that his government favored a peaceful solution to the Eritrean question and was "perturbed greatly by the sight of blood being shed from both sides." He further indicated that, if the need arose, Ethiopia would even welcome mediation by the Sudan so that a speedy settlement might be reached. The ELF responded favorably to the initiative and announced through its foreign mission that it welcomed "any political initiative from any source in order to arrive at a political solution that is in line with the aspirations of the Eritrean people to win their national independence." It stipulated, as conditions for negotiation, that Ethiopia recognize the ELF as the sole legitimate representative of the Eritrean people and that negotiations be held in a neutral capital.[8]

The response of the Ethiopian armed forces in Eritrea contrasted strongly with these peace overtures. About the same time, Ethiopian troops in Umm Hajar, a town in western Eritrea, killed 200 people and caused an exodus of 4,000 others.

The Umm Hajar incident and the fact that the Eritreans who were taken captive by the Ethiopian army were excluded from the general amnesty granted to political prisoners (at the insistence of the coordinating committee of the armed forces) led 23 Eritrean members to walk out of a session of the

Ethiopian Parliament and to resign. Soon afterward, the prime minister addressed Parliament and declared his government's determination to "use dialogue rather than force in order to reach a negotiated settlement."[9]

Furthermore, though the state of emergency was not lifted, in an attempt to appease Eritrean pride, an Eritrean governor, Emanuel Ande Michael, was appointed to administer the province, for the first time since the annexation of Eritrea in 1962. At the same time, General Aman Andom, an Eritrean by birth and the recently appointed chief of staff of the armed forces, was sent on a fact-finding mission to evaluate the Eritrean situation and the background to the Umm Hajar incident. During his visit to Eritrea, Aman addressed mass rallies and stated that Eritrea had chosen of its own volition to federate with Ethiopia. Placing the blame for past misdeeds on the previous administration, he appealed to the Eritreans to join the rest of Ethiopia in bringing about changes that had been set in motion by the army. The fact that Aman did not indicate that the central government was prepared to grant any concrete concessions to Eritrea did not go unnoticed. ELF reactions were reflected in the *Eritrean Review*, one of the organs of the movement:

> The Eritrean revolution suspects the sincerity of Haile's prime minister who did not take any serious steps to implement what he called his determination to restore peace and stability in Eritrea except sending his defense minister, General Aman Andom—an Eritrean traitor and a stooge of the Ethiopian government—to Eritrea to remedy the situation . . . to arrive at a political solution cannot be accomplished by means of sending stooges to Eritrea. . . .[10]

In any event, before any concrete steps were taken, on September 12 the army deposed the emperor and took over power, establishing a provisional military government. General Aman Andom was placed at the helm of the government. During the first few days he appeared confident that the Dergue, and all Ethiopians, were behind him. It was inconceivable, from his viewpoint, that former antagonists—including Somalia and the ELF—could disagree with the policies of the new government. When pressed on Eritrea, Aman's response was that the PLF, by virtue of its Marxist-Leninist ideology, necessarily had a common identity with the aspirations of the new socialist Ethiopia.

If the conflict could not be resolved politically, he reasoned, Ethiopia's interests would best be served by collaborating with the PLF to eliminate the ELF. The two groups were already divided over the objectives of their struggle, with the ELF concerned primarily with Eritrean independence. Although the Marxist-oriented PLF also favored independence of Eritrea, it viewed the struggle in a broader revolutionary framework that included all Ethiopia and the Middle East.

Aman's reasoning, however, was accepted neither by the separatists nor by his fellow members in the Dergue, which was deeply divided on a number of issues. In October 1974, a Dergue majority moved to purge opposition within the army, the university, and the trade unions. A month later, the Dergue decided to eliminate leaders of the old regime. At least 59 former top government officials were executed in what came to be known as Bloody Saturday; General Aman lost his life at the same time, while resisting arrest, and was accused, inter alia, as a traitor because of his refusal to order 5,000 troops to Eritrea.

A new phase of violence and repression followed, and the campaign to crush the revolutionary movement in Eritrea was begun with renewed vigor. The Dergue chose Brigadier General Teferi Banti as Aman's successor. As commanding officer of the Second Battalion in Eritrea, he had been committed to a military solution to the Eritrean crisis; his demand for an additional 5,000 troops had been one of the principal causes of the rift between General Aman and the rest of the Dergue. Teferi immediately sent those troops to Eritrea, and simultaneously replaced the Eritrean civil governor with a Shoan general, which was a fatal mistake.[11]

Late in December 1974 the Dergue announced that it was still trying to find a peaceful solution to the Eritrean conflict. In conjunction with this policy statement, several senior Ethiopian officials visited President Jaafar al-Nimeiry in the Sudan to follow up his offer of mediation. At the same time, the military council in Eritrea issued a conflicting statement: "Since our policy of patience failed to have the peaceful results we expected, what is the use of patience? We must change our peaceful attitude."[12]

Encouraged by instability within Ethiopia, the Eritrean liberation movement intensified its operations in an effort to attract world opinion to its cause. On December 28 the ELF announced that it was stepping up its fight for independence. In response, the military increased its efforts to eliminate the ELF and PLF by employing a "scorched-earth policy" of "kill all, burn all." Roughly 20,000 troops, half of the Ethiopian army, massed against ELF and PLF forces numbering 5,000–6,000.[13] On the order of the Dergue, over 1,000 villagers were massacred in bombing raids and paratrooper attacks, and thousands more Eritreans were rounded up and detained in specially prepared camps around Addis Ababa.[14] Eritrean wells and rivers allegedly were poisoned, crops burned and defoliated, and cattle slaughtered.[15] The provisional military government also was accused of blocking foreign relief supplies during a period of severe drought.[16] The embargo on food supplies imposed by the military government lasted from September 1975 to February 1976, severely affecting the whole population of Eritrea. These combined tactics forced more than 100,000 Eritrean refugees into the Sudan.[17]

As the military offensive continued and more and more people were killed, prospects for a solution became more remote. Thus far the Afars inhabiting the Danakil area of Eritrea had remained aloof from the liberation movement. However, attempts by the Dergue to expropriate all the holdings of their chief, Bitwoded Ali Mira, turned the Afars against the dictatorship and caused them to join the ELF. As a result, access to Assab, principal port of entry to Ethiopia and site of the oil refinery, was made extremely hazardous and costly. The assassination of 50 young Eritreans in Asmara precipitated the defection to the ELF of a large number of commandos especially trained to operate against the rebels. By mid-January 1975, the ELF and the PLF had signed an agreement in the village of Coazien, a few miles outside Asmara, to establish a united front. In February this united front launched full-scale hostilities, and a key Eritrean member of the Dergue, Major Michael Gabre Negus, defected to it. Eritreans apparently were becoming convinced that the government intended to exclude them from all political participation, and their support for the ELF's new position—that recognition of Eritrea's right to independence was a prerequisite to any talks—presumably was growing accordingly.

Despite the shared goal of independence and attempts to consolidate, the liberation forces have been unable to maintain a united front. At present, four rival groups exist. The largest and senior group is the ELF under Ahmed Nasser, numbering about 23,000. The radical break-off wing, the EPLF (Eritrean People's Liberation Front) under Rahmadan Mohammed Nur, counts approximately 17,000 adherents. Then there is the ELF-PLF faction under the long-time leader of the EPLF, Osman Saleh Sabbe. This group was formed at the Khartoum meeting in 1976 by which the two groups settled their differences at least temporarily. This faction has approximately 5,000 followers. Finally, there is the smaller, fourth group led by Afe Work Essayas. Among them, these four groups claim to have captured 85 percent of the countryside and the cities of Tesennei, Nacfa, Keren, Decamare, and Agordat, and to have sealed off Barentu.[18]

As indicated above, by the late 1960s Muslim-Christian antagonism had led to the defection of a large number of Christian elements. Today, with the exception of the small splinter party under Afe Work Essayas, all the groups are Muslim-led and Muslim-financed. This would leave a momentous problem if independence were to become a reality. For decades, the Muslim elements of the Eritrean population were engaged either in nomadic pursuits or in commerce and trade, leaving the administration of governmental affairs to the Christians except in Massawa and the Western Province. Now, however, given the support furnished by the Arab states to the separatist movement, the Muslims have, for the first time, seized the opportunity to gain control of the leadership of the movement. If independence should occur, they would hardly resist the temptation to assert a monopolize administrative positions, to the exclusion of the Christians. This would throw the Christians into opposition, fearful that an independent Eritrea would in reality be an Arab *vilayet* (subordinate region) and member of the Arab League.

EXTERNAL ACTORS

For the separatists, then, the source and extent of external aid have decisively affected tactics and, to a lesser extent, goals; they have also helped to determine the religious identification of the movement's leadership. For the supporters of the separatists, the Arab-Muslim links were no doubt important to the Arab states, although the salience of these affective ties varied considerably. Similarly, the Arab states that supported the Eritreans were mindful of the strategic location of Eritrea along the Red Sea coast and, by extension, the importance that Eritrea was assumed to have for the survival of Ethiopia. Support for the Eritreans was for some Arab states a means to demonstrate their commitment to orthodox Arab nationalism by assisting a Muslim-led movement in opposition to a Christian government that Arab states suspected of being more pro-Israel than neutral in the Arab-Israeli conflict. Beyond these general considerations, a multiplicity of factors determined the extent of support and the shifts over time.

Egypt provided the first base for the ELF after the OAU refused in 1963 to accept the front as a genuine liberation movement. However, Nasser soon terminated his support, partly as a result of the personal diplomacy of Emperor Haile Selassie and the emperor's leading role in the OAU at this time.

The potentially or actually most important outside actor in the Eritrean-Ethiopian conflict is the Sudan, which has a long border with Ethiopia adjacent to Eritrea. Ethiopian-Sudanese relations have fluctuated considerably, and Sudanese aid to the Eritreans has varied accordingly. The separatists turned to the Sudan for aid in the early 1960s, but close personal relations between the emperor and the Sudanese leaders—Ismail al-Azhari and General Ibrahim Aboud—for a long time kept the Sudanese government from aiding the Eritreans. Of great significance in this respect was the support that the emperor gave the Sudanese leaders in suppressing the revolts in the Sudan. Nevertheless, the Sudan provided some unofficial aid in 1965, despite an agreement with Addis Ababa to curtail the activity of guerrillas operating against both governments. In 1967, the Sudanese government showed more willingness to cooperate with the Ethiopian government by agreeing to move the refugee camps at least fifty miles from the border, and apparently did so.

However, between 1969 and 1971 relations again deteriorated and the Sudan, now led by Jaafar al-Nimeiry, resumed unofficial aid to the separatists. When Nimeiry visited Addis Ababa in 1971, another agreement was reached, this one to deny sanctuaries to the guerrillas operating from Ethiopia and the Sudan. It was implemented after the Ethiopian emperor, in collaboration with the World Council of Churches, succeeded in arranging a peace settlement between the Sudanese Anya Nya rebels and the Sudanese government. The Sudan made an effort to close the border, and many Eritrean and southern Sudanese refugees were returned to their respective countries. Reports in

March 1973 claimed that Sudanese troops had forced Eritrean guerrillas out of the Sudan and into confrontation with Ethiopian units, costing the separatist severe casualties.[19]

The coincidence of progressive radicalization in the Ethiopian military regime and several attempted coups in the Sudan resulted in a reversal of this policy. President Nimeiry openly backed the ELF-PLF movement to counter alleged conspiracy by the Dergue and President Muammar al-Qaddafi of Libya to overthrow him, and in response to Soviet ascendancy in Addis Ababa. On January 30, 1977, Nimeiry announced he would no longer attempt to mediate in the conflict, and offered full support to the Eritrean independence movement. By April, the chief spokesman for the Ethiopian regime, Lieutenant Colonel Mengistu Haile Mariam, was charging that Sudanese troops equipped with tanks and heavy artillery were being deployed in support of both the ELF and the Ethiopian Democratic Union (an anti-Marxist coalition opposed to the Marxist regime). He specifically accused Nimeiry—who he said, was acting in league with Egyptian President Anwar Sadat—of having decided to destroy Ethiopian unity and reverse its revolution "within the next three months," and alleged that Egyptian troops had joined Sudanese units along the Ethiopian-Sudanese border.[20]

The common denominator in Sudanese and Egyptian policies at this time was represented by Soviet activities in the area, particularly by Ethiopia's turn to the Soviet Union for aid in 1976. The Sudan and Egypt both face a hostile Soviet-supported Libya and neither wishes to have, in addition, to confront a similar challenge from an Eritrea controlled by a Soviet-supported Ethiopia, nor to admit Soviet influence over the Eritrean coast and islands in the Red Sea south of Port Sudan. This fear of extended Soviet influence led to the proposal made by Nimeiry for a regional grouping of the Sudan, Somalia, the territory of Afars and Issas (Djibouti), North Yemen, South Yemen, and Eritrea. It should be noted that the proposal was made at a meeting held in North Yemen with the presidents of Somalia, the Yemen Arab Republic, and the People's Democratic Republic of Yemen on March 22, 1977, shortly after the visit of Premier Fidel Castro of Cuba to Addis Ababa, Mogadisho, and Aden, at which time Castro proposed what some interpreted as a "Pax Sovietica"—a socialist federation of Ethiopia, Somalia, Djibouti, and South Yemen.

Like the Sudan, Somalia's policy toward Ethiopia has been a crucial external factor in the development of the Eritrean-Ethiopian conflict. Unlike the Sudan, however, the significance of Somalia lies in its ability to open a second front in the southeastern part of Ethiopia bordering on Somalia. Somalia has long claimed this part of Ethiopia, and its support for Somali irredentism and Balle separatism in this area has served to maintain a southern front, diverting Ethiopian troops and other resources otherwise available for use in Eritrea.

The degree of Somali intervention has fluctuated. During the administration of Prime Minister Ibrahim Egal (1967–1969), relations between Ethiopia and Somalia improved considerably and the Somali government withdrew its support for the southern separatist/irredentist groups. This changed with the Marxist-led military coup in Somalia in 1969, after which relations between the two states immediately deteriorated. Ethiopian-Somali tension was further sharpened in the early 1970s, when the Somali government benefited from Soviet arms supplies, and there were preliminary signs of oil and gas deposits in the disputed Ogaden area. The downfall of the monarchy and the consequent turmoil and violence in Ethiopia made it inevitable that the Somalis would actively press their claims on Ethiopia. That major Somali-supported offensives in the south did not take place until early 1977 can probably be attributed to two factors: Soviet restraint, flowing from the simultaneous Soviet support for both the Ethiopian and the Somali governments, and the possibility that such moves might be counterproductive by uniting Ethiopians against the traditional adversary to the south.

The limited or uncertain assistance provided the Eritreans by the above countries made the movement solicit support from other states as well. The radical Arab governments—Syria, Iraq, and Libya—provided considerable aid during the monarchy in Ethiopia. The ELF headquarters were moved to Damascus after the shift in Egyptian policy in the mid-1960s, and spokesmen have emphasized that the first automatic weapon the ELF received was from Syria (in 1963) and that the "first rocket the revolution received for the purpose of liberating the cities was also from Syria."[21] Radio Damascus has claimed that ELF guerrillas in Syria and Iraq have received training alongside Palestinian *fedayeen.* Both Syria and Iraq have given financial support to the Eritrean movement, and have served as intermediaries for (second-hand) Soviet arms destined for the separatists.[22] Libya has also provided arms (apparently most of them Soviet), sometimes channeling them through South Yemen and Aden. South Yemen became particularly important as a conduit for arms after the improvement in Ethiopian-Sudanese relations in 1972.

Saudi and Kuwaiti support for the Eritreans was of much less significance during the imperial regime in Ethiopia. Saudi support seemed to decline further after the 1967 war, at a time when the Eritrean separatists became more radical ideologically.

The changes in the government of Ethiopia affected this pattern of support. Libya's Qaddafi announced at the Islamic Conference of Foreign Ministers in Tripoli in May 1977 that the conference should promote a settlement between the Dergue and the Eritreans. While taking credit for arming the Eritreans at an earlier stage, he now called on the Eritreans to work with the Dergue.[23] In contrast, Saudi Arabia and Kuwait became more forthright in their support for the Eritreans. The Kuwaiti minister of defense and interior issued a statement on February 18, 1975, proclaiming full support for the

Eritreans. ELF spokesmen further claimed that Saudi Arabia and Kuwait had extended promises of financial aid to Addis Ababa (presumably during the visit of a high-level Ethiopian mission to these and other Arab countries early in 1975), provided Eritrea was granted independence.[24] Similarly, the impact of Soviet support for the Dergue was noted in the changing policies of Sudan and Egypt toward greater support for the Eritreans.

Ethiopia's turn to the Soviet Union after 1974 reflected the government's increasing isolation as American support declined markedly. Moreover, it was a logical response of a government that not only was Marxist but also was desperately seeking aid to counter what it perceived as a profoundly hostile regional environment and imminent threats to the survival of the state itself. The importance of retaining Eritrea was emphasized by the recent Somali successes in large parts of Ogaden, and the uncertain future of Djibouti—previously the French Territory of Afars and Issas, which provided Ethiopia's only outlet to the sea except the Eritrean ports.[25] The developments in Djibouti and Ogaden raised the prospect that Somalia, with or without Soviet assistance (and if without, then with Saudi Arabian assistance), would see its long-standing claims to Djibouti and Ogaden vindicated. It was feared that even if Djibouti were not annexed outright by Somalia, it would be heavily influenced by the coastal Arab states and a member of the Arab League.

This prospect, of course, made the central government in Addis Ababa even more determined to prevent the loss of Eritrea, which was seen as the only realistic hope for Ethiopia to escape strangulation by loss of access to the sea. Mindful that the defeat in the 1935–36 war with Italy was sealed when the port of Djibouti was closed off, the Ethiopian government viewed the retention of Eritrea as necessary for the country's survival. This made the government both intransigent and desperate for help. Soviet support was formalized in a series of agreements signed during Mengistu's visit to Moscow in May 1977. Details of the agreements were not publicized, but they were believed to include economic and technical assistance in addition to earlier provisions for military assistance concluded in December 1976.

The de facto alliance with the Soviet Union resembled Ethiopia's earlier relationship with the United States. Between 1953 and 1974, the United States was Ethiopia's main supporter, providing crucial military and economic assistance as well as diplomatic support. In that period military assistance grants totaled $182 million. In February 1974, as internal conflict in Ethiopia accelerated, the Ethiopian government asked to purchase emergency military equipment from the United States. The request precipitated a debate in Washington involving considerations of Ethiopian domestic policies (toward the famine and dissidents) as well as U.S. foreign policy interests in the area, but the decision was ultimately to allow sale of the arms. Following the massacres of November 1974, the U.S. government appealed to the military regime not to execute more members of the former Ethiopian government, and announced that "as a precautionary measure" all military supplies to Ethiopia would be suspended. That suspension was lifted early in 1975, in response to urgent entreaties by the military regime.

In 1977, however, the Carter administration's emphasis on human rights made it probable that no military aid would be provided. The Ethiopian government responded by closing U.S. consulate offices in February 1977 and ordering 300 U.S. personnel to leave the country by April. There were several, partially contradictory elements in U.S. policy in addition to the human rights question. In particular, it was recognized that refusal to supply aid would leave the central government exclusively dependent on the Soviet Union and give the latter another foothold in the Middle East that might affect the Indian Ocean oil and shipping lanes. The American administration is equally aware, however, that the Ethiopian government is considerably more radical than the Eritrean separatists, who are supported by many of the Arab states whose goodwill the United States is trying to cultivate. There have been reports from various sources of American contacts with the Eritrean movement and of indirect aid. Moreover, the decision by the United States to phase out the Kagnew station in Asmara was an indication that it had no basic interest in keeping Eritrea as part of Ethiopia.[26]

Ethiopia's relations with Israel reflect a basic and continuing dilemma. On the one hand, both states are, although to varying degrees, keenly aware of their isolation in a region dominated by Arab states; and Israel would be a natural ally in Ethiopia's quest to avoid full Arab control of the Red Sea. On the other hand, closer relations with Israel would constitute a provocation to the Arab states and make coexistence policies more difficult. Consequently, the Ethiopian government under the emperor deliberately stressed its neutrality in the Arab-Israeli conflict. It refrained from establishing full diplomatic relations with Israel until the late 1960s, and even then never sent an ambassador to Israel.

Nevertheless, economic and even military relations were maintained. During the 1960s Israel provided Ethiopia with commando training for the armed forces, specifically for counterinsurgency operations against the Eritreans. The latter, and the Arab states, naturally seized on this to "demonstrate" that Ethiopia's neutrality was in fact a cover for pro-Israeli attitudes, and have further alleged (incorrectly) that Ethiopia leased some strategically located islands off the Eritrean coast to Israel. Arab suspicion of Ethiopian collusion with Israel lingered after the imperial government, in a shift of policy, broke diplomatic relations with Israel following the 1973 war, insisting that Israel must relinquish the occupied territories in accordance with U.N. Resolution 242. On the surface the military government maintained the policy of severing diplomatic relations with Israel, but in fact there were secret communications and some Israeli officers in disguise came to Ethiopia to train a special army unit (NEBELBAL, or "Flame") in counterinsurgency tactics.

The diversity of external involvement and interests in the Eritrean conflict has made it impossible for organizations such as the OAU and the Islamic Conference to play an active role. The Eritreans were represented by Osman Saleh Sabbe at the Islamic Conference of Foreign Ministers in Kuala Lumpur in June 1974, but did not succeed in obtaining a formal resolution referring to the conflict. The following year, the conference called upon member states and international organizations to promote a "just solution." Similarly, the 1977 conference in Tripoli did not go beyond a stated collective desire to "achieve peace in this important area."[27] These statements were nevertheless significant, in that they indicate a concern to settle the conflict, and specifically avoid any endorsement of independence for Eritrea as a condition for settlement. Such endorsement would not only raise the general consideration of setting a precedent for greater ethnic self-determination, but would make the Ethiopian government more intransigent, more prepared to obtain any aid possible to resist the separatists, and thus further complicate the pattern of international relations in the area. Similar considerations have prevailed in the OAU, although when the Eritreans first appealed for assistance in 1963, the OAU rejected the movement as a genuine liberation force, primarily for fear of setting a precedent for secessionist movements elsewhere.

CONCLUSION

In view of the foregoing considerations, it would seem that some realistic form of association between Ethiopia and Eritrea must be devised for the sake of preserving the peace and tranquillity of the area, and in the interests of the local protagonists. Mutual accommodation within Ethiopia is thus inextricably linked to reduced tension in the area, just as internal and external forces of conflict have been mutually reinforcing in the past. The unrest that gradually emerged in Eritrea during the federation was stimulated through the campaign by Arab states against any association of Eritrea with Ethiopia. However, although the propaganda and funds gradually succeeded in building up resistance to the federation, it was in large part due to the ineptitudes, failures, and egregious errors of the Ethiopian government. Far too frequently it overwhelmed the relatively exiguous social and administrative structures of Eritrea with federal institutions, counterparts, or innovations. What was worse, it suppressed the trade unions, prohibited the use of the local flag, and eventually, by devious means, eliminated the federation. It then prohibited the teaching of Tigrinya and Arabic in government schools, using Amharic and English as the only languages of instruction, as in the rest of Ethiopia.

Under continued Arab attacks against the federation, Ethiopia inevitably became more and more concerned with the necessity of preserving the association with Eritrea against foreign attack, and less and less sensitive to mounting local sentiments. Whatever may have been the abuses and mistakes on the part of the previous regime in Ethiopia—and they were many and deplorable—they were nothing compared with the treatment meted out to Eritrea by the Dergue. Apart from the incredible savagery of its attacks on Eritrean farmers and city dwellers, which have appalled Ethiopians themselves, as well as foreigners, the Dergue has indulged in a studied campaign of discrimination and of playing off the various elements of the Ethiopian population against each other. Today there is not one Eritrean in any significant decision-making post in the new Marxist government, whereas before 1974 there were some who held prominent roles in the highest ranks of the army, the air force and the police, as well as in the cabinet and the civilian administration. The savage repressions, the "Peasants March" of 1976 and its planned 1977 version, the attempts to set Christians against Muslims, southerners against northerners—all have created a climate of hostility, animosity, and violence that is as unnatural to the entire region as it is reprehensible.

There can be no solution to the problem of Eritrea until the Ethiopian government returns to the basic principle that a settlement must be achieved through negotiations. So long as Mengistu, the head of state and chief of government, proclaims as he did after the killing of his predecessor, Teferi Banti, that there would be no further attempts to negotiate with the rebels in Eritrea, there can be no hope for any solution. The Dergue's preoccupation is to secure more arms from the Soviet Union so that it can at last impose its own draconian solution on Eritrea. So long as the Dergue and the Soviet Union dominate Ethiopia, there is no possibility of accommodation with either the Eritreans or the neighboring Arab states. The neighboring Arab states that feel threatened by the Soviet Union will seek to create a buffer between themselves and the areas already under Soviet influence. However, such efforts—witness the Sudan proposal to this effect, supported by Saudi Arabia—would create both international and internal turmoil. The large Christian element of the Eritrean population could not accept the creation of a new Arab state of Eritrea that would be a member of a regional Arab federation and presumably of the Arab League. The opportunity for bringing about a consolidation of the diverse elements of the Eritrean population would be foreclosed—indeed, a new Lebanon would be created—and Ethiopia would resort to extreme measures of preemptive defense against perceived Arab encirclement.

NOTES

1. For a discussion of factors linking Ethiopian peoples, see Donald N. Levine, *Greater Ethiopia: The Evolution of a Multiethnic Society* (Chicago: University of Chicago Press, 1974), esp. pp. 40–68.

2. Patrick Gilkes, *The Dying Lion: Feudalism and Modernization in Ethiopia* (London: Julian Friedman, 1975), p. 195.

3. *Harnet (Liberation)* 2 (Mar. 1973):11–12.

4. Gilkes, op cit., p. 197.

5. *Report of the UN High Commissioner for Refugees*, UN General Assembly Official Record, 23 sess., Supplement No. 11 [A/7211] (New York: United Nations, 1968), p. 28.

6. Gilkes, op. cit., p. 200.

7. Interview with Saleh Sabbe, ELF-PLF spokesman, *Al-hawadith* (Beirut), June 21, 1974.

8. *Eritrean Review* no. 16 (Sept. 1974), p. 9.

9. Ibid., p. 7.

10. Ibid, p. 8.

11. *Africa Contemporary Record* (London), 7 (1974–1975):B186–B187.

12. *Washington Post*, Dec. 18, 1974.

13. *Financial Times* (London), Feb. 24, 1975.

14. *EDU Advocate* (London), Dec. 1975.

15. *U.S. Policy and Request for Sales of Arms to Ethiopia*, hearings before the Subcommittee on International Political and Military Affairs of the Committee on Foreign Affairs, U.S. House of Representatives, 94th Cong., 1st Sess. (Washington, D.C.: U.S. Government Printing Office, 1975), p. 28.

16. *Economist*, Sept. 27, 1975, p. 51.

17. Statement of President Nimeiry in an interview, *Middle East Review* 8 (Apr. 1976):28.

18. *Le Monde*, Mar. 16, 1977; *Economist*, Apr. 30, 1977, pp. 66–69; *New York Times*, July 11, 12, 13, 1977.

19. Cited in Gilkes, op. cit., p. 201.

20. *Washington Post*, Apr. 13, 1977.

21. *Al-Ba'ath* (Damascus), Oct. 19, 1975.

22. *Africa Confidential* 16, no. 7 (Apr. 11, 1975):6; *Africa* (Apr. 1975):1. Also see *Le Monde*, Feb. 8, 1975.

23. *ARNA*, May 16, 1977, cited in *Foreign Broadcast Information Service*, May 17, 1977, p. A-3.

24. *Keesings Contemporary Archives* (1975), p. 27031.

25. *Washington Post*, May 24, 1977.

26. See *U.S. Congressional Record*, July 19, 1976, pp. 7338–44; *Ethiopia and the Horn of Africa,* hearings before the Subcommittee on African Affairs of the Committee on Foreign Relations, U.S. Senate, 94th Cong., 2nd Sess. (Washington, D.C.: U.S. Government Printing Office, 1976).

27. *Washington Post*, Feb. 8, 1977.

CHAPTER

7

THE KAZAKHS IN CHINA

June Teufel Dreyer

THE PROTAGONISTS

The Sino-Soviet frontier in Central Asia is an artificial boundary that divides several minority groups. This paper will focus on one of these groups, the Kazakhs, and their relations with their fellow Turkic Muslim peoples and with the Soviet and Chinese governments.

There are 700,000 Kazakhs in China, most of them living in or near the Ili Kazakh Autonomous Chou of Sinkiang province,[1] which is contiguous to the Soviet republic of Kazakhstan. According to the 1970 census, there are nearly 5.3 million Kazakhs in the Soviet Union. Both Soviet and Chinese Kazakhs are minority groups, not only in relation to the populations of their own countries (China has an estimated 900 million people and the Soviet Union, according to its 1970 census, has 241,720,000), but even in the provinces in which they live. Sinkiang has a population of approximately 11 million persons and Kazakhstan, 12.13 million. However, the importance of the Kazakhs lies not in their numbers but in their interactions with the other minority peoples of the area, and in the strategic positions of these groups with regard to the Soviet and Chinese leaderships.

The ethnic mosaic of Central Asia is complex, formed over centuries of nomadic migrations and the rise and fall of invading warrior tribes. The emergent picture is one of constant reshuffling of alignments and of a steppe constantly in flux. The word "Kazakh" first appeared during the fifteenth century. Of Turkish origin, it is derived from a term meaning a masterless person or freebooter and came, by extension, to refer to nomads as well. The Kazakhs, a Muslim people, are closely related to other Central Asian Muslim peoples, such as the Kirghiz and the Uzbeks. The traditional nobilities of the Kazakhs and these other groups trace their origins to Genghis Khan, a Mongol. While the accuracy of historical records, and particularly of genealogical tables, from this period is often diluted by fanciful embellishment, it would appear that the Mongol conquests of the twelfth century effected a fundamental redistribution of the separate nomadic groups of the Central Asian steppes. In the following centuries the culture of the Kazakhs, Kirghiz, and Uzbeks was formed. Because of this, different ethnic groups may have the same ancestor. Whether the presence of the ancestor in several different genealogical tables is genuine or fictive often is less important than the fact that the table is credible to the groups involved. Normally, these kinship groups were loosely organized and spread over extensive areas. Unless united under a single leader, such as Genghis Khan, they did not pose a large-scale threat to more centralized governmental systems.

A complete elucidation of the factors that came to distinguish one ethnic group from another would entail a lengthy anthropological treatment far beyond the scope of this paper; moreover, the clan subdivisions within each ethnic group contained variations of their own that often rendered a clan of one ethnic group closer, in some ways, to the clan of another ethnic group than it was to some of the clans in its own group. Among the nomadic people of the area, linguistic differences typically were rather slight, since their constant movements and interchanges with each other tended to inhibit the development of divergent speech patterns. Kazakh, Karakalpak, Kirgiz, and Kazan Tatar are similar enough that a speaker of one can readily be understood by speakers of the others. Dialectical differences tended to be more marked among settled peoples such as the Uzbeks, Uighurs, and Tajiks; different speech patterns might well exist from valley to valley. Typically, however, speakers were less aware that they were using a different language than they were of using a regional dialect; they tended to identify with a dialectical unit rather than an ethnic group. The same held true of differences in weaving patterns, costumes, and other manifestations of folk art.

Other differences tended to be rather slight as well. Among the Kazakhs, horses were the most common mode of transportation; the Kirghiz seemed to prefer Bactrian camels. Both groups were rather nominal Muslims, though they were, nonetheless, ready to avenge any perceived slights to their faith. Kazakhs seemed somewhat more amenable to strong leadership than the more belligerent Kirghiz. The Karakalpaks were generally semi-, rather than fully, nomadic, and utilized cattle more than horses or camels. Also, they tended to be more devout Muslims.

The differences between the oasis culture of the settled peoples and that of the nomads were often more prominent than the differences of any one group within a category from the others of that category. Oasis culture was characterized by larger, more substantial dwellings containing a greater variety of luxury items; had a marked specialization of labor; and secluded its women. Nomads tended to possess few nonessential items, to have less specialization of labor, and to allow women a more meaningful role in the social and economic activities of the group.[2]

All groups showed keen interest in genealogical tables; and members thereof, on meeting a newcomer, would spend considerable time searching for a common ancestor. This kinship, real or imaginary, often manifested itself in cooperation during hostilities, and even resulted in a certain amount of crossing of ethnic lines.[3] In addition to the potential binding force of kinship, cooperation has been facilitated by the Muslim faith common to most of these groups. The Islamic admonition to join together in time of holy war generally was accepted enthusiastically by most members of the group, even when the cause might appear to outsiders as rather tenuously related to religious matters. The circumstance of finding themselves in the paths of two expanding empires was to provide the peoples of the steppe with many causes for uprising.

Several factors converged to give the Kazakhs a central role in the ethnic tensions between the Chinese and Russian (later, Soviet) empires. First, unlike several groups that are also found in both countries, and to which they are ethnically and historically related, the Kazakhs live close to the border. Second, being nomadic, Kazakh groups frequently crossed the border in the course of their migrations. And third, since their culture emphasized superb horsemanship, cultivation of the martial arts, and the satisfactions of combat, the Kazakhs were relatively easily roused to battle. Thus, for cultural, geographical, and historical reasons, the Kazakhs play an important role in Sino-Soviet hostilities, and have been chosen as the focus of this study.

THE COURSE OF EMPIRE

Imperial China had traditionally claimed jurisdiction over Central Asia, but rarely exercised it in fact. Chinese civilization was based on sedentary agriculture; and the mountainous, arid cold of much of Central Asia did not attract Han Chinese settlers. Except for a small area of moderate climate, the territory referred to rather vaguely in Chinese sources as "the Western Regions" could not be considered part of either the Chinese cultural or the Chinese administrative sphere. A few caravan routes traversed the area from earliest times, allowing trade between Han dynasty China* and imperial Rome, but the hazards of the route combined with the anticommercial bias of official Confucian philosophy to limit the effects of this contact. It would be difficult to consider Central Asia an integral part of the Chinese economic unit. Culturally, since the inhabitants of these lands did not partake of Han civiliza-

---

*The Han dynasty, commonly divided into Former or Western Han (206 B.C.-A.D. 23) and Eastern Han (A.D. 25–220) is regarded as one of China's most glorious, and gave its name to the majority (94 percent of the present-day population) ethnic group of the country.

tion, they were regarded by the Han Chinese as barbarians. The expert horsemanship and martial skills that characterized their lifestyles were frequently threats to Han culture.

These peoples could be, and several times were, conquered by Chinese armies; but garrisoning such far-flung areas was difficult and expensive. One solution devised to reduce the problem of maintaining armed forces in distant areas was the military agricultural colony: soldiers were charged with raising their own food and were expected to form self-sufficient outposts of the empire. The scheme, though ingenious, had several drawbacks, not least of which was the fact that soldiers tended to marry local women and eventually became assimilated to the very people they had been sent to subdue. In general, Chinese policy toward these and other border peoples aimed at control rather than absorption: the inhabitants were permitted to maintain their traditional lifestyles and cultures so long as they did not disturb the order and peace of empire.

Meanwhile, shortly after the Kazakhs began to appear as a separate people, the Russian empire began to expand eastward. Between 1689 and 1860, the Ch'ing government, which became progressively enfeebled in its later years, ceded over 300,000 square miles of its Central Asian domains to the czar's government.[4] The Chinese bitterly resented these cessions. Together with other concessions that had to be made to various foreign countries, they came to be referred to as the "unequal treaties." The fact that these settlements were forced on an unwilling government forms the basis for the present-day Chinese government's claim to large portions of Kazakhstan and other parts of Soviet Central Asia.

One result of czarist expansion was the colonization of Kazakhstan by peasants from European Russia. The Russian government originally maintained restrictions on migration but, on realizing its value, began to offer attractive inducements to settlers. Their arrival aroused considerable resentment among the Kazakhs, then estimated to number 3 million.[5] The nomads had pastured their herds over large portions of the steppe. Russian colonization took land away from grazing, and denied many Kazakhs the use of their traditional winter camps. Many of them fled south, to land still held by China.

The increasing weakness of the Ch'ing dynasty had other repercussions besides the cession of territory to Russia. In the period immediately following China's reconquest of the Western Regions in 1759, efficient and relatively honest officials had been sent to administer those territories. In time, however, they were gradually replaced with less competent and greedy types who oppressed the peoples under their charge and aroused their hostility. Both this and the arrival of the Kazakhs, whom the Russian government could claim as subjects of the czar, played into Russian hands.

Accumulated grievances against the Ch'ing government flared into a Muslim rebellion in 1862 that eventually encompassed the entire Chinese northwest. In 1865 a Turkic Muslim named Yakub Beg took advantage of the rebellion to set up an independent state in Sinkiang; tacit support from Russia helped him to maintain his position.[6] However, in the attendant chaos, Russia's trade was disrupted and its consulates burned. There was also a substantial exodus of refugees into Russia. Seeing a territorial opportunity as well as a way to reassert its trading position, Russia moved into the rich Ili Valley, in Kazakh territory, and annexed it. The enfeebled Ch'ing dynasty, in a costly campaign it could ill afford, finally put down the northwest Muslim rebellion and destroyed Yakub Beg's state. The subsequent Chinese demand that Russia withdraw from Ili led to a major diplomatic confrontation between the two states. Eventually, a convention was signed providing for Russian withdrawal on China's cession of some territory west of Ili, its granting of special trading concessions in nearby areas, and the payment of a 9 million ruble indemnity to cover Russia's expenses in "administering" Ili.[7]

Fearful of further Russian moves, the Ch'ing government decided to incorporate what had been the Western Regions into the regular administrative system of China. In 1896 it was formally created a province with the name Sinkiang ("New Territory").

In the following years, the czarist government attempted to cope with mounting domestic problems, a costly and ultimately humiliating war with Japan, and international intrigues on its European borders. But the colonization of Kazakhstan continued: between 1896 and 1916, more than 1.4 million new settlers poured into Kazakhstan and implanted a strong Russian presence there. Its economy became firmly tied to that of European Russia, supplying it with meat, hides, and dairy products.[8]

Further escalation of tensions between China and Russia over Central Asia were limited by domestic difficulties that prevented each state from further consolidating its hold over its Central Asian domains. In 1911 the Ch'ing dynasty fell, being replaced by a series of warlord governments that were preoccupied with quarrels with other warlords; even Chiang Kai-shek's Kuomintang (KMT) government, which assumed power in 1928, was unable to exercise more than nominal control over Sinkiang. In Russia, a 1916 decree ordering Kazakhs, who were traditionally exempt from military service, to be drafted to help fight in World War I caused a bloody rebellion that further weakened the faltering czarist government. During the ensuing disruptions on the steppe, additional numbers of Kazakhs fled to China.[9]

THE 1917 REVOLUTION AND ITS EFFECTS ON CENTRAL ASIA

The success of the Bolshevik Revolution that began in 1917 changed the power equation in Central Asia in favor of the newly formed Soviet Union. The new government's success did not come easily, and its relations with the non-Russian peoples of the former czarist empire were among its more difficult problems. In an earlier bid for the support of these peoples, called minority nationalities in Marxist parlance, it had promised self-determination to all who wished it. However, when the Communist party's struggle against the czarist government actually came to fruition, the party came to view self-determination as "profoundly counterrevolutionary" and ruthlessly suppressed such movements. The Kazakhs' Alash Orda provisional government was one of the victims, and a bitter anti-Bolshevik struggle took place in which many Kazakhs joined the White Army of Admiral Aleksandr Kolchak.[10] The economy of the area was badly affected: in the Kazakh province of Semirechie, livestock decreased by 51.67 percent between 1917 and 1920.[11] In 1920 and 1921, the Kazakh areas were hit by famine. The Kazakhs were more seriously affected than the Russian colonists: their herds had been depleted in the fighting and they did not receive their fair share of the emergency food supplies sent in by the new government. An estimated 1 million persons died of hunger and related conditions in 1921 alone, and a necessary preoccupation with sheer survival reduced the Kazakhs' organized resistance to the Bolshevik government.[12]

In contrast with the czarist government's relatively cautious attitude toward altering the traditional lifestyles of its Central Asian subjects, the Soviet government promoted rapid change. Although Kazakhstan was constituted an "autonomous" socialist republic in 1920 and given the consitutional right to secede from the Soviet Union, its non-Russian inhabitants had very little to say about the governance of their area, and it was clear that any attempts to exercise the right to secede would be regarded as counterrevolutionary. Measures were introduced to force the nomads to settle down, to destroy tribal and kinship ties that might facilitate resistance to the new government, to promote agriculture as an alternative to pastoralism, and to introduce the Kazakhs and other Central Asian peoples to the Russian language and Marxist culture. While motivated by a desire to improve the lives of Central Asian peoples and to facilitate the new government's control of the area, the reforms were not perceived as improvements by many of those affected. The fictional nature of autonomy was patently obvious. The Kazakh intelligentsia, influential despite its small numbers, was irked by the introduction of a new Cyrillic-based written language that the government alleged would suit the nationality's needs better than the traditional Arabic script. They would have preferred a system devised by a Crimean Tatar, Ismail Bey Gaspirili, which would have been suitable for all Turkic peoples, and viewed the Soviet government's choice of a Cyrillic script as an attempt to separate them from these other peoples.[13]

In addition, there was a cultural contradiction between the Soviet leadership's implicit belief that agriculture was a more desirable way of life and the nomads' attachment to their animals and to a peripatetic mode of existence. A collectivization program begun in 1928 was conducted without adequate planning and far in advance of collectivization in Russian areas. Forced into collectives where grazing was often insufficient, thousands of Kazakhs watched their herds starve. Others killed their animals and tried to escape. Some of them fled to Afghanistan, others to China. The Kazakh population of the Soviet Union fell by almost 900,000 between 1926 and 1939, and there was also a sharp drop in numbers of animals.[14] Soviet policies were the worse in their effect on the Kazakhs in that they administered through the local Russian-colonist elite. As described by Richard Pipes, this group

> . . . utilized the Soviet government and party machines to intensify the economy and political exploitation of the native population. The Revolution, therefore, brought to the Moslem areas not an abolition of colonialism, but colonialism in a new and much more oppressive form. . . . the classes which in Russia proper constituted the lower orders of society formed in the eastern borderlands a privileged order, which itself was engaged in exploitation and oppression.[15]

The Kazakhs' situation, like that of other Soviet nationalities, has been better since the death of Stalin, though not so much so as to eliminate discontents. Nikita Khrushchev's reforms in higher education allowed a higher percentage of Kazakhs and most other nationalities to attend universities and to take advantage of better job opportunities. Standards of living in Central Asia have improved markedly. Local factories turn out desired consumer goods. The infamous Soviet housing shortage is markedly less in Central Asia than in European Russia, as is the supply of fresh meat, milk, and vegetables. There is a Kazakh member of the Politburo.[16]

Still, the results of raised living standard and two generations of pressure have not made significant numbers of Kazakhs into either committed Soviet citizens or assimilated Russians. Nomadism has survived, albeit in a modified form. It has been pointed out that although Soviet propaganda describes nomads as "roving" *(otgonnyi),* rather than nomadic *(kochevoi),* herders as "specialists skilled in the care of livestock" and the nomadic family as a "brigade" with each member holding an official title, the end result continues to be pastoral nomads moving seasonally in family groups to find grazing for their animals.[17]

A recent study concludes that the Kazakhs and other Muslim peoples have been extraordinarily resistant to assimilation. This is true even of persons who have been exposed to Russians for long periods of time. One scholar, using the self-reported first languages of Soviet citizens as an index of assimilation, puts the russification level of urbanized Kazakh communities that have had over two centuries of extensive contact with Russians at only 3.2 percent; that for rural Kazakhs is 2.7 percent.[18] Interestingly, the 1970 Soviet census listed a slightly higher percentage of Uighurs reporting Uighur as their native language than in the previous census of 1959 (88.5 percent versus 85.0 percent). That for Kazakhs remained almost exactly the same as in 1959.[19] Similar figures are reported for other Central Asian minorities, thus tending to support the conclusion that "the effect of exposure to Russians on the russification of Muslims is exceedingly small."[20] An American student in Tashkent in 1970 was told by a recent Russian arrival that at first it was hard for him to believe that Russian rule extended to Central Asia.[21]

A Western social scientist, analyzing the significantly higher rates of population increase among Central Asian minorities than among Russians, describes these peoples as pursuing *la vengeance des berceaux*—getting even through the cradle, or compensating for heavy immigration to their homelands and some assimilation losses through a high birth rate. In Kazakhstan the Muslim school-age population is significantly higher than the Muslim percentage in the total population of the province, even though children of the Muslim minorities, particularly female children, are more likely to drop out of school than are Russian children. The fact that available labor now seems to be directed to Siberia rather than Kazakhstan makes russification still less likely.[22] Nonetheless, Russian dissident Andrei Sakharov has pointed out that Soviet prisons are filled with ethnic dissidents.[23]

ACTIVITIES OF THE SOVIET AND CHINESE COMMUNIST PARTIES IN SINKIANG

While the Soviet government was extending and consolidating its power over the former czarist domains in Central Asia, it did not lose interest in those Central Asian territories still nominally under Chinese control. At this point it is necessary to backtrack to 1917, to examine the situation in Sinkiang during the years following the October Revolution.

When the Bolshevik government assumed power in Russia, it issued a declaration abrogating the unequal treaties concluded during the czarist era. However, none of the land obtained under them was returned to China, and the Soviet Union proved even more interested in Sinkiang than czarist Russia had been. The warlord of Sinkiang, Sheng Shih-ts'ai, was concerned with maintaining his independence from the government of China, then headed by Chiang Kai-shek; and the Soviet Union provided financial assistance that helped Sheng in this endeavor. In return, the Soviet Union received a privileged position in Sinkiang. Soviet geologists explored the province's rich natural resources, Soviet engineers surveyed railways, and Soviet pilots staffed Sinkiang's air routes.

Propaganda activities aimed at forming a pro-Soviet Communist party; the atmosphere in Sinkiang was for the most part distinctly unfriendly to the Chinese Communist Party (CCP). In 1934, when the beleaguered CCP fled its

Kiangsi Soviet base to escape annihilation by Chiang Kai-shek's forces, it wandered for many months in search of a reasonably safe haven. The Soviet Union, ostensibly its fraternal socialist ally and adviser, never told the CCP of its position in Sinkiang. A former CCP leader who later defected has speculated that this was because Stalin had designs on Sinkiang and wished to exclude Chinese influence of any sort from the province.[24]

In 1938, Sheng, seemingly attempting to gain a degree of independence from the Soviet Union by playing off the Soviet and Chinese parties against one another, welcomed several CCP advisers into his government and even announced his intention to join the CCP. A few years later, however, alleging their involvement in a plot against him, he had those advisers arrested and executed. Mao Tse-tung's brother, Mao Tse-min, was among these martyrs to Chinese Communist concern with Sinkiang.

When, due to its involvement in World War II, the Soviet Union could no longer sustain its aid to Sinkiang and, in fact, seemed to be losing the war, Sheng mended his fences with Chiang Kai-shek's KMT government. Accepting a cabinet-level position in Chungking, he left Sinkiang and the KMT was able to choose its first governor of the province. Sinkiang's non-Han groups were not pleased by the reassertion of Chinese control, and the new administration of the province proved neither tactful nor honest. Han settlers were arriving, and would presumably occupy minorities' lands, a Han army stationed there had to be provisioned and paid, and the province's economy was deteriorating.

Meanwhile, the Soviet Union, miffed at losing its position in Sinkiang, had taken the offensive in World War II and was able to reassert its interest in the province. The previous government-to-province special relationship having failed, the Soviet Union began to work through Sinkiang's aggrieved non-Han groups. Sympathetic Soviet agents provided dissident ethnic group leaders with financial aid and advice. A major rebellion ensued, with a multiethnic alliance representing Uighurs, Kazakhs, Kirghiz, White Russians, and others cooperating in the establishment of an independent state, the East Turkestan Republic (ETR). Its capital was at Ining, in the predominantly Kazakh territory bordering Soviet Kazakhstan. Its leader, Akhmedjan, was a Uighur, though the ETR's mainstay was its Kazakh cavalry, commanded by Osman Bator. At one point the rebel cavalry threatened the provincial capital of Urumchi;[25] the fact that it pulled back only when the Soviet Union, having offered its services as mediator, advised ETR leaders to do so seems to indicate the movement's dependence. However, the abundant evidence of KMT mismanagement makes it clear that the Soviet Union was exploiting existing grievances rather than creating them.

Chiang Kai-shek's KMT government was amenable to compromise, especially since the Sinkiang rebellion was tying down troops and materiel that Chiang could have put to better use in his battle with the CCP. Eventually a compromise was worked out, providing for increased minority representation in government and a greater degree of autonomy for the province. Burhan, a Tatar who had managed to create a certain amount of rapport with all sides, was made governor. The troops of the ETR would remain undispersed as a partial guarantee that the KMT would observe its part of the bargain, and a KMT garrison also remained in Sinkiang.

Meanwhile, however, Chiang Kai-shek was losing his battle with the CCP. The Soviet Union not only did not aid the CCP in this effort but actually entered into publicly announced negotiations with the KMT. Although the exact bargaining terms were not revealed, the Soviet Union clearly was offering Chiang Kai-shek's government arms—which surely would have been used against the CCP—in return for some form of control over Sinkiang.[26] Eventually, the CCP's military success foreclosed this option. By the late summer of 1949 its armies had been victorious in most of the rest of China and were pressing hard on Sinkiang. At this point virtually the entire provincial government of Sinkiang, from governor Burhan on down, and including most of those who had been leaders of the ETR, defected to the CCP en masse.

Thus Sinkiang, with its large Turkic Muslim majority (estimated at 75 percent Uighur, 10 percent Kazakh, and less than 6 percent Han at this time), formally became part of the People's Republic of China (PRC). Exactly how the province's leadership was persuaded to defect is not known. However, in addition to the certainty of CCP takeover regardless of their wishes, the provincial leaders surely were influenced by promises that Sinkiang would receive autonomous status (the nature of this autonomy probably being somewhat ambiguous), that there would be concessions to the ethnic groups and their cultures, and that the leadership role of the present elite would continue. The CCP did not have to make good on the last in several significant cases: the plane carrying most of the high-ranking ETR leaders, including Akhmedjan, crashed en route to a conference in Peking. The Chinese did not release news of the disaster until many months later, thus fanning speculation that the crash might not have been accidental.[27] The only remaining ETR leader of note was Saifudin, a young Moscow-trained Uighur who spoke Chinese rather poorly at this time. He had been engaged in fomenting anti-Han Chinese riots in Sinkiang during the early 1940's, had been Minister of Education in the ETR government, and was a member of the Communist Party of the Soviet Union (CPSU).

Saifudin was not the only reminder of the Soviet Union's privileged position in Sinkiang. The new Chinese People's Republic began its political career as an international outcast, and was forced to turn to the USSR for help. Negotiations over a treaty dragged on for many months, leading observers to conclude that the Soviet Union was driving a hard bargain. The full provisions of what would become the Sino-Soviet Treaty of 1950 were not announced by either side, but are known to have included a special consular position for the USSR in Sinkiang, plus joint exploration of Sinkiang's resources and the creation of joint stock companies to exploit those resources.[28]

The Chinese did not send People's Liberation Army work teams* to the three predominantly Kazakh districts in December 1949, when such teams were sent to the rest of Sinkiang, explaining that "conditions were as yet unsettled" in those areas.[29] The work teams did not appear in the three districts until the latter half of 1950, after the Sino-Soviet treaty was signed (on March 27). One may speculate that the "unsettled conditions" may therefore have included the unsettled question of who should administer the three districts, and that the Soviet Union was arguing for jurisdiction over them. Though it did not receive jurisdiction over the three districts, the Soviet Union retained an influential position there. When, toward the end of 1950, the organs of local power in Ili, Tacheng, and Tarbagatai were "reorganized," the administrative control boards that replaced them included many Kazakhs who has been members of, or sympathetic to, the ETR government (though a Han Chinese generally held the final decision-making power). In urban areas of the three districts, the pro-Soviet Kazakh intelligentsia remained in power and generally was not made to undergo intensive ideological remolding or reform. The local clan headman structure was left largely unaltered as well, save for those who overtly resisted the new government. Osman Bator, whose Kazakh cavalry had been so important to the success of the ETR, was one such holdout. He fled south, but was captured and executed. As for Saifudin, while he was in Moscow helping to negotiate the 1950 treaty, it was announced by Peking that he had become a member of the CCP and that he had resigned from the CPSU.

In 1951 a purge, probably undertaken in connection with the "three-anti" campaign then being conducted in the rest of China, reportedly removed pro-Soviet figures in the Kazakh areas; a large-scale pacification and re-education campaign was conducted in 1953. The official New China News Agency explained that "it was only after all this that the entire Kazakh people returned to the fold of the ancestral land."[30]

In general, however, strenuous efforts were made to conceal any differences between the Chinese and Soviet governments over Kazakh lands. The national boundary was referred to as "Friendship Border," and Kazakhs of both nationalities—who were virtually indistinguishable without reference to passports—crossed it frequently to graze their herds and to visit kinfolk. Soviet technicians were lavishly praised in the Chinese press for the selfless way in which they were helping their socialist neighbor to develop its resources, and

---

*Work teams were charged with unifying and mobilizing the masses, helping in the formation of peasants' and herders' associations, preparing for the establishment of local representative organs, and similar organizational "spadework." In addition, they engaged in propaganda and indoctrination work, the recruitment and training of cadres, and the "guidance" of local-level mass campaigns.

Soviet ethnographers worked with the Han Chinese among Sinkiang's minorities.[31] Soviet aid helped build a railroad connecting Lanchow, capital of China's Kansu province, with Urumchi, the capital of Sinkiang. It was planned to continue the line on through Ili, ultimately to reach the Soviet border. Meanwhile, the Soviet Union would extend the terminus of its Turk-Sib Railroad from Aktogai to the border; the two lines would connect at a new town, Druzhba (Friendship).

Wishing to avoid antagonizing the Kazakhs and risking the reinforcement of any pro-Soviet tendencies they might have, Chinese policy was cautious and followed a modified Soviet plan. "Land" reform was carried out under slogans such as "herdowners and [poorer] herders both profit" and "no struggle, no liquidation, no division of property." Chinese state trading organs offered relatively high prices for herders' products. While presented as evidence of China's high regard for its minority nationalities and its desire to ensure their prosperity, this was also a way for the new government to gain control in the herding areas by linking them with the Chinese market system, and to redirect trade away from the Soviet Union as well. Lenient attitudes were also taken toward most religious practices, even toward polygamy.

In 1954, Nikita Khrushchev visited Peking, hoping to obtain Chinese support in his bid to succeed Stalin. This he did, but not before the Chinese exacted a quid pro quo. Khrushchev agreed, among other things, to terminate the joint stock companies in Sinkiang. Soviet influence, however, remained in the form of advisers, technicians, and the need to order equipment and spare parts from the Soviet Union. The Chinese also announced that Uighur, Kazakh, and the other Turkic Muslim languages would henceforth be written in the Cyrillic script. Since many of the intelligentsia of these minorities had been educated in the Soviet Union and were already acquainted with Cyrillic, this was understandable. However, the use of Cyrillic in writing Uighur and Kazakh also created a bond between these Chinese minorities and their fellow Uighurs and Kazakhs in the Soviet Union while creating a linguistic distance between the Chinese minorities and the Han majority in China. Sheng Shih-ts'ai, from his vantage point in Taiwan, later recalled his own misgivings when his Soviet advisers declared repeatedly that "the peoples along the Sino-Soviet frontier are all brethren. The racially related peoples will one day be united as citizens of the same nation."[32] It is inconceivable that the leaders of the PRC would not have seen the implications of allowing Cyrillic to replace Arabic in Sinkiang, and the fact that this decision was announced at all* is indicative of

---

*There is no evidence that the decision to use Cyrillic was actually implemented on a significant scale, though the break with the USSR, and China's development of its own Latin-based *pin-yin* system as a standard orthography for all the CPR's linguistic groups, occurred too soon after the decision to use Cyrillic to draw any meaningful conclusions from this.

the degree to which the Chinese government felt it necessary to placate the Soviet Union at this time.

A month after Khrushchev's visit to China, the Ili Kazakh Autonomous Chou was created, encompassing the three predominantly Kazakh districts of the former ETR and, like the ETR, having its capital at Ining. The chairperson and a vice-chairperson were Kazakhs, but there was also significant (and presumably more powerful) representation from regular units of the Chinese People's Liberation Army (PLA) and from the Sinkiang Production and Construction Corps. The latter, with its motto "on the one shoulder a rifle, on the other a hoe," was intended to garrison the area while helping local people develop their economy. The possibility of American and other imperialist intervention always existed, and there surely were ways in which the local economy could be improved. But it was also possible for the Soviet Union to view the Production and Construction Corps as guarding the border against it. And the local people, noting the large number of corps members and their preoccupation with agriculture, as opposed to animal husbandry, could see the corps as yet another Han Chinese plan to usurp their lands, turn the nomads into sedentary agriculturalists, and assimilate them. The corps also bore an uncomfortable resemblance to the military agricultural colonies of imperial China, whose minorities policies were regularly and vehemently denounced by Mao. In 1956, there began a large-scale transfer of Han Chinese into Sinkiang, with many of them being absorbed into the corps or onto newly created state farms.

Curiously, and quite at variance with the practice elsewhere in China, the Ili Kazakh Autonomous Chou's creation in 1954 and Sinkiang's reconstitution as the Sinkiang Uighur Autonomous Region (SUAR) during the following year occurred although elections in 14 counties of Ili *chou* could not be held until 1956.[33] Normally, such administrative units would not be constituted until elections had been held in their component parts.

Also in 1956, the CCP began a major investigation of its policies toward minority nationalities; this was carried on at the same time that persons throughout China were encouraged to voice their opinions of socialism in a campaign to "let a hundred flowers bloom, let a hundred schools of thought contend." The results, as they became known in 1957, were profoundly disquieting to party leaders. As they pertained to the Kazakhs and other minorities of Sinkiang, the campaign revealed lurking preferences for the Soviet Union over China, often strongly voiced preferences for an independent Kazakh, Uighur, or Turkic state, and the repeated conviction that if ETR leader Akhmedjan were still alive, he would be extremely dissatisfied with what had become of the autonomy he thought he had been promised. There were also charges that the Han were exploiting the minorities, and demands that they leave Sinkiang en masse.

Saifudin, who had been made governor of the SUAR in 1955, attempted to refute these charges in the expected ways: Sinkiang had "always" been part of China, the Han were sacrificing themselves to build a better Sinkiang, and there was sufficient wealth in the province for all. Those who thought otherwise were either counterrevolutionaries or had been duped by counterrevolutionaries.[34] As might be anticipated, many of the "hundred flowers" were found to be poisonous weeds; Kazakhs who had voiced them were among those removed from the socialist Garden of Eden and sent for "reform through labor." These included the talented young poet Kazhykumar Shabdanov; Jahoda, the head of the Ili Kazakh Autonomous Chou; the vice-director of the chou's propaganda department, and the president of its People's Court.[35] Significantly, Zunin Taipov, a former leader of the ETR army who had been absorbed into the Chinese military, was removed as well.

Public mention of the pro-Soviet predilections of those purged was of necessity muted, in order to avoid creating a confrontation with the Soviet Union. The anti-Soviet component of the antirightist campaign is sworn to by later refugees in the Soviet Union and can be read into the Chinese criticisms of local nationalism in Sinkiang. While pro-Kazakh and pan-Turkic sentiments obviously are not the same as pro-Soviet sentiments, the role of the Soviet Union in supporting such separatist movements must be kept in mind. Thus every nostalgic recollection of Akhmedjan, Osman Bator, or the ETR inevitably reminded the Chinese leadership of Soviet machinations in Sinkiang. Also very much on the minds of Chinese leaders was the example of Mongolia, where the Soviet Union had successfully encouraged "local nationalists" to set up a state "independent" of China when in fact it was almost completely dependent on Soviet aid and trade. Hence local nationalism in Sinkiang, while not the same as pro-Sovietism, is perceived by the Chinese leadership as having a high degree of overlap with it.

SINKIANG MINORITIES AND THE SINO-SOVIET DISPUTE, 1958–76

In 1958 China began the Great Leap Forward, which represented a sharp break with the social, economic, and ideological policies it had pursued during the previous nine years. There were many reasons behind the launching of the Great Leap and why it was begun at this particular time. Among the more important were the growing conviction among an influential segment of the Chinese leadership that continued adherence to the Soviet model would be detrimental to China's development, and the feeling that the Soviet Union had abandoned its commitment to true Marxism. Communes encompassing many tens of thousands of persons were created, the use of material incentives in production was sharply curtailed, and there was a large-scale confiscation of private property. The relative tolerance accorded to minority nationalities' languages, customs, and lifestyles under the influence of the Soviet model also ended.

The Kazakhs and other minorities of Sinkiang were expected to contribute their animals to the communes, learn Han Chinese, adopt Han cultural forms, and give up various "decadent" customs, including polygamy. Communes were not generally established in Kazakh areas until several months after they had been set up in much of the rest of China, by which time their major deficiencies had become known. Although there is some evidence that Kazakh communes were created in a somewhat modified form, their effects were as dysfunctional as in other areas of China. Production fell drastically, and there was widespread hunger and dissatisfaction with both the economic and social policies of the Great Leap Forward. There were rumors of small-scale uprisings in Sinkiang in 1958 and 1959.[36]

The Soviet leadership was contemptuous of the Chinese policies and annoyed at the repudiation of the Soviet Union's model that the Great Leap represented. Khrushchev was publicly critical of the communes; the Soviet press treated China's ensuing economic difficulties with smug "concern." In 1960, all Soviet technicians still remaining in China were abruptly withdrawn. The strains in the Sino-Soviet relationship became increasingly evident to outside observers. A combination of intense minority dissatisfaction with Chinese rule in Sinkiang and growing hostility between the Soviet and Chinese leaderships provided the backdrop for the internationalization of the Kazakh situation.

The first public manifestation of this internationalization (or, perhaps more accurately, reinternationalization) of the Sinkiang borderlands question occurred during the spring of 1962. In view of the subsequent exacerbation of the Sino-Soviet dispute, and of the ethnic component of that dispute, the incident was to take on enormous significance. The direct antecedents of the disturbances of 1962 can be traced back four years. The culturally repressive social policies introduced during the Great Leap Forward and the critical economic situation that followed it strained Sinkiang minority groups' tenuous allegiance to Han China. The belief that Han residents received perferential treatment in the allocation of food and other rationed commodities exacerbated these strains. On the southeast coast of China, authorities were allowing those citizens who wished to leave for Hong Kong to do so. Those who left could be presumed to include a high percentage of the malcontents, thus reducing the task of enforcing social order.

In addition, whatever the political beliefs of the persons involved, the emigration would certainly ease pressure on China's scarce food resources. Apparently the authorities in Sinkiang at first were similarly disposed to allow Uighurs and Kazakhs to leave for the Soviet Union, but subsequently began to worry over the large size of the migrant population, the fact that they were taking their herds with them, and the uses to which the now openly hostile

Soviet Union could put the refugees. Chinese officials also discovered that Soviet consular authorities had been issuing thousands of false Soviet passports to those who wished them.[37] The exodus was ordered halted, to the annoyance of many would-be emigrants. There seems to have been a demonstration of some size in front of CCP headquarters in the Ili Kazakh Autonomous Chou, during which the demonstrators were fired upon. Several dozen Uighurs and Kazakhs were killed. News of the massacre spread quickly, resulting in rioting and disorder in other parts of Sinkiang. The Chinese suspected the Soviet Union of having fomented the incident—which closely resembled the incidents preceding the formation of the ETR two decades before—while the Russian press used the incident to "prove" the repressive, racist nature of Chinese policy toward its non-Han peoples.

The above events have been pieced together; the Chinese side has said virtually nothing publicly. Chou En-lai, as part of a lengthy report to the National People's Congress over two and a half years after the incident, said only that

> In 1962, under the instigation and direct direction of external forces, a group of the most reactionary protagonists of local nationalism staged a traitorous counterrevolutionary rebellion in Ining, Sinkiang, and incited and organized the flight to foreign territory of a large number of people near the frontier. Under the leadership of the Party, the people of all the fraternal nationalities in Sinkiang resolutely crushed these subversive and traitorous activities.[38]

The Soviet side claimed to present an eyewitness account, and was somewhat more graphic:

> Forty residents of Ili Kazakh Province [sic] went to the local Party committee for permission to leave for the USSR. But there they did not even want to listen to them. And when more than 2,000 persons gathered before the Party Committee building, bursts of machine-gun fire from the windows lashed the crowd. From the military district headquarters, which was across the street, they also opened fire, shooting people in the back. Ordinary people —shepherds, farmers—cursing the maniacs mad with thirst for power, fell, mowed down by a scythe of lead.
>
> The crowd scattered. Only several dozen bodies of men, women, old men and children remained lying before the windows of the Party Committee building as testimony to the bankruptcy of the nationalities policy pursued by the Chinese leaders, as a reproach to their unclean conscience.
>
> And after this, they call themselves Communists! After all, one of the chief perpetrators of the crime, Chang Shu-chi, Secretary of the Ili-Kazakh Party Committee, was not even censured; he is at liberty and occupies a high post. Who knows, perhaps he will again arrange a "bloody Sunday" somewhere in the outlying nationality districts.[39]

However different their emphases, the official Chinese and Soviet accounts agree on the essence of the story. The incident touched off an ongoing public confrontation between China and the Soviet Union that has been carried out through overt military means, clandestine infiltration, and propaganda. This confrontation has had important repercussions for the political, economic, and cultural lives of the minority peoples on both sides of the border.

Militarily, both sides complain of border incursions by planes, troops, and ostensibly private citizens.[40] Only once has fighting on any significant scale been reported from the Sinkiang/Kazakhstan area; in August 1969, there were clashes involving several hundred Chinese and Soviet troops, with casualties on both sides. The Chinese accused the Soviet Union of sending helicopters, tanks, armored vehicles, and several hundred troops two kilometers over the border, where they were repelled. The Chinese Foreign Ministry's note charged that larger numbers of troops and vehicles were being assembled to provoke even larger conflicts in the future.[41] The Soviet Ministry of Foreign Affairs replied that the Chinese authorities had been "deliberately exacerbating" the border situation for several months, and had purposely provoked both this and a previous clash in the Ussuri River area. The fact that the Chinese soldiers were equipped with movie cameras was held indicative of the planned nature of the Chinese attacks,[42] and captured documents were released that purported to prove Chinese guilt in the Ussuri clashes.[43] More recently, however, an analyst of the U.S. Central Intelligence Agency has taken the position that while the Chinese did indeed provoke the Amur/Ussuri confrontation, that in Sinkiang/Kazakhstan was perpetrated by the Soviet side.[44]

A smaller-scale confrontation on the Sinkiang border occurred in March 1974, when a Soviet helicopter landed inside Chinese territory at Altai and was seized by the Chinese. The Soviet Foreign Ministry protested that the vehicle had been sent to pick up a seriously ill serviceman who was in urgent need of hospitalization, but that it had lost its bearings and made a forced landing, in what proved to be China, when its fuel supply ran out.[45] The Chinese Foreign Ministry's reply formally accused the Soviet Union of "cook[ing] up a bunch of lies to cover the crime," noting that the helicopter carried neither medical personnel nor medical equipment, but did possess arms, ammunition and reconnaissance equipment. Documents on board had indicated that the crew was on a "special mission"; morever, this intrusion was not an isolated incident.[46] Mass rallies were held throughout Sinkiang in which the participants accused the Soviet Union of carrying out provocations, planning a large-scale invasion, and wishing to add to the 560,000 square kilometers it had already "stolen" from Sinkiang[47] (a reference to the treaty of 1881). Despite the Soviet Union's threat of "serious consequences" if the helicopter and crew were not returned, the confrontation gradually subsided. More than two and a half years later, the helicopter and its crew were returned, with a statement explaining that "investigation has established the veracity of the Soviet crew's contention that they crossed into Chinese territory unintentionally.[48] In both Soviet and Chinese accounts of the 1969 and 1974 incidents, indigenous ethnic names among the personnel mentioned are conspicuously lacking, leading one to conclude that each side considers border defense in the area too important to be left to the natives. The Chinese side did belatedly note that "people of all nationalities" had helped in apprehending the Soviet helicopter and paraded one of them, variously referred to as Chiyatapieke and Muyatapiehko, at National Day rallies in Peking several months later, where he declared that "the militia and people of various nationalities. . . . are not to be bullied."[49]

Most Sino-Soviet confrontations on the Sinkiang border were not so spectacular, though carrying no less potential for rapid escalation. A more typical situation was described by a Soviet soldier in 1968:

> A fisherman comes, sticks a pole with Mao's portrait on it in the snow and begins to dig a hole. We explain that it is forbidden to cross the border. We escort him back. The next day 20 fishermen come. Three have nets and each one has a booklet of quotations. They wave them around so that fishing will be better. We escort them back to the border. About 500 people are brought to the border. There are women and children among them. They organize a rally and beat drums. They are loaded on trucks and head for the Soviet shore. Our fellows stand in a chain. The trucks race at them, intending to frighten them. Nothing happens, and they go away. [Then] they come with streamers: quotations are attached to sticks and there are iron pipes on top of the sticks. Again our men form a wall. Their people put the quotations in their pockets and start swinging the sticks. Never mind, we drove them away.[50]

It is quite likely that the infiltration, subversion and sabotage activities each side accuses the other of contain substantial elements of truth.

Although the physical presence of the minority peoples is scarcely noticeable in these post-1962 confrontations, propaganda channels for both parties to the dispute have sought to fill in the gaps with lengthy discussions of the feelings of Kazakhs and Uighurs on each side of the border. The 1962 incident touched off a major media "war," with both China and the Soviet Union increasing minority-language broadcasting to areas where transborder reception is possible. The Soviets were immeasurably aided in this by the reemergence in the Soviet Union of leading Kazakhs and Uighurs who had been imprisoned or purged by the Chinese government, many of them during the anti-rightist campaign. Just how they made their escape has never been made clear, but it is plain that they are of great value to the Soviet Union as propagandists.

Uighur, Kazakh, and Kirghiz programs beamed from Tashkent, Alma Ata, and Frunze were instituted in 1964 and expanded in 1967. Special correspondents from Tass, *Kazakhstanskaya pravda,* and others joined the refugee newscasters, who could truthfully claim to have seen both sides of the border. Much of the content of the programs seems to present a factually accurate description of the situation in Sinkiang, presumably in order to establish the credibility of the broadcasts. Other themes, however, include the material advantages possessed by Kazakhs, Uighurs, and others in the Soviet Union, the higher level of labor-saving technology available, and the greater cultural freedom and diversity allowed there. The broadcasts frequently hark back to the Ili revolt of 1944, the founding of the ETR, the historical independence of the Turkic Muslim peoples and their praiseworthy struggle to maintain this independence, the 1962 incident, and other items with similarly subversive content. Sympathy is expressed for those who are persecuted by the Chinese authorities for having relatives in the Soviet Union or who are suspected of pro-autonomy or pro-Soviet feelings.[51]

A few examples may serve to transmit the flavor of these broadcasts. Zunin Taipov, the former head of the ETR army referred to earlier, reported from his new home in Kazakhstan:

> . . . how many bitter stories have I heard from my fellow countrymen about those who have remained behind the cordon, who have not yet succeeded in returning home! . . . how bitter it is to realize that thousands of my brothers, Uighurs and Kazakhs, Kirghiz and Mongols, have remained there, beyond the barricade, and are being subjected today to incredible persecution and repression . . . Peking does not hide its intention of "Sinifying" Sinkiang.[52]

A correspondent for *Kazakhstanskaya pravda* added:

> It seems almost unbelievable that one is standing on the farthest limit of the motherland. The windows of the neat houses on the collective-farm village face through the poplars onto the empty village road, the wire fences and a narrow control strip. Just beyond it is the grassy bank of a small ordinary river . . . and yellow mountains rising like a wall. On their table-flat tops one sees bright patches of crops that have not been harvested.
>
> "They'll be there 'til the snow flies," the collective farm chairman said to me, pointing across to the other side. "Even if they are tiny plots, no one can do much by hand, with sicles and rollers. And especially this year."
>
> "Why?"
>
> "The Chinese authorities ordered all the Kazakhs and Uighurs out of our part of the border area into the interior of the country. Do you see that over there?"
>
> Yes, I did see the adobe ruins of some resettlement just to the right, at the foot of the mountains.
>
> Why, I wondered, did they have to chase from their native haunts hundreds of peaceful people—farmers and herdsmen—and destroy their houses?

"Why?" the chairman asked in astonishment. "They were afraid. They were beside themselves to show how badly the Kazakhs and the Uighurs were living here in the Soviet Union. And every day, from morning to night a showcase of life was visible over here. They could look and compare."

The borderland collective farm we were talking about is a middling one in the production administration, but it long ago finished grain mowing and it was now harvesting a rich corn crop. It was typical that all the field work here was mechanized. The output per corn-harvesting combine had reached record levels.

Naturally, our neighbors saw all this. They saw it and, of course, they made comparisons. Frankly, the comparisons were not flattering to the Chinese authorities. Just last year dozens of families—representatives of the so-called "national minorities"—fled across the border here into the Soviet Union. These people were wasted with hunger and were dressed and shod in all sorts of unthinkable rags and foot bindings. The Chinese border guards fired at them, but they kept on coming. Many of them are now working on the collective farm. From now on they will work not from fear but from conscience. They were given outright grants and helped to build houses.

I talked to some of these people. Among them were those with relatives and friends on the other side. For this reason alone I shall not give their names in this account. It is known that the Chinese authorities, extending their anti-Soviet campaign further and further, have, in their mad fury, undertaken to persecute the Kazakhs and Uighurs living in the Chinese People's Republic.

Obviously they put their prison camp on the border also for purposes of visual propaganda. From the pastures of the collective farm one could see with the naked eye little chained figures moving huge stones to clear a road into the mountains.

"My brother might be there," said an old shepherd peering out with eyes as sharp as an eagle's. For more than six months he had had no news from the other side. He had spent almost all his life in Western China . . . Was he in one of the people's communes? Yes, but just as before, he saw nothing but the tattered yurt and the herds of sheep. He had to tend a flock of 600 by himself. It was no easier for the peasants in the "commune." Just try living for a long time in a barracks where life is measured by the ringing of a gong, and where you march in ranks from field to field!

I looked at the shepherd in his fine fox-fur cloak and his sheepskin hat (it is now wintry cold high in the mountains) and I found myself thinking: "How many years did this man waste in vain? . . ."[53]

In the passages quoted above, as in many other Soviet propaganda releases, there is a clear implication that the minorities' sympathetic kin, backed by the Soviet government, are ready to welcome their Chinese relatives to the Soviet Union. A Western journalist who visited Alma Ata in 1976 noted the publication there of a thrice-weekly paper called *Yeni khayat* (new life), for the refugees. It employs Arabic script, since, its editor explained, Soviet authorities discovered that the refugees had difficulty adjusting to the Cyrillic-based script used by other Turkic-Muslim language newspapers published in the Soviet Union. It should be noted that the Soviet authorities probably had other reasons for not using the Latin-based alphabet that the Chinese introduced in 1960 after the break with the Soviet Union.

Yeni khayat's editor claimed that over 100,000 persons had crossed the border (Chinese sources say 60,000) and that they had been provided with food, clothing, and medical attention, and eventually settled on collective farms; most apparently have continued as sheep herders.[54] Seemingly to enhance the contrast between its picture of the cultural genocide of minorities in China and their happy life in the Soviet Union, the Russians have allocated funds to refurbish Islamic monuments, including Tamerlane's tomb,[55] and have published multivolume compendiums on Uighur, Kazakh, and other nationality heritages.

The Chinese Communists have countered by accusing the Soviet Union of being a "big prison for nationalities,"[56] of forcing the nationalities to learn Russian—this last juxtaposed with a quotation from Lenin on the advantages of linguistic diversity[57]—and of exploiting its nationality republics. Chinese analysts were delighted to note that while a 1974 edition of the book *Problems of the CPSU Economic Policy and Reclamation of Virgin Lands in Kazakhstan* quoted Communist party leader Leonid Brezhnev as saying, "We must spare no expenditure to carry out material encouragement, for such expenditure will bring returns a hundredfold," a 1976 reprint had deleted these words, thus showing the deliberately "exploitative nature of the Brezhnev government."[58]

Just how seriously each party takes the propaganda efforts of the other is unclear, though neither has exerted much effort to jam its antagonist's broadcasts. In 1964, Saifudin publicly accused the Soviet Union of using radio transmissions to "spread lies and slander attacking the leadership of the CCP and to distort the history of Sinkiang in an effort to undermine the unity of the Chinese people of all nationalities,"[59] thus seemingly being concerned enough to issue the statement.

In 1967, Ivan Spivanhov, deputy chief editor of *Kazakhstanskaya pravda,* was quoted as saying that Chinese broadcasts "beam in hot and strong" but that "few people take any notice. It is so rude and clumsy."[60] However, the efforts made to answer Chinese charges may indicate a somewhat less nonchalant attitude. China's claim to much of Soviet Central Asia on the ground that "many hundreds of years ago, Chinese troops came to these parts and the Chinese emperor once used to collect tribute from the local inhabitants" was termed

> . . . childish . . . one could say that England was French territory because it was once the domain of a Duke of Normandy, or that France is an English

> possession since during the Hundred Years' War it was almost completely conquered by England . . . or that the boundary of the CPR passes only along the line of the Great Wall, less than 100 kilometers from Peking: the boundary of China did once pass there, the wall being evidence of this.[61]

The Soviet Union also reacted sharply to evidences of collaboration between the CPR and Ukrainian separatists,[62] and answered Chinese charges that Kazakhstan was being exploited:

> . . . the republics are no longer divided into agrarian and industrial or raw-material and processing republics . . . The Party has consistently carried out Lenin's behest in the economic and cultural fields and in all spheres of social life; without this it would have been impossible to strengthen the mutual trust of the working people of all nationalities, to put an end to their alienation and to bring about unprecedented cohesion among the peoples of the USSR . . . this special feature of our Party's nationalities policy is reflected, in particular, in the Law on the USSR State Budget for 1972 . . . almost all the money from all-Union turnover tax receipts from the territory of [five] republics will be deducted into these republics' state budgets, while the Kazakh Republic's budget will receive 100% of these funds. In addition, Kazakhstan will receive a large subsidy from the Union budget—more than 456,000,000 rubles.[63]

Izvestia also announced plans to publish a ten-volume dictionary of the Kazakh language[64] and a multivolume Kazakh Soviet Encyclopedia.[65] There was renewed evidence in civil defense in Kazakhstan,[66] and Brezhnev personally made highly touted visits to the republic in 1970 and 1972.[67]

Chinese media have attempted to refute Soviet charges of cultural repression with lengthy articles discussing the exact numbers of pamphlets, books, and texts printed in Uighur, Kazakh, Mongolian, Kirghiz, and Sibo, "publication of which has had considerable use in developing the languages and literatures of the various nationalities, enriching their culture and accelerating the progress of the socialist revolution and reconstruction in Sinkiang."[68] A post-Cultural Revolution attempt to renew pressure on these minorities to use the Latin alphabet was carried out at the same time that many of China's non-Sinkiang minority groups were being urged to study Han;[69] apparently it was considered sufficient to separate Chinese Uighurs and Kazakhs from their Soviet counterparts on the basis of script.

The death of Mao's heir-apparent, Lin Piao, coincided with a further liberalizing of attitudes toward minorities. Uighurs and Kazakhs reportedly were adapting the new revolutionary operas introduced under the egis of Mao's wife to their own languages and art forms, and were receiving more consumer goods manufactured to the specifications of their customs and traditions.[70] A protégé of Lin Piao, who had become first party secretary of the SUAR after the Cultural Revolution, was removed from office and replaced by Saifudin; thus a minority group member was in charge of the SUAR for the first time since 1949. Other Uighurs and Kazakhs were given prestigious, although not necessarily influential, positions in government and party, and a campaign was begun to recruit more of them into leadership positions at lower levels of society.[71]

Chinese propaganda tended to treat the 1962 incident as instigated by the Soviet Union, and as constituting one more proof that the Russians were following in the footsteps of their czarist predecessors. The Soviet Union's explanation of the nineteenth-century territorial cessions was flatly rejected: the lands thus obtained should have been returned, presumably with their inhabitants. An NCNA report circulated in the capitals of several African states implied that the peoples of Soviet Central Asia desired to "enter into a close union with China."[72]

Thus, while the Soviet side has been less overtly fearful of the effect of Chinese propaganda than the Chinese have seemed of Soviet propaganda, both parties have attempted to answer each other's charges, and have accompanied these refutations by actions significantly liberalizing policies toward minorities.

Nonetheless, neither side remains certain of the loyalties of its minorities. Within a few years of one another, two books were published in the Soviet Union to disprove "falsifiers of history who claimed that Soviet rule was established artificially and against the wishes of the population of Central Asia and Kazakhstan."[73] At approximately the same time, a Soviet journal commented that although

> . . . there is no socio-economic basis in the USSR for nationalistic ideology . . . survivals of nationalism and chauvinism still persist in the minds of some people. They are viable and are often combined with religious survivals and, "what is particularly dangerous, are capable of reviving relatively rapidly under certain conditions." Difficulties in inter-national relations are encountered where there were violations of the national policy under the Stalin personality cult . . . nationalistically minded and religious elements are speculating on the mistakes of the past and trying to kindle nationalist dissension and spread national mistrust.[74]

A few years later, several Kirghiz scholars were severely criticized for various "errors," including the assertion that even if a nationality's demands for separation and political self-determination conflict with the interests of the nation, no one has a right to intervene forcibly in the nation's internal life and "correct" its errors. Another view that was officially declared mistaken was historians' treatment of attempts in the 1920s to establish a separate Mountain

Province in the Turkestan Autonomous Republic as the desire of the Kirghiz people to set up an independent state.

> Everyone knows that this proposal was advanced by bourgeois nationalists, in opposition to the fundamental interests of the Kirghiz people. The proposal was rejected by the Bolshevik Party and its proponents were removed from their posts and expelled from the Party.[75]

In China, the media show almost frenetic joy at each new archaeological find in Sinkiang that links that province with China proper. A rally is held, with banners and headlines proclaiming, for example, that "T'ang [Dynasty] Relics Prove Sinkiang Historically Part of China." Rally leaders dutifully reiterate the most recent twist in the party line, and explain that these latest discoveries will give the lie to nationalistically minded internal "splittists" and to the Soviet revisionists who wish to separate Sinkiang from the ancestral land.[76]

The group accompanying James Schlesinger to China recently has testified to their Chinese hosts' extreme nervousness while guiding the American guests through Sinkiang. In a newspaper account admittedly modified for diplomatic reasons, one of them writes:

> A Caucasian waiter in Sinkiang . . . reacts stiffly to a Chinese "hsieh-hsieh" and warmly to an English "thank you." . . . Or take the crowds in Ining, less than 50 miles from the Soviet border. As our caravan goes from stop to stop, the crowds on the streets grow, until at last the local citizens virtually climb into the cars. The crowds are nearly all Kazakh and Uighur, though the town is supposed to be half Chinese. They break into almost joyous applause at every wave. Our hosts from Peking grow testier than at any other point in the trip. A few nights later they are relaxed in their reaction to a large crowd in Huhehot. In the second crowd, the faces were yellow and the mood merely curious. In the first, the mood stirred by American faces was implicitly anti-Chinese.[77]

A West German magazine has published the story of two recent refugees from China to the Soviet Union, one a Kazakh and the other a Kirghiz. On apprehension, both had been placed in a Soviet prison where a fellow prisoner, an ethnic Russian hostile to the Soviet government and familiar with the cruelties of the Gulag Archipelago, was amazed to learn that they were happy with their new lot. He quoted one as saying, "I have a bunk, a light bulb in the cell, we get food every day, even fish. What else do I need?"[78] Members of the Schlesinger party have confided that their Chinese hosts seemed taken aback by the relatively low standards of living in Sinkiang, speculating that the Chinese guides were shocked by the discrepancy between reality and what their own propaganda had led them to believe.[79]

CONCLUSIONS

It has been seen that the principal factors in the internationalization of the Kazakh question were the hostilities between the two host countries and the deteriorating economic conditions in China during the late 1950s and early 1960s. The many references in Chinese media to the existence of local nationalism throughout the 1950s make it clear that Kazakh and Uighur dissatisfaction with Chinese Communist rule existed prior to the catalyzing incident of May 1962, but that the appearance of Sino-Soviet friendship muted the public manifestation of these dissatisfactions.

The exact nature of Kazakh and Uighur demands on the Chinese government has never been made clear. There are references to separatism, implying an independent Sinkiang; to joining with other Turkic Muslims (some of whom undoubtedly would come from Soviet Kazakhstan) in a larger separate state; and to demands for the greater autonomy of Sinkiang within the Chinese state, some of them including demands that the Han Chinese leave Sinkiang and others simply asking that they relinquish their commanding positions in the province's economic and administrative infrastructure.

Whether or not Soviet intrigues were behind the May 1962 incident, as the Chinese charge, the Soviets hastened to make use of Kazakh and Uighur dissatisfaction thereafter. Championing the cause of China's Turkic Muslim peoples, they sought to contrast the economic hardship and cultural repression on the Chinese side of the border with the much better situation on the Soviet side. The Soviet Kazakhs and other Central Asian minorities seem to have profited as a result, being granted various cultural and material benefits in an effort to provide suitable anti-Chinese propaganda. In that the Chinese have perceived it necessary to refute Soviet charges, Chinese Kazakhs and Uighurs have benefited as well. Compilations have been made of folksongs. Resources have been transferred to Sinkiang via a preferential revenue redistribution plan that has returned more money to the province than is collected there, thus allowing the construction of mining and other industries and helping to raise living standards. There has been an increase in the number of Uighurs and Kazakhs in leadership positions in the SUAR.

While Chinese and Soviet Kazakhs and Uighurs have gained leverage over their respective governments as a result of the Sino-Soviet situation, there are limits to how far either government can be manipulated. Past experience has shown that overzealous catering to minority cultures simply reinforces the continued perception of ethnic separatism and prevents the drawing together of its peoples that each of the countries desires. Moreover, the granting of more autonomy may lead to subsequent demands for separatism. In addition, the more liberal policies of China and the Soviet Union doubtless are looked upon with justifiable skepticism by minorities on both sides of the border. In some instances, the liberality of a pronouncement may be tempered by other words spoken in a different context; in other instances, the policies are known to be subject to rapid reversal. For example, Leonid Brezhnev, on presenting the Order of Friendship of Peoples to Kazakhstan, might say:

> In speaking about the new historic community of peoples, we certainly do not mean that national differences are already disappearing in our country or, all the more, that a merging of nations has taken place. All nations and nationalities populating the Soviet Union retain their features, national character traits, language and their best traditions.[80]

Yet one must understand this in the context of other statements, such as the following:

> The peoples of the Caucasus had a custom in ancient times: The warriors mixed drops of their blood in a common bowl and were bound together forever by ties of brotherhood, honor and glory. The Union of Soviet Socialist Republics became this blood brotherhood for us, a brotherhood of peoples. Since then, this brotherhood has become our sun.
>
> Cherish the sun, people![81]

And Chinese minorities have become familiar with "soft line" policies toward the retention of their customs and languages that change virtually overnight with the launching of new mass campaigns or shifts in leadership, as occurred during the Great Leap Forward and Cultural Revolution.[82]

Given the higher degree of ideological orthodoxy demanded, and lower living standards prevailing on the Chinese side, the Soviet Union would probably enjoy an advantage in any contest between the two states for the loyalties of the Central Asian peoples. Still, for reasons discussed earlier, the Soviet Union cannot be fully certain of the loyalties of its own minorities. This, plus recent Chinese efforts to raise living standards in Sinkiang, to co-opt more Uighurs and Kazakhs into the province's elite, and to relax some of the more culturally repressive aspects of the past, make it unlikely that the Soviet Union will decide to employ the incitement of China's Kazakhs and Uighurs in any large-scale way. Anti-Chinese propaganda and infiltration directed toward Sinkiang probably will continue on a small scale, in an attempt to impress the Chinese with the potentially damaging effects of a larger-scale effort. The probability that the Soviet Union does not intend to support Chinese Kazakh separatism or autonomy in any meaningful way, when added to the ever-larger Han Chinese presence in Sinkiang—and Russian presence in Kazakhstan—makes it highly unlikely that those Turkic Muslims in Central Asia who desire a separate state will ever see their wish fulfilled. The most feasible scenario for the creation of such a state would entail a major destabilization of the present equilibrium on the border, such as a Sino-Soviet war. This possibility has already occurred to at least one Soviet citizen. The dissident Russian intellectual Andrei Amalrik has written:

> Simultaneously [with the Russian middle class becoming increasingly anti-Soviet government and extremist organizations playing a greater role] the nationalist tendencies of the non-Russian peoples of the USSR will intensify sharply, first in the Baltic area and along the Volga.
>
> In many cases, party officials among the various nationalities may become proponents of such tendencies and their reasoning will be "Let Russian Ivan solve his own problems." They will aim for national separatism for still another reason: if they fend off the growing general chaos, they will be able to preserve their own privileged positions.[83]

Amalrik's vision is apocalyptic and does not discuss what might be the outcome of such a situation. Recently he has revised his timetable, and does not envision the dismemberment of the Soviet Union by his original target date of 1984.[84] Moreover, his hostility toward the Soviet Union may lead him to overstate its weaknesses. Given the unlikely eventuality of a Sino-Soviet war and the resurfacing of autonomy demands, there is a high probability that the Soviet Union would win and, as part of the settlement, might detach Sinkiang from China and establish it as an autonomous state, albeit one highly dependent on the Soviet Union for its existence. At first glance, given the Soviet Union's not wholly successful record of relations with its own Central Asian minorities, the effort might not seem worth the potential gains. On the other hand, the example of the Mongolian People's Republic (MPR) may indicate that the venture is indeed worthwhile.* The MPR is, and Sinkiang could be, a buffer state between the Soviet Union and China. The MPR is rich in minerals and has been usefully integrated into the Soviet economy; Sinkiang could be as well. Moreover, though Mongolians would probably, under other circumstances, wish a higher degree of international maneuverability, their actions indicate their strong preference for an independence circumscribed by the Soviet Union to the risk of inclusion within the Chinese state. Thus, there are very real prospects for gain for the Soviet Union in such a situation. This

---

*Outer Mongolia had a very small proportion of Han Chinese residents in 1911, when it severed its relationship with China. This is one aspect in which its position is quite different from that of Sinkiang now. The Chinese government has been reticent in giving an exact nationality breakdown of the population of Sinkiang, but Soviet sources estimated that the Han proportion had increased from 3 percent in 1949 to almost 45 percent in 1966. See T. Rakhimov, "The Great-Power Policy of Mao Tse-tung and His Group on the Nationalities Question," *Kommunist* no. 7 (May 1967): 114–19; *CDSP* 19 (June 7, 1967): 3–4. Given the large-scale population transfers into Sinkiang since the Cultural Revolution, the 45 percent figure, which I consider plausible, would be significantly higher now, perhaps by as much as 10 percent.

scenario of a Sinkiang detached from China and dependent on the Soviet Union is the most feasible in the context of a general Sino-Soviet war; as an independent policy goal, the gains to the Soviet Union would not seem worth the efforts involved.

Chinese foreign policymakers have shown themselves to be highly skilled and fully cognizant of the realities of, and limitations on, Chinese power. The existence of the MPR is a constant reminder of what may happen in Sinkiang. It is therefore probable that the Chinese will do their utmost to prevent an escalation of Sino-Soviet violence. The influx of Han to Sinkiang, and specifically to the border areas, including Ili, probably will continue to the extent that the local economy can absorb the immigrants. Sinkiang's minorities will be treated in such a way as to diffuse resentments through the granting of some privileges while not courting the minorities to such a degree that further demands for separatism will be encouraged.

The Sino-Soviet conflict is potentially so serious that both parties have been wary of sparking a confrontation. Thus, at least some of the hesitancy displayed by both sides on the specific issue of the Kazakhs is explainable: the risks are so great that they induce restraints on the governments involved. The resulting low intensity of the Kazakhs' conflicts with their respective governments is difficult for an outside power to take advantage of: there is no general chaos to exploit, dissident army to support, or large-scale genocide to denounce.

The best-laid plans of government policymakers have gone astray before, and it is not beyond the realm of possibility that this may happen again. History is replete with instances in which a relatively minor incident occurring in a context of tension and hostility touched off an "accidental" war. A Sino-Soviet armed struggle is but one of several possible scenarios that might rekindle hopes for separatism in Sinkiang and/or Kazakhstan. It is conceivable, for example, that such a minority uprising might occur independent of any impetus from Peking or Moscow. Here the social mobilization phenomenon may be of crucial importance. In destroying the traditionally loose-knit kinship groups of the Central Asian peoples and in giving them a common written language, making them literate, and drawing them into factories and mass organizations, the Chinese and Soviet governments may inadvertently be creating the preconditions for large-scale, well-organized resistance to their respective rules, rather than the small-scale and loosely organized hostilities they have successfully handled so far.

It is difficult to tell how much genuine feeling Chinese Kazakhs and Uighurs have for their kinfolk across the border, and vice versa; but the constant propaganda of both sides, particularly that of the Soviet Union, that they are indeed one people would surely reinforce such feelings as do exist, and may even create them where they do not exist. This may spark desires for irredentism that operate independently of official Chinese or Soviet wishes.

At present, however, these possibilities remain remote and the outlook seems to portend a continuation of low-level resistance that may occasionally be exacerbated by local economic shortages or a misguided or misinterpreted order from Peking or Moscow. There seems little probability of either an escalation or a solution to the Kazakh question.

NOTES

1. *Peking Review (PR)* 19 (May 28, 1976): 28. Other Chinese population figures are, unless otherwise specified, drawn from John S. Aird, *Population Estimates for the Provinces of the People's Republic of China: 1953 to 1974* (International Population Reports, Series P-95, no. 73, Washington, D.C.: U.S. Department of Commerce, 1974). Soviet population data are, unless otherwise specified, drawn from the 1970 census, as reported in *Current Digest of the Soviet Press (CDSP)* 23 (May 18, 1971): 14–18.

2. Elizabeth E. Bacon, *Central Asians Under Russian Rule* (Ithaca; N.Y.: Cornell University Press, 1966), pp. 27, 47–48.

3. Lawrence Krader, *Peoples of Central Asia* (Bloomington: Indiana University Press, 1963), p. 193. Also see Alfred E. Hudson, *Kazakh Social Structure,* (New Haven, Conn.: Yale University Publications in Anthropology, no. 20, 1938). Repr. New York: Human Relations Area Files Press, 1964.

4. W. A. Douglas Jackson, *The Russo-Chinese Borderlands* (Princeton: Princeton University Press, 1962), pp. 112–113, 116.

5. George J. Demko, *The Russian Colonization of Kazakhstan, 1896–1916* (Bloomington: Indiana University Press, 1969), pp. 121–22.

6. Yuan Tsing, "Yakub Beg and the Moslem Rebellion in Chinese Turkestan," *Central Asiatic Journal* 6 (June 1961): 154.

7. Immanuel C. Y. Hsu, *The Ili Crisis: A Study of Sino-Russian Diplomacy 1871–1881* (Oxford: Clarendon Press, 1965), pp. 186–87.

8. Demko, op. cit., p. 182.

9. Bacon, op. cit., pp. 116–117. Also see Richard Pipes, *The Formation of the Soviet Union* (Cambridge, Mass.: Harvard University Press, 1964), p. 83.

10. Pipes, op. cit., pp. 108, 172–173.

11. Bacon, op. cit., p. 117.

12. Pipes, op. cit., p. 174.

13. Bacon, op. cit., p. 114.

14. Ibid., p. 118.

15. Pipes, op. cit., p. 191.

16. Ann Sheehy, "The Central Asian Republics," *Conflict Studies* 30 (Dec. 1972): 13–27.

17. Bacon, op. cit., pp. 119–20.

18. Brian Silver, "Social Mobilization and the Russification of Soviet Nationalities," *American Political Science Review* 68 (Mar. 1974): 63.

19. *CDSP* 23 (May 18, 1971): 16.

20. Silver, op. cit., p. 62.

21. David C. Montgomery, "An American Student in Tashkent," *Asian Affairs* 59 (February 1972): 37.

22. Rein Taagepera, "National Differences Within Soviet Demographic Trends," *Soviet Studies* (Glasgow) 20 (Apr. 1969): 478, 481, 489.

23. Andrei Sakharov, *Sakharov Speaks* (New York: Alfred Knopf, 1974), p. 43.

24. Allen S. Whiting and Sheng Shih-ts'ai, *Sinkiang: Pawn or Pivot?* (East Lansing: Michigan State University Press, 1958), p. 54.

25. Excellent accounts of this period may be found in ibid. and in Owen Lattimore, *Pivot of Asia* (Boston: Little, Brown, 1950).

26. *New York Times (NYT)* Feb. 1, 1949, p. 1; Feb. 2, 1949, p. 18; Feb. 6, 1949, Sec. 4, p. 1; Mar. 22, 1949, p. 22.

27. Whiting and Sheng, op. cit., pp. 142–43.

28. Ibid., p. 86.

29. K. F. Kotov, *Autonomy of Local Nationalities in the Chinese People's Republic* (Moscow: State Publishing House, 1956), trans. in U.S. Department of Commerce, Joint Publications Research Service (JPRS) 3547: 56.

30. New China News Agency (NCNA), Lanchow, May 6, 1954, quoted in Whiting and Sheng, op. cit., p. 144.

31. See, Kotov, op. cit.; and S. I. Bruk, "Ethnic Composition and Distribution of the Population in the Sinkiang-Uighur Autonomous Region of the People's Republic of China," *Sovetskaya etnografiya* 2 (1956), trans. in JPRS 16,030: 27–56.

32. Whiting and Sheng, op. cit., p. 168.

33. Bruk, op. cit., p. 16.

34. Saifudin, speech to the Party Committee of the SUAR on Dec. 16, 1957, Peking Radio, Dec. 25, 1957.

35. Li Hui-yu, "The Ili Autonomous Chou Has Very Extensive Powers; Why Do the Local Nationalists Say It Has No Powers?" *Ili jih-pao,* Aug. 30, 1958, quoted in George Moseley, *A Sino-Soviet Cultural Frontier: The Ili Kazakh Autonomous Chou* (Cambridge; Mass.: East Asian Research Center, Harvard University, 1966), p. 68.

36. See Moseley, op. cit., pp. 107–10.

37. "China Said to Send Troops to Sinkiang" *NYT,* Apr. 16, 1964, p. 6, quoting a White Russian refugee interviewed in Hong Kong; Moseley, op. cit., p. 108.

38. Chou En-lai, "Report on the Work of the Government," speech to first session of third National People's Congress, Dec. 30, 1964, trans. in U.S. Consulate General, Hong Kong, *Survey of the China Mainland Press (SCMP)* 3370 (Jan. 5, 1965): 12.

39. Zunin Taipov, "Eyewitness Account: On the Other Side of the Barricade," *Kazakhstanskaya pravda (KP),* Sept. 29, 1963, p. 4; *CDSP* 15 (Oct. 16, 1963): 16. Also see A. Mirov, "Sinkiang Tragedy," *Literaturnaya gazeta,* May 7, 1969, in *CDSP* 21 (May 28, 1969): 5–6.

40. See "The Chinese Ministry of Foreign Affairs Protest to the Soviet Union," NCNA, Sept. 17, 1968; and the Soviet Union's reply, "Provocative Fabrication of the CPR Ministry of Foreign Affairs," *Izvestia,* Nov. 2, 1968; *CDSP* 20 (Nov. 13, 1968): 42.

41. *PR* 12 (Aug. 15, 1969): 3.

42. S. Borzenko et al., "On Stony Hill," *Pravda,* Aug. 16, 1969, p. 6; *CDSP* 21 (Sept. 10, 1969): 4.

43. Published in both *Pravda* and *Izvestia,* Sept. 11, 1969; *CDSP* 21 (Oct. 8, 1969): 9.

44. Roger Glenn Brown, "Chinese Politics and American Foreign Policy," *Foreign Policy* 23 (Summer 1976): 3–23.

45. Text of note in *Pravda,* Mar. 21, 1974, p. 9; *CDSP* 26 (April 17, 1974): 4.

46. NCNA (Peking), Mar. 23, 1974; *SCMP* 5585 (Apr. 12, 1974): 66.

47. See Urumchi Radio (Sinkiang), Mar. 28, 1974, in *Foreign Broadcast Information Service, China, (FBIS-CHI)* 62 (1974): A1-A3.

48. Tass, Dec. 27, 1976; *CDSP* 27 (Jan. 28, 1976): 14

49. Peking Radio, Oct. 1, 1974; *FBIS-CHI* 192 (1974): D6, and 201 (1974): A4.

50. "That's How It Is on the Border," *Pravda,* Mar. 12, 1969, p. 6; *CDSP* 21 (April 2, 1969): 3. This particular incident occurred on the Ussuri border, between northeastern China and southeastern Soviet Union. It has been included because, save for the participants being fisherfolk

(whereas on the Sinkiang/Kazakhstan border they are typically sheepherders), it represents a composite picture of elements reported in similar confrontations there.

51. Gretchen S. Brainerd, "Soviets Intensify Propaganda to Moslem Nationalities in China," Radio Liberty dispatch (Munich), Feb. 14, 1972, pp. 1–4.

52. Taipov, op. cit.; *CDSP* 21 (May 28, 1969): 5.

53. O. Matskevich, "Along the Border," *KP,* Sept. 24, 1963, p. 3; *CDSP* 15 (Oct. 16, 1963): 17–18.

54. Christopher S. Wren, "Kazakhstan Beckons Refugees from China," *NYT,* Apr. 24, 1976, p. 8.

55. Hedrick Smith, "Tamerlane Stirs Soviet Controversy," ibid., June 2, 1974, p. 2.

56. "Soviet People's Struggle Against New Tsars," *PR* 19 (Nov. 12, 1976): 21–22.

57. "Analysis of Soviet Revisionists' Policy of 'National Rapprochement,' " ibid. 17 (July 19, 1974): 18–20.

58. "Soviet Social Imperialism Pursues a Policy of National Oppression," ibid. 19 (May 28, 1976): 19–23.

59. NCNA (Urumchi), Apr. 28, 1964.

60. Brainerd, op. cit., p. 2.

61. *Pravda,* Sept. 2, 1964; *CDSP* 16 (Sept. 16, 1964): 4–5.

62. M. Panchuk, "The Chinese Splitters and the Ukrainian Nationalists," *Rabochaya gazeta,* Feb. 27, 1972; *CDSP* 24 (Mar. 22, 1972): 13–14. For a representative sample of Chinese propaganda in favor of the Ukrainian nationalists, see NCNA (Peking), Oct. 15, 1974; *FBIS-CHI* 201 (74): A1.

63. E. Bagramov, "The Drawing Together of Nationalities Is a Law of Communist Construction," *Pravda,* June 22, 1972; *CDSP* 24 (July 17, 1972): 10–11.

64. *Izvestia,* Nov. 23, 1972, p. 5; *CDSP* 24 (Dec. 20, 1972): 23.

65. *Izvestia,* May 12, 1972; *CDSP* 24 (June 7, 1972): 26. The effect of showing the Soviet Union's encouragement of nationality cultures may have been somewhat diluted by the newspaper's observation that the encyclopedia's first entry was that of Abas, "the great Kazakh poet and educator, whose ardent dream was to educate his people and bring them closer to Russian culture."

66. V. Titov, "Our Common Duty," *Pravda,* Aug. 14, 1972; *CDSP* 21 (Sept. 10, 1972): 6–7.

67. See *CDSP* 22 (Sept. 29, 1970): 1–8, and 24 (Sept. 27, 1972): 6–7, for accounts of Brezhnev's visits.

68. *Kuang-ming jih-pao,* Oct. 23, 1963; JPRS 22,246: 91–95.

69. Contrast *Jen-min jih-pao,* Aug. 22, 1971, with Urumchi Radio, Dec. 10, 1970.

70. Urumchi Radio, Oct. 9, 1974.

71. NCNA (Urumchi), May 17, 1972; *SCMP* 5143 (May 30, 1972): 22–23.

72. Tass, Apr. 21, 1969; *CDSP* 21 (Sept. 17, 1969): 17. Tass's evident anger at this, plus Russian fears of the potentially subversive effects of such statements, make it unlikely that the NCNA report was a Soviet fabrication. However, information available to the author indicates that the report may well have been fabricated by U.S. intelligence sources.

73. Khamid Inoyatov, *Central Asia and Kazakhstan Before and After the October Revolution,* trans. D. Fidlon (Moscow: Progress Publishers, 1966); and I. I. Mints, *The Triumph of Soviet Rule in Central Asia and Kazakhstan* (Tashkent: USSR Academy of Sciences Branch Publishing House, 1967). The latter was reviewed in *Pravda,* Nov. 22, 1967, p. 3; *CDSP* 19 (Dec. 13, 1967): 22.

74. L. M. Drobizheva, "On the Social Homogeneity of the Republics and the Development of National Relations in the USSR," *Istoria SSR* no. 1 (Jan. 1967); *CDSP* 19 (May 24, 1967): 28–29.

75. D. Malabayev and M. Dzhanuzakov, "Protect and Strengthen Our Great Fraternity," *Sovetskaya Kirghizia,* Dec. 7, 1972, p. 3; *CDSP* 25 (Apr. 18, 1973): 17.

76. Urumchi Radio, Mar. 16, 1975; *FBIS-CHI* 54 (1975): E5.

77. Robert L. Bartley, "In China, Trust What You Feel," *Wall Street Journal,* Oct. 1, 1976, p. 10.

78. A. Uchitel, "Escape to an Adjacent Cell," *Possev* 2 (Feb. 1976), in *Freedom at Issue* (Sept.-Oct. 1976): 10.

79. Information made available to the author on a private basis.

80. Quoted in E. Tadevosyan, "A State Based on the Friendship of Peoples," *Izvestia,* Jan. 23, 1974, p. 3; *CDSP* 26 (Feb. 20, 1974): 28.

81. Leonid Gurunts, "Cherish the Sun, People," *Pravda,* May 3, 1968, p. 3; *CDSP* 20 (May 22, 1968): 23.

82. See June Teufel Dreyer, *China's Forty Millions* (Cambridge, Mass.: Harvard University Press, 1976), for an examination of the shifts in policies toward minorities under the PRC.

83. Andrei Amalrik, *Will the Soviet Union Survive Until 1984?* (New York: Harper and Row, 1970), p. 63.

84. Raymond H. Anderson, "Author Sees Soviet Lasting Beyond '84," *NYT,* Dec. 12, 1976, p. 8.

CHAPTER

8

MUSLIMS IN THE PHILIPPINES AND THAILAND

Astri Suhrke
Lela Garner Noble

Muslims in the southern Philippines and in southern Thailand are clearly distinguished minorities in those countries. In both cases their numbers are comparatively small—5 percent of the population in the Philippines and 3 percent in Thailand—and in both cases they inhabit regions remote from the national capital and adjacent to Malaysia. Finally, the Muslim communities in both countries have given rise to movements that have resorted to violence in attempts to create independent or autonomous political structures of their own.

Differences between the two minority groups are as obvious as their similarities. The ethnic identity of Muslims in the Philippines is based on religion; other characteristics distinguishing them from the Christian majority are derived primarily from the religious factor. Internally, Filipino Muslims are divided into 13 subgoups, characterized generally by different languages and customs. Muslims in southern Thailand share a broader range of ethnic characteristics and distinguish themselves from Muslims in other parts of the country, notably those in or near Bangkok, who present no political problem as a minority group.*

In terms of total numbers, Filipino Muslims are a much larger group than those in southern Thailand. Estimates of Filipino Muslims range from a claim of 5 million by militant Muslims to slightly over 1.5 million, the figure cited in the government's census figures for 1970. If 2.2 million is taken as a reason-

---

*We will discuss only the Muslims in southern Thailand. For the sake of brevity, they will be referred to throughout as "southern Muslims" or "Thai Muslims." These terms are not used by the minority, but are also used to refer to Malay Muslims in Malaysia. "Pattani Muslim" is occasionally used, but may be misleading, because Pattani today is only one of the provinces inhabited by the southern Muslims. "Pattani" is a transliteration from Thai; "Patani" is the Malay version.

able compromise, the Philippine Muslims would outnumber the southern Thai Muslims by about three to one (the Thai 1960 census estimates 700,000 Muslims in the south).[1] The Philippine Muslims, moreover, identify with a much greater territory than they in fact dominate. They claim Mindanao, the Sulu Archipelago, and Palawan as their "homeland" and perceive it as the "heartland" of the pre-Hispanic island grouping, yet they constitute a majority of the population in only five of the 21 provinces in the area. One estimate cites figures of 14 million for the total population in the area claimed as Muslim "homeland": 10 million Christians, 2 million Muslims, and 2 million people identified with neither religion. In southern Thailand, by contrast, the Muslims are concentrated in four provinces (Pattani, Narathiwas, Yala, and Satul) where they represent 70–80 percent of the local population. Generally, demands for autonomy and separatism have covered only these four provinces, although occasionally they have included the predominantly Thai Buddhist province of Songkhla in order to prevent the isolation of Satul.

The separatist movement in the Philippines has been more extensive in its organization and operations than its equivalent(s) in Thailand, and markedly more successful in gaining external support. Consequently, the extent of devastation from the fighting has been much greater in the Philippines than in Thailand. Success, however, has been equally elusive.

THE PHILIPPINES

Internal Dimensions

The nature of Muslim identity in the Philippines is suggested by a declaration drafted by Muslim leaders in 1935 for submission to the U.S. government:

> . . . we want to tell you that the Philippines as it is known to the American people is populated by two different peoples with different religions, practices and traditions. The Christian Filipinos occupy the islands of Luzon and the Visayas. The Moros predominate in the islands of Mindanao and Sulu. . . .
>
> [F]rom time immemorial these two peoples have not lived harmoniously. . . . Should the American people grant the Philippines an independence, the islands of Mindanao and Sulu should not be included in such independence. . . . Our public land must not be given to people other than the Moros. . . . Our practices, laws and the decisions of our Moro leaders should be respected. . . . Our religion should not be curtailed in any way. All our practices which are incidents to our religion of Islam should be respected because these things are what a Muslim desires to live for. . . . Once our religion is no more, our lives are no more.[2]

That this statement has been quoted by both Muslim separatists and loyalists in recent years suggests that it reflects widely shared and enduring perceptions:

Muslims see religion as basic to their identity and as clearly distinguishing them from Christian "Filipinos," whose domination they fear.[3]

Islam came to the islands in the fourteenth century; and by the time the Spaniards arrived in the sixteenth century, it had affected socioeconomic and political structures in the southern islands and was spreading northward. Because the Muslim sultanates in the south were better organized than the more localized structures in the north, the Muslims were successful in staving off Spanish conquest and, hence, Christianization. For religious, economic, and political reasons, however, the Spaniards persisted in their effort to subjugate the sultanates and co-opted their Filipino converts into the battle. When the Muslims retaliated, the Spaniards branded them as "pirates" and propagandized an image of "Moros" that still persists.

The centuries of warfare took their toll on Muslim society, diverting it from its natural patterns of development and draining it of resources. Because of this war-induced weakness and their own superior military strength, the Americans succeeded in doing what the Spaniards had never done: consolidating control over the Muslim region and integrating it into the governmental system of the Philippines. Economically, Muslims lagged behind the Christian Filipinos, and their fears of Christianization led to many to isolationist policies that only increased their feelings of comparative disadvantages and vulnerability. Actions of the independent Philippine government corroborated Muslim fears. Muslims were granted exemptions from Philippine law having to do with marriage and divorce, but the exemptions were deliberately legislated as temporary. Christians dominated the national government and nonelected offices in Muslim areas, and the government encouraged Christian migration into Mindanao. Because much of the land Muslims considered to be theirs was held in accordance with their own rather than Philippine legal concepts of landholding, Christians frequently succeeded in getting title to land claimed by Muslims, who were then left with the options of fighting or capitulating. If they fought, they confronted not only Christian settlers but also the predominantly Christian Philippine Constabulary.

Because of this historical context, in the Muslim view being Muslim meant not only having in common religion and, because of the nature of Islam, a set of norms regulating personal and political life and a notion of the nature of community. Being Muslim also meant having an identification with territory, a memory of past glories, a consciousness of present deprivation and powerlessness, and—for many—a feeling of being continuously under siege.

Being Muslim, however, related only to one level of consciousness and to particular contexts. Muslims spoke a variety of languages; and language differences generally were reinforced by differences in territorial identifications, economic activities, social and political structures, art forms, and hierachies of values. In contexts where Muslims were dominant and communication was limited, these sociolinguistic groupings—and the smaller clan structures that existed within them—were most significant as a basis for identification. When there was contact among various groups of Muslims, the differences frequently provided the bases for group stereotyping, friction, and rivalry.

Among Muslims educated in the Philippines, a sense of being Filipino frequently coexisted with a sense of being Muslim. The coexistence was particularly obvious among Muslim politicians, who used Muslim clans, symbols, and practices to build bases allowing them to participate in the benefit network that was the essence of Philippine politics before 1972, and who identified each other as Liberals or Nacionalistas rather than Muslims. Since the benefit network extended to followers, other Muslims tended to regard Manila as a distribution center, a perception they had in common with non-Muslim Filipinos at least during election campaigns.[4]

There was, however, a series of developments in the 1950s and 1960s that tended to make Muslims more conscious of their Muslim identity, to increase their expectations, and to lead many to believe that they were incapable of fulfilling these expectations within the context of the Philippine political system. A resurgence of Islam and concomitant politicization, together with accelerated Christian migration, increased Muslim consciousness. Muslims expected to participate in the benefits of the Philippine system and to do so as Muslims. Many of those trained in the Middle East explicitly identified themselves with the world of Islam, and were aware that many of their coreligionists exercised significant power elsewhere. Motivated by Islamic ideas of justice and equality, they became committed to change in the structures of Muslim society in the Philippines as well as in relation to Christian society. Others moved from initial politicization through radical or reformist student organizations in the Philippines to an explicitly Islamic ideology.*

But while consciousness and expectations increased, shifts in the population balance in many areas of Mindanao resulted in the reduction of Muslim political representation. This, in addition to the growing bankruptcy of the Philippine political system and the closure of political bargaining with the imposition of martial law, indicated diminishing Muslim political capabilities within the system.† At the same time, Muslims were developing other kinds

---

*Nur Misuari, chairman of the MNLF's central committee, was originally a member of the Kabataang Makabayan, the student group linked with the Maoist New People's Army, but broke with it because he felt it disregarded Muslim interests. Interviews with other MNLF members suggest that his experience was not atypical.

†It was significant that when the level of fighting increased drastically in 1970 and 1971, the areas most affected were those in which politicians were challenged by Christians who had Christian majorities at least potentially behind them. For descriptions of the effects of the election campaigns and Marcos' declaration of martial law, see Lela G. Noble, "The Moro National Liberation Front," *Pacific Affairs* 49 (Fall 1976): 405–24; and Robert D. McAmis, "Muslim Filipinos: 1970–72," in Peter Gowing and Robert McAmis, eds., *The Muslim Filipinos* (Manila: Solidaridad, 1974), pp. 42–57.

of capabilities. Muslim organizations had proliferated. At least one, the core of what was later identified as the Moro National Liberation Front (MNLF), was developing a fairly cohesive structure and ideology and connections with Muslims outside the Philippines who were willing to provide training, weapons, sanctuary, money, sympathy, and/or pressure against the Philippine government. It had a new kind of leadership, generally educated in universities in the Philippines or the Middle East; self-consciously Muslim rather than Maranao, Tausug, or Maguindanao; and committed to change in the distribution of wealth and power.

Because of this new pattern of capabilities, the MNLF quickly became the dominant Muslim organization when local fighting between Muslims and Christians escalated into a full-scale war between Muslim groups and the "Christian" government after the declaration of martial law in 1972. The MNLF's leadership was able to articulate Muslim grievances to Muslims inside and outside the Philippines, to mobilize Muslim discontent, and to sustain fighting capacity despite a major buildup and deployment of government forces.* Thus by 1973, at the height of its power, the MNLF had 15,000–20,000 armed men associated with it and a solid base of support in Muslim communities in the southern Philippines.

External Factors

Inside the Philippines, Islam provided a basis that circumstances developed into ethnic identity, politicized ethnic discontent, and a separatist movement. Outside the Philippines, Islam created linkages with Muslim political communities. External factors were significant in increasing Muslim self-consciousness and self-confidence, and in subsidizing a greater scale of fighting than would have been possible without outside assistance. Equally or perhaps more important, external factors were significant in limiting the goals and tactics of both separatists and the Marcos government, and in facilitating peace negotiations.

Consciousness-Raising

In the 1950s Islamic teachers from several Muslim countries—particularly Egypt, Pakistan, and Indonesia—began coming to the southern Philip-

---

*There were, however, limits on the MNLF's capacity for mobilization. Many Muslims fighting remained unaffiliated with the MNLF. See Lela G. Noble, "The Moro National Liberation Front," *Pacific Affairs* 49 (Fall 1976): 405–24.

pines. Their activities were directed primarily at reforming Philippine Islam, but they also encouraged contacts between Philippine Muslims and the wider Islamic world. Frequently under the sponsorship of Muslim politicians, more Filipino Muslims began studying in the Middle East, attending Islamic conferences, and making pilgrimages to Mecca. The newsletter of the King Faisal Center at Mindanao State University later reflected some of their reactions:

> Muslims are now in transition. In dynamic quest for their rightful place in the world are about one fourth of humanity. They are in command of almost a quarter of the globe's land area, where about two thirds of the oil reserves are found.[5]

Malaysian and Libyan Aid

Aside from the diffuse consciousness-raising that resulted from contacts with the Islamic world and the specific demonstrations of political potency of the oil cartel and the conferences of Islamic foreign ministers, contacts with two Muslim states enabled Muslims in the Philippines to mount major military activity against the government. Malaysia was the first of these states, and its policy was clearly affected by factors other than religious ties with discontented Muslims in the Philippines. The clandestine training and supplies given to the leaders of the MNLF, apparently beginning in late 1968, was a direct reaction to Philippine governmental policy, as revealed by the Corregidor incident in March 1968. Presumably in pursuit of the Philippine claim to the Malaysian state of Sabah, the Philippine armed forces had enlisted Muslim recruits whom they trained to infiltrate Sabah. Training began on the island of Simunul in Sulu and later shifted north to Corregidor. According to Muslim accounts, the trainees rebelled against their officers when they learned they were to be sent into action against fellow Muslims, and about 30 of them were killed. Non-Muslim accounts (which in this instance seem more reliable) generally attributed the cause of the rebellion to the officers' failure to pay the recruits.

Whatever the provocation, the incident provided an incentive for cooperation between Muslims in the Philippines, who were incensed at the disregard for Muslim lives shown by the administration of Ferdinand Marcos, and Muslims in the Malaysian government, who were outraged that after they had made significant concessions in response to Marcos' desire to reestablish diplomatic relations, he had "stabbed them in the back." When Udtog Matalam, a Muslim political leader in Mindanao, founded the Muslim Independence Movement (MIM) in May 1968 he attributed its secessionist goals to the Corregidor incident. Malaysia began giving military training to members of MIM's youth section soon thereafter, and the MNLF was organized and the central committee selected at a training site off the coast of West Malaysia.[6]

How long the Malaysian government itself was directly involved in aiding the MNLF cannot be ascertained. It may be that only minimal aid was given after 1969, as the Philippines and Malaysia began to move toward cooperation in the Association of Southeast Asian Nations (ASEAN) in the wake of elections that had dire consequences in both countries. The Malaysian federal government never publicly admitted that it was giving any aid at all, and generally lobbied at Islamic conferences in favor of noninterference in an "internal affair" of the Philippines. It did not, however, intervene to stop the assistance given by Tun Mustapha, the chief minister of Sabah, in cooperation with the government of Libya. Failure to restrain Mustapha probably resulted both from a conviction that Marcos deserved what he was getting and from an awareness that it would have been very difficult to control Mustapha's actions. Mustapha delivered votes critical to the Malaysian leadership; he was generally supportive of the federal government; but he was capable of acting independently, and he might—if faced with an ultimatum—move toward secession himself. When the Malaysian leadership finally decided in mid-1975 to push Mustapha into resigning, his policy toward the Muslim separatists (and its consequent effect on Philippine-Malaysian relations) was undoubtedly a factor in the decision; how critical it was cannot be ascertained.[7]

As for Mustapha's own motives, his antipathy toward the Philippine government dated from the Diosdado Macapagal administration, which first announced a claim to Sabah in 1962. He had consistently opposed any concessions to the Philippines, and the Corregidor incident could only have confirmed his worst suspicions of Philippine intentions. He is identified as a "Suluk" (accounts vary as to whether he was born in the southern Philippines or in Sabah), has relatives living in the Philippines, and is a Muslim zealot. It is widely believed that he had ambitions to become sultan of Sabah, in or out of Malaysia, with or without parts of the southern Philippines. The combination of all these factors motivated his allowing Sabah to be used as a training ground, supply depot, communications center, and sanctuary by the MNLF.

The extent to which Sabah's involvement was a direct result of Mustapha's personal commitment and ambition became evident as his power declined beginning in mid-1975. Accounts citing separatist sources reported that the flow of arms into the southern Philippines decreased in August and stopped completely in December.[8] After Tun Fuad Stephens was named chief minister following the defeat of Mustapha's party in the April 1976 elections, he indicated that he would not allow the separatists to use Sabah as a base for operations against the Philippines or as a sanctuary.[9] Stephens had a record for opposition to the Philippines because of its claim to Sabah dating back to 1962, when he was Sabah's first chief minister. However, he was a Kadazan and, until his conversion to Islam, a Christian, and had ample reason to be unenthusiastic about Mustapha's activities in behalf of militant Muslims. There is no evidence that Datuk Harris Salleh, his successor (Stephens was killed in a plane crash in June 1976), has reversed his policy.

Libya's involvement with the separatists grew out of contacts between Rascid Lucman, a Muslim political leader from Lanao del Sur, and Colonel Muammar al-Qaddafi. As violence escalated in the southern Philippines in 1970 and 1971, Qaddafi reacted to reports of Muslim massacres by charging the Philippine government with genocide and openly threatening to support the Muslims. Libyan spokesmen later publicly admitted giving aid—to the MNLF rather than Lucman since 1971—and lobbied vigorously for the imposition of sanctions against the Marcos regime by Islamic states.[10]

Libya's support was never an unqualified asset, since that nation's popularity with other Muslim states is limited, but it was important both because it financed the lobbying activities as well as some of the fighting of the separatists and because its generally strident support of the cause forced other Muslim states to deal with it.

Other limits of Libyan support became obvious in late 1976, when Qaddafi and other Libyan officials became involved in negotiations with the Marcos regime. There is evidence that at least initially the Libyans put considerable pressure on the separatists as well as the Philippine government to make concessions, and that at least one compromise worked out between Qaddafi and the Marcoses was not approved by the MNLF leadership. Even after the negotiations collapsed at the end of April 1977—amid angry recriminations —Qaddafi's statements at the Islamic foreign ministers' conference in Tripoli were comparatively mild. For various reasons (concern over Libyan prestige with other Muslim states, compassion for civilians killed in the fighting, disappointment with the performance of the separatists?), Libya clearly preferred to support compromises rather than continued fighting.*

Conferences of Islamic Foreign Ministers

In contrast with the changes in Malaysian and Libyan policies, the efforts of the yearly conferences of Islamic foreign ministers and the Islamic Secretariat, which is responsible for implementation of joint decisions, have consistently been directed toward affecting the goals and tactics of the Philippine protagonists. At their conference in Benghazi, Libya, in March 1973, the foreign ministers resolved "to appeal to peace-loving states, religions and international organizations to exert their good offices with the Government of the Philippines to halt campaigns of violence against the Muslim community, to ensure their safety and realize their basic liberties." They also named a

---

*It is interesting—and significant—that as Qaddafi moved toward compromise with the Philippine government, a policy more in line with those pursued by other Islamic states, he was shifting his support from the Eritrean separatists to the Ethiopian government, a policy that brought him into direct conflict with other Islamic states.

five-man team to visit the Philippines in three months, establishing a voluntary fund to help Philippine Muslims, and asked Indonesia and Malaysia to exert their good offices within ASEAN.[11]

When the team visited the Philippines in mid-August, the Philippine News Agency quoted the delegates as saying that they were convinced that Marcos was sincerely trying to find solutions to the problem and that Filipino Muslims could expect some aid but should not allow themselves to be used by extremists or Communists.[12] The team's official report (which was more critical of Marcos' policies than the Philippine account indicated) was submitted to the Islamic summit meeting in Lahore, Pakistan, in February 1974, and a decision was made to keep it secret. There was, however, a full discussion of the issue at the foreign ministers' meeting in Kuala Lumpur, Malaysia, in June 1974. In their final communiqué the ministers first called on the Philippine government to stop all actions resulting in "the killing of Muslims and destruction of their properties and places of worship," then stated their conviction

> . . . that the socio-economic measures proposed by the Philippine Government to improve the condition of the Muslims would not by themselves solve the problem and urged the Philippine Government to find a political and peaceful solution through negotiation with Muslim leaders and particularly, with representatives of the Moro National Liberation Front in order to arrive at a just solution to the plight of the Filipino Muslims within the framework of the national sovereignty and territorial integrity of the Philippines.[13]

They appealed to "peace-loving States and religions and international authorities, while recognizing the problem as an internal problem of the Philippines," to use their good offices to insure the safety and liberties of Philippine Muslims. They also announced a decision to create a Filipino Muslim Welfare and Relief Agency and called for contributions to support its operation.*

In late 1974 and early 1975 Hassan al-Tohamy, the secretary general of the Islamic Secretariat, made a series of visits to Manila that resulted in a meeting between the MNLF leadership and a Philippine delegation headed by Executive Secretary Alejandro Melchor in Jiddah, Saudi Arabia, in mid-January 1975. That meeting deadlocked, and a second one scheduled for Jiddah in April was not held.

Instead, the Philippine government recruited Muslims inside the Philip-

---

*MNLF spokesmen demanded the creation of an internally sovereign, politically autonomous Bangsa Moro State that would include all of Mindanao, the Sulu Archipelago, Basilan, and Palawan; would have its own security force and exclusive responsibility for maintaining internal order; and would be loosely associated with the Philippines. *New York Times,* Mar. 9, 1975.

pines to come to Zamboanga City for "peace talks." Between the first of these meetings, which was held in April, and the second, in June, al-Tohamy sent the Philippine government a draft agenda for further negotiations that had been prepared by a four-member committee (from Saudi Arabia, Libya, Somalia, and Senegal) representing the Islamic foreign ministers. The nine points of the agenda were virtually the same as the four points presented by the MNLF as a basis for negotiation in Jiddah.* They provided for Islamic self-government (in the framework of Philippine sovereignty and territorial integrity) in Mindanao, Basilan, Sulu, and Palawan: the territory owned by Muslims before 1944, including that which had been taken from Muslims since then.[14] Christians and non-Christian minorities historically present in Islamic territories would have the status of minorities in a Muslim land.

The second session of the Zamboanga talks rejected this plan of action and endorsed instead Marcos' version of "autonomy," a fact that was duly communicated to the Islamic foreign ministers when they met at Jiddah in July. Nevertheless, the Jiddah conference approved the committee of four's plan as a basis for further negotiations between the MNLF and the Philippine government, and instructed the committee and the secretary-general to arrange those negotiations as soon as possible.[15]

There was little evidence of the committee's activity during the next year. Al-Tohamy's replacement as secretary-general, Ahmadu Karim Gaye of Senegal, reportedly talked with Marcos at the U.N. Commission on Trade and Development meetings at Nairobi, Kenya. At their meeting in Istanbul in May, the foreign ministers again called on the Marcos administration and the MNLF to resume negotiations for a solution in accordance with the plan of action and resolutions approved at the Jiddah conference, expressed appreciation for the efforts of the committee of four, and renewed its mandate to work toward a settlement. The ministers also specifically requested the Philippine government "to halt its military operations against Muslims, adopt necessary measures for the immediate withdrawal of its troops and honour its commitment to grant autonomy to Muslims in [the] south Philippines within the state of [the] Philippines."[16]

Then, after the Colombo nonaligned summit in August, the committee of four visited Manila. Ali Trekki, Libya's vice-foreign minister, reportedly told Philippine officials that he had persuaded MNLF leaders to relax their preconditions for further negotiations. The committee also promised approximately $1 million for relief of victims of the earthquake in the southern Philippines.

---

*The wording of the statement does not make clear whether there is an intended distinction between the general statement in regard to Mindanao, Basilan, Sulu, and Palawan and the specific mention of territories held by Muslims before 1944.

Libyan delegates met with Marcos again in October, during the International Monetary Fund and World Bank conference in Manila, and invited the Marcoses to visit Tripoli. Marcos invited Qaddafi to visit Manila, and later announced that his wife would accept the Libyan invitation.

The result of Imelda Marcos' trip to Tripoli in November 1976 was a series of talks involving officials of the Philippine government, the MNLF, and the Islamic conference. Between December 5 and 23 the negotiators reached agreement on a cease-fire and tentative terms for a peace settlement; the terms were to be finalized at further talks in Libya February 5-March 3, 1977, initiated at Jiddah during the first week in March, and signed in Manila.*

The cease-fire went into effect on December 24, 1976; though there were continuing skirmishes in isolated areas, it was generally successful. The timetable for the talks, however, was not followed because of disagreements over the substance of autonomy, the role of the MNLF, and procedures for implementation. Controversy centered on whether or not the consent of the people in the proposed region should be solicited through a referendum or plebiscite (both terms were used). Marcos insisted that a plebiscite was necessary because the Philippine constitution required the consent of the people affected by any changes in jurisdictions: the proposed region involved the merger of two existing regions and the inclusion of three other provinces not in either of those regions. The MNLF opposed the plebiscite on the grounds that the Philippine government had made other jurisdictional changes without consulting the people involved and that the Tripoli agreement—which defined the region's geographical scope and the nature of its autonomy—did not provide for a plebiscite.

The issue was more fundamental than the arguments indicated. Though the new region was smaller than the territory the MNLF had originally demanded (13 rather than 21 provinces), Christians still constituted approximately two-thirds of the population and could be expected to vote against any arrangement giving Muslims predominant influence; even many Muslims

---

*The cease-fire was to be supervised by a committee representing the Philippine government, the MNLF, and the Quadripartite Ministerial Commission (the committee of four). The terms, which were not released in the Philippines, provided for an "autonomy for the Muslims" in 13 provinces. The "autonomy" was to have Muslim courts, a legislative assembly and executive council, an administrative system, special regional security forces and representation in the central government; control over education, finance, and the economic system; and a right to a "reasonable percentage" from the revenues of mines and minerals. The central government was to maintain responsibility for foreign policy and national defense affairs. The role of the MNLF forces in the Philippine armed forces and relationships between structures and policies of the "autonomy" and those of the central government were to be discussed later. "Agreement between the Government of the Republic of the Philippines and Moro National Liberation Front with the Participation of the Quadripartite Ministerial Commission, Members of the Islamic Conference and the Secretary General of the Organization of Islamic Conference," Dec. 23, 1976.

could be expected to vote against the arrangement, if they opposed the role of the MNLF. Hence a plebiscite would invalidate the negotiated settlement.

In an effort to resolve the imbroglio, Marcos twice postponed the plesbiscite and, after the talks in Tripoli deadlocked almost as soon as they resumed, again sent his wife to talk directly with Qaddafi. The resulting compromise, announced April 8, 1977, provided that Marcos would declare an autonomous region of the 13 provinces agreed to in the December negotiations, appoint a provisional regional government, and hold a plebiscite to decide administrative details.

Marcos implemented that agreement by appointing a government, which he invited the MNLF to join and Nur Misuari to chair, then specifying that the questions to be asked voters in the referendum/plebiscite included whether or not they wanted the two regions merged into one, the three provinces added, and the nature of autonomy to be in accordance with what the Marcos regime identified as the MNLF's plan. The plebiscite produced a rejection of the procedures by the MNLF, which advocated a boycott and also refused to participate in the provisional government; a rejection of Marcos' interpretation of the agreement with Qaddafi by the Libyan government; and, according to the Philippine Commission on Elections, a rejection of the proposed changes by 96 percent of the 3 million people voting. The Islamic Conference sent a team to Manila to try to salvage a settlement; but each side rejected the other's compromise proposals, and the talks collapsed. Spokesmen for the Islamic team strongly denounced the position of the Philipine government, claiming it violated both of the Tripoli agreements, and warned that the resumption of fighting appeared inevitable. The Marcos government carefully limited its criticism to the adamance of the MNLF and dispatched Secretary of Foreign Affairs Carlos Romulo to explain the Philippine position in Malaysia, Indonesia, and some Middle Eastern states. Concern, however, focused on the Islamic foreign ministers' conference scheduled to meet in Tripoli on May 16.

The Philippine government fared better at that meeting than it feared. In his opening speech Qaddafi expressed his sincere wish for peace, though he warned that fighting might resume. The final communiqué blamed Manila for shirking its international responsibilities and obligations under the Tripoli agreement and called on Islamic countries to support the MNLF "in all ways and means to achieve all the demands of the Muslims in the area," but it once again stopped short of imposing economic sanctions. It mandated its committee of four to "continue . . . efforts to mediate between the Marcos government and the MNLF."[17]

Indonesia

Indonesian policy deserves separate treatment, since it has been significant outside as well as inside Islamic meetings. The feelings of Indonesian leaders are doubtless based in part on the nation's own experience with militant Muslim movements in the 1950s and 1960s. These feelings are reflected in the restrictions currently placed on explicitly Muslim political activity in the country and in the fact that in 1976 Indonesia had neither an office of the Palestine Liberation Organization nor a Libyan embassy, despite frequent announcements of negotiations toward the establishment of both. The primary motivation of Indonesian policy toward the Philippine situation, however, seems to be what is reiterated by Indonesian spokesmen as the goal of Indonesian foreign policy generally: the preservation of regional stability. To this end Indonesian leaders, including both President Suharto and Foreign Minister Adam Malik, have tried to mediate between Malaysia and the Philippines, either at their own initiative or at the request of the Philippine leadership. In 1973 and early 1974 there seemed to be considerable optimism in Jakarta and Manila about the possibility of Indonesian mediation and an assumption (by journalists—and presumably also by officials) that a possible quid pro quo was a Philippine renunciation of its claim to Sabah in exchange for a Malaysian agreement to clamp down on Tun Mustapha. Specific terms of a settlement could be worked out in a tripartite meeting. The Malaysians, however, refused to bargain (they denied that they had anything to concede) and refused to attend a "summit" at which they might be pressured into bargaining. In April 1974 Malik commented that Indonesia had twice mediated, but neither party had accepted the Indonesian proposals.[18]

It has also been reported that the Indonesian government tried to mediate between Marcos and the MNLF leadership—specifically, that Suharto tried to persuade Marcos to meet with MNLF representatives, whom he had on hand for that purpose, when Marcos met with Suharto at Menado in May 1974.[19] Marcos refused to do so. At the end of the Suharto-Marcos meeting, the Indonesian statements referred to the desirability of participation by Muslims in the Philippine government and reflected the Indonesian conviction that Manila should make every effort to talk to the separatist leadership.[20]

Yet at Islamic meetings Indonesia has consistently taken a pro-Philippine position.* There were rumors that Tun Mustapha was called to Jakarta before the Islamic foreign ministers' meeting at Benghazi in 1973 and warned about his collaboration with Libya, which was then lobbying for sanctions against the Philippines. A Foreign Office spokesman would only confirm that Mustapha was there as a friend of "Pak Adam" Malik.[21] At the Benghazi meeting, Indonesian spokesmen emphasized the dangers of interfering in the internal affairs of states. Before the Islamic summit at Lahore in February 1974, Malik

---

*Since Indonesia does not consider itself an Islamic state, in the sense that Islam is the state religion or provides the directing principles for state policy, it is not formally linked with the Islamic Secretariat and attends meetings only by invitation.

was quoted as saying that Indonesia had agreed to participate on the condition that discussion be confined to the question of peace in west Asia, and that he had told Qaddafi not to "interfere" in the Philippine situation, since Indonesia was already doing everything possible to persuade all parties to find a reasonable settlement.[22] At Kuala Lumpur in June 1974, Indonesia reported that the Philippine government had accepted the establishment of a Muslim Welfare Agency, financed through the Islamic Secretariat in cooperation with the Philippine government, and that "the sincerity and willingness of President Marcos to work toward an integrated Philippine society in which Muslims could assume their rightful place were not to be doubted."[23] At Jiddah in July 1975, Malik reportedly said that "no sovereign government worthy of its name" could accept the measure of autonomy spelled out in the proposals of the committee of four.[24]

An MNLF communiqué claimed that at the Istanbul meeting in 1976, Malik called on Marcos to grant Philippine Muslims local autonomy, stop military operations, and talk directly to the MNLF leaders rather than to the Muslims "employed under him," and warned Marcos that Indonesia would sever relations with the Philippines unless there was a political and peaceful solution to the conflict.[25] No confirmation of this claim is available—nor was there subsequent evidence of a shift in Indonesian policy.

The MNLF

The Islamic meetings have provided a focus for the lobbying activities of the MNLF, shaped the nature of its appeals, and determined its negotiating position toward the Philippine government.* MNLF spokesmen came to the Kuala Lumpur foreign ministers' meeting with an "appeal letter" and a description of "the rise and fall of Moro statehood." The appeal to the foreign ministers was that they extend "unanimous and unequivocal support behind our people's right to the full enjoyment of their national freedom and independence." The document identified Philippine policy with Western colonialism and Christianization, but charged that it was more ruthless and brutal than either Spanish or American colonialism had been. Armed rebellion was justified as an act of self-determination, since "between us and the Christian Filipino people, there is an irreconcilable contradiction which no human con-

---

*The MNLF also timed its military offensives to coincide with the Islamic meetings, obviously seeking to call attention to the continued fighting. The extortion attempts, kidnappings, and hijackings that occurred particularly in late 1975 and 1976, however, resulted from the decline in foreign support and the Philippine government's own military offensives: the objectives were to get money or supplies or simply to escape. Most of the incidents appeared not to have official MNLF approval.

trivance can permanently resolve. The only solution is our separation into two distinct and separate political entities." Marxist or Maoist influences were disavowed: "We are born Muslims and we will die as Muslims . . . the ideological aspiration of our Revolution is no other than the paramount interest of our oppressed people, our homeland and Islam."[26]

After the conference two MNLF spokesmen said they were "fully in accord" with the letter and spirit of the communiqué, but Marcos' failure to meet the demand for a political solution would mean that "we will continue our struggle for liberation until we can enjoy the blessing of national freedom and independence."[27] It was clear, however, that the provision in the communiqué that a solution be reached within the framework of Philippine sovereignty and territorial integrity constituted a rejection of the MNLF's announced goals of complete independence. Certainly the MNLF's leadership considered the provision a mandate to change its goal. During the Jiddah talks with the Philippine team, it explicitly identified its demand for autonomy as a concession made in response to the foreign ministers' recommendation.

Both the similarities between the MNLF's conditions for negotiations and the plan of action drafted by the foreign ministers' committee and the pattern of negotiations in late 1976 and 1977 suggest that there has been further collaboration between MNLF negotiators and the committee. MNLF statements indicate that its central committee regards the legitimation provided by its conformity with Islamic conference recommendations as an important asset in achieving a negotiated settlement, which is also the object of the fighting. Other reports, particularly in 1977, indicate some opposition within the MNLF leadership to compromises proposed by their Islamic supporters.

The Philippine Government

The Philippine government initially responded to the concern expressed by Muslim states over its "treatment" of Muslims by arranging for tours of the southern Philippines, by emphasizing the socioeconomic programs that it regarded as evidence of its concern for Muslim welfare, and by branding the separatists as Maoists and/or outlaws. After the oil boycott accompanying the Middle East war in 1973 began to affect Philippine oil supplies and prices, President Ferdinand Marcos publicly condemned Israel and called for a withdrawal of Israeli forces from occupied Arab territory. The Arab summit meeting in Algiers then decided to spare the Philippines from further cuts in oil deliveries. Nevertheless, the message that the Philippine oil supply was contingent on Muslim goodwill had been delivered. Libya explicitly linked the oil supply with Marcos' treatment of Philippine Muslims. Hence Philippine diplomatic initiatives in relation to the Middle East increased markedly.

The Kuala Lumpur communiqué demonstrated that diplomatic efforts had only partial success. While the Philippine government had cause for relief that the foreign ministers refused to endorse secession, the rejection of socio-economic programs as inadequate and the insistence on a political settlement represented criticism of Marcos' strategy. Whether or not the regime realized this at the time of the January 1975 Jiddah negotiations with the MNLF is not clear. Alejandro Melchor's opening statement stressed that the "New Society" had not been given a chance to institute reforms and development plans because of a lack of peace and order—a lack for which Nur Misuari was blamed—and argued that the logical move was to stop the "senseless enmity" and proceed to implement reconstruction and development. Melchor rejected any form of autonomy except local administrative autonomy (the content of which was not clear, particularly in the context of martial law) as being incompatible with the Philippine constitution. Both these remarks and the "draft of preliminary understanding," prepared by the Melchor team and rejected by Misuari, suggest that the Philippine government had no expectations for the talks beyond a desire to placate al-Tohamy and certain Muslim states, and to persuade Misuari and the other MNLF leaders that they were misguided. The message was that if the MNLF would agree to a cease-fire and a cooling-off period, the Philippine government could be trusted to appoint qualified Muslims to civilian and military positions and, more generally, to look after the economic, cultural, and religious well-being of Philippine Muslims.[28]

After the stalemate at Jiddah, the Marcos government adjusted its tactics in an apparent effort to appeal to both its internal and its external audiences. The immediate internal concern was a referendum scheduled for February 27, in which voters were asked to endorse a continuation of martial law. Marcos began to emphasize the seriousness of the Muslim insurgency, identified the MNLF's definition of autonomy as equivalent to secession, and suggested that the MNLF was controlled by an outside force. The "outside force" was presumably Libya; the Maoist label used earlier apparently was judged inappropriate because Marcos was seeking to normalize relations with Peking. After the referendum overwhelmingly endorsed the continuation of martial law, the government began to stress its amnesty programs and held the two major "peace talks" in Zamboanga described earlier. The second of these meetings, attended by Muslims who had been loyal to the government or who had recently "returned to the folds of the law," rejected the negotiating plan of the foreign ministers' committee of four and endorsed Marcos' plan for "autonomy short of independence." The Marcos plan, as relayed to the Jiddah meeting of the Islamic foreign ministers, involved the creation of four regions in the southern Philippines that would be headed by commissioners appointed by Marcos and directly responsible to him; the appointment of Muslims to economic and social welfare offices; and the absorption of "sincere" higher-ranking Muslim defectors into the armed forces.[29]

Militarily, the Marcos regime may have limited the level of force used against the separatists, again out of consideration for its foreign audience. It has frequently been alleged that factions in the armed forces have advocated a more militant posture but have been restrained. Nevertheless, the buildup of the Philippine armed forces, the arming of civil defense units, and estimates of casualties suggest that a high level of force has in fact been used. A major offensive launched against the rebels in North Cotabato and Lanao del Sur in February and March 1976 coincided with an announced ban on foreigners' traveling in parts of the southern Philippines. The ban was justified officially as a precaution against kidnappings, but it had the obvious effect of limiting foreign press coverage of the fighting.

Throughout 1976, Philippine newspapers continued to report large numbers of defections from the MNLF and other Muslim groups. The numbers appeared to be exaggerated (the government's figures on defections exceeded its estimates of MNLF members) and included many the MNLF would identify as "bad elements." Still, a combination of policies of attraction, military offensives, exhaustion, and a decline in the flow of supplies undoubtedly encouraged surrenders.

By late 1976 the Philippine government had accompanied these domestic policies with another diplomatic effort. Taking advantage of Islamic Conference mediators—and Qaddafi—the Marcos regime made significant compromises in an effort to get a cease-fire, and then a final settlement. Yet its simultaneous commitment to a plebiscite predictably resulted in a rejection of the compromises earlier agreed to. Internal factors—the resistance of Christians to what they perceived as Muslim dominance, the resistance of many Muslims to what they perceived as MNLF dominance, the resistance of Filipinos to what they perceived as foreign intervention—and external factors—the Islamic states' control of oil and financial resources—clearly produced conflicting pressures and contradictory policies.

Summary

While external Muslim factors neither caused the conflict between Muslims in the southern Philippines and the Philippine government nor resulted in its resolution, these factors have had significant effects on that conflict. As a result of connections with the larger world of Islam, the expectations of Philippine Muslims were increased in ways that, in the Philippine context, had separatist implications. The separatists received military support from two Muslim states. Libya was originally motivated by Qaddafi's Islamic fervor, which was doubtless increased by a general tendency to oppose the international establishment, and was unaffected by any concern over regional stability. Later, when some of the costs of its policy became evident, Libya gave priority to a compromise settlement, and shifted from military to diplomatic assistance. In Sabah, Tun Mustapha's Islamic fervor was supplemented by broader ethnic links with Philippine Muslims, but was critically encouraged by his opposition to specific Philippine policies. The value of his assistance was largely related to the proximity of Sabah to the Philippine war zone. Malaysian policy was almost entirely a reaction to Philippine policies connected with the claim to Sabah, and support was limited by a concern over regional and internal stability; nevertheless, its early assistance and later tolerance were important assets to the MNLF.

Other Islamic states—whose attention had been aroused by reports of escalating violence in the southern Philippines—were motivated exclusively by a concern over the mistreatment of Muslims. For this reason they separately and jointly tried to facilitate a settlement of the conflict along lines favorable to the Muslims. But because of reservations over the separatists' goals and/or ideology, over setting precedents supporting interference in the internal affairs of states, and, in the case of at least Indonesia and Malaysia, over the risk of jeopardizing cooperation with the Philippine government, they were unwilling to use all the forms of leverage which they possessed.* The Philippine government has reason to fear an oil boycott only if it should escalate warfare to a point approximating genocide, but not if it simply refuses to grant meaningful autonomy. The general willingness of Islamic states—thus far—to give credence to Philippine announcements of intentions has meant that they have had a greater effect on the vocabulary and form than on the substance of Philippine policy. The beneficiaries of offers of amnesty and positions frequently have been unprincipled bandits and old-style political leaders. Loyal Muslims who are professionally competent and honest have lacked power bases inside the Philippines and contacts outside it. When they have been given positions, they have seldom been given adequate authority to "deliver" change; hence they risk being discredited within Muslim society. The creation of new structures has not been accompanied by any significant devolution of power.

Thus the basic causes of Muslim-Christian conflict remain unresolved. The separatists and their overseas sympathizers have succeeded in getting concessions that have benefited Muslims, including many against whom the rebellion was presumably directed; they have not succeeded in getting fundamental change.

---

*Both Malaysian and Indonesian spokesmen have argued that ASEAN provided a better forum for handling the issue than did the Islamic foreign ministers' meetings. When an ASEAN summit was being discussed for early 1976, however, the Malaysian prime minister, Tun Razak, reportedly refused to attend unless Marcos agreed not to raise the issue of the Muslim insurgency and Sabah's role in it. Thus Malaysian and Indonesian arguments seemed to be based at least partially on the assumption that ASEAN would provide a better forum because it would not handle the issue, and hence would avoid a confrontation that might jeopardize its existence. Nevertheless, there is some evidence that private discussions have taken place at ASEAN sessions.

THAILAND

Internal Dimensions

The Muslim population in southern Thailand has a long history of intermittent conflict with the central government, going back to the early thirteenth century, when the Sukothai kings claimed the Muslim sultanates as vassals.* However, the sultanates probably were neither more nor less unruly than other vassal territories in the outer reaches of the kingdom. When the Siamese kings were strong, the vassals generally accepted their status, which in principle and practice meant a great deal of local autonomy. When the Siamese throne was weak, the Muslim rulers tended to defy the sovereign, refusing to provide tax and manpower contributions.

Toward the end of the nineteenth century, the vassal system was gradually replaced by a Western-inspired, centralized administration. Local autonomy was no longer permitted, and Thai government officials took the place of Muslim rulers. The relationship between the central power and the local population became more intimate, governed in principle by the demands for uniformity of the centralized administration that expressed the values and norms of the majority population, the Thai Buddhists. Since then, the relationship between the minority and the majority has remained an uneasy one, reflecting the tendency of ethnic cleavages to coincide with socioeconomic and political distinctions.

The ethnic boundaries of the southern Muslims are both clear and parallel. The Muslims profess a religion that sets them apart from the Theravada Buddhist majority; they are of Malay race, while the Thai people originated in northern China and later intermarried with other arrivals from the north; they speak a local dialect of the Malay language and only perhaps 20–30 percent have a reasonable command of the nationally spoken Thai language (although Thai is more widely spoken in Satul than in the other Muslim provinces); they have maintained Malay customs, some of which—like the manner of dress—are easily visible; and they are conscious of having a long history of self-government under Muslim rulers who in some instances belonged to proud dynasties and lived and ruled in a grand manner. (The descendants of the most significant dynasty, the Pattani, still live in respected if rather faded circumstances in the South.)

These ethnic boundaries are reinforced by other cleavages. The economic structure of the Muslim provinces is dominated by Thai Buddhist government

---

*They were later called third- and fourth-class provinces, implying geographic remoteness from the seat of central power and less central control than in the first- and second-class provinces.

officials and Thai Chinese capitalists (merchants and rubber plantation owners). Although it is easy to demonstrate that, on a nationwide scale, there are Thai Buddhists who are as poor as the southern Muslims, the focus of the latter is more narrow, usually confined to the border provinces. In this universe the Muslim is generally a rubber tapper, a fisherman, or a vendor, while the Thai Chinese and the Thai Buddhists occupy the higher socioeconomic strata.

Since virtually all government officials from the district office to the gubernatorial level are Thai, ethnic distinctions also parallel that between the rulers and the ruled.* That relationship is not a particularly trusting one anywhere in rural Thailand. It is exacerbated in the south by language differences (the bilingual government official is an even more rare phenomenon than a bilingual Muslim), endemic lawlessness and banditry, and cumulative instances of open clashes between government officials and the local population —the Muslims accusing the officials of violating their civil and human rights, and the officials accusing the Muslims of disloyalty to the government.

The parallel cleavages encourage politicization of ethnic antagonism and "ethnicization" of economic and political disputes. Mediation of such disputes is encumbered by the governmental structure of Thailand. Governmental power was traditionally centered in the administrative branch, and has remained so despite the change to a constitutional monarch and occasional functioning of parliamentary institutions after 1932. Effective political power continues to be exercised through the bureaucracy (civilian and military). The bureaucracy, not the political parties and the legislative branch, is the source of political power, patronage, protection, and funds. Entry into it requires, at a very minimum, a Thai education and a high degree of Thai acculturation. The southern Muslims have been unable and/or unwilling to enter the bureaucracy in any significant number, even in local administration in the south; and they play no role whatsoever in national bureaucratic politics. Consequently, they have neither the access nor the power that would enable them to participate effectively in settling minority-majority disputes.†

This situation has led a number of prominent southern Muslims to advocate autonomy for the four border provinces with a predominantly Muslim

---

*The only notable exception is the appointment of a southern Muslim to be governor of Pattani after the so-called Pattani massacre in December 1975, when five Muslim youth were killed, allegedly by government soldiers. The governor, Termsakdi Samantarath, comes from a distinguished family of public servants in Satul province and served previously in Narathiwas and Satul—both southern, predominantly Muslim provinces.

†The contrast with another minority group, the Chinese, is interesting. The success of the Chinese in surviving and advancing within the Thai political system stems largely from their possession of special skills and resources valued by the Thai elite. The southern Muslims do not have any equivalent resources that make them a "valued" minority group in the polity.

population. The Thai government, however, has considered autonomy to be as unpalatable as secession and has suppressed its Muslim advocates.* The result has been a growing polarization within the leadership of the minority group, between those who argue the need to accept the present system and those who categorically reject it in favor of secession.†

The secessionist alternative is strengthened by other factors. The southern Muslims are territorially concentrated in an enclave, representing approximately three-fourths of the local population in the four southernmost provinces. Moreover, and of central importance, these provinces border on Malaysia.‡ The present northern states of West Malaysia were vassals of Siamese kings until the British succeeded in establishing their authority in this area, culminating in the Anglo-Siamese border agreement of 1909. The present border is consequently viewed by southern Muslims as a highly artificial one that arbitrarily confines them to Thai rule, while other Malay Muslims are included in Malaysia. Ties between Malays on both sides of the border, and particularly in the western sector, have traditionally been close, including dynastic links and the sharing of a common dialect. Much traffic (legal and illegal) continues across the border, and several Muslims on the Thai side have dual nationality.

The significance of proximity to Malaysia goes further. Malaysia is a Muslim state in the sense that the constitution establishes Islam as the official

---

*One outstanding leader, Haji Sulong, was killed in 1954. Circumstantial evidence pointed to the Special Branch of the Thai police as responsible (cited in *Suara Siswa* [Kuala Lumpur], Dec. 1970, p. 30). This conclusion was confirmed by a less partisan source, a British former officer of the Malay police, in an interview with the author. Another leader advocating autonomy, Tunku Abdul Yala (Abdul Na Saiburi), found it prudent to seek exile in Kelantan, Malaysia, where he became associated with separatist leaders.

Muslims in the Bankok region have tried to mediate, arguing that the southern Muslims who advocate autonomy "merely" want decentralization and "that is not treason." Statement by the (ad hoc) Siam Muslim Group, *Bangkok Post,* June 27, 1974. The Thai government has not censored members of this group, nor occasional political splinter parties composed of Thais who also advocate a measure of autonomy for the southern Muslims, such as Palang Mai and the Socialist Party of Thailand. See *Bangkok Post,* Jan. 6, 1975. The government's reaction clearly depends upon who is advocating autonomy.

†Autonomy may conceivably reappear as a compromise alternative if the Thai government becomes unable to retain even a semblance of control in the south, and if both the government and the militant Muslims could be persuaded that autonomy is a more realistic or desirable option than secession or merger with neighboring Malaysia.

‡One of the separatist movements, the United Patani Freedom Movement, claims a larger territory than that inhabited primarily by Muslims. Its map of a projected independent Republic of Patani, presented to the author in 1971, included a large slice of the Thai Buddhist-inhabited provinces of Songkhla in addition to the four Muslim provinces.

religion. Although the Malay Muslims in Malaysia do not constitute a numerical majority, they enjoy special constitutional and political privileges as *humiputra* ("sons of the soil"), and the Malaysian government has been particularly attuned to improving the position of the Malays relative to the Chinese and the Indians since 1969. This has a powerful demonstration effect on the Thai Muslims; the contrast accentuates their own position as a Malay Muslim minority ruled by "idol-worshipping" Thai Buddhists. The contrast is viewed as relevant precisely because the southern Muslims consider themselves not only Muslims but also Malays, just like those on the other side of the border.[30]

The strength of autonomy and/or secessionist movements has fluctuated. In the post-World War II period, one can identify some years when the movements seemed particularly active and assertive—notably in 1947, the mid-1950s, and the late 1960s. At no time, however, did the conflict reach the proportions it has had in the southern Philippines after martial law (1972), in terms of the level of violence, the relative violence, the relative numbers involved, and the degree of organization among the Muslims. In the early 1970s the separatists were estimated to have only 700–1,000 armed activists who were organizationally divided and, by their own admission, fighting an uphill struggle.[31]

The dissatisfied, militant leaders evidently have been unable to mobilize the greater part of their community in a sustained fashion. This may seem strange, in view of the minority-majority relationship described above. There are, however, mitigating factors that help to restrain deliberate rejection of Thai rule and, indeed, have produced some active "loyalists" among the southern Muslims.

The "loyalists" generally comprise those who are able and willing to take advantage of the opportunities for a Thai education and consequent upward mobility. They also include a group of local leaders who recognize that they can exercise limited, perhaps symbolic, leadership either locally (as village headmen or municipal councillors) or nationally (in the National Assembly—when it functions). Once a Muslim obtains a Thai education and masters the Thai language, there is little if any discrimination in employment in either the public or the private sector. The "loyalists" recognize that Thai rule generally permits considerable ethnic diversity—the main exception was Phibul Songkram's first regime on the eve of World War II, when stringently assimilationist policies were applied to all ethnic minorities in the country. To some extent, majority tolerance has been a matter of practicality; the Thai bureaucracy has not been sufficiently well-organized to administer with ruthless efficiency, particularly in the provinces remote from Bangkok. But it has also been a question of principle. Religious freedom has been permitted to the extent of allowing Islamic law to apply in matters of family and inheritance contracts, and the southern Muslims have maintained private Islamic schools *(pondok)* that teach the vernacular and local history, in addition to Arabic and the Islamic religion.*

A majority of the southern Muslims probably have not accepted the legitimacy of Thai rule in the deliberate manner of the "loyalists." Their attitude and behavior seem, rather, to reflect political apathy that, in a negative sense, is conditioned by what the Thai government does not do. As long as Thai officials do not interfere markedly with Malay Muslim ways of life (notably in educational and religious questions), and as long as the government does not make its presence too strongly felt by police actions and administrative corruption, large segments of the minority group tend to remain politically inactive. Moreover, land disputes between the majority and the minority have not yet been sufficiently serious to instill an acute sense of relative deprivation among the minority in this respect.†

External Dimensions

The periods of increased violence and articulation of discontent in the past demonstrate that the southern Muslims can be mobilized against the Thai government on a broader scale than was the case in the early 1970s. External factors have been significant in this mobilization process; and, in a broader sense, the importance of outside developments is indirectly shown by the ability of external parties to moderate the local conflict.

Malaysia

As noted, the very presence of Malaysia and its pro-Malay communal politics exerts a continuous demonstration effect on the Thai Muslims. At one stage, in 1947–48, developments in Malaysia also gave the Thai Muslims some reason to hope for a border adjustment that would include the four Muslim provinces in the Federation of Malaya, and this contributed to the most

---

*A program was under way in 1970–71 to convert all *pondok* into private schools that would teach a standard Thai curriculum. The program was to be gradual, and monetary incentives were offered to *pondok* headmasters. It was an extremely controversial program, and Thai officials freely admitted they had insufficient administrative control to implement it completely.

†This may change, however, if the Thai government proceeds with plans to settle Thai Buddhists on large tracts of land organized collectively *(nikom sang kong eng)* in the border provinces. The land settlement policy has been denounced by the separatists as a means to "destroy all political, economic and cultural activity among the Muslims." United Patani Freedom Movement, "Declaration of Warning," Aug. 1, 1971. (Leaflet.)

widespread support for secession in southern Thailand to date.* The government of Malaysia has subsequently disassociated itself from any irredentist demands, thus narrowing the realistic options available to the dissatisfied southern Muslims. The federal government also has adhered to a strict nonintervention policy vis-à-vis groups advocating autonomy or separatism, thus depriving them of their most logical supporter and undoubedly deflating some enthusiasm among the southern Muslims for the separatist or autonomy cause. The latter may still be considered desirable, but it seems impossible without considerable Malaysian assistance. The separatists would need an external protector to proclaim and maintain their ministate, which would have to be established in defiance of Thai authority and power. Since the Thai government would hardly accept autonomy unless it were perceived as the lesser of two evils, the separatist alternative would have to be credible in this case as well.

The reasons why Malaysia would be the most logical external supporter lie in a combination of ethnic ties, geographic proximity, and the historical links noted earlier. These links are strongest with respect to the Malays in the northern state of West Malaysia, Kelantan, where political leaders frequently have expressed support for the Thai Muslims. This goes back to 1945, when the Malay Nationalist party proclaimed ". . . the right of the Malays in the four southern provinces of Thailand to determine their own future."† One of the founding members of the party was Burhanuddin al-Helmy, a Kelantanese who later became the first president of the Pan-Malayan Islamic Party (PMIP). The PMIP and its successor, PAS (Parti Islam), have controlled state politics in Kelantan since the first state elections in 1954; and party leaders have made similar claims on behalf of the Thai Muslims. Datuk Mohamed Asri thus stated in 1970 that since the four southern provinces of Thailand were not "released" from Thai rule in 1909, the Malay Muslims there "feel that they are states which ought to be free like their sister states in Malaysia," and declared this struggle a "holy one."[32] In June 1974 Asrin, who was then chief minister of Kelantan as well as a minister in the federal government,

---

*Great Britain was then negotiating the terms for the Federation of Malaya with the Malay leaders. The British had already compelled Thailand to return those provinces that Thailand had occupied during the war—Trengganu, Kelantan, Kedah, and Perlis—and British hostility to Thailand at that time was well-known. If further border adjustments were to be made, this was clearly an opportune moment.

†The party program also included the following item: "The struggle for independence of the Malay race must be dynamic and should start immediately, encompassing the former Dutch Indies, [and] British North Borneo. . . ." Foreword by Machtiar Djamily to Burhanuddin al-Helmy, *Asas falsafah kebangsaan Melayu* ("Basic Philosophy of the Malay People") (Jakarta: Tedak, 1963). I am indebted to John Funston of the Australian National University for bringing this to my attention.

restated this theme in more cautious terms: "The request for autonomy with specific conditions for the four provinces as put forward by the freedom front seems credible if well received."[33] While PAS leaders have confined their statements to expressions of sympathy and concern, there is a great deal of suspicion in Bangkok that the party condones tangible support for the autonomy-separatist groups as well. Since PAS controls state politics in Kelantan, and since Kelantan is just across the border, with easy access from the Thai Muslim provinces of Pattani and Narathiwas, this suspicion may be well-founded.*

Kelantanese concern for the Thai Muslims partly reflects particularist ethnic ties between the two communities: a common dialect and memories of dynastic ties in the past. Beyond that, Kelantan is one of the most orthodox Islamic states in the Federation of Malaya; and orthodoxy implies special concern for a situation in which fellow Muslims are governed by non-Muslims, as in southern Thailand. Another element in Kelantanese support for the Thai Muslims—a Pan-Malay doctrine—has not been stressed in recent years. This doctrine was seriously discredited in Malaysia during the confrontation with Indonesia in 1963–65, and Burhanuddin, whose interest in the Thai Muslims was part of a greater vision of Pan-Malay unity, was twice interned by the federal government in this period.

The particularist ties between Kelantan and the Thai Muslims are not shared by other Malays in Malaysia. Moreover, PAS is a splinter party in Malaysian national politics: it has had only a small proportion of the seats in the federal Parliament (12 out of 154 in 1969), and has consistently carried only Kelantan in state elections. When PAS was an opposition party in national politics (then as the PMIP), it was attacked by the leading Malay party, the United Malays National Organization (UMNO), whose leaders regarded PAS' orthodoxy and communal appeal as an injury added to the insult of remaining outside the broader alliance of communal parties forged by UMNO. In 1972, PAS joined the alliance's successor, the National Front, in a coalition on both the federal and the state level; but this has hardly muted its inclination to express sympathy for the Thai Muslims, as Datuk Mohamed Asri's speech of June 1974 indicates.

PAS' concern is to some extent shared by two other groups in Malaysia that may have more influence on the policy of the federal government. There are, first, "communal watchdogs" in UMNO and a younger generation of politicians and technocrats who believe in "the primacy of the Malay race in

---

*Tunku Abdul Yala, now an old man but apparently still active, reportedly lives on a 600-*rai* estate in Kelantan provided by PAS leaders, where he allegedly keeps arms caches and supervises his followers in Pattani. The estate conveniently faces the sea, facilitating traffic to and from Pattani by small crafts. *The Nation* (Bangkok), May 8, 1974.

Malaysian politics."[34] This group will be quite apprehensive if the Thai government moves toward a more suppressive and/or assimilationist policy toward the southern Muslims, on the ground that it violates "Malay rights". Second, there is the National Union of Malaysian Muslim Students, which twice in recent years has succeeded in straining Thai-Malaysian official relations by demonstrating on behalf of the Thai Muslims.*

Unofficial concern, possibly material (unofficial) aid, and expressions of sympathy in Malaysia have a dual effect on the situation in south Thailand. They help to keep alive the hope for autonomy, separatism, and perhaps even irredentism among the southern Muslims—thus contributing to continuation of the conflict. But they also serve to attenuate the conflict by restraining Thai policy toward the minority group. Increased suppression or a rigid assimilation policy would make it difficult for the Malaysian federal government to maintain its nonintervention policy.† At the very least, it would be politically very embarrassing to censor expressions of sympathy and discourage unofficial, material support to the southern Muslims, as the federal government consistently has done in the past. The Thai government is quite aware of this and of the value to itself of the present nonintervention policy.

The Malaysian government's policy rests in a general sense on the importance attached to good relations with the Thai government. The two states have enjoyed close, harmonious relations since Malaysia's independence, reflecting similar elite attitudes in domestic politics (pragmatic, conservative, and strongly anti-Communist) and in foreign policy (Western-oriented, conservative, and for a long time aligned with Great Britain and the United States, respectively). Both states are members of the regional organization ASEAN and have stressed the need to strengthen cooperation among its members after major changes took place in the region in the early 1970s: the British completed their military withdrawal from Malaysia; the United States reduced, and was eventually asked to terminate its military presence in, Thailand; Communist forces were victorious in Vietnam, Laos, and Cambodia; and the ASEAN states proceeded to normalize relations with these countries as well as with China. In this context, the Malaysian government considers Thailand a necessary ally to disprove the "domino theory" in any of its versions.

---

*Its publication, *Suara siswa,* devoted its Dec. 1970 issue to the "plight" of the southern Muslims. The following June the students organized a demonstration against Thai Prime Minister Thanom Kittikachorn during his visit to Kuala Lumpur.

The Malaysian government banned the publication, and police promptly broke up the demonstration and pressed charges against the student leaders.

†As a spokesman for the prime minister's office noted, a forceful Thai policy "would reverberate in Trengganu and Kelantan—all over the country. It would be an extremely difficult situation for us." Interview with author, Kuala Lumpur, May 1971.

A more specific and compelling reason for the Malaysian nonintervention policy is the continued insurgency by the Communist Party of Malaya (CPM). The CPM retreated to the Thai side of the border after it failed to "liberate" Malaya in the late 1940s and the early 1950s. It has continued to use the Thai border provinces as a sanctuary for raids into Malaysia. The Thai government agreed to cooperate, first with the British and then with the Malaysian government, in suppressing the CPM; and a revised border agreement was concluded in 1965. It provided for "hot pursuit" by Malaysian forces within a five-kilometer zone on the Thai side of the border, and the permanent stationing of a Malaysian police field force just inside the border. A high-level border committee was set up to meet twice annually; and the arrangement worked remarkably well, despite an underlying problem that surfaced continuously.

The CPM offered the Thai authorities a live-and-let-live policy, repeatedly assuring local Thai officials that the CPM had no interest in Thailand but were "merely" using Thai territory as a base for operations against Malaysia. This was a welcome signal to Thai officials, who were preoccupied with problems caused by bandits, Muslim separatists, and Thai Communists who ventured into the border provinces from the midsouthern region. In Bangkok, the inclination was similarly to accept the CPM's offer of peaceful coexistence in view of insurgency problems in the northeast, the north, and, more recently, repeated political crises in Bangkok. The CPM thus enjoyed its sanctuary to the point that it was the de facto government in Betong (Yala province). This status caused consternation in Kuala Lumpur, but the border agreement allowed Malaysian forces to chase the CPM into Thailand and, to that extent, make up for Thai laxity.

The tacit but clearly understood quid pro quo for the border agreement (which benefited Malaysia more than Thailand) was Malaysian nonintervention with respect to the Muslim separatists (where the benefits tended to be reversed). This understanding was nullified by the suspension of the border agreement in May 1976, following a major Malaysian military operation in the Thai border zone. The CPM organized huge rallies in Betong, involving several thousand persons who denounced the border agreement for permitting violations of Thai sovereignty. The Thai government, somewhat unexpectedly, took up the demands of the demonstrators and asked that the border agreement be renegotiated. In the meantime, the "hot pursuit" clause was revoked and the Malaysian police field force was withdrawn to the Malaysian side of the border. The Thai government, then headed by Seni Pramoj, initially seemed prepared to renew the border agreement along lines acceptable to Malaysia. The Malaysian prime minister, Datuk Hussein Onn, announced on June 7, 1976, that a new agreement would be signed when Seni visited Kuala Lumpur later that month.[35] Seni's visit, however, produced no agreement but, rather, a clarification of the problem. The Thai government was unwilling to permit a one-sided "hot pursuit," claiming that Malaysian operations against the CPM on the Thai side should be reciprocated by permission for Thai soldiers to pursue Muslim separatists taking refuge on the Malaysian side of the border.[36] The Malaysian government refused openly to endorse such a license to hunt Malay Muslim "brothers," and the negotiations came to a standstill.

The Thai position did not simply reflect a desire to accommodate the CPM as part of a general reorientation in foreign policy, as some Malaysian officials speculated. There had just been a national election in Thailand (April 1976) that had aroused a great deal of emotion over the issue of foreign (specifically American) troops stationed in Thailand, and had heated nationalist sentiments. And there was a further injury to Thai pride and sensitivity in having "Malaysian forces . . . in those areas inhabited by people of Malay descent with whom they can converse in a common tongue," as one Thai paper phrased it.[37] (Thai officials in the border provinces, it will be recalled, very rarely speak Malay.) A lingering Thai suspicion that the Malaysian government might be tempted to use the separatist movement for its own ends was brought to the surface.

What these ends might be was not clearly articulated, but one possibility was that the Malaysian government, impatient with the level of Thai cooperation in suppressing the CPM, could utilize the links between the southern Muslims and Kelantan to compete with the CPM and the Thai government in governing the border provinces. There is also evidence that the CPM has succeeded in converting some Thai Muslims to their cause, thus giving added impetus to a possible preemptive strategy by the Malaysian government to infiltrate the Muslim separatist ranks and prevent the CPM from demonstrating that Islam and Communism are compatible.[38] It is clear, however, that any deviation from the official nonintervention policy will be taken very seriously by the Thai government. Even rather innocuous statements, such as Datuk Mohamed Asri's speech in June 1975, caused a furor in Bangkok, despite immediate assurances from the Malaysian government that the speech in no way represented official policy.

The differences between the two governments should not obscure a common recognition that the elites in both countries have infinitely more to gain by cooperating than by risking serious tension—not to mention war—through pursuit of conflicting policies in the border region. As the venerable old statesman of Malaysia, Tunku Abdul Rahman, observed during the 1976 debacle: the CPM would be the principal victor in a conflict between Malaysia and Thailand, and the CPM's strategy is precisely to provoke such a development.[39] From Bangkok's perspective, there is the additional worry that a Thai-Malaysian conflict would help to mobilize the southern Muslims behind the separatists, in the expectation that a border adjustment was possible. The basic consensus between Bangkok and Kuala Lumpur has nevertheless permitted disagreement on the nature and scope of cooperation. The differences that surfaced in early 1976 subsequently were resolved as a coup d'etat in Bangkok brought a staunchly anti-Communist government to power. The military-backed regime of Thanin Kraivichien was prepared to allow Malaysian forces expanded pursuit of CPM units and bases in the south; Kuala Lumpur, gratified by what it saw as a new determination in Bangkok, was ready to concede mutual hot pursuit. This might involve Thai forces hunting down Muslim separatists seeking refuge in Malaysia; but the understanding was that the reciprocity principle would be used to suppress the CPM and, beyond that, simply reflected the equality of the two states in this cooperative endeavor. In any event, the situation in the south is sufficiently fluid to permit official identification of the enemy as Communist in any particular operation. A carefully worded border agreement was signed in March 1977, and massive joint operations against the CPM started earlier in the year.

Other Outside Parties

Outside involvement in the conflict has primarily been limited to Malaysia. Neither the territory in question nor the dispute has any great strategic or political value to other governments. Conceivably, adversaries of the Thai government might find support of the separatists a useful tool to embarrass or weaken the Bangkok regime. The Chinese-supported Communist Party of Thailand has routinely given verbal support to the "fraternal" Muslims in the four provinces and endorsed autonomy for the region; but to the extent that Peking (or Hanoi or Moscow) is prepared to support insurgents in Thailand, there are clearly more promising candidates for assistance than a weak rebel movement in the south whose leaders have traditionally looked to fellow Muslim groups or governments for aid. Of these, Indonesia and the conference of Islamic foreign ministers are of particular interest here, in view of their involvement in the somewhat similar conflict in the Philippines. However, two factors have greatly limited their interest in the Thai Muslims. First, the level of violence involving Muslims in southern Thailand is much lower than that in the Philippines. While it is sufficient to stir the sensitivities of Malay Muslims in Malaysia, who have a sense of close identification with their "brothers" across the border, it has rather less impact in Indonesia and more remote countries, where the only shared bond with the Thai Muslims pertains to religion. Second, the Malaysian government, in order to protect its delicate border arrangement with the Thai government, has stressed to the Indonesians and in the Islamic conference that the problem is entirely a domestic, Thai affair.

Indonesia. The only plausible reason for the present Indonesian government to intervene would be to mediate in order to promote ASEAN cooperation and its own image of regional leadership; but this might well be counterproductive, since the Thai and Malaysian governments are likely to view Indonesian efforts as meddling in their own, generally amicable, bilateral relations. Against this, there are several considerations in favor of nonintervention. The Suharto government is anxious to live down the heritage of the confrontation policy of the previous government, which involved some clandestine support for the Thai Muslim separatists—apparently justified on both ideological and ethnic grounds (that is, to "liberate" Malays ruled by a conservative, "Old Established Force" government). Also, as pointed out above, the Suharto government is not partial to Muslim movements of any militant persuasion. Finally, Suharto, like previous leaders, is extremely sensitive to the multiethnic composition of Indonesia and has justified its nonintervention policy primarily on this ground. As Foreign Minister Adam Malik said when he returned from the Islamic conference at Kuala Lumpur in 1974: "We cannot have a separate state for every minority in a country."[40] The government has an obvious interest in limiting the principle of ethnic self-determination: the centrifugal forces of Indonesian politics have been manifested in the past, and may well increase as the government tries to digest the more recent territorial additions of West Irian and East Timor.

It is interesting to note that although Malaysia is also a multiethnic state, this is rarely if ever mentioned as a rationale for the Malaysian nonintervention policy. Admittedly, mutual dependence among the ethnic groups of Malaysia, and the absence of territorially distinct groupings of the Malays, the Chinese, and the Indians, make separatism a quite remote prospect in West Malaysia; but this is not true for East Malaysia in relation to the federation as a whole. The explanation is, rather, that the Malaysian government has more concrete reasons to adopt a nonintervention policy—these happen to coincide with the principle of limiting ethnic self-determination, but that principle is not stressed in the formulation and explanation of policy. In Indonesia's case, the principle is emphasized because there are no reasons of a more concrete nature, or at least none that lend themselves to public statements.

Conference of Islamic Foreign Ministers. The Indonesian position echoes the general attitudes at the various conferences of the Islamic foreign ministers. The conferences have not, as of April 1977, included any reference to the Muslims in southern Thailand in the final communiqués, in contrast with the references and activities on behalf of the Philippine Muslims. Only once did the conference produce a limited "fact-finding mission." After the 1974 conference, held in Malaysia, the Egyptian secretary-general of the Islamic Secretariat, Hassan al-Tohamy, traveled from Kuala Lumpur to Bangkok, with brief stops in the southern provinces, where he conferred with the governors. He concluded that there was no problem in the southern provinces, merely a "lack of understanding," and assured the Thai government that he had "no intention of interfering in the internal affairs of Thailand."[41]

The Islamic indifference should not be credited entirely to Malaysian efforts to protect the understanding with the Thai government concerning the border region. The relatively low level of violence in southern Thailand, as compared with that in the Philippines, is no doubt an important factor. It apparently requires a great deal of violence and destruction involving Muslim minorities for the Islamic conference as a collectivity to recognize that "a problem" exists.

A related explanation may be the failure of the southern Muslims to develop contacts with radical Muslim states that can act as their advocates within the conference. Although there have been reports in the Thai press of Libyan support to the separatists, no evidence has been offered; and separatist spokesmen have not named Libya as a source of assistance. Possibly this reflects a structural characteristic of the movement. Some of its leaders are old men, steeped in their own community, wary of links with any outsiders, and unprepared to associate their cause with a more general, radical doctrine that demands a new politico-economic order within and among states. The parochialism of these leaders is a counterweight to the inclination of other sections of the movement to seek outside support.* One may discern here a self-reinforcing cycle: a low level of internal violence justifies a parochial distrust of outside groups and limits the ability of the minority to obtain the attention of potentially interested outside parties; lack of outside partisan support in turn reduces violence and strengthens parochialism. As suggested above, however, this cycle is not necessarily dominant or inevitable.

CONCLUSIONS

In the cases of both the Thai and the Filipino Muslims, there is close interaction between internal and external dimensions of the conflict; indeed, it is difficult to distinguish between the two in some respects. Outside factors contributed to the Muslims' consciousness of themselves as distinct groups and helped to sharpen this consciousness into demands for autonomy and secession. In Thailand these stimuli came primarily from neighboring Malaysia, reflecting the close ethnic ties with groups in that country, while in the Philippines there was a wider range of international stimuli, corresponding to the broader international contacts of the Filipino Muslims. For both, the stimuli

---

*Thai newspapers at one time claimed the National Liberation Front of Pattani had distributed a leaflet announcing that children of the former royal family of Pattani were studying in Egypt, other Arab countries, and India to prepare themselves to rule an independent state of Pattani. *Bangkok World,* June 21, 1974. The dynastic ties apart, Muslims from south Thailand study or have studied in Muslim countries, primarily in Malaysia and Egypt, but no statistics on their numbers are available. There is no evidence that this group has emerged as an identifiable leadership segment within the Muslim community, nor within the separatist movement(s).

consisted of demonstrations of the possible and, more directly, of expressions of sympathy and material assistance.

The concern of outside actors for the minority groups served to restrain the central governments' policies. In Thailand, anticipated strong reaction from the Malaysian government if the Thai government were to proceed toward a rigid assimilationist policy or increased suppression of Muslims helped deter the Thai government from doing either. In the Philippines, the continuing concern of the Islamic foreign ministers over the conflict in the southern Philippines may have restrained the government's conduct of the war; it clearly affected the timing and content of government announcements of new policies. There is some reason to hope that it will yet facilitate a genuine compromise.

The outside actors who modified the internal conflicts in these ways were all linked to the minority groups by some form of ethnic ties. In fact, ethnic ties were the only basis for support to the minority groups except in one instance—Malaysian assistance to the Philippine Muslims. The goal of the outsiders was primarily to prevent actions that might produce consequences deemed unacceptable; they did not commit themselves to support the maximum goals of the Muslims. Indeed, in the Philippines the refusal of the Islamic foreign ministers to support secession influenced the Muslims to reduce their demands. These instances, then, support one of the initial hypotheses of the study: ethnic links help to keep a conflict between a minority group and the majority-dominated government it challenges within the bounds of total defeat and total victory.

It is important to note, however, that in neither case was there intense hostility between the government experiencing internal conflict and outside actors that conceivably might have led to a policy of supporting total victory for the minority group. The Malaysian attitude is instructive in this regard; more generally, it points to the interaction between ethnic and nonethnic factors in the policy of an interested outside party.

With respect to the Thai Muslims, the Malaysian government perceived the conflict in three contexts. First, there was a general desire by the government to cultivate good relations with the Thai government. This suggested at least a policy of strict nonintervention and at most, cooperation to suppress the minority group. Second, these policy suggestions were reinforced by a specific bargain between Thailand and Malaysia whereby the Thais would facilitate suppression of Communists troubling the Malaysian government, and the latter would help to control the separatists troubling the Thai government. Third, the Thai Muslims were seen as fellow Malay Muslims—that is, as sharing ethnic identification with the politically dominant group in Malaysia; hence the Malaysian government could not openly commit itself to active suppression of this kin group. Nor could it endorse the demands for a policy supporting the ethnic kin that emanated from more restricted circles in Malaysia without jeopardizing the benefits from good relations with Thailand.

The government compromised by proclaiming a nonintervention policy, which included censoring of unofficial support for the Thai Muslims and, by 1977, might facilitate Thai military suppression.

In the Philippines, the ethnic links between the minority group and the Malays in Malaysia generally were weaker, although they were salient to the political group led by Tun Mustapha in Sabah. The Malaysian government did not prevent this group's assistance to the Philippine Muslims, and at times facilitated it. It was more difficult politically for the Malaysian government to censor Tun Mustapha than to preach restraint to the sympathizers for the Thai Muslims, but a more important explanation for the different policy lies elsewhere. There was a specific quarrel between the Malaysian and the Philippine governments that recommended a strategy to embarrass and weaken the rival, in contrast with the specific bargain between the Malaysian and the Thai government, which recommended a policy of utmost restraint. Yet the Malaysian government was deterred from giving greater support to the Filipino Muslims by the desire to maintain a modicum of good relations with the Philippine government, for the same reasons that applied to its general relationship with the Thai government.

The different intensities of the conflicts in Thailand and the Philippines also help to explain the variations in the policies of outsiders. They were undoubtedly the most important factor accounting for the different responses of the Islamic foreign ministers, who became closely involved in the Philippine conflict, partly mediating and partly supporting the Muslims, but had no similar involvement in the conflict in Thailand. A second factor should also be mentioned: because parochialism was greater among the Thai Muslims than among the Filipino Muslims, the Thai Muslims were less willing or able to develop outside contacts, except with closely related groups in Malaysia.

Finally, the two regional states that most influenced the course of the conflicts—Malaysia and Indonesia—are both multiethnic states. The Indonesian government explained its noninvolvement in the Thai dispute by denying the validity of ethnic self-determination as a general principle; but this policy, and Indonesia's limited mediative efforts in the Philippine conflict, also rested on other considerations. The Malaysian government rarely invoked this principle to justify its refusal to support the Muslims in southern Thailand, although it might have served a legitimizing function. With regard to the Philippine conflict, the effect of multiethnicity in Malaysia is more difficult to analyze. Clearly it did not prevent direct federal assistance to the Muslims in 1968 and early 1969, nor did it lead to early restraints on Tun Mustapha's assistance. It is true, however, that Malaysian-Philippine relations improved significantly, and aid to the Muslims presumably decreased, after the elections in 1969, which most clearly demonstrated the potential for ethnic violence in Malaysia. Moreover, the decision of the Malaysian federal government to withdraw its support of Tun Mustapha followed his circulation of a memorandum raising the issue of Sabah's status within the federation.

NOTES

1. For a discussion of the problem of estimating numbers of Muslims in the Philippines, see "The Muslim Population in the Philippines," an information sheet published by the Dansalan Research Center (Marawi City: Dansalan College, Apr. 1976). (Mimeographed.)

2. Published in *Philippine Muslim News* (Manila) 2 (July 1968): 7, 21; repr. in *The Rise and Fall of Moro Statehood,* prepared by the Central Committee of the MNLF for the conference of Islamic foreign ministers in Kuala Lumpur, Malaysia, June 1974, pp. 16–17.

The term "Moro" was introduced by the Spaniards and was their name for all Muslims, after the Islamized Mauritanians ("Moors," in English) who had conquered Spain in the eighth century under Arab leadership. In the 1950s and 1960s the term was rejected by many Philippine Muslims as derogatory, but it has recently been rehabilitated.

3. For Muslim Filipino perspectives on their history, see the MNLF's *Rise and Fall of Moro Statehood* and the many essays of Cesar Majul, for example, his "The Muslims in the Philippines: An Historical Perspective," in Peter Gowing and Robert McAmis, eds., *The Muslim Filipinos* (Manila: Solidaridad, 1974), pp. 1–12.

4. There is an interesting discussion of the relationship between the premartial-law political process and ethnic identifications in Crawford Young, *The Politics of Cultural Pluralism* (Madison: University of Wisconsin Press, 1976), pp. 327–72.

5. *Islamic Digest,* Mar. 1976.

6. *Straits Times,* Mar. 11, 1974; *Far Eastern Economic Review,* Mar. 25, 1974, pp. 12–13.

7. For more information on relations between the Malaysian government and Tun Mustapha, see Robert O. Tilman, "Mustapha's Sabah, 1968–1975: The Tun Steps Down," *Asian Survey* 16 (June 1976): 495–509.

8. *Far Eastern Economic Review,* May 7, 1976, p. 21.

9. *Daily Express* (Manila), Apr. 18, 1976. There were reports in Manila that Mustapha had met with Misuari at Mecca in January; hence it was assumed that a victory by Mustapha's party would have resulted in a resumption of aid.

10. *Far Eastern Economic Review,* July 1, 1974, p. 12. Nur Misuari was a protégé of Lucman and was linked with him in the Muslim (or Mindanao) Independence Movement and the Ansar el-Islam. Reports presumably based on interviews with Lucman attribute the break to his realization that Misuari was diverting funds to the Bangsa Moro Army, which Lucman denigrated as "Communist." See *Far Eastern Economic Review,* Mar. 25, 1974, p. 13. An MNLF affiliate interviewed in 1976 reported that both Misuari and Abul Khayr Alonto, vice-chairman of the MNLF, became disillusioned with Lucman and other "old politicians" during the 1971 elections, and that Alonto was called to the "Middle East" after the elections (he was himself elected vice mayor of Marawi City) to confirm reports of Lucman's corruption. Thereafter funds went directly to the MNLF leadership.

11. *Asia Research Bulletin* 2 (Mar. 1–31, 1973): 1699. ASEAN is a regional organization including Malaysia, Singapore, Indonesia, Thailand, and the Philippines.

12. Ibid. 3 (Aug. 1–31, 1973): 2077.

13. *Straits Times,* June 26, 1974.

14. "Copy of Resolution No. 10, Passed in the Sixth Islamic Conference of Foreign Ministers Held at Jeddah, Saudi Arabia, July 12 to 15, 1975"; distributed by the MNLF, northern Mindanao.

15. "Istanbul Conference Communiqué," repr. from *Muslim World,* May 22, 1976.

16. *Far Eastern Economic Review,* Nov. 12, 1976, pp. 32–33.

17. *FBIS Daily Report: Middle East and North Africa,* May 17, 1977, from ARNA (the Libyan news agency); *Far Eastern Economic Review,* June 3, 1977, p. 8.

18. *Daily Press Summary,* U.S. Embassy, Jakarta, Apr. 4, 1974.

19. *Far Eastern Economic Review,* Nov. 7, 1975, p. 23 (insert).

20. Ibid., June 10, 1974, pp. 16–17.

21. *Daily Press Summary,* U.S. Embassy, Jakarta, Mar. 27, 1973.

22. *Asian Recorder* 20 (Feb. 12–18, 1974): 2535.

23. *Straits Times,* June 24, 1974.

24. *Far Eastern Economic Review,* Nov. 7, 1975, p. 23 (insert).

25. "News on the Progress of the Istanbul Conference of Islamic Foreign Ministers," issued by the MNLF, northern Mindanao.

26. "Appeal letter to the Islamic Foreign Ministers' Conference, Kuala Lumpur, Malaysia, June 21, 1974," from the Office of the Chairman, Central Committee, MNLF. The letter quoted a Philippine general as saying, at the height of the Kamlon rebellion in Sulu in the 1950s, "The only solution to the Moro problem is to Christianize them."

27. *Far Eastern Economic Review,* July 8, 1974, p. 11.

28. The MNLF's reply to Melchor's statements was published in the Feb.-Mar. 1975 issue of *IQRA,* the newsletter of the MNLF, northern Mindanao.

29. *New York Times,* Aug. 15, 1975.

30. This has been recognized by leading "loyalist" Muslims such as Governor Termsakdi Samantarath in his *Kawbanyasarob satangen si changwad paktai* ("An Account of Conditions in the Four Southern Provinces") (Bangkok: National Defense College, 1970), pp. 7–8.

31. For an elaboration, see M. Ladd Thomas, *Political Violence in the Muslim Provinces of Southern Thailand* (Singapore: Institute of Southeast Asian Studies, 1975) pp. 15–17; Norman Peagram, "Boiling Point in the Troubled South," *Far Eastern Economic Review,* May 21, 1976, pp. 12–13; and Astri Suhrke, "Loyalists and Separatists: The Muslims in Southern Thailand," *Asian Survey* 18, no. 3 (Mar. 1977): 237–50. Various names of secessionist organizations have been mentioned: the Pattani Islamic Revolution, the National Revolutionary Front, the National Liberation Front of Pattani, and the United Pattani Freedom Movement. It is not entirely clear how, or if, these organizations overlap.

32. *The Muslim* (London), July 1970, p. 230.

33. *Straits Times,* June 18, 1974. This speech was made in Malaysia, which probably explains the more subdued tone in comparison with the previous statement, which was made to a Muslim paper published abroad.

34. Yong Mun Cheong, "The Malaysian Setting," *Southeast Asian Affairs, 1974* (Singapore: Institute of Southeast Asian Studies, 1974), p. 138.

35. Kuala Lumpur Domestic Service, June 6, 1976; *Foreign Broadcast Information Service* FBIS, *Daily Report: Asia and the Pacific.*

36. For an elaboration, see Richard Nations, "Hot Pursuit After Whom?" *Far Eastern Economic Review,* Aug. 27, 1976, pp. 33–35.

37. *Bangkok Post,* May 5, 1976.

38. A Malaysian white paper, *The Path of Violence to Absolute Power* (Kuala Lumpur: Ministry of Home Affairs, Malaysia, 1968), claims the CPM has set up party schools in the Thai border region for special training of party cadres to carry out "religious subversion"—that is, to promote "the spurious doctrine that Islam and Communism share the same ideals" (pp. 28–29). The Malaysian home affairs minister, Tan Sri Ghazali Shafi, told the Malaysian Parliament on July 12, 1976, that the CPM had organized a front (PAPERI, Parti Persudaraan Islam) that since 1965 had been recruiting Thai Muslims, especially in Waeng district (Narathiwas province). See *New Straits Times,* May 16 and 27, 1976, for elaboration.

39. *The Nation* (Bangkok), May 7, 1976.

40. Jakarta Domestic Service, June 25, 1974; *FBIS, Daily Report: Asia and The Pacific.*

41. Agence France Press, dateline Bangkok, June 27, 1974; *FBIS, Daily Report: Asia and the Pacific.*

CHAPTER

9

SPREAD OR CONTAINMENT: THE ETHNIC FACTOR

Astri Suhrke
Lela Garner Noble

We must now return to the questions posed at the outset: Are domestic ethnic conflicts peculiarly conducive to external involvement? If so, to what kind of involvement? Is there a "multiplier effect" whereby domestic ethnic conflict generates further conflict as it involves outside parties? If so, is the circle of outside parties likely to be small or large?

Let us start with a simple categorization based on two dimensions: the scope of involvement (the number of outside parties involved) and the nature of international or transnational relations arising from such involvement (whether they are conflicting or cooperative). The more new conflict is generated among the larger number of parties, the greater the "multiplier effect" and —from a perspective of international peace and stability—the more disturbing such conflicts would be. The diagram below may help to conceptualize the relationship between these two dimensions.

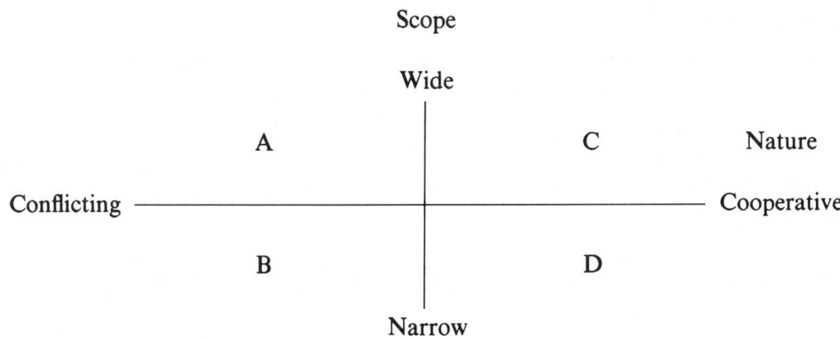

While it would be difficult, if not impossible, to place any one case exactly in this figure, a tentative placement can be suggested.

The cases of Cyprus, Lebanon, and Eritrea would fall somewhere in quadrant A. They share the following characteristics:

- Each protagonist in the local conflict received outside, partisan support in direct response to the local conflict
- There was a chain-reaction type of response as many other external parties reacted or adjusted in ways that had a bearing on the conflict
- There was typically an "inner ring" of participants whose policies were conflicting, and an "outer ring" whose activities were more mediatory or interpositional.

The cases of the Kazakhs and the Kurds fall in quadrant B, with the Kazakh case closer to the "narrow" point on the axis than the Kurdish case. Generally, both cases share the following characteristics:

- Only one of the local protagonists received outside active, partisan support
- There was little, if any, chain reaction in the form of policy adjustments by other states that had a bearing on the conflict
- The partisan involvement that took place created considerable conflict between the states concerned.

None of our cases falls clearly in quadrant C, although developments at a particular time, such as the U.N. Peacekeeping force in Cyprus, would qualify.

The case of the Thai Muslims fits in quadrant D. Its characteristics are the following:

- A very small number of outside parties played an active role
- None of the local protagonists received active, partisan support of any magnitude in direct response to the conflict
- The conflict to some extent stimulated—or at least did not prevent—interstate cooperation among the parties concerned.

In recognition of these characteristics, cases under A might be termed "complex conflict expansion"; under B, "simple conflict expansion"; under C, "complex conflict containment"; and under D, "simple conflict containment." To the extent that cases in the two latter categories are located toward the "cooperative" point on the axis, we can also speak of "conflict transformation," in that the process of containing the conflict stimulated international cooperation.

The categorization thus far does not include the cases of Northern Ireland and the Philippine Muslims, which seem to be intermediate cases. Several outside parties were involved in the Philippine Muslim rebellion, but the foreign involvement was not competitive. Nor did it produce a great deal of interstate conflict among the parties concerned; rather, the relations were somewhat mixed, both conflicting and cooperative. Let us therefore place this case at the intersection point of the two axes. Similarly, Anglo-Irish relations relative to the conflict in Ulster involved a combination of conflict and at least tacit cooperation, but outside involvement was primarily limited to these two parties. This case would therefore be further toward the "narrow" point on the vertical axis, and at a midpoint on the horizontal axis. The term "conflict equilibration" might be appropriate for both cases.

What, then is the relevance of ethnic factors in determining these various patterns? Specifically, we wanted to examine the impact of three ethnic dimensions: the type of issue raised in the ethnic conflict (separatism, irredentism, or limited sharing of power within the state), cross-boundary ethnic ties, and the ethnic characteristics of the interested or actually intervening outside parties.

COMPETITIVE CONFLICT EXPANSION

All three cases under this rubric—Cyprus, Lebanon, and Eritrea—were centrally connected to much broader patterns of international conflict or cooperation. This connection generally explains the wide scope of involvement in the initial conflict. In two of the cases (Lebanon and Eritrea) it also decisively influenced the policies of the "inner ring" participants.

Eritrea's centrality to a broader pattern of international relations is partly unrelated to the ethnic dimensions of the conflict. A wide array of Arab states supported the Eritreans because they heartily disliked Ethiopia's pro-Western, pro-Israeli policy that characterized the reign of Emperor Haile Selassie. Some of them were not mollified by the radicalism of the subsequent government, while others feared the radicalism and pro-Soviet policies of the new regime. Most external parties were sensitive to the strategic location of Eritrea along the Red Sea. Competition for access to this area by regional and extraregional actors became enmeshed with the internal struggle between the Eritrean separatists and the central government in Addis Ababa. While the strategic consideration was not a central factor for all external supporters of the Eritreans, Addis Ababa tended to believe so, and intensified its search for countervailing outside assistance to prevent greater Arab encirclement. As individual states became involved, their rivals, friends, and adversaries in turn found it desirable to adjust accordingly. Competitive involvement was further encouraged by the accessibility of the local protagonists to outside parties. The consequent alignments heightened tension in the area, but in an important sense were also a product of previously conflicting forces.

Ethnic factors were mainly relevant in two respects. Some Eritreans self-consciously portrayed the separatist movement as an Arab Muslim struggle against a non-Arab Christian government. This identification was an important factor in generating outside support. For some Arab states, the Arab nationalist link was most significant, while for others it was the Muslim identification. In either case, the salience of these ties was emphasized by their symbolic value to Arab states in different contexts: the Arab-Israeli conflict and inter-Arab rivalry. Support for the Eritreans was a means of demonstrating a commitment to orthodox Arab nationalism. More tangibly, an independent Eritrea beholden to Arab states for its independence would be a likely client, at least for a while, that would extend Arab influence along the remaining Red Sea coast.

The combination of affective ethnic ties, strategic-political considerations, and, for some (notably Sudan and Somalia), more particularist quarrels with the central government in Addis Ababa determined the extent of outside support for the Eritrean separatists. When these factors were mutually reinforcing, or at least not internally conflicting, they generated a significant amount of support for the separatists. This stands in contrast with the generally lukewarm support that the Muslim states extended to the Muslim rebels in the Philippines. One restraint on external support to the Philippine Muslims was a reluctance to set a precedent for greater ethnic self-determination; in Eritrea, this reluctance was overshadowed by the benefits the external parties hoped to receive for their support. Yet, the ethnic nature of the initial Eritrean conflict raised another dimension of cost. The Ethiopian government was determined to suppress the separatists at almost any cost, not merely because Eritrea was its main outlet to the sea but also because it feared the Eritrean rebellion signaled a general fragmentation of multiethnic Ethiopia. This determination promised a protracted, violent conflict that, given Ethiopia's centrality to a broader pattern of international relations, would likely lead to sustained tension in the region and invite further extraregional participation. Consequently, some external parties considered mediation based on a compromise solution of internal autonomy short of full secession for the Eritreans.

In Lebanon, the wide scope of international involvement is similarly explained by Lebanon's central link with other international conflicts. This link was even less related to ethnic dimensions of the conflict between the Lebanese protagonists than was the case in Ethiopia. Lebanon, bordering both Syria and Israel, is geographically a part of the Arab-Israeli equation; the large Palestinian presence in southern Lebanon directly linked developments in Lebanon to the Palestinian struggle. Involvement by external parties in the Lebanese civil war generally reflected their interests in these two questions. The consequent tension in the region—attenuated by elements of convergence in the policies of Syria and Israel, as well as efforts by Arab League members to concert their policies—was thus related to ethnic identification, but not the Christian-Muslim distinction that divided the local Lebanese protagonists.

The internal Christian-Muslim division between the Lebanese cut across state boundaries, but these ties were not the basis for external support. They either proved irrelevant or, as at one time during Syrian involvement, were grossly violated. Syrian objectives—to assure a balance in Lebanon that would not lead to a confrontation with Israel, to assert Syrian influence in Lebanon generally, and to control the Palestinian movement—required a shifting policy. At one time these objectives dictated an alliance with fellow Muslims in Lebanon, at another time an equivalent alliance with the Christians. Shared ethnic ties, in the sense of shared religion, were thus subordinated to Syria's strategic-political aims.

It should be noted that the Syrian government is self-consciously secular, and Baathist indifference to the fate of Muslims, qua Muslims, in Lebanon is hardly surprising. It is interesting, though, that domestic criticism in Syria over Hafez al-Assad's policy did not focus on the religious identity of the Lebanese parties, but on their political stance. Assad was criticized for supporting a conservative group against a leftist alliance, not for allying with Christians against Muslims. This point supports the contention that the internal conflict in Lebanon was largely a struggle between socioeconomic groups that generally happened to be divided along religious—or ethnic—lines.

In Cyprus, by contrast, cross-boundary ethnic links were highly relevant, in that they rendered external involvement along ethnic lines inevitable. Greek and Turkish involvement triggered initiatives and adjustments by several other states and international organizations. This "outer ring" of involvement only marginally reflected ethnic ties (the Greek and Turkish diaspora in Great Britain and the United States) but clearly showed broader strategic-political considerations flowing from Greek and Turkish membership in NATO, their (and Cyprus') importance to NATO's southern flank, and, at an earlier period, the anticolonial movement.

There are several reasons why cross-boundary ethnic ties were more salient in Cyprus than, for example, in Lebanon. The ties were close and multidimensional; they were reinforced by a parallel Greek-Turkish enmity of long standing and, for Turkey, supported by a psychological attachment to Cyprus that has national security implications. Cyprus is geographically close to Turkey and was once part of the Ottoman Empire, and Turkey has traditionally tried to deny an actual or potentially hostile power access to the island. Turkish demands that the identity of the Turkish Cypriot community must be preserved are designed to forestall Greek control over the island through *enosis;* thus they neatly harmonize with sentiments demanding protection for the kin minority. For Greece, ethnic arithmetic would favor enosis, and certainly underpins whatever attachment there has been to this idea in Greece. Inclusion of Cyprus would mean the addition of only a small foreign minority (about 100,000 Turkish Cypriots, compared with Greece's present population of about 8 million), and the Turkish Cypriot minority presumably could be treated on the same basis as other small minorities (including Turkish) in

Greece. Actual Greek policy, however, has generally been low-key and open to compromise solutions; and Greece has demonstrated a willingness to restrain Greek Cypriots demanding enosis. This restraint results principally from the fear of war with Turkey, and the certainty that Greece would be by far the weaker party in such a contest. Greek deviations from a restrained policy (as in 1974) are explained both by a miscalculation of Turkish response and by the perceived need to move preemptively to secure Greek influence on the island.

The internationalization of the Cyprus conflict thus derives from, and contributes to, a parallel Greek-Turkish enmity. Their bilateral relations have fluctuated; their policies toward Cyprus similarly contain a measure of tacit agreement alongside conflicting pulls that at times produce sharp hostility. The point to be stressed here is that precisely because cross-boundary ties are conflicting, they carry some inherent restraint on the policies of the mother countries. From a Greek perspective, the adverse power ratio between the two mother countries inhibits support for a radical solution to the internal conflict in Cyprus (enosis or unitary independence). This, in turn, moderates the potential for conflict generation on the state-to-state level arising from the internal conflict. Moreover, both Greece and Turkey recognize American opposition to a confrontation between the two NATO partners over Cyprus and have shown some receptivity to American efforts to defuse the situation.

SIMPLE CONFLICT EXPANSION

The Kurdish and Kazakh cases involve dissatisfied minorities whose kinship ties connect them with minorities in the adjoining states. The willingness and ability of the latter to give aid were limited by their own minority status. The most significant external involvement came from governments of adjoining states that seized upon the ethnic conflict as a pretext, or a tool, to promote wholly or partly unrelated foreign policy interests. Soviet meddling in China's Kazakh problem reflected the intrinsic value of this area in Moscow's view, but Soviet policy was heavily conditioned by the Sino-Soviet conflict and closely followed its dynamic. In the Kurdish case, the shah of Iran found it convenient to support the Kurdish rebellion in Iraq in order to weaken what he considered a rival (the Baghdad government). The slightly wider scope of involvement in the Kurdish conflict reflects the relative openness of the Persian Gulf area to competitive large-power penetration. Typically, though, these cases are characterized by one-sided partisan support for dissatisfied minorities, and the international consequences are mainly evident in the bilateral relations between the states concerned. Of interest here is the apparent reluctance by friendly governments to support the central government facing an externally supported rebellion in a Holy Alliance type of concerted suppression, even when the central government faces a protracted and difficult struggle, as the Iraqi government did at one stage.

In both cases we have a close, circular relationship between the causes of involvement and the effects on the external environment. External intervention, and the form it took, was determined primarily by existing enmity relations between the states concerned, and in turn accentuated or increased that enmity. However, state-to-state rivalry also produced restraint in that the intervening party wished to avoid an unregulated or greatly intensified confrontation with its adversary. Both the Soviet Union in the case of the Kazakhs, and Iran in the case of the Kurds, shied away from massive intervention that would risk a major confrontation with China and Iraq, respectively. Yet, it is reasonable to postulate that if state-to-state relations worsened significantly for other reasons, a more substantial intervention on the side of the minorities might be justified as a tool in a conflict where the risks were already considerable.

The ethnic dimensions of the internal conflict entered primarily to restrain the degree of external partisan support. Iran and the Soviet Union had their own minorities that were ethnically related to the Kurds in Iraq and the Kazakhs in China, respectively, and the extent of central government control over these minorities clearly influenced their interventionist policy. The shah had his own Kurds fairly well under control at the time he gave substantial aid to the Kurdish rebels in Iraq (the Turkish government was more worried about the political activities of its Kurds and hence adopted a pro-Iraqi neutrality, despite a not-so-cordial relationship between Ankara and Baghdad). Though there were ethnic dissenters in the Soviet Union, including Kazakhs, the government exercised a great deal of control. It should be noted, however, that neither the Soviet Union consistently, nor Iran at all, endorsed a separate state for the Kazakhs in China or the Kurds in Iraq. Such endorsement of the principle of ethnic self-determination would have been politically unwise, in view of the probable demonstration effect on their own minorities. It is hardly coincidental that the Soviet Union had sponsored an East Turkestan Republic only during the Stalinist era, when domestic controls were most rigid.

There were other considerations of cost relating to the characteristics of the initial conflict. The minorities were relatively small compared with the total population of the country (tiny in the Kazakh case, more substantial in the Kurdish case), and the kind of external support necessary to bring the dissatisfied minorities toward something like a victory clearly would be very substantial. Moreover, because the central governments viewed greater autonomy for rebellious minorities as a possible step toward territorial fragmentation, they were firmly determined to prevent this. The issues at stake and the balance of forces between the local protagonists thus promised a long, uphill struggle for the minorities. This prospect further discouraged the external supporters from embarking on a massive intervention designed to bring the minorities to victory, and recommended instead a limited investment (subsequently terminated in Iran's case). Indirectly, then, these restraints limited the degree of international conflict arising from partisan involvement.

SIMPLE CONFLICT CONTAINMENT

In the Thai Muslim case, the dissatisfied minority was weak and, to the extent that it solicited external support, looked primarily to ethnic kin who constituted majorities in neighboring or more distant countries. The failure of the latter to extend partisan support was partly due to the low level of the local conflict, and partly because the most closely connected kin group commanding governmental power—the Malays in Malaysia—did their best to ensure that the conflict would not be internationalized.

Malaysia's containment policy illustrates how far an outside government will go in ignoring cross-boundary ethnic ties in order to maintain a useful cooperative relationship on the state-to-state level. The affective ethnic ties linking the local minority with the outside majority were strong and multidimensional, but the Malaysian government had a more important reason to maintain good relations with the government of Thailand: a specific cooperative bargain of great significance. The Malaysian government declared a strict nonintervention policy with respect to the local conflict, and at one stage even facilitated Thai suppression of the kin minority. As a result, the internal conflict was contained, was isolated from intergovernmental cooperation between the two states, and indirectly stimulated further cooperation.

CONFLICT EQUILIBRATION

In the case of the Muslim minority in the Philippines, the initial conflict was linked to a broader set of international relations, specifically to the Association of Southeast Asian Nations (ASEAN) and the U.S.-Philippine alliance, but was not central to either. The external actors who became involved in the conflict were principally motivated by other reasons. The local minority had an ethnic link with outside majorities, and this link constituted the major (but not sole) reason for the latter to render assistance. The ethnic tie was weak in the sense that for most external actors it involved only one dimension of ethnicity—the Islamic religion—but it did provide a sense of commonality that helped the Muslim minority to obtain support from the Islamic Conference as a whole, as well as from individual Muslim states in the region (Malaysia) and outside it (Libya).

As noted, the affective tie was not the sole basis for external support. It became a salient policy consideration to the external majorities partly because of the intensity of the local conflict. There were also motives of a nonethnic nature. The Malaysian government had a specific quarrel with the Philippine government and considered partisan support for the rebels a suitable revenge for a previous Philippine initiative. Libya no doubt found some satisfaction in supporting rebels who were not only Muslim but also leftist-radical, in opposition to a conservative central government allied to the United States.

Just as in the Kazakh and Kurdish cases, external involvement was primarily one-sided on behalf of the rebels (American support for the central government of the Philippines was not a direct response to the conflict but part of a continuing, broader policy). The absence of competitive, external involvement—partly because cross-boundary ethnic ties were not in themselves competitive, and partly because the initial conflict was not central to another international conflict system—signified a limited spillover of the conflict to the external environment. Certainly, external government support for the rebels served to increase tension between these supporters and the central government in the Philippines. But even here we see tension moderated by efforts to find a compromise solution. Governmental relations among the parties concerned rarely reached the point of open recriminations. Within the smaller ASEAN circle, patterns of cooperation remained undisturbed by the conflict.

International conflict was moderated for two reasons. First, the ethnic dimensions of the conflict served to restrain the extent of outside partisan support for the rebels. Outside governments were explicitly unwilling to support the extreme separatist demands of the rebels and encouraged them to compromise in favor of autonomy. The Islamic states apparently considered ethnic self-determination in its extreme logic an undesirable precedent; and multiethnic states in the region, such as Malaysia and Indonesia, seemed particularly concerned. Related cost factors were also relevant: the rebels represented a quite small minority that would need sustained and substantial external support to compel the central government to accept separatist demands, which it considered wholly unacceptable.

Second, broader foreign policy considerations of a nonethnic nature recommended restraint. None of the intervening parties had a preexisting, strongly hostile relationship with the Philippine government. On the contrary, Indonesia and Malaysia stressed the need to regulate intraregional disputes in order to strengthen ASEAN as a regional organization. Libya's quarrel with the Philippine government was part of a more broadly diffused radical challenge. Its role in the negotiations in late 1976 and early 1977 clearly indicated that its opposition to the Philippine regime was not sufficiently fundamental to prevent compromise when other concerns made it desirable. Many other Islamic states viewed their relations with Manila in the context of the Arab-Israeli conflict and were pleased by the Philippine government's adjustments on this issue.

The internationalization of the Ulster conflict has primarily involved the Republic of Ireland and Great Britain (which has official jurisdiction over the area and therefore is not an "external" actor in the sense that the Republic is), and some unofficial support to the Ulster Catholics from Irish-Americans. The lack of involvement by other parties is explained by the relative strategic-political unimportance of Ulster to any other party, and the effects of ethnic and jurisdictional ties in limiting "legitimate" involvement to Britain and the Irish Republic. The consequences of such involvement for Anglo-Irish relations have been mixed. At times relations have been strained, but tension has also been moderated by a tacit recognition that both governments have common interests in Ulster. Neither has consistently pursued an unambiguous policy of partisan support for the opposing extremist groups in Northern Ireland.

For Dublin, cross-boundary ethnic ties produce conflicting stimuli. Strong, multidimensional ethnic ties and geographic proximity to Ulster's Catholic minority suggest partisan support and—to some groups in the Republic—merger. On the other hand, since Ulster's Catholics are in a minority, merger would mean inclusion of the militantly opposed Protestant majority, who would constitute a sizable minority in a United Ireland (1 million out of less than 4.5 million). Unlike the Greek case, ethnic arithmetic does not favor the radical solution of merger. There is also the recognition that a substantial segment of the Ulster Catholics does not support merger if it can be obtained only through violence and if it does not promise an end to violence. Moreover, the radical vanguard for merger, the Irish Republican Army, constitutes the greatest domestic challenge to the Dublin government, which understandably is reluctant to support violent republicans even when their efforts are concentrated in Ulster. On the other hand, the strength of affective ethnic ties does not permit indifference to the fate of Catholics in Northern Ireland, especially in periods of intensified local violence, when pressures in the Republic to support Ulster kin increase. This was clearly demonstrated by Dublin's response to the increased violence and dispatch of British troops to Ulster in 1969. The result is an ambiguous policy: support for power-sharing formulas also sought by the British government and the moderate segments in Ulster, but a partisan reflex to protect the Catholics when their position appears to take a decisive turn for the worse.

Contemporary British involvement in Ulster has centered on attempts to stabilize the situation in order to end the violence and destruction—which at times has spread from Ulster to other areas of the United Kingdom—and to stop the drain on British resources. While stability through reform has not been attained, British governments have firmly rejected the radical alternatives of either ruthlessly suppressing the Catholic minority or forcing the Protestant majority to be incorporated in a united Ireland—principally because these alternatives violate basic norms of how to solve domestic political problems, but also because the Republic of Ireland could not tolerate the first alternative and is not enthusiastic about the second.

The Ulster case provides an interesting contrast to Cyprus, in that the reasons for external moderation toward the local conflict differ. Britain does not have the close, affective ties with Protestant Ulstermen that form the basis for Turkish support to its kin group in Cyprus. The Republic of Ireland has a close identity with its kin in Ulster, and for over four decades after 1922 refused to accept the *de facto* division of the island—not dissimilar to the Greek attachment to Greek Cypriots in the context of the "Megali Idea" (although in the Greek case the attachment has been diluted by physical distance). Restraint on actual Greek policy to obtain merger, however, rests on considerations of state-to-state relations with Turkey, while Dublin's unwillingness to support merger stems primarily from characteristics of the internal conflict itself, notably the unfavorable ethnic arithmetic. These factors also help to explain why there is a somewhat more conflicting external involvement in Cyprus than in Northern Ireland, and a consequent difference in the interstate tension generated.

THE ETHNIC FACTOR

The significance of ethnic factors in conflict expansion or containment can now be summarized in general terms.

Scope of External Involvement

Among the three ethnic dimensions to be considered (cross-boundary ties, issues in the initial conflict, and ethnic characteristics of the intervening party), the nature of cross-boundary ties is most directly relevant in determining whether the scope of external involvement is wide or narrow.

Cross-boundary ethnic ties do not in themselves create a wide scope of external involvement in the internal conflict except when they include outside parties that play an important role in other systems of international conflict or cooperation and whose actions trigger something like a chain reaction (such as Greece and Turkey in Cyprus), and when attenuated ties, typically involving only one dimension of ethnicity, link populations in a number of states (such as Muslim support for Muslims in the Philippines, Arab nationalist/Muslim support for Eritreans). If internal ethnic conflict does become enmeshed in a wide set of international relations, it will be due primarily to strategic/political reasons (as in Lebanon). Indeed, one can discern a tendency for cross-boundary ethnic ties to limit the scope of external involvement when these ties are multidimensional and link a local protagonist to an outside majority (as in Northern Ireland). In these cases the strength of the ethnic factor is likely to discourage the involvement of outside parties that might otherwise act on the basis of nonethnic considerations.

Consequences of External Involvement on the International System

External involvement in the form of active partisan support to one or both of the local protagonists is likely to generate further international conflict and tension. Let us therefore initially focus on the relationship between ethnic factors and active partisan involvement by outside parties.

Cross-boundary ethnic ties stimulate partisan intervention primarily in cases where internal minorities are linked to outside majorities. They are also relevant in a majority-majority relationship when the issue involves merger. However, these ties are rarely, if ever, sufficient to produce sustained partisan support for a radical change in the status quo favorable to the kin group (notably merger and separation). Such support usually requires additional, weighty reasons of a nonethnic nature (like those motivating Arab states—with the possible exception of Syria and Iraq—to support the Eritreans) and/or unambiguously positive cost-benefit calculations in ethnic terms (clearly Ireland found these negative). Even when ethnic ties favor strong partisan intervention, the stimulus can easily be blunted and subordinated to nonethnic factors recommending restraint. The salience of ethnic ties is greatest when the kin group appears to be in great physical danger. At this stage, restraints on active partisan intervention are likely to be set aside, but only temporarily or until the status quo ante has been restored (as exemplified by the Philippine Muslim case and Turkish response to communal violence in Cyprus).

Cases involving separatism and autonomy produce restraint on partisan intervention that seems to apply whether or not involvement is based on ethnic ties. One set of restraints applies mainly when the intervening party is a government: the reluctance to set a precedent for greater ethnic self-determination. This consideration is especially relevant for governments presiding over multiethnic populations and/or a minority linked to the rebel group. The other source of restraint has more general applicability. When the separatist/autonomist rebels constitute a small minority (which seems typical in such cases), they will require a great deal of outside assistance to achieve victory. The intervening party must thus consider this cost, as well as the cost of provoking unambiguous hostility from the central government of the embattled state. The latter will view demands for separatism, and probably autonomy, as a fundamental challenge to the integrity of the state, and hence will resist at all cost. This promises a long, costly conflict and, in some cases, further complications because of the possibility of other external actors entering the fray. The prospect is likely to moderate external partisan support and to encourage the less committed partisans to mediate (as was true in regard to the Eritreans and the Philippine Muslims). In these cases, then, we can conclude that ethnic factors relating to the initial conflict tend to restrain the degree of outside partisan involvement, and to that extent moderate the potential for international tension arising from involvement.

In conflicts involving merger (or irredentism), we have by definition an immediate "internationalization" in that the goal requires at least the acquiescence of an external government (the mother country). However, an appropriate ethnic arithmetic is a necessary, but not sufficient, factor even for acquiescence (witness Greece relative to Cyprus).

In conflicts where internal power distribution short of partition, separation, or merger is at issue, we hypothesized relatively fewer pressures for outside partisan involvement than in separatist or merger cases. There was insufficient comparability of cases discussed here to permit a detailed examination of this question. In several cases, the impact of this issue on the form of external involvement was blurred because several issues coexisted or competed. Still, it may be noted that in the Lebanese case—where power distribution within the state constituted the central issue between the Lebanese protagonists—the local factions accepted an alignment with Syria as a necessary evil. Suspicion of Syrian motives stemmed partly from the fear that Syria wanted to influence Lebanese developments in general, and signified a distaste for foreign alliances that might jeopardize Lebanese exclusive sovereignty over domestic affairs. Similar reservations were not evident in separatist or autonomy movements, although these certainly had other reasons to distrust their external allies.

With respect to the intervening party, we have already seen that cases involving separatism or autonomy tend to produce restraint, in part because of the reluctance of outside parties to set a precedent for greater ethnic self-determination. This restraint does not apply in conflicts involving adjustment of the internal power-sharing formula and may facilitate a strong partisan involvement in such instances, provided the outside party has other reasons for doing this (as Syria had in Lebanon). When the internal conflict involves a diversification of issues and protagonists along a radical-moderate spectrum, however, we can observe a familiar dynamic: the possibility of a radical solution (merger, partition, separation) encourages at least some outside parties to stress the need for a moderate solution by adjusting the power-sharing formula (as Britain did in Ulster and the United States in Cyprus).

Ethnic Characteristics of the Outside Party

The impact of the third ethnic dimension—the ethnic characteristics of the outside party—has in part been dealt with. Governments are generally reluctant to support a policy of greater ethnic self-determination as a matter of principle, and governments of multiethnic states are especially sensitive to the possible adverse demonstration effects at home. The ability of a government to control its own minorities, or generally to maintain a stable pluralist formula, conditions its policy toward ethnic conflict elsewhere in a straightforward manner: the more control in domestic politics, the more willingness to support ethnic self-determination in other countries (consider Soviet and Iranian policies in the Kazakh and Kurdish conflicts). Autocratic governments have an edge over polyarchic systems in this respect. Strong autocratic governments likewise will have less difficulty in pursuing a foreign policy that ignores, or even violates, affective ethnic ties between their domestic constituencies and kin engaged in conflict elsewhere (for instance, Syria in Lebanon). This further suggests an answer to a question raised at the outset: when are we most likely to find a divergence between official policy toward ethnic conflict in another state, and the unofficial activities of domestic ethnic sympathizers? A divergence seems most probable in two situations: political systems ruled by autocratic but weak regimes (allowing little opportunity for domestic ethnic sympathizers to influence official policy, but being unable to control their activities), and an open system where the government cannot, or will not, fully control the transnational activities of local sympathizers who find they are too weak to shape official policy according to their desire.

POLICY IMPLICATIONS

The policy implications of these generalizations are brought out more clearly if we distinguish between affective intervention (based on cross-boundary ethnic ties) and instrumental intervention (in the absence of, or unrelated to, such ties).

International Stability and Conflict Regulation

Let us first adopt a perspective that emphasizes the value of international stability and conflict regulation. From this perspective, there is reason to be content: the case studies reviewed here do not suggest that internal ethnic conflict is particularly prone to develop into international conflict.

Instrumental Intervention

Internal ethnic conflict can provide a convenient pretext for external intervention, partly because its festering quality promises a "cheap" involvement in some respects. The extent of intervention, however, and hence the full consequences for international order, are principally regulated by broader policy considerations extraneous to the ethnic conflict. There is nothing inherent in the ethnic conflict that suggests either extensive or intensive partisan involvement. Similarly, the initial conflict can become entangled in a broader international conflict because of the strategic significance of the territory involved or the political alliances of the main protagonists. In this case, the dynamic of the broader conflict is largely unrelated to the ethnic dimensions of the initial conflict.

To the extent that ethnic dimensions play a role in the internationalization process, they tend to have a restraining effect. We have noted the restraints on external governmental support for separatist and autonomy movements. One cost factor—the principle of greater ethnic self-determination—is especially pertinent to governments of multiethnic states. Since instrumental intervention seems a convenient option for governments of adjoining states that have easy access to the rebels, and since minorities frequently straddle national boundaries, restraint stemming from considerations of precedent may be somewhat typical. From the perspective of the central government facing separatist or autonomy groups, the prospect for active international support is also limited. Traditional friends tend to retain a supportive policy; other states will need particularist, instrumental reasons for becoming involved. Unless such reasons obtain, the tendency in the international community, particularly in international and regional organizations acting as a collectivity, is to adopt a neutral attitude that indirectly supports the central government by accepting its claim that the ethnic conflict is an internal affair of the country concerned (for instance, Organization of African Unity and U.N. resolutions on the Eritrean question and the U.N. response to Kurdish pleas).

Ethnic conflicts that are perceived as involving a great deal of internal violence encourage external mediation to regulate and stabilize the initial conflict and thus prevent it from becoming a source of wider international conflict. The ethnic factor here appears as an intervening variable: ethnic identification contributes to the intensity of the local conflict (witness Ulster, Lebanon, and Cyprus), and intensification reinforces whatever inclinations to mediate outside parties may have had earlier.

Affective Intervention

When cross-boundary ethnic ties form the basis for outside involvement in the internal conflict, we have a potentially more explosive international situation for reasons directly related to ethnic dimensions. Although ethnic ties in these cases may limit the scope of external involvement, they suggest strongly partisan support for ethnic kin and consequent international tension. Nevertheless, the cases discussed here demonstrate that cross-boundary ethnic ties rarely are unambiguous sources of partisan support. First, these ties are potentially most significant when they link either one or both of the local protagonists to outside majorities. Because the latter are in a position to render support of some magnitude through official channels, the conflict will spill over into international relations. But if the internal conflict concerns separatism, the outside majorities will tend to restrain their support for reasons discussed above (particularly in the Philippine Muslim case). If incorporation in another state is the goal of the ethnic dissidents, the government of that state is likely to consider full support only if the arithmetic and geography of ethnic distribution are favorable (they were not in the Irish case). If the ethnic arithmetic is appropriate, but if merger would include a local minority that also has strong affective ties with another outside majority, there is a potential for intense international conflict—but that potential in itself can have a deterrent effect (witness the Cyprus case). There remains the "classic" irredentist case of European pre-World War II history, where, as in the Italian case, a kin group was cut off from its "homeland," territorially concentrated and relatively homogeneous internally, and waiting to be "redeemed." Only in this case would the cross-boundary ethnic ties be free of internal contradictions and stimulate unqualified partisan support from the homeland.

Even in the classic irredentist case, of course, sentiments of ethnic solidarity had to compete with other policy considerations in determining the extent of support for the ethnic kin. This is also demonstrated in the case of the Thai Muslim militants, who initially wanted merger with Malaysia but, precisely because Malaysia did not take up the irredentist claim, changed their goal to independence. Although ethnic ties in this case are strong and rather unambiguous in suggesting partisan support from the external majority, the latter has subordinated its sentiments to the need to maintain good state-to-state relations with the central government ruling their ethnic kin group. When ethnic ties are ambiguous—simultaneously suggesting support and restraint toward the kin group—it can be assumed that considerations of state-to-state relations acquire even more significance in the final determination policy. Consequently, unqualified support from outside majorities for either merger or separatism involving ethnic kin—that is, the kind of support most likely to create international conflict of some significance among the states involved—would seem to require a special combination of ethnic and nonethnic circumstances, and it may well be a rare case that meets these requirements.

Parties to the Domestic Conflict

If we adopt a different perspective—that of the parties to the domestic conflict—the cases reviewed here do not give much reason for comfort. In particular, embattled ethnic groups seeking a radical change in their position to obtain security and justice will find the conclusions grim indeed.

Instrumental Intervention

A small minority that has no powerful outside kin can count only on very uncertain assistance. It can find allies who will assist for reasons of their own, and whose support is consequently conditioned by a dynamic over which the minority has little control and that it finds difficult to predict. If the minority's case is purely incidental to that of its allies, it is likely to find an inverse relationship between its need for support and the amount it can obtain. When the minority is weakest—desperately seeking international recognition and support either to gain momentum or to prevent an imminent defeat—the outside ally tends to limit its assistance, since even a "cheap" intervention may be a wasted asset. If the challenge of the minority grows more formidable and increases the prospect for a favorable settlement, the minority is likely to find its ally reconsidering: what are the costs of risking intensified conflict with the central government (and its allies) against the absence of any intrinsic benefit, and possible disadvantages, to be derived from victory for the minority? If the central government at this point is weak and/or isolated internationally, the local challengers probably will find their ally steadfast—but they need an ally less than if the central government retains considerable strength and international support. In the latter instance, of course, the risks and costs of maintaining support for the rebels are increased for the ally. The main modification of this cycle of support occurs when the ally has strong instrumental reasons for continuing to assist the minority, including intrinsic strategic benefits attendant on an eventual victory. In these situations the external ally would be prepared to accept greater risks and costs from supporting the minority group.

Affective Intervention

When the ethnic minority has affective ties with outside majorities, the cycle of support differs in one important respect: the minority can expect considerable support when it is most needed, that is, when its position is at the point of marked deterioration. Perceptions of that point will vary. If the cross-boundary tie is weak, a heavy casualty rate for the minority appears to be a critical point. If affective ties are strong, any decrease in the physical security or political status of the minority may be sufficient to jolt the kin majority into rendering substantial assistance (consider Turkish response to violence on Cyprus and Ireland's policy toward Ulster in 1969, and variations in Islamic Conference attention to Muslims in the Philippines and Thailand). However, support adequate to obtain a radical, positive change in the position of the minority is another thing. As in the case of instrumental intervention, consideration of such a policy requires a broader cost-benefit calculation, going beyond the simple moral imperative of rescuing ethnic kin from what is seen as imminent defeat (violent suppression or assimilation into an alien body politic). In the cases considered here, these calculations produced restraint following the initial demonstration of support. When the position of the minority appears to be somewhere between the extremes of defeat and victory, kin may maintain their moral support but are less prone to give material assistance.

When the local ethnic group constitutes a dominant majority, it will by definition be less dependent upon outside support than the local minority will; but if the question of merger with the homeland arises, it of necessity requires external support along ethnic lines. The local proponents of merger probably will find that the homeland government's response is heavily influenced by what they see as extraneous foreign policy considerations. In the Cyprus case, these considerations generally recommended restraint in Athens. The absence of ethnically based merger between independent states in the post-World War II era indicates that these restraints may be typical or, more basically, that the structure of the Cyprus conflict is unique.

The prospects of dissatisfied, radical ethnic groups' exploiting the international environment to achieve their purposes generally seem limited, but possibly there is more hope for the moderate segments. While radical groups, as suggested in one of our initial hypotheses, seem more likely to be outward-looking than are loyalists of either a reformist or traditionalist orientation, and hence more likely to get outside support, their involvement in the escalating violence is likely to be ultimately counterproductive for the achievement of their own goals. When outside parties move toward a mediatory role emphasizing compromise, the local moderates are likely to be the beneficiaries of the radicals' initiatives. There is some indication that this is happening in Ulster, Cyprus, and the southern Philippines, where moderates are either seeking out and cooperating with the external parties that are playing a mediating role or are simply available to cooperate with the domestic government in formulating and implementing a compromise settlement.

In a broader sense, this point should be of interest to observers who fear that ethnic relations in a postcolonial society move from an initial coalition toward greater polarization, culminating in the defeat of the centrist forces. Under some circumstances, it appears, external involvement—even if initially or partially partisan—can help to check this development. A more precise identification of these circumstances must await further research, which is clearly warranted from both academic and policy perspectives.

CONCLUSIONS

The tenor of the conclusions drawn from these case studies contradicts what we called the Wilsonian postulate (see Ch. 1), namely that internal ethnic conflict constitutes a major source of international conflict. We have tried to show that instances of affective intervention leading to considerable international conflict required a special combination of circumstances that rarely exists, and was not fully present in the case studies considered here. More frequent, probably, are cases where internal ethnic conflict is used as a vehicle for outside parties to promote unrelated interests. Even here, the specifically ethnic dimensions of the initial conflict tend to have a restraining effect. When and if such conflicts generate substantial international tension, it usually will be despite, rather than because of, the ethnic dimensions, and due to the overriding importance of other foreign policy considerations.

Eight case studies admittedly offer a limited basis for generalizing about such a complex topic. Moreover, all but one of the case studies have a common feature that possibly has biased our conclusions. Except for the Ulster case, the studies involved Islamic religion as a component of ethnicity. Conceivably, this has skewed them toward greater international involvement of an affective kind because this particular ethnic identity has been given institutional expression in the form of an international, explicitly political organization: the Islamic Conference of Foreign Ministers and its permanent Secretariat. If so, this should give even greater force to our contradiction of the Wilsonian postulate. Even though the sample is biased in favor of this postulate, the conclusions differ. It does, of course—perhaps paradoxically—also substantiate the Wilsonian case for the value of international (or transnational) organizations in achieving at least comparatively peaceful settlements.

Another objection might be that our sample is biased in favor of "developing" states, which, for a variety of reasons, are commonly believed to be particularly "penetrable" by external parties. This may be so, and some interesting insight might be derived from focusing specifically on the differences between preindustrial and postindustrial societies as they affect external involvement in internal ethnic conflict. However, this variable is sufficiently complex and potentially important to justify separate treatment. Our case studies already contain a great deal of variation, which, as noted initially, has both advantages and disadvantages.

Finally, we have not included any cases where radical challengers of the ethnic status quo have been successful. The obvious candidate for consideration in this respect is Bangladesh. It should be noted that the decisive external involvement in this conflict rested on instrumental considerations rather than affective cross-boundary ties. Instrumental reasons were dominant in determining Indian support for the Bengalis in East Pakistan, although ethnic animosities were an important factor in creating the preexisting hostile relationships between India and Pakistan that fueled Indian desires to weaken its enemy. Strong partisan support for the rebels was further favored by considerations of costs. The weakness of the Pakistani government, and the international publicity given to its "atrocities" in East Pakistan, reduced the military and moral costs of supporting the challengers. A critical factor finally, was geographical: the people of East Pakistan were in reality already separate; the task was simply to give legal status to that separation.

The Bangladesh case is thus in some respects atypical—which accounts for its being the only example of successful separatism in the post-World War II period. There is another case of ethnic conflict where the challengers are likely to be successful in the near future: Rhodesia. Rhodesia is also atypical or, more accurately, it is typical of another kind of conflict, generally associated with another historical era. While the conflict in Rhodesia is ethnic—with race being the primary component of ethnic differentiation—the institutionalized minority rule of the settler regime is perceived as a legacy from the colonial era. Thus it involves a particular definition of self-determination that commands considerable international consensus: the right of the people of a state to self-government, or, more specificially, to independence from white colonial rule. Efforts of peoples within states to obtain self-determination, by contrast, are characteristic of a postindependence era; and the evidence is that they generate a different international response.

INDEX

Acheson Plan, 62
Addis Ababa Agreement (1972), 133
Afars, 128, 137
affective intervention, 10, 16, 227–28, 229–30; Cyprus, 229–30; Ireland, Republic of, 229; irredentism, 228; Thai Muslims, 228
Afghanistan, 152
Africa, 3, 13, 43; multiethnic characteristics of, 13
Agame, 128
Agew, 128
Agordat, 137
Ahdab, Abdul Aziz al-, 112
Ahmid, Ibrahim, 78
Ain al-Rummaneh massacre, 104, 105–106; blame for, 105–106
Akele Guzai, 128
Akhmedjan, 154, 155, 159
Akkar, 98
Akritas, Dighinis, 48
Al-hawath, 134
al-milhaq al-watani (*see,* National Pact)
ALF, 109
Algeria, 88
Algiers, 192
Ali Ilahis, 69
Alliance party, 29
Alma Ata, 163, 165
Amalrik, Andrei, 172
Amharic, 128
Amman, 108; Hashimite regime of, 108
Amur/Ussuri confrontation, 162
Anatolia, 70
Andom, Aman, 135–36; death of, 136
Anglo-Irish relations, 35–36
Angola, 40
Ankara, 56, 75
anticolonialism, 46
anticommunism, 46
Anya Nya rebels, 138
Arab Empire, 94
Arab Summit Conference, 120
Arab League, 93, 100, 110, 116, 216; Lebanese crisis, 116, 216
Arab Liberation Front (*see,* ALF)
Arab States, 99, 102; Israeli raids into, 102
Arafat, Yasser, 107, 108, 110, 120
Arif, Abdul Rahman, 79–81; Barzani, Mulla Mastafa, relations with, 80; downfall of, 81; Moscow visit of, 80
Arif, Abdul Selam, 77–80; military operations of, 79–80
Asberom, Ras Tesemma, 129
ASEAN, 11, 184, 203, 206, 220, 221
Asmara, 129, 137
Asri, Datuk Mohamed, 201, 202, 205
Assad, Hafez al-, 102, 107–108, 112, 115, 117, 217; Israel, strategy toward, 108
Association of Southeast Asian Nations (*see,* ASEAN)
Autocephalous Orthodox church, 48

Baath party, 75–77, 81–89, 217; anticommunism of, 76; Communist party, relations with, 83–84, 86; DPK, response to, 76, 86; ethnic rights, 81; Kurds, relations with, 75–77, 81–85; military actions of, 77, 82, 86–89; overthrow of, 77; pan-Arabism of, 75, 81, 82, 85; persecution of, 75; return to power of, 81–85; Revolutionary Command Council, 82; Soviet condemnation of, 76–77; Syria, 77
Baathism, 103
Bakhtiar, Timour, 70, 83
Bakr, Ahmad Hasan al-, 84, 85; 15-point peace plan of, 84
Bangkok, 204, 205
Bangladesh, 231–32
Banti, Teferi, 136
Baradost tribe, 72
Barakat, Antoine, 111
Barentu, 137
Baghdad, 70, 71, 72, 73, 74, 75, 76, 77, 78, 79, 80, 83, 86, 87, 88, 89
Baria, 128
Barth, Fredrik, 4
Barzan, 72
Barzani, Mulla Mastafa, 70, 71–90; Arif, Abdul Rahman, relations with, 79–81; Arif, Abdul Selam, relations with, 77–80; Baath regime, 75–77, 81–85; Bakr, Ahmad Hasan al-, 84; Bazzaz, Abdul Rahman, 80–81; Communist party, relations

with, 72, 78; DPK, attitude toward, 74, 78–79, 81; exile of, 71; failure of, 85–89; 15-point program, 81, 84; goals of, 72; Kassem, Abdul Karim al-, relations with, 72–73; Kurdish separatism, involvement in, 71–73; power of, 78; return to Iraq of, 71; Soviet Union, relations with, 71, 73, 74, 76; Talib, Naji, relations with, 81; 12-point program, 81, 84; U.S. aid, 88; the West, relations with, 74, 75

Barzani tribe, 70–73, 78, 86, 87; failure of, 71; hostility to, 71; rebellion of, 70–71; religious leadership of, 78; rivals of, 72

Bator, Osman, 154, 156, 159

Bazzaz, Abdul Rahman, 80–81; 12–point program of, 81

Beg, Yakub, 150

Beirut, 81, 95, 98, 102, 103, 104, 105, 107, 111; poverty in, 98; wealth in, 98

Belfast, 25

Beni Amer, 128

Bet Asghede, 128

Bet Juk, 128

Betong, 204

Bilen, 128

Biqaa Valley, 95, 98, 107

"Bloody Sunday" (1972), 31, 35, 36

Bolshevik Revolution (1917), 100, 150–153; Central Asia, effects on, 150–51

Boumedienne, Houari, 88

Brademas, John, 63

Brezhnev, Leonid, 171

British Empire, 43

Burhan, 155

Byron, Lord, 60; *Memoirs*, 60

Byzantine Empire, 44, 94

Cairo, 76, 77, 127

Cairo Agreement, 101, 120

Canada, 3

Cambodia, 64, 203

Carey, Hugh, 37

Carter, President Jimmy, 64

Carter administration, 142

Castle, Barbara, 61

Castro, Fidel, 139

Catholic Social Democratic and Labour Party (*see,* SDLP)

Catholics in Northern Ireland, 17, 21–40, 222; Belfast violence toward, (1969), 25; British intervention, attitudes toward, 26; civil rights of, 25, 26, 27, 30; conflict, attitudes toward, 27; cross-border ethnic ties, 30, 222; governmental attitudes toward, 24, 25; Great Britain's attitude toward, 32; IRA, 24–28, 29, 30–31; Londonderry violence toward (1969), 25; minority status of, 24, 26; nationality identification of, 21, 23; NICRA, 25, 30; peaceful demonstrations, 30; political force of, 30; politicians, 25; "power-sharing," belief in, 27, 28, 29; proportional representation given to, 27; racial identity of, 21–22; riots of, 25–26; SDLP, 28, 30; security, need for, 27, 29; supporters of, 30–31; unification with Republic of Ireland, attitudes toward, 27, 28; violence, attitudes toward, 27

CCP, 153–56, 158–59, 161, 166; Chiang Kai-shek, 154, 155; minorities, policy toward, 158–59; Sheng Shih-ts'ai, 154; Sinkiang, 155; Soviet relations with, 154, 155

CENTO, 77, 83

Central Asia, 146–53, 160–74; Bolshevik Revolution, effect on, 150–53; China, 148–49; collectivization program, 151–52; cultural differences, 147; ethnic groups of, 146–47; Han dynasty in, 148–49; language differences, 147; Muslimism, 146, 148; nomads in, 151; Sino-Soviet border, 146, 156–57, 160–74; Soviet Union, 149–74; "the Western Regions," 148, 149, 150

Central Intelligence Agency (*see,* CIA)

Central Treaty Organization (*see,* CENTO)

Chamber of Deputies, 96, 97

Chamoun, Camille, 97, 100, 105, 106, 111, 114

Chiang Kai-shek, 150, 153–55; CCP, 155; Sinkiang rebellion, 154–55

Ch'ing government, 149–50

China, 2, 6, 8, 9, 146–74; CCP, 153–56; Central Asia, 148–50; Ch'ing government, 149; communes, 159; economic problems, 160–61, 170; Great Leap Forward, 159; Han dynasty, 148–49; minorities, attitudes toward, 159, 171; population of, 146; PRC, 155; propaganda, 163–69; Soviet Union, relations with, 148–74; territorial concessions of, 149; Turkic

Muslims, 170; "unequal treaties," 149, 153; "the Western Regions," 148, 149, 150
Chinese Communist Party (*see,* CCP)
Chou En-lai, 161
Christian independence party, 130
Church of England Ascendancy class, 23, 24
Churchill, Winston, 61
CIA, 61, 65, 83, 118, 162; Cyprus involvement of, 65; Kurdish rebellion, 83
Clan na Gael, 36–37
Claude, Inis, 9
Clerides, John, 63
Coazien, 137
Colombo nonaligned summit, 187
Command Council, 85
Communist Party of Malaya (*see,* CPM)
Communist Party of the Soviet Union (*see,* CPSU)
comparative politics, 1, 2
competitive conflict expansion, 215–18
Conference of Islamic and Non-Aligned Nations, 44
Conferences of Islamic Foreign Ministers, 185–89, 190–94, 207–208; Benghazi meeting, 185, 190; Filipino Muslims, 185–89; Indonesian actions at, 190–91; Istanbul meeting, 187, 191; Jiddah conference, 187, 193; Kuala Lumpur meeting, 187, 191–92; Lahore meeting, 186, 190; Philippine involvement of, 185–89; Thai Muslims, 207–208; Tripoli Agreements, 188–89; Zamboanga peace talks, 193
conflict equilibration, 220–23
conflict extension, 11
conflict transformation, 11
Cooley, John K., 118, 119; *Christian Science Monitor,* 118, 119
Coser, Lewis, 11
containment, 16
Corregidor incident, 183
Covenant of Cooperation, 72
Cosgrave, Liam, 33, 34; power-sharing, support of, 34
Council of Ireland, 27, 32, 34, 36
CPM, 204–206; in Thailand, 204
CPSU, 155, 156
cross-boundary ethnic links, 6–7, 9, 11, 14–16, 30, 45–46, 68, 89, 217, 222, 223–24, 228; Catholics in Northern Ireland, 30, 222; in Cyprus, 45–46, 217; Kurds, 68, 89
Crouzet, Francois, 49
Cuba, 40
cultural identity, 4
cultural pluralism, 4
Cultural Revolution, 168, 171
Cypriot National Union, 51
Cyprus conflict, 1, 9, 43–65, 214, 217–18, 223, 224; British involvement, 43, 47, 48, 49–52, 53, 61; CIA, 61; civil war in, 43, 56, 57, 61; communal conflict, 51–52; communal division of, 46, 48, 54, 56; communal talks, 63, 65; Communist party, 50; Constitution, 52, 53, 55; coup (1974), 44, 61, 62, 63; cross-boundary ethnic ties, 217; economic backwardness, 48; "enosis," 44–45, 47–59, 62, 65, 217–18; EOKA, 44, 50–52, 53; "ethnarch," 47; ethnic conflict, growth of, 48–52; ethnic differentiation, 46–52, 54; ethnic factors, 45–52, 59; ethnic identity, 48; geography as factor, 43; government under Turkish rule, 47; Greco-Turkish relations as factor in, 44, 47, 53, 58–59, 62, 65; Greece's involvement, 43–65; Greek Orthodox church, 47; Greek-American attitudes, 62–64; history of, 43–46; independence of, 43, 53, 54, 55, 61; internal self-government of, 48; international intervention, 43, 44–46; invasion of (1974), 58; location, importance of, 43, 45, 47, 62; Muslims, 45, 46–47, 48, 51, 57, 60; NATO, 44, 45, 53, 54, 59, 60, 62; peace-keeping force in, 56; political groupings, 49–50; public education, 48; Regional Cooperation for Development as factor in, 60; separatism, 52; social services, 48; Soviet Union's involvement, 44, 45; Turkish forces in, 58, 65; Turkey's involvement in, 43–65; United Nations in, 43, 45, 52, 53, 56; U.S. involvement, 44, 45, 46, 53, 59, 61–65; violence in, 49, 51–52;
Cyprus Is Turkish party, 51
Cyrillic script, 151, 157–58

Damascus, 76, 108, 113, 127
Damour, 111
Dankalia, 128
Dbaye, 111

Decamare, 137
Dembia, 128
Democratic Party of Kurdistan (*see,* DPK)
Denktash, Rauf, 65
Dergue, 133, 136–37
Dighenis (*see,* Grivas, George)
domestic ethnic lobby groups (*see,* lobby groups)
"domino theory," 203
Douglas, William O., 68
DPK, 72, 73, 74, 75, 76, 78–80, 81, 86; autonomy, 76; Baath party, contacts with, 75, 76; Barzani, Mulla Mastafa, attitude toward, 74, 78–79, 81; Communist sympathies of, 76, 78, 80; Soviet support of, 80; urban intellectualism of, 78
Druze, 94–95, 111; minority status of, 95; peasant rebellion, 94
Dublin, 24, 31, 34, 36, 222; Easter week uprising (1913), 24
Duroselle, Jean-Baptiste, 49

Eagleton, Thomas, 63
East Turkistan Republic (*see,* ETR)
Edde, Raymond, 107, 114
Eden, Anthony, 50, 53
EEC, 36
Egal, Ibrahim, 140
Egypt, 60, 73, 77, 85, 100, 102, 108, 110, 116–17, 138, 182–83; Eritrean-Ethiopian conflict, 138; Great Britain's occupation of, 100; Iraq, relations with, 77, 85; Israel, negotiations with, 110; Kurdish rebellion, attitude of, 73; Lebanese civil war, 116–17; Philippines, involvement in, 182–83; Soviet Union, relations with, 100; Syria, crisis with, 110
Eisenhower Doctrine, 100
ELF, 132–42; Afars joining of, 137; Egypt's support of, 138; international lobbying of, 134; OAU, 134; PLF agreement with, 137; political exiles, 132
"enosis," 44–45, 47–59, 62, 217–18; British reaction to, 52, 53, 61; Communist party, 50; EOKA, 50–52, 53; Greece's aid to, 53; Greek Cypriot reaction to, 50; growth of, 49–50; Orthodox church's reaction to, 50; Turkish Cypriot reactions to, 48, 49, 50; Turkey's attitude to, 58, 217; U.S. attitude to, 62; violence because of, 49, 50, 51–52
EOKA, 44, 50–52, 53, 54, 55, 57, 58, 61; communal conflict because of, 51–52; "enosis," 44, 50–52; Makarios, Archbishop, influence on, 52; violence because of, 51–52
EPLF, 137
Eritrean Democratic Front, 132
Eritrean-Ethiopian conflict, 127–44, 215–16; Addis Ababa Agreement (1972), 133; Arab Muslim identification, 216; Arab states, 138; "creeping coup," 133; cultural factors, 130–31; economic factors, 131; Egypt, 138; ELF, 137–42; ethnic factors, 130, 131–32, 216; foreign involvement, 138–43, 215–16; geographic factors, 130; history of, 129–37; international factors, 131; Iraq, 140; Libya, 140; martial law, 133; military response to, 134–35, 136–37; Muslims, 130, 132, 137, 138; political factors, 130–31; peaceful solutions, attempts at, 135, 136; "scorched-earth policy," 136; Somalia, 139–40; Soviet Union, 139; Sudan, 138–39; Syria, 140; terrorism, 133; Umm Hajar incident, 134–35; violence, 136–37
Eritrean Liberation Front (*see,* ELF)
Eritrean People's Liberation Front (*see,* EPLF)
Eritreans, 2, 4, 5, 127–44, 214, 215–16, 224; Arab states, 127; Christians, 132–33, 137; ethnic identity of, 4, 128, 130, 131–32; external support, 127, 215–16; federation, 130–31; fighting capacity of, 133; food embargo, 136; Great Britain's administration of, 129; Italy's administration of, 129; military response to, 136–37; Muslim links, 130, 131; Muslim-Christian friction, 132–33, 137; political arrangements of, 130; refugees, 136; separatist movement, 127, 130, 132, 216, 224; United Nations involvement, 130
Essayas, Afe Work, 137
Ethiopia, 2, 4, 5, 127–44; "creeping coup," 133; Dergue, 133, 136–37; Eritreans in, 2, 4, 5, 127–44; ethnic groups in, 127–29; Great Britain's involvement in, 129; international lobbying, 134; Israel, 142; Italy's involvement in, 129; language families, 128; military regime of, 139; Muslim-Christian distinctions, 128–29;

regionalism of, 128; "scorched-earth policy," 136; Soviet Union, 141; U.S., 141–42
Ethiopian Democratic Union, 139
"ethnarch," 47, 51
ethnic conflicts: boundary disputes, 2, 4; characteristics of, 3–7; China, Kazakhs, 2, 6, 8, 9, 146–74; Cyprus, 1, 9, 43–65; decolonization as factor in, 2; economic aspects of, 8; Ethiopia, Eritrean conflict in, 2, 4, 5, 8, 127–44; ethnic factors, 6–8, 223–26; exploitation of, 3; external responses to, 7–9, 11–16, 213–32; festering quality of, 5–6, 7, 17–18; foreign involvement in, 1, 2, 3, 5–6, 7, 10, 11–18, 213–32; foreign policy formulation, 3; geography as factor in, 68; internal pressures for involvement in, 3, 12–13, 15–16, 213–32; Iraq, Kurdish rebellion in, 1, 5, 6, 68–90; leadership as factor in, 68; Lebanon, civil war in, 1, 8, 93–122; Lenin's interpretation of, 10–11; literature of, 2, 9–11; lobby groups, 2; migration, 2; Northern Ireland, 1, 21–40; Philippines, Muslim separatist movement, 2, 11, 178–95; policy implications of, 226–28; policy problems of, 2–3; politics as factor in, 3, 5, 68; reasons for, 11–13; Thailand, Muslim separatist movement, 2, 4, 8, 196–210
ethnic groups, 3, 4–5, 11, 14–16, 68, 146–47; Central Asia, 146–47; cross-boundary links between, 14–16; demands of, 11–12; extremists in, 4; Kurds, 68; nationalities, resemblances to, 4; policy problems of, 2–3; self-determination, 4–5
ethnic identity, 2, 4, 6–7, 8, 39–40, 127–44, 178–79; definition of, 4; Eritreans, 127–44; Filipino Muslims, 178–81; history of, 2; Muslim-Christian, 128; Northern Ireland, 21–23, 39–40; Thai Muslims, 196–97
ethnic kinship ties, 7, 13, 14–18, 38–39, 59, 60, 68, 148, 182–83, 208, 210, 216; Cyprus, 59, 60; Eritreans, 216; involvement because of, 16–18; international, 7; Kazakhs, 148; Kurds, 68; Muslims, 182–83, 184, 198–99, 200–206; Philippines, 210; Thailand, 208
Ethniki Organosis Kypriakou Agonos (see, EOKA)
ETR, 154–56, 158–59, 161, 164; Soviet involvement with, 154
European Commission on Human Rights, 36
European Economic Community (*see,* EEC)
external forces, 2, 3, 11–16, 39–40, 43–65, 50, 200–208, 213–32; consequences of, 224–25; in Cyprus, 43–65; ethnic characteristics of, 13–14, 225–26; ethnic kinship ties, 14, 15–16; geographical proximity, 14–15; ideology, 14; Kurdish rebellion, 68; noninvolvement, 12, 13–14; in Northern Ireland, 39–40; in Thailand, 200–208

Faisal, King, 70
Fateh, 108–109
Faulkner, Brian, 29
fedayeen (*see,* Palestinian resistance movement)
Fertile Crescent, 99–100; Jewish immigration into, 100
Fianna Fail, 34
Filipino Muslim Welfare and Relief Agency, 186
Fitchett, Joseph, 117; *Washington Post,* 117
Ford, Gerald, 113
Ford administration, 36
foreign involvement, 6, 7, 10, 11–18, 26–40, 44–46; affective, 10, 16; costs, 17; in Cyprus, 43–65; ethnic ties as factor in, 7, 13, 14–18; forms of, 16–18; instrumental, 10; in Northern Ireland, 26–40; political entrepreneurism, 13; resource allocation as factor in, 12, 13; territorial integrity as factor in, 12, 13, 17
France, 94, 95, 99–100, 101; Fertile Crescent, involvement in, 99–100; Lebanese mandate of, 95, 100; Ottoman Empire, 99; Syrian mandate, 100
Franjieh, Suleiman, 94, 105, 106, 110, 112, 113, 114
Frunze, 163

Gaels, 21, 23
Gaye, Ahmadu Karim, 187
Gaza Strip, 108
Geertz, Clifford, 4
Gemayel, Pierre, 103, 104, 105–106, 110, 114; defense policy of, 103; Israeli raids, actions of, 104

Genghis Khan, 146, 147
genocide, 6, 16
Gladstone, William, 61
Golan Heights, 107, 108
Gondarine, 129
Great Britain, 26–40, 44, 45, 47, 48, 49–52, 53, 56, 60–61, 94, 99–100, 101, 129; "Bloody Sunday" (1972), 31; concessions of, 30; Conservatives, 32; in Cyprus, 44, 45, 47, 48, 49–52, 53, 54, 60–61; Eritrean involvement, 129; "enosis," reaction to, 49–50, 53, 61; Fertile Crescent, involvement in, 99–100; Greek Cypriots in, 61; human rights charges against, 36; IRA, view of, 32; Iraqi mandate of, 100; Ireland, Republic of, relations with, 33, 35–36; Labor Government's attitude toward Cyprus, 53, 61; Northern Ireland, intervention in, 26–40; Ottoman Empire, 99; Palestinian mandate of, 100; peacekeeping role of, 38, 39; philhellenism of, 60–61; Transjordanian mandate of, 100
Great Leap Forward, 159–60, 171
Greco-Turkish relations, 44, 47, 53, 58–59, 62, 65
Greece, 43–65; Cyprus, involvement in, 43–65; "enosis," 44–45, 47–48, 53–59; EOKA, attitude toward, 53; geographic location, importance of, 59; Great Britain, dependence on, 53, 54; indifference of, 56–57; junta, 62; "Megali Idea," 44; nationalism of, 59; NATO, withdrawal from, 64; politics of, 44; Turkey, secret meetings with, 54; Turkish Cypriots, recognition of, 56; U.S., dependence on, 53
Greek Catholic Christians, 95, 96, 107
Greek Cypriots, 44, 45–65; anti-British attitudes of, 49, 61; "enosis," 44, 47–52, 53, 54; "ethnarch," 47; ethnic links of, 45–46, 47; Greece, dependence on, 54; guerrilla warfare of, 44; majority status, 44, 45; political grouping of, 50; power of, 54, 57
Greek Orthodox, 95, 96, 98
Grivas, George, 48, 52, 53, 54, 55, 56, 62; "enosis," 55; Greece's support of, 53; guerrilla activity of, 53; international stature of, 54
Gurr, Ted Robert, 2

Hadendowa, 128
Haile Selassie, 132, 133, 138, 215; coup, 133
Han dynasty, 148–49
Hanafi Sunii Arabs, 69
Hanafi Sunii Turks, 69
Hanna, Major General, 112
Hawatmeh, Nayef, 109
Helmy, Burhanuddin al-, 201, 202
Herder, Johann, 9
Hermel, 98
Heslinga, M. W., 22
Homs refinery, 113
Horowitz, Donald, 8
Husayn, Saddam, 85, 87–88
Hussein, King, 113

Ili Kazakh Autonomous Chou of Sinkiang province, 146, 158–59, 161; creation of, 158
Ili Valley, 150
Indonesia, 182–83, 186, 189–91, 195, 206–207; Muslim activity in, 189–90; Philippines, involvement in, 182–83, 189–91, 195; Thailand, involvement in, 206
Institut International de Recherche et de Formation en vue de Développement (*see,* IRFED)
International Monetary Fund and World Bank, 188
Ioannides, Demetrios, 56–57
iqta', 94
IRA, 24–28, 29, 30–21, 32, 33, 36–37, 40; anti-British feelings of, 24–25, 26; Clan na Gael support, 36–37; ethnic identification, 24, 40; goals of, 31; guerrilla tactics, 31, 33; Ireland, Republic of, attitudes toward, 31, 34–35; Northern Command, 11, 31; "provisional," 26; strength of, 31; unification, belief in, 25, 27, 31; U.S. attitudes toward, 36–37; violent orientation of, 26, 27, 31, 32
Iran, 60, 69, 70, 71, 73, 79–80, 83, 86, 87–89; Barzani, Mulla Mustafa in, 71; Iraqi relations with, 70, 83, 87; Kurdish rebellion, assistance to, 73, 79–80, 86, 87–89; Kurds in, 69, 70; Soviet involvement in, 69
Iraq, 1, 5, 68–90, 100, 109, 127; Arif, Abdul Rahman, 80–81; Arif, Abdul Selam, 77–80; arms shipments to, 80; Baath regime, 75–77, 81–85; Bakr, Ahmad Hasan al-,

84, 85; Bazzaz, Abdul Rahman, 80–81; British mandate of, 100; Communist party, 72, 73, 80; coup attempts, 82; economic growth, 85; Eritrean-Ethiopian conflict, 140; Egypt, relations with, 85; Iran, relations with, 70, 83, 87; Kassem, Abdul Karen al-, 71–73; Kurds in, 1, 5, 68–90; Lebanese civil war, 113; military response to Kurdish rebellion, 73–74, 79–80, 86–89; monarchy, 71; oil revenue, 76; revolution (1958), 71; Revolutionary Command Council, 82; Six-Day (Arab-Israeli) War, 81; Soviet involvement in, 71, 80, 83–84, 85, 88; Syria, federation with, 76, 85; Talib, Naji, 81; Turkey, relations with, 70, 75
Iraq Petroleum Company, 74
Ireland, Republic of, 17, 23–24, 27, 31, 32, 33–36, 38–39; anti-terrorist legislation, 34, 35; British conquest of, 23; Catholics, treatment of, 23–24; civil war (1922–23), 24; Council of Ireland, 27, 32; Dail, 34; economic competition in, 24; ethnic factors, 38–39; financial aid to Northern Ireland, 34; government's attitude to Northern Ireland, 33–36; Great Britain, relations with, 35–36; guerrilla war (1916–21), 24; history of divisions in, 23–24; IRA in, 31, 34–35; Presbyterians in, 23, 24; Protestants, treatment of, 23–24; Public Accounts Committee, 34; public opinion, 35; social divisions, 23; terrorism, attitudes toward, 36; violence, history of, 24
IRFED, 97–98
Irish Free State, 24
Irish Northern Aid Committee (*see,* Noraid)
Irish Republic Army (*see,* IRA)
Irish republicanism, 24
Isaacs, Harold, 4
Islam (*see,* Muslims)
Islamic Conference, 46, 60, 143
Islamic Secretariat, 185
Israel, 78, 80, 82, 94, 98, 100, 101–103, 107–108, 109, 110, 112–13, 142, 192, 216; Egypt, negotiations with, 110; Ethiopia, 142; inter-Arab division toward, 107; Kurdish rebellion, 80; Lebanese civil war, 94, 112–13, 118–19; Lebanon, relations with, 100; October War (1973), 108–109; Philippines attitude toward, 92; PLO, 101–102; retaliation policy of, 102–103; Soviet Union's backing of, 100; Syria's attitude toward, 107–108; U.S. backing of, 100
Issas, 128
"Italian Empire of East Africa," 129
Italian Somaliland, 129
Italy, 129

Jabal Amil, 95
Jahoda, 159
Jalloud, Salam, 116
Jibril, Amhed, 109
jihad, 132
"Johnson letter," 62
Jordan, 101, 102, 108; PLO, 101, 102, 108
Jumblatt, Kamal, 105–106, 109, 110, 111, 113, 114; socialist secular philosophy of, 106

Kadiri dervish order, 69
Karakalpak, 147
Karamanlis, Constantine, 63
Karame, Rashid, 105, 107, 112
Kassa, Ras Asrate, 133
Kassem, Abdul Karim al-, 71–75; Baath party, persecution of, 75; Barzani, Mulla Mustafa, relations with, 71–73; Kurds, relations with, 71–73; overthrow of, 75; Soviet Union, relations with, 73
Kassis, Charbel, 107, 114
Kazakh Soviet Encyclopedia, 107
Kazakhs, 2, 6, 8, 9, 146–74, 214, 218–20, 226; Alash Orda government, 151; anti-Chinese propaganda, 170; assimilation, resistance to, 152–53; birth rate, 153; Bolshevik resistance by, 151; Bolshevik Revolution's effect on, 150–53; China's policy toward, 157; culture of, 148; ETR, 156, 158–59; famine, 151; Han dynasty's attitude toward, 148–49; Khrushchev, Nikita, reforms of, 152; "land" reform, 157; minority status of, 218–19; Muslims, relations with, 146, 148; nomadism of, 147, 151, 152; pro-Soviet tendencies, 156, 158–59; purge of, 156; self-determination, Soviet suppression of, 151; Sino-Soviet border, 146, 156–57, 160–74; Stalin's death, effect on, 152; standard of living, 152; Soviet involvement with, 9, 149, 171–72, 219

Kazakhstan, 146, 149, 150, 151; economy, 150; Soviet colonization of, 149, 150
Kazakhstankaya pravda, 163, 164, 166
Kazan Tatar, 147
Keating, Kenneth, 63
Kelantan, 201–202
Kemalism, 59, 60
Kennedy, Edward, 37
Keren, 128, 137
Khaddam, Abdel Halim, 107
Khalid, King, 12
Khartoum, 134
Khatib, Ahmad al-, 111
Khleifawi, Abdel Rahman, 117
Khouly, Hassan Sabry el-, 116
Khouri, Bishara al-, 96
Khrushchev, Nikita, 152, 157, 160
Khusistan Liberation Movement, 79
Kirghiz, 146, 147, 163, 168
Kirkuk, 72, 86; rioting, 72
Kirmanji, 69
Kissinger, Henry, 61, 63, 113
KMT, 150, 154–55; Soviet relations with, 155
Kolchak, Aleksandr, 151
Kosygin, Aleksei, 85
Kraivichien, Thanin, 206
Kremlin, 71, 73, 80, 84
Kuala Lumpur, 204, 205
Kunama, 128
Kuomintang, (*see,* KMT)
Kurdi, 69
Kurdish rebellion, 1, 5, 6, 68–90; anti-Western attitude of, 73, 741; Arab attitude toward, 73; Arif, Abdul Rahman, 79–81; Arif, Abdul Selam, 77–80; autonomy, 76, 84; Baath regime, 75–77, 81–89; Barzani, Mulla Mastafa, 71–90; Barzani tribe, 70–73; Bazzaz, Abdul Rahman, 80–81; cease fire (February 1964), 78; cease fire (June 1966), 79; cross-boundary ethnic links, 89–90; DPK, 74, 75, 76; Egypt's attitude toward, 73; external forces, 68, 75, 77, 79–80, 83–85, 87–89; failure of, 85–89; 15-point peace plan, 84; foreign response to, 72–73; government's response to, 73–74; Iran's assistance of, 73, 79–80, 83, 86, 87–89; Iraqi-Iranian relations as factor in, 88–89; Iraqi-Soviet relations as factor in, 85; Israel, 80; kidnappings, 75; March 1975 Agreement, 85–89; military response to, 73–74, 77, 82, 86–89; "national rights" as factor, 76, 78; oil companies, violence to, 74–75; origins of, 70–73; Outer Mongolia, 76; pan-Arabism, 78, 79, 82, 85; publicizing of, 74; Soviet response to, 73, 74, 76–77, 80, 83–84, 85, 88; Syria's response to, 77; Talib, Naji, 81; terrorism of, 74–75; tribal divisions, 73, 74, 78, 89–90; Turkey's influence on, 70, 75; 12-point program, 81; United Nations, 76, 82; U.S. response to, 75, 87, 88
Kurds, 1, 5, 68–90, 214, 218–19, 226; Communist influence on, 70, 71; DPK attitude toward, 78–79; ethnic disunity of, 69; European exiles, 72; geographical isolation of, 68–69; independent nature of, 68; internal rivalry of, 69, 73, 74; military operations against, 73–74, 79–80, 86–89; minority status of, 218–19; nationalist movement of, 50; "nationalist rights" recognized, 75–76; outside contacts of, 5; religion of, 69; separatist movement of, 69–70, 71; tribal nature of, 69
Kuwait, 73, 77, 116, 127, 140–41

Lahoud, Fuad, 102–103
Laos, 203
Lasta, 129
Le Monde, 74, 112, 114
Le Nouvel Observateur, 104
League of Nations, 95, 99
Lebanese civil war, 8, 93–122, 216–17, 225; Arab states, 116–17; armed forces, break up of, 111; beginning of, 105; Cairo Agreement, 120; causes, 94–116; cease fire, 93; Christian-Muslim linkages, 99, 216–17; conclusion of, 120; devastation of, 93; ethnic identity, 121; ethnic-socio-economic forces as factor, 94, 99–104; external causes, 99–104, 122; foreign involvement, 216–17; internal causes, 99–104, 122; Israeli raids as factor, 101–104; Israel's involvement in, 94, 99, 101–103, 107, 112–13, 118–19; military government, 105; Muslims demands, 106; Palestinian exiles as factor, 94, 98, 99, 101–105; peacekeeping force, 93; PLO, 101–103, 104, 106, 107–110; political structures as factor, 94–97; rightist factions, 113–14; Saudi Arabia's involvement in, 110–11; social injustices as

factor in, 98, 103, 106; Syria's involvement in, 94, 107–116; U.S. involvement in, 94, 118
Lebanon, 8, 93–122, 214, 216–17, 223; Arabism of, 96; armed forces, 111; autonomy, 94; Cairo Agreement, 101; Chamoun, Camille, 100; Christians in, 94–99; civil war in, 8, 93–122; Communist party, 103; demography, 95; Druze, 94–95; economic aspects, 8, 93, 97–99, 103; Eisenhower Doctrine, 100; feudalism, 94–95; French mandate, 95; geographic location, 93; history of, 94–97; inflation, 104; Israel, relations with, 100, 101; Israeli raids into, 98, 101–103; Maronites, 94–95, 103; Muslims in, 94–99; National Pact, 96, 98, 99, 100, 106; Palestinians in, 100–101; Phalangists, 104; PLO, 101–102, 106; political structure of, 94–97; poverty, 98; "sectarian balance" formula, 96–97, 99, 100; social reforms needed, 99; underdeveloped regions, 98; United Nations, 103
Lenin, V. I., 10, 166
Liberal Progressive party, 129
Libya, 15, 37, 38, 109, 113, 116, 139, 140, 185, 187, 195, 208, 220; Eritrean-Ethiopian conflict, 139; IRA, 37; Lebanese civil war, 116; Marcos', Imelda, trip to, 188; Philippines, involvement in, 185, 195; Thailand, 208
Lin Piao, 167
Loizos, Peter, 51
London settlement, 62
Londonderry, 25, 31; "Bloody Sunday" (1972), 31
Lucman, Rascid, 185

Macapagal, Diosdado, 184
Macedonia, 47
Mahabad Kurdish Republic, 69, 71
Makarios, Archbishop, 43, 48, 50, 52, 53, 54, 55, 56–57, 61, 63, 64–65; assassination attempt on, 56; CIA involvement of, 65; constitution, suggested amendments by, 55; coup (1974), 61, 63; "enosis," 48, 54, 55; Great Britain, relations with, 61; Greco-Turkish tensions, cause of, 65; independence, attitudes on, 53, 54, 61; international stature, growth of, 54
Malay Nationalist party, 201
Malaya, Federation of, 200, 202
Malaysia, 183–84, 195, 198–99, 200–206, 220–21; border agreement, 204, 206; CPM, 204–206; Muslims, 198–99, 203; nonintervention, 204; Philippine involvement of, 183–84, 195; Thailand involvement of, 198–99, 220
Marcos, Ferdinand, 183, 184, 185, 186, 187, 188–89, 192, 193–94; Conference of Islamic Foreign Ministers, 186; Israel, attitude toward, 192
Marcos, Imelda, 188, 189
Malik, Adam, 190, 191, 207
Mariam, Ato Wolde Ab Wolde, 129, 132
Mariam, Mengistu Haile, 139
Mao Tse-min, 154
Mao Tse-tung, 154
Maronites, 94–99, 103, 104, 106, 109, 111, 112; attacks on, 111; government participation of, 96; majority status of, 95; National Pact, 98–99; peasant rebellion, 94; Palestinians, attitude toward, 99, 103
Matalam, Udtog, 183
Mazzini, Giuseppe, 9
"Megali Idea," 44, 53, 59, 223
Melchor, Alejandro, 186, 193
Menelik, Emperor, 129
Mensa, 128
Mesopotamia, 69
Michael, Emanuel Ande, 135
Middle East, 60, 71, 100, 181, 182
Mill, John Stuart, 9
MIM, 183; Malaysian aid to, 183
Mindanao, 179, 180, 181; Christian migration to, 180
Mira, Bitwoded Ali, 137
Misuari, Nur, 189, 193
MNLF, 182–94; autonomy, belief in, 191; cease-fire agreement, 188; committee of four, 187; Conferences of Islamic Foreign Ministers, 191; Indonesia's attitude toward, 190–91; Jiddah Conference, 187, 193; Kuala Lumpur meeting, 191–92; Libyan aid to, 185; Malaysian aid to, 184; Tripoli agreements, 188–89
Modelski, George, 5
Mogadisho, 127
Mohammed, Idris, 132
"molla," 49
Mongol conquests, 147
Mongolian People's Republic (*see,* MPR)
Moro National Liberation Front (*see,* MNLF)

Moros, 180, 191
Moscow, 71, 76
Moslems (*see,* Muslims)
Mosul, 72, 74; meeting (March 1959), 72
Moynihan, Daniel P., 37
MPR, 172–73
Mulla Mastafa (*see,* Barzani, Mulla Mastafa)
multiethnic states, 5, 13–14; intervention of, 13–14
"multiplier effect," 213
Murphy, Richard, 112
Mushin, Zuheir, 109
Muslim Independence Movement (*see,* MIM)
Muslim League, 129
Muslim Welfare Agency, 191
Muslims, 2, 4–5, 11, 15, 17, 45, 46–47, 51, 57, 60, 94–99, 102, 104, 105, 106, 109, 112, 128, 132, 137, 146, 164, 178–210, 220, 223, 224; Central Asia, rebellion of, 149–50; Ch'ing government, 149–50; Corregidor incident, 183; in Cyprus, 48, 60; Eritreans, 130, 131, 132, 137; ethnic identity in Philippines, 178–81; ethnic identity in Thailand, 178–79; ethnic links in Philippines, 182–83; Ethiopia, 128, 129; Kazakhs, 146, 164; in Lebanon, 94–99, 102, 105, 106; Libyan support of, 15, 184; in Malaysia, 198–99; Malaysian aid to, 182–83; Middle East, role of, 60; Palestinian support of, 102, 106; Philippine government's attitude toward, 192–94, 220; in Philippines, 11, 17, 60, 178–95; in Thailand, 4–5, 17, 178, 196–210, 220; Tripoli agreements, 188–89
Mustapha, Tun, 184, 190, 210

Nacfa, 137
Nakshbandi, 69
Narathiwas, 179, 202
Nasser, Ahmed, 137
Nasser, Gamal Abdel, 60, 85, 100, 138
Nasserism, 103
Nasserite insurgents, 72
National Command Congress, 81
National Liberal Party (*see,* NLP)
National Organization of Cypriot Struggle (*see,* EOKA)
National Pact (1943), 96, 98, 99, 100, 106, 112; domestic politics, 96; foreign policy, 96; military alliances, 100; Muslim's attitude, 106; sectarianism of, 99
National Security Agency (*see,* NSA)
National Union of Malaysian Muslim Students, 203
nationalism, 4–5, 9, 47, 49; Cyprus, 49
NATO, 44, 45, 53, 54, 59, 60, 62, 63, 218; Cyprus conflict, 44, 45, 53, 59, 60, 62; Greece, 59, 64; Turkey, 63, 64
Nayif, Abdul Razzaz, 82
NCNA, 156, 168
NEBELBAL, 142
Negus, Michael Gabre, 137
New China News Agency (*see,* NCNA)
NICRA, 25, 30
Nilotic people, 128
Nimeiry, Jaafar al-, 136, 138–39
Nixon administration, 36
NLP, 106
nomads, 147, 151, 152; Soviet suppression of, 151
Noraid, 37
North Atlantic Treaty Organization (*see,* NATO)
North Yemen, 139
"Northern Command," 31
Northern Ireland, 1, 17, 21–40, 214–15, 221–23; British conquest of, 23; British intervention in, 26–40, 221–23; Catholics in, 17, 21–40; civil rights movement, 25, 26; civil war (1922–23), 24; constitutional convention, 27, 28; cross-boundary ethnic ties, 222; cultural differences in, 22, 23; emergency powers legislation, 26; ethnic factors, 38–40; ethnic identification, 21–23, 38–40; foreign involvement in, 26–40, 221–23; internment, 26; IRA, 24–28, 29, 30–31; Ireland, Republic of, attitudes toward, 33–36; isolation, 23; peace movements in, 31; polarization in, 26; "power-sharing," 27–28, 32–33; Protestant Unionist government, 25; Protestants in, 21–40; riots (1969), 34; Rose, Richard, opinion survey of, 21–22; social interaction in, 22; unification, 25, 27, 28; U.S. attitudes toward, 36–27
Northern Ireland Civil Rights Association (*see,* NICRA)
Northern Ireland Labour party, 29
NSA, 118

Nur, Rahmadan Mohammed, 137
Nurcular, 69

OAU, 134, 138, 143, 227
October War (1973), 108–109
O'Dwyer, Paul, 37
Ogadin region, 131
oil boycott (1973), 192
O'Neil, "Tip," 37
O'Neill, Terence, 25
Onn, Datuk Hussein, 204
Orange Order, 24
Orangemen, 24
Organization of African Unity (*see,* OAU)
Ottoman Empire, 47, 58, 94, 99; Fertile Crescent, 99; nationalism, 47
Outer Mongolia, 76

Pakistan, 60, 182–83, 231–32; Philippines, involvement in, 182–83
Palawan, 179
Palestine, 100, 101
Palestine Liberation Army (*see,* PLA)
Palestine Liberation Organization (*see,* PLO)
Palestinian nationalism, 101
Palestinian refugees, 98, 100–105, 111; in Lebanon, 98, 100–101, 103–104
Palestinian resistance movement, 101–104
Pallani, 179
Pan-Arabism, 77, 78, 79, 85
Pan-Malay doctrine, 202
Pan-Malayan Islamic Party (*see,* PMIP)
Papadopoulos, George, 56
Papagos, Alexandros, 53
Papandreou, George, 56
Parliamentary Defense Committee, 102
Parsons, Talcott, 4
Parti Islam (*see,* PAS)
partisan cooperation, 16
partisan intervention, 14, 15
PAS, 201, 202
Pattani, 196, 197
Pax Syriana, 116
PDFLP, 109
Peck, Winslow, 118
Peking, 163
People's Democratic Republic of Yemen, 127, 139
People's Liberation Army, 156
People's Republic of China (*see,* PRC)
Persian Gulf, 84, 89
PFLP, 107
Phalange party, 103, 105–106
Philippine Commission on Elections, 189
Philippines, 2, 11, 15, 17, 60, 178–95, 214–15, 216, 220–21; Arab oil boycott (1973), 192, 195; autonomy, Muslim, 188; cease-fire agreement, 188; Christians in, 180, 191; Conferences of Islamic Foreign Ministers, 185–89; Corregidor incident, 183; Egypt's involvement in, 182–83; external factors, 182–94; 209–10, 216, 220–21; history of Muslimism in, 180–81; Indonesia's involvement in, 182–83, 189–91; Libyan involvement in, 185, 188, 189; Malaysian involvement in, 183–84, 195; MNLF, 182–92; Muslims in, 2, 11, 15, 17, 60, 178–95; Mustapha, Tun, 184, 195; Pakistan's involvement in, 182–83; "peace talks," 187, 188; plebiscite, 188–89; politicalization of Muslims in, 181; religion as factor, 179–80, 188–89; separatist movement, 179, 185; Tripoli agreements, 188–89; Zamboanga talks, 187
Pipes, Richard, 152
PLA, 111–15
PLF, 132, 135, 136–37, 139; ELF agreement with, 137; Marxist-Leninist orientation, 132, 135
PLO, 98, 101–103, 104, 107–110, 117, 118; Arab armies, clashes with, 101; Arab people's support of, 101, 102; Cairo Agreement, 101; Egypt, 117; goals of, 101; Israel, attitudes toward, 108, 118; Jordan, 108; Lebanese civil war, 107–110; Palestinian state, hope of, 109; Phalangist hostility, 107; strategy of, 101; Syria, 108
PMIP, 201, 202
Popular Democratic Front for the Liberation of Palestine (*see,* PDFLP)
Popular Front for the Liberation of Palestine (*see,* PFLP)
Popular Liberation Front (*see,* PLF)
power-sharing Assembly, 28, 32–33, 34; Cosgrave, Liam, support of, 34; failure of, 33
Pramoj, Seni, 204
Pravda, 76, 77, 84
Problems of the CPSU Economic Policy and Reclamation of Virgin Lands in Kazakhstan, 166

PRC (*see,* China)
Progressive Front, 109, 111, 113, 114, 119–20, 122; PLO alliance with, 119
Protestants in Northern Ireland, 21–40; civil rights for Catholics, attitudes toward, 25, 26, 27; ethnic identification of, 24; extremists, 25, 31; general strike, 28, 30; Great Britain's attitude toward, 32; industrial action, 29–30; IRA threat to, 28; liberals in, 29; "loyalists," 29; majority status of, 29; nationality identification of, 21, 23; paramilitary groups, 30; political parties of, 29–30; political parties of, 29–30; "power-sharing," attitudes toward, 27–28, 32; racial identification of, 21–22; Scotland, ethnic ties with, 29; security, need for, 28, 29; strength of, 29–30; terrorists, 30; unification with Ireland, Republic of, 27, 28; Unionist government of, 25; United Kingdom, integration with, 28, 32–33; UUUC, 28; violent confrontation, 30, 34
Public Accounts Committee, 34

Qaddafi, Muammar, 37, 139, 140, 185, 188, 189, 191, 195; Philippine separatist movement, involvement in, 185, 188, 189, 195

Rahman, Tunku Abdul, 205
Rashaida, 128
Red Sea, 127
Regional Cooperation for Development, 46, 60
Rejection Front, 109, 116
resource allocation, 11, 12, 13
Revolutionary Command Council, 82, 84
Rezzak, Arif Abdul, 81
Rhodesia, 232
Riyadh, 93
Rogers, William, 36
Romulo, Carlos, 189
Rose, Richard, 21–22
Rosenau, James, 6
Rouleau, Eric, 74, 112, 114; *Le Monde,* 74, 112, 114
Royal Ulster Constabulary, 30, 35
Rwandiz, 79

Sabah, 183, 184, 190, 210
Sabah, Amir Sabah al-Salim al-, 120
Sabbe, Osman Saleh, 129–30, 132, 137, 143
Sadat, Anwar, 85, 115, 116, 120, 139; Syrian invasion of Lebanon, 116
Saho of Samhar, 128
Said, Nuri al-, 70
Saifudin, 155, 156, 158–59, 166
Sa'iqa, 109, 112, 113
Sakharov, Andrei, 153
Salleh, Datuk Harris, 184
Sampson, Nicos, 52, 58
Sarkis, Elias, 93, 114, 120
Satul, 179
Saudi Arabia, 93, 110–11, 116–17, 127, 134, 140–41, 187; ELF, 134; Eritrean-Ethiopian conflict, 140–41; Lebanese civil war, 116–17
Schlesinger, James, 169
Schmidt, Dana Adams, 74; *New York Times,* 74
Scotland, 23, 29
SDLP, 28, 30
Self-determination, 2, 4–5, 9, 10, 53, 151; Bolshevik promise of, 151; Communist suppression of, 151; Cyprus, 53; literature, 9–10; Versailles Conference, 9
Semirechie, 151
Senegal, 187
Separatism, 170–71, 224–25
separatists, 12, 13
Seychelles, 43
Shabdanov, Kazhyduniar, 159
Shatt al-Arab boundary, 70, 83, 89
Shafii Suniis, 69
Shehab, Fuad, 97, 100; Eisenhower Doctrine, repudiation of, 100
Sheng Shih-ts'ai, 153–54, 157; CCP, 154; Soviet support of, 153
Shoan, 128, 130
Shute Iranians and Arabs, 69
Shute Muslims, 95, 98
Sidon, 95, 103, 104
Sinai Disengagement Agreement, 110, 115
Sinkiang ("New Territory"), 150, 153–59, 160–74; CCP, 153–56; Chiang Kai-shek, 154; Cyrillic script, 157–58; emigration from, 160–61; ETR, 154–56, 158; Han people, 158–59; non-Han groups, 154; People's Liberation Army work teams, 156; Production and Construction Corps, 158; purges, 156; rebellion in, 154; Sino-Soviet border, 160–74; Soviet involvement in, 153–59; SUAR, 158

Sinkiang Uighur Autonomous Region (*see,* SUAR)
Sino-Soviet relations, 6, 9, 146–74; Central Asia as factor in, 149, 150; importance of, 173; Kazakhs as factor in, 9, 148, 149, 150; media "war," 163–69; military actions, 162–63; Sinkiang border disputes, 160–63;
Sino-Soviet Treaty (1950), 155
Six-Day (Arab-Israeli) War, 81
Smyrna, 57
Solh, Reyad as-, 96, 105
Somalia, 131, 139–40, 187
South Yemen, 139
Soviet-American relations, 3; Jews as factor in, 3
Soviet Union, 3, 38, 44, 45, 47, 56, 69, 70, 71, 73, 74, 76, 80, 82, 99–100, 119–20, 139, 141, 146–74; Arab states, relations with, 100; Arif, Abdul Selam, attitude toward, 80; arms shipments, 80, 82; Bolshevik Revolution, 150–53; Central Asia, 149–59; China, relations with, 6, 9, 148–74; Communist party, 44; Cyprus conflict, 44, 45; Czarist government, 150; Egypt, relations with, 100; Eritrean-Ethiopian conflict, 139, 141; expansion of, 149, 153; Fertile Crescent, involvement with, 99–100; Iran, 69; Iraq, attitude toward, 71, 73, 85; Israel, relations with, 100; Kazakhs, 9, 148–74; Kurdish rebellion, 73, 74, 76–77, 80; Lebanese civil war, 119–20; Middle East, involvement in, 100; Muslims, 45; Northern Ireland, 38; population of, 146; propaganda, 163–69; Sino-Soviet border clashes, 160–63; U.S., relations with, 3
Spivanhov, Ivan, 166
Stalin, 152, 154, 157
Stephens, Tun Fuad, 184
SUAR, 158–59, 168, 170
Sudan, 127, 133, 136, 138–39; Addis Ababa Agreement, 133; civil war, 133; Eritrean-Ethiopian conflict, 136, 138–39
Suez Canal, 100
Suharto, President, 190
Sultan, Ibrahim, 129
Sulu Archipelago, 179
Sunni Muslims, 95, 98
Sunningdale conference, 34
Syria, 76, 77, 85, 87, 93, 94, 95, 100, 102, 107–116, 127, 140, 216; Eritrean-Ethiopian conflict, 140; French mandate, 95, 100; Israel as factor to, 107; Lebanese civil war, 94, 107–116; mediator, role of, 107; peacekeeping troops, 93

Taipov, Zunin, 159, 164
Tajiks, 147
Talabani, Jelal, 74, 76, 81, 82, 85, 86; Baath party support, 82
Talib, Naji, 81
Tashkent, 163
Teheran, 73, 83, 87, 88, 89
territorial integrity, 12, 13
terrorism, 6
Tesennei, 137
Thailand, 2, 4–5, 17, 196–210, 214, 220; border agreement, 204, 206; Buddhists, 196–97, 199; Conference of Islamic Foreign Ministers, 207–208; coup d'etat in, 205–206; CPM's involvement in, 204–205; ethnic ties, 208; external forces, 200–209; government in Muslim provinces, 197; history of Muslims in, 196; Indonesian involvement in, 206–207; Kelantanese concern, 201–202; Libya, 208; "loyalist" Muslims, 199–200; Malay race in, 196; Malaysian involvement in, 198–99, 200–206, 208; Muslims in, 3, 4–5, 17, 196–210, 214, 220; secessionist movement, 197–98, 199, 201; violence, 206
Theravada Buddhists, 196
Third World, 53
Thrace, 47, 59
Tigrai, 128
Tigre, 128, 129
Tigrinya, 128, 129
Tohamy, Hassan al-, 186, 187, 193, 207
Transjordan, 100
Treaty of Guarantee, 57
Trekki, Ali, 187
Tripartite Conference, 57
Tripoli, 95, 103, 104
Truman Doctrine, 59
Turcomans, 72
Turkey, 43–65, 69–70, 75, 87, 88; arms embargo by U.S., 46; Cyprus, involvement in, 43–65; emigration from Cyprus, 57; Empire of, 43; "enosis," attitude toward, 48, 49, 57, 58; ethnic links, 57, 58; geo-

graphical location, importance of, 59; Greece, secret meetings with, 53; Kurdish rebellion, response to, 75, 87, 88; Kurds in, 69–70; Muslim relations, 60; nationalism, 59; settlement of Cyprus conflict, attitude toward, 58; Turkish Cypriots, protection of, 57–58; U.S. pressure on, 62
Turkish Cypriots, 44, 45–65; communal identity, 55; countermemorials, 51; counterterrorist organization of, 52; economic blockades against, 52; "enosis," reaction to, 48, 49, 50–52; ethnic links of, 45–46, 47; minority status of, 44, 45, 47, 50, 55; modernization of, 51; Muslim support of, 60; political parties of, 51; political representation of, 54; power of, 54; refugees, 58; Turkey, aid from, 57–58, 60; Turkish National Congress, 51; village self-rule, 51
Turkish Empire, 43, 47; in Cyprus, 47
Turkish National Congress, 51
Turkish National Pact, 60
Turkistan Autonomous Republic, 169
Tyre, 95, 103, 104

Uighurs, 147, 161, 163, 164, 167, 170; China, demands on, 170
Ulster (*see,* Northern Ireland)
Ulster Defence Regiment, 30
Ulster Unionist, 29
Ulstermen (*see,* Protestants in Northern Ireland)
Umm Hajar, 134
Umm Qasr, 84
Unionists, 130
United Democratic Party of Kurdistan, 71, 72; Communist party, relations with, 72; Covenant of Cooperation, 72
United Irishmen, 24
United Kingdom, 28, 32, 36
United Nations, 43, 44, 45, 52, 53, 54, 56, 57, 58, 61, 62, 73, 76, 82, 88, 100, 103, 108, 130, 227; in Cyprus, 43, 45, 52, 53, 56, 58; "enosis," 44, 53, 61, 62; Eritrean-Ethiopian conflict, 130; General Assembly, 44, 108; Kurdish rebellion, 73, 76, 82, 88, 227; Lebanon, 103, 108; Palestinian involvement, 100; Security Council Resolution (242), 108
United States, 36–37, 38, 44, 45, 46, 53, 54, 61–65, 75, 87, 88, 100, 101, 103, 113, 118, 134, 203; Arab states, relations with, 100; Clan na Gael, 36–37; Congress, 64; Cyprus conflict, 44, 45, 46, 53, 59, 61–65; Eisenhower Doctrine, 100; "enosis," attitude toward, 54, 62; Eritrean-Ethiopian conflict, 134; Ethiopia, 141–42; Greek-American community in, 62–64; IRA support in, 36; Israel, relations with, 100; Kurdish rebellion, 75, 87; Lebanese civil war, 94, 113, 118; Middle East, involvement in, 100, 103; NATO, 62; Northern Ireland, government attitudes to, 36; peace initiatives, 103; Turkey, attitude toward, 63; Turkish arms embargo of, 46, 61–62, 64
United Ulster Unionist Council (*see,* UUUC)
Ussuri River clashes, 162
UUUC, 28, 29
Uzbeks, 146, 147

Vanezis, P. N., 48
Venizelos, Eleutherios, 53
Versailles Conference, 2, 9
Vietnam, 64, 203

Warsaw Pact nations, 56
West Bank-Gaza Strip state, 109
West Malaysia, 201
Wilson, Harold, 33, 35
Wilson, Woodrow, 10
Wilsonian postulate, 230
World Council of Churches, 138
World War I, 9, 14, 24, 69, 95, 99, 150
World War II, 2, 24, 48, 50, 100, 154

Yahya, Tahir, 75
Yala, 179
Yarmouk Brigade, 111
Yemen, 131
Yemen Arab Republic, 139
Yeni khayat, 165–66
Young, Crawford, 4

Zahle, 107
za'ims, 100, 106
Zaza, 69
Zgharta Liberation Army, 106
Zibari tribe, 72
Zionism, 82
Zurich settlement, 62

ABOUT THE EDITORS AND CONTRIBUTORS

ASTRI SUHRKE is Assistant Professor of International Relations at American University, Washington, D.C. She has written articles on the Muslims in Thailand which have been published in *Comparative Politics* and *Pacific Affairs,* and a chapter in *Studies of Contemporary Thailand* (Australian National University Press). She has also written in the field of comparative foreign policy, including an article in *World Politics,* and has co-authored *Strategies of Survival: Smaller Asian States in a Changing International Environment,* which is to be published by Queensland University Press.

LELA GARNER NOBLE is Professor of Political Science at San Jose State University, San Jose, California. She received her Ph.D. from the Fletcher School of Law and Diplomacy, Tufts University. She wrote *Philippine Policy toward Sabah: A Claim to Independence,* which is to be published in the Monograph Series of the Association of Asian Studies. She is the author of several articles on Philippine foreign policy and the Philippine Muslims published in *Asian Survey* and *Pacific Affairs.*

NAOMI BLACK is Associate Professor of Political Science at York University, Toronto. Her Ph.D. dissertation for Yale University was titled "Peace with Honour: British Policy in Cyprus." She has published articles on Cyprus in the *Canadian Journal of Economics and Political Science* and the *Canadian Journal of Political Science.* She edited *Readings on the International Political System* (New York: Prentice-Hall, 1970) and has written several articles on foreign policy and international relations.

TERRANCE G. CARROLL is Assistant Professor of Politics at Brock University, St. Catharines, Ontario. He received his Ph.D. from Carleton University. In 1970–71 he and two colleagues designed and carried out a national survey on the political socialization of Canadian schoolchildren. In 1971–72 he did extensive interviewing in Northern Ireland as a part of his study of the attitudes and behavior of disaffected Catholic political activists. Both projects have resulted in a number of papers and articles, including two which have been published in edited volumes on political culture and local government.

JUNE TEUFEL DREYER is Associate Professor of Political Science at Miami University, Oxford, Ohio. She received her Ph.D. from Harvard University and has been a Fellow at the Harvard East Asian Research Center and the Berkeley Center for Chinese Studies. She wrote *China's Forty Millions* (Cambridge: Harvard University Press, 1976) and has published articles in *Problems of Communism, Pacific Affairs, China Quarterly,* and the *Far Eastern Economic Review.* She has also served as northwest editor for the two-volume *A Provincial Handbook of China,* which Stanford University Press is publishing under the general editorship of Edwin A. Winckler.

"ETHIOPIAWI" is an Ethiopian scholar.

GEORGE S. HARRIS is Director of the Office of Research and Analysis for Western Europe, Bureau of Intelligence and Research, U.S. Department of State, and was formerly Special Assistant to the Director, Office of Research and Analysis for Near East and South Asia. Since 1968 he has also been a Professorial Lecturer in Middle Eastern Studies at the School of Advanced International Studies, The Johns Hopkins University. He studied at Ankara University and received his Ph.D. from Harvard University. He is the author of *The Origins of Communism in Turkey* (Stanford, Cal.: The Hoover Institution, 1967) and *Troubled Alliance: Turkish-American Problems in Historical Perspective, 1945–1971* (Washington, D.C.: The American Enterprise Institute, 1972), and of numerous articles.

LEILA MEO is Visiting Professor in Middle East Studies at the University of Cincinnati. She studied at the American University at Cairo and received her Ph.D. from Indiana University. She wrote *Lebanon: Improbable Nation, A Study in Political Development* (Bloomington, Ind.: Indiana University Press, 1965) and is currently working on a book entitled *The Arabs: Their Heritage and Their Future.* She served as editorial writer and consultant for the U.N. Department of Information and the U.S. Information Agency.